"I know I can never be forgiven, I know my heart is illegal.

I have crossed the line into freedom land.

I have become one with trees, dirt, fangs, musk,

high water, and howls in the night."

—Charles Bowden

A WILD LIFE

For Reba, Ian, and Eli
—Nick

For my parents
—Melissa

MELISSA HARRIS

A WILD LIFE

A VISUAL BIOGRAPHY OF PHOTOGRAPHER MICHAEL NICHOLS

aperture

Michael "Nick" Nichols and a silverback mountain gorilla in Zaire (now Democratic Republic of Congo), 1991. Photograph by Peter Wilkins.
All photographs in *A Wild Life* are by Michael Nichols, unless otherwise noted.

SOME GIRLS

Vumbi pride (robot-camera photograph), Serengeti
National Park, Tanzania, 2011

Sirens. His appetite, first, is for their physical magnificence. Their comportment, their musculature. Their suppleness, their lean goldenness transfix him. Their indifference seduces him. Enigmatic eyes set in heart-shaped faces—serenely closed one minute, burning with intentionality the next. Mouths to be reckoned with: stretched open in a primordial call, or lips pursed in what resembles calm, or impish delight. Sinuous curves. They have been licking each other: subtle hues seem to wash over them in a soft caress. Everything glistens as the five lionesses loll in the brush.

He is overwhelmed. Undone—yet again—by such penetrating femininity. He is almost breathless.

"I never expected to fall in love like this. I never imagined I could feel this way." Their watchful intelligence, their soulfulness, "the way," he whispers, "they look inside me."

These are the lionesses of the Vumbi pride in the Serengeti, in northern Tanzania.

Vast and primal, the landscape here undulates forward in spectra of sand to gold to green grasslands, with dots of purple and red-blue-orange, wildflowers and brush. The plains crest in sculptural mounds, smooth and gray—rocky formations known as kopjes. Clusters of acacia trees filter the noonday sun, offering a break in the horizon line as well. The breeze is restorative.

Michael Nichols—or Nick, as he has been known for decades—is in Tanzania's Serengeti National Park with Reba Peck, his wife, and Nathan Williamson, his assistant and videographer. It is October 2011, and they are in the early stages of a seventeen-month project photographing the Serengeti lion for *National Geographic*. Nick has been with the magazine for more than two decades, working always in close collaboration with scientists. In this case he has joined forces with ecologist Craig Packer, longtime director of the Serengeti Lion Project. One of the world's longest-running large-animal studies, the project was founded in 1966 by the eminent biologist and wildlife conservationist George B. Schaller. Schaller's original studies concentrated on prides in the Serengeti's richly biodiverse Seronera region—although he worked throughout the park "to census lions and record the movements of the 155 lions I had ear-tagged."

At Packer's recommendation, Nick and his team have set up camp in the Serengeti's Barafu Valley. Here they can work alone—or rather, without the company of other humans, as the park's Seronera area is now overrun by tourists on safari. Barafu Valley, by contrast, is deemed a "marginal" landscape for lions, in part because there is no steady water source—a fact of the ecosystem that affects the behavior of all animals, in terms of both movement and predation. Packer was adamant that Nick must witness the "feast-or-famine" existence of one of the plains prides in the project's study—and this is possible in Barafu.

Nick, Reba, and Nathan Williamson began their time in the Serengeti with a few weeks in the wild Lamai Triangle, or Lamai Wedge, farther north. It was there that Nick first encountered the wondrous diversity of the Serengeti, and where he first became entranced by this terrain and its inhabitants.

As a photographer, Nick has always worked this way: he must feel before he can truly see. In the Serengeti, he makes his way through the Darwinian landscape, sensing and beginning to understand how to convey visually its lifeblood, its ravages, its songs, its laments.

The Serengeti thrives on its legendary annual migration of animals—wildebeest, gazelles, zebras— and in his first weeks in Tanzania, Nick begins by photographing galaxies of creatures confronting countless trials on their respective odysseys.

By the time Nick brings his full focus to the lions, the Serengeti is coursing through him. He is now at home here, poised to render this place's harsh tensions, to go deep, to get close.

Nick is a photojournalist working in a time of crisis. Habitat and species are continually threatened by humans—some have already been eradicated, others are beyond the possibility of regeneration if action is not taken soon. Poaching—with planes, guns, poison, snares, and other lethal weapons—is an unrelenting threat. The slaughter of big cats, elephants, great apes, rhinoceroses, and other animals, by poachers is feeding an estimated multibillion-dollar illegal wildlife trade industry.[1] Park guards and rangers attempting to care for and protect these animals are regularly murdered in the process. Environmentalists have been killed as well. The long-term destructive impact on wildlife populations is huge and unconscionable.

It is in part as basic as supply and demand. If people stop believing that ivory trinkets are worth the slaughter of elephants, the killings will stop. The same is true for rhinoceroses, killed for their horns; lions and tigers, killed for their skins, bones, and organs. If people stop finding amusement in the humanoid antics of captured apes, the animals may be left in peace. Except that entire habitats are being raped for their resources, decimated by logging and other practices—leaving many animals without a home.

Land is everything.

For nearly thirty years, Nick has conspired with scientists, naturalists, journalists, and activists to take on these issues. They painstakingly consider the complicated questions, from every angle: How may we manage land and natural resources in a manner that is sustainable for all who share the planet? National parks, from Yellowstone to the Serengeti, abut people's farms and backyards. In countries that are economically devastated, the poorest communities are often in close proximity to predators. In some places, deeply rooted cultural traditions clash with conservation efforts. And yet there must be a way, Nick and his colleagues firmly believe, for wild and human cultures to coexist, with respect and security for all.

"Wildlife photography" is not the right term to describe what Nick does. To begin with, "wildlife photography" is a genre that until recent years has been consistently undermined by questionable ethics, often trivialized by sentimentality, and represented by one-hit visual wonders. Missing, for the most part, has been the in-depth, fact-based storytelling and testimonials that define the most trenchant photojournalism. Nick approaches his work in this reportorial tradition: he is a photojournalist in the wild. And like other photojournalists in areas of crises, he sheds light on the inner workings of communities, the intrinsic significance—even magnificence—of what's at stake, and the horrors of the battlefield.

I first saw Nick's 1989 book *Gorilla: Struggle for Survival in the Virungas* shortly after its publication, when I became an editor at Aperture Foundation.[2] What immediately riveted me about his photographs was that they seemed to depict the animals on their own terms, with profound intimacy; there was no whiff of saccharine, no overt anthropomorphism. In fact, I had never before encountered such an approach to what is also termed "natural history photography." While I respected the work I'd seen in that genre, it had seldom captivated me photographically, beyond my curiosity about the subjects. Nick's photographs in *Gorilla* demanded that attention be paid, and I have since come to see that demand as a central energizing component of his work. Moreover, his galvanizing images form narratives, complete with protagonists, antagonists—lovers, caregivers, heroes, and other archetypes—all rendered with a sensibility that straddles documentation and interpretation.

His process (as I have learned) is taxing, to say the least: there are Herculean labors and triumphs, and sometimes epic failures from which to recover. There are the nuanced cultural complexities that surround his projects, and that have taught Nick to avoid a unilateral point of view and to consider his subjects from a fully encompassing perspective.

I contacted Nick shortly after seeing *Gorilla*, asked him about his current projects and dreams, and proposed that we collaborate. In the years since, I've had the privilege of working with him on three books, and a number of projects for *Aperture* magazine, of which I became an editor in 1992, and was editor-in-chief from 2002 to 2012.

Aperture—which originated as the magazine founded in 1952 by Ansel Adams, Dorothea Lange, Barbara Morgan, and Minor White, among others—is now a far-reaching foundation devoted to photography. It has long had a reputation as a publisher of groundbreaking work by inspired artists and deeply courageous, often advocacy-driven photojournalists. It was the perfect home for Nick in every respect. Fresh in my mind's eye when I began working with him were narratives by some of the other photographers whose work we were publishing—among them Donna Ferrato, Nan Goldin, Sally Mann, Mary Ellen Mark, Richard Misrach, and Eugene Richards. As incongruous as it may seem, their work formed the personal visual context into which I fitted Nick's stories and images. Similar tensions vitalize the work of all these photographers—often disquieting interpretations of violence, beauty, poverty, desire, exploitation, and love—as they turn their cameras toward the dramas of families, communities, and environments. They look without flinching at sometimes unsettling truths: psychological, racial, and political. There is no exoticism, nothing remotely cloying in their work. That Nick's protagonists are nonhumans in no way diminishes the work's relevance or its ability to get under one's skin.

We worked on projects together over the next two decades, yet I still had no real idea how he does what he does, how he achieves such shattering intimacy in his work, or what compels him as he chases images of these elusive psyches.

And then, in March 2012, I went into the field with Nick for the first time.

I joined him, Reba, and Nathan Williamson in the Barafu Valley at their isolated campsite in the Vumbi pride's territory, on the savannas of the Serengeti. I arrived at what seemed a propitious time: after the rains and before the yearly migration. It was here, tent-side—as curious giraffes, camouflaged by the trees defining the tip of our camp, eavesdropped—that Nick and I began a discussion that would continue over the course of the next four years: unfettered, free-flowing, Nick-unplugged, ever-digressing conversations.

Through those talks, and in those I've had with many of Nick's colleagues and collaborators over the years, I grew to understand more acutely certain aspects of his self-described "alpha" nature. Nick's Dude-ish charm and Alabama drawl belie a tireless and competitive perfectionist with a healthy ego, a flaring temper, and relentless drive. Those conversations have also revealed a person who is, both on evidence and by his own admission, surprisingly fragile; a man who continues to delight in the world, and whose speech is inflected with giggles and cackles, almost always.

Nick is six-foot-one, carries his ample height nimbly and with self-assurance. His gait is easy, his gestures fluid—working with wild animals as he does, there can be no abrupt moves, no lurches. (Like many other photo-documentarians, he must play the fly on the wall, habituating his subjects to his presence over a time and with patience and consistency.) His wide-set eyes, though ringed with lines of fatigue, are always animated, always searching. Over the years, his once dark-brown hair has variously flowed down his back, been bandana'd or ponytailed; it has weathered severe croppings and has often been drenched in sweat and itchy with bugs. Lately, his facial hair evinces his age, flecked with silver scruff.

Baby Thompson gazelle and hyena, Lamai Wedge, Serengeti National Park, 2011

In conversation, Nick's modifiers of choice are "fucking" and "goddam," and they insert themselves with the frequency of someone else's "you knows" and "ums"—but they're never intended as coarse expletives. (Still, I've deleted many here because they are better said than read.) To my own ear, perhaps because of his Southern cadence, they resonate a bit like the punctuation and exclamatory speech bubbles in comic books.

Earth to Sky[3] is the title of Nick's 2013 book about African elephants—but the words *earth to sky* could easily serve as a metaphor for the pathways of Nick's life. From the backyard hideouts of his childhood in Alabama to the last untrodden places on Earth, from the unfathomable depths of caves to the lofty canopies of the world's tallest trees, from immediate surroundings to larger, often fantastic ecosystems, Nick has always been a man of boundless embrace, with an innate sense that anything and everything he imagines is within reach.

His photographic projects reflect this expansive sensibility while hinging on his larger inquiry about wildness itself. Nick:

> What is *wild*? It is the essence of what I believe in. It means untamed. It means free. And it is the thing that most human beings have no concept of, because we think that we are in charge. The fundamental thing we have to do in this whole game is put that idea, that need to be in control, aside.

Something of a paradox, then, that the imperative to save what remains of true wild is within the controlling hands of humans—who so often polarize wildlife as "other," read: lesser. Nick's work

OPPOSITE: Wildebeest, Mara River, Lamai Wedge, Serengeti National Park, 2011. ABOVE: Giraffes, Lamai Wedge, Serengeti National Park, 2011

implicitly suggests the ultimate folly in forgetting that we humans, too, are animals—with the capacity of permanently destroying this shared habitat.

Parks, from Congo's Nouabalé-Ndoki to India's Bandhavgarh to California's Prairie Creek, are helping to protect designated landscapes and their inhabitants. However, many conservationists have long questioned the "anointing" of pockets of wilderness—through land management and protection—in both theory and practice. While concurring with the larger goal of saving habitats and species, these advocates don't believe that consecration of land will shift minds and hearts, will effect a true cultural departure from exploitative lust. The value judgment, the embrace of relativism, also imply that nonprotected land is therefore less important, and fair game.

As Barry Lopez wrote in 1990, in the pages of *Aperture* magazine:

> To have this fundamental problem of land ethics defined, or understood, as mainly "a fight for wilderness" hurts us in two ways. It preserves a misleading and artificial distinction between "holy" and "profane" lands, and it continues to serve the industries that most seriously threaten wilderness. . . . What we face is a crisis of character. Our relationships with the land

are essentially still colonial—exploitive, indifferent, romantic, and cruel. They are largely untouched by a sense of wonder or by the sense of a universe shaped by other than human perception and orderings. We are, it is possible to argue, blind to creation; we do not scruple or hesitate to improve upon it or to disturb it.[4]

Still, protecting regions remains our most efficient and immediate solution, until humans adopt a less tyrannical attitude toward nature. The isolation of areas of land and the labeling of "endangered" species are pragmatic stopgaps, not cures. To halt the hunting of an animal only because it is endangered does not nurture a true sense of the worth of that animal's life, nor does it necessarily result in the desired regeneration of a population. Worse, as soon as a species is removed from the endangered list—or "delisted"—it is hunted again, and once more the ecological balance is potentially disrupted. The campaign against logging the redwood forest cannot be about saving a last piece of land along a scenic highway; it must be about valuing redwoods as part of the larger ecosystem—understanding their interdependence with rivers, fish populations, birds—and the consequences of their loss for all these elements, and for humans, too.

In the mid-twentieth century, pioneering ecologist Aldo Leopold argued for what he termed a "land ethic" (conceiving *land* in widely inclusive terms): "All ethics so far evolved rest upon a single premise: that the individual is a member of a community of interdependent parts."[5] A land ethic, he wrote,

> reflects the existence of an ecological conscience, and this in turn reflects a conviction of individual responsibility for the health of the land. *Health is the capacity of the land for self-renewal. Conservation is our effort to understand and preserve this capacity.*[6] (Emphasis mine.)

ABOVE: Nick, Serengeti National Park, 2012. Photograph by David Griffin. PAGES 16–17: Wildebeest and zebras, Serengeti National Park, 2012

In his *Sand County Almanac* (1949) and his journal entries in *Round River* (1953), Leopold does not separate his discussion of the wild from his discussion of humans. Rather, his land ethic "enlarges the boundaries of the community to include soils, waters, plants, and animals. . . ."[7]

Nick Nichols, through his life's work photographing in the wild—blazing his own path, in his own way—has reached a similar understanding of humanity's relation to the land: he does not come from a nature- and animal-photography tradition or a landscape-photography tradition or an expedition/adventure-photography tradition, although his work is infused with characteristics of all these genres. As a young man, he more or less educated himself in the history of photography, looking at publications by Edward Weston and Henri Cartier-Bresson in his college library, taking note of Ernst Haas's 1971 book *The Creation*[8] and Mitsuaki Iwagō's work in the Serengeti. Nick also saw George Schaller's and Dian Fossey's images of their respective studies, as well as the films of Alan Root, and the photographs and films of Hugo van Lawick (collaborator and former husband of Jane Goodall), and those of Bob Campbell on Fossey.

Still, the tradition from which his work and sensibility more clearly derive is that of straightforward hard-hitting photojournalism. There is perhaps no clearer evidence of this than Nick's thirteen years as a Magnum photographer, from 1982 to 1995. Magnum Photos, the prestigious international photography cooperative, has since its founding been lauded for its commitment to "concerned photography"—generally focusing on human subjects—by some of the world's most respected photojournalists. If there is a Magnum mindset, it may have to do with seeing and then photographing with a sense of purpose and context, with an emphasis on storytelling rooted in a social conscience. These are among the qualities that characterize Nick's photography and distinguish it from others that focus on wildlife.

Perhaps his most distinctive feature is the ability to get very, very close to his subjects in every sense. The viewer doesn't just see what the photographer saw, but experiences the intensity of his encounters, his feral instincts—which have been continuously tested and sharpened.

"Should trees have standing?" This question was posed elegantly in a 1972 paper by environmental law and ethics scholar Christopher D. Stone.[9] What, indeed, are the *rights* of flora and fauna?

These questions relate directly to the ethics of being a photojournalist in the wild. Beyond the usual journalistic demands for honesty and full disclosure is the challenge of how one may function in such environments without leaving a damaging footprint, without influencing the situation being documented. The confluence of photography and technology, advocacy, science, and conservation are stunningly complex and uniquely invoked in Nick's work. These elements must be considered through the complicated lenses of human rights, endemic poverty and unemployment, agricultural demands, along with politics, corruption, and myriad power struggles—often deadly struggles; the resulting contextual layers of understanding are critical to any conscionable decision-making about land and resource management, as well as sustainable wild populations of all species.

Here, Nick will be our ecological Virgil, visually guiding us through many of these issues, as well as the very notion of wild, and where and how it brushes up against man.

MY HOMETOWN

Muscle Shoals, Alabama, April 1985

The legendary *Muscle Shoals sound.* That defining Muscle Shoals rhythm section—a group of brilliantly funky session musicians known as the Swampers. Until a few years ago, that was basically all I knew about Nick's hometown of Muscle Shoals, Alabama: its history as a kind of musical utopia, where gifted musicians played off each other's talents and passions—the results subsequently captured in the town's famous recording studios known for producing a distinct, achingly soulful sound.

What is the alchemical force of this stretch of Alabama along the south bank of the Tennessee River, 150 miles from Memphis and 115 miles from Birmingham? I wanted to hear the river sing, as it is fabled to do, and to feel the magic that catalyzed such innovation with the likes of Aretha Franklin, Wilson Pickett, Percy Sledge, the Rolling Stones, Etta James, Lynyrd Skynyrd, Duane Allman, Clarence Carter, and so many others who recorded here, and who found solace or inspiration in this landscape. Jimmy Cliff, who made his 1971 album *Another Cycle* in Muscle Shoals, described the particular convergence of moment and place as "a field of energy."[1]

The town's Fame and Muscle Shoals Sound studios managed somehow to transcend divides in musical genres, and also—to the surprise of all concerned, it seems—with regard to race.

When I was growing up in New York City in the 1960s and '70s, the civil rights movement was a big and central topic, both in my family and at my school. But the specifics of racism, of the South's struggle with its seemingly entrenched bigotry—the violence, the riots, the cruelty and demoralizing effect of segregation—were for me something of an abstraction, and seemed distant (although racism was certainly a part of life in the North as well). It was not until I was a teenager that I began to really pay attention to photographs—by Charles Moore, by James Karales, and others—in magazines my parents subscribed to and held onto such as *Life* and *Look*, as well as reportage in the *New York Times*. These images brought the reality of the civil rights struggle into our lives, and had a galvanizing effect on America. It was largely through my experience of those photographs that I formed my picture of the South—and of what it must have been like when Nick was growing up there.

Michael Keith Nichols was born in Muscle Shoals in 1952. The town is of course its own place with its own unique history—but seminal events were happening close by, and Nick might have had at least some awareness of them. Montgomery is only a couple hundred miles from Muscle Shoals: Rosa Parks was arrested there in December 1955 for refusing to give up her seat on a bus to a white passenger. Two months later, the Montgomery home of Martin Luther King Jr. was bombed by segregationists; he was the spokesman for the Montgomery Bus Boycott at the time. In 1961 the Freedom Riders' buses were stopped by disruptive violence in Anniston, Alabama—and again in Birmingham, and again in Montgomery. George C. Wallace, the ultimate segregationist, began his four terms as Alabama's governor in 1963. And in 1965 Reverend King led more than three thousand marchers in support of civil rights from Selma to Birmingham. Not long after, President Lyndon Johnson signed the Voting Rights Act into law.

These landmark events, along with the Vietnam War, dominated the larger social and political context of Nick's childhood. Surprisingly, though, the subject of civil rights is almost entirely absent from my conversations with Nick and his family and childhood friends, as well as Reba—who was raised in nearby Killen—as we discuss their experiences growing up in Alabama. The issues of racial strife and equality, of social justice didn't touch their lives directly, it would seem, until they went off to college or were drafted. That said, the debate over "states' rights" pervaded, feeding off people's prejudices and fears (as it does to this day in parts of the country), cloaking racism in an argument against the federal government's unwelcome interference in local self-determination.

At the same time, the advent of a seductive counterculture challenged authority and its givens, and this shaped Nick's burgeoning sense of self. His close childhood friends, Jamie and Ken Kelley (now married), explained that being hippies—as Nick and his friends were—in that period was a form of rebellion against deeply rooted mores. "For us," they told me, "it was about breaking from the ways of the past. And that included racism."

Nick wore his hippiness in long, dark waves—at first only down to his shoulders—but that was a statement in itself. In Alabama in the early 1960s,

> the worst thing—worse than anything—was to have long hair. It meant to everyone that you were questioning authority, in ways that were related to civil rights and Vietnam, but that we didn't understand entirely then. Men where I lived hated the Beatles' hair . . . there was fire about hair in Alabama. So if you wanted to rebel, hair was a good place to start. . . .

> I had pretty hair.

> And then the Crosby, Stills, Nash and Young song underlined it—"Almost Cut My Hair." I was not a redneck. I was a *hippie*, and embraced all that that meant . . . peace and love and not war. The music, and all that came with it, formed me. I read *Rolling Stone* from its inception. It was the times. Then one day . . . now away at college, I heard the Stones' "Street Fighting Man" and saw that there could be anger attached to peace and love. . . .

> We were just kids but the time was ripe.

But this is the macro. To look with a close-up lens: Nick's childhood was often horribly fraught. His father, James Cloyd Nichols, bolted angrily from their home when Nick was three years old, leaving Nick and his older sister and brother in the care of their mother Joyce. Money was scarce at best— their father forked over the minimal court-ordered support. Their mother, while managing to provide for them—often just barely—was an unreliable alcoholic. It is perhaps not surprising that Nick's

Nick, eight years old, 1960

The Nichols family, 1964. Left to right: Joyce, Pat (fifteen), Nick (twelve), James Jr. (Jim, sixteen)

older sister, Pat Charette, was somewhat oblivious to the civil rights turmoil that was happening nearby: "We really didn't know that there was a race issue," she tells me, indicating that their very survival was at times at stake, and this was the focus.

The children's maternal grandmother, Bonnie Mae Stutts Hall, was by all accounts a broadminded, openhearted woman—Pat uses the word "antiracist" to describe her. Pat recalls Bonnie Mae's regular visits with "an elderly, blind African American woman named Mattie. Our grandmother would read her mail to her, and pay her bills, pick up a few little groceries for her. . . . Mattie could not do those things for herself."

Like Bonnie Mae, their mother, Joyce, was also vehemently nonracist. Nick and Pat concede, however, that not everyone in their family was: the word "nigger" was a regular part of their father's lexicon until the last few years of his life. Eventually their older brother, Jim, went to live with their father, while Pat and Nick stayed with their mother. Influenced by Joyce, the two younger siblings did not grow up hating anyone; their father's bigotry was one of many traits that pained them.

Life with Joyce, however, was often brutal and scary. She was a chain smoker and a binge drinker whose bouts with alcohol could be terrifying. According to Nick: "The smallest amount of whiskey could turn her into a monster." One of Nick's childhood friends refers to her as "a belligerent, raging drunk," and Jamie and Ken Kelley remember Joyce as "very moody," saying, "there was a lot of verbal abuse— she would play a lot of emotional games and guilt trips." Among the day-to-day dilemmas, as Pat remembers, were: "What are we going to eat? Are we going to be warm? Are we going to be clothed? . . . If you stopped to really see the situation you were in, you wouldn't make it."

After Nick's father left home, he stayed close by until Nick went into the army, at which point he moved to Montgomery, where he married for a third time. Nick's memories of his parents' life together are minimal, but he has a vague recollection of the violence the day James Sr. left: his mother caustic, screaming, while his father punched holes in the wall with his fist. "After my dad left," recalls Nick, "it was always so hard to visit him as a kid. He was mean and prejudiced. As difficult as my mother was when she was drunk, my father was worse. He was cruel. But," he concedes, "that was *our* experience. Most people loved my father— he was outgoing and charismatic." Nick tells me that as an adult, he had scarcely any relations with his father until shortly before James Nichols's death in 2007: "It was like a renaissance. He had stopped hating . . . I got to know and care for my father—I had a real father—at the end of his life."

It was a year or two after their father moved out that Nick's brother, Jim, went to live with him. A year older than Pat and four years older than Nick, Jim seemed to have a mean streak that came out when he visited his younger siblings on weekends. In Pat's recollection, he was a selfish bully who took pleasure in flamboyantly treating himself to little extravagances that Nick and Pat couldn't afford—indulgences funded by working odd jobs for their father. James Nichols's income from an array of jobs—he was a milkman when Nick was born, at other points the owner of a grocery store, a long-haul freight truck driver, a prison guard—far surpassed their mother's meager means.

I telephoned Jim Nichols in early 2014 to ask him about his memories of his younger brother. He stayed on the phone just long enough to declare, gruffly and definitively, that they had no relationship at all, that he had nothing to say about Nick.

Pat married at sixteen, happy to get out of the house—but leaving Nick alone at home with his mother. She cringes, thinking of her younger brother, forced to face Joyce's binges by himself. There were many times, Pat tells me, when no one knew Joyce's whereabouts or when she might find her way back home. At one point, Nick's father tried to gain custody, but Nick, loyal to his mother, refused: "I wouldn't have that."

I spoke with Joyce at her home in Charlottesville in early autumn 2013, just months before she moved to a hospice where she died in January 2014. When we met, she was very frail, and tethered to an oxygen tank, but still somehow fierce, ready to rumble. In the course of our discussions, Joyce was filled with self-reproach—about her drinking, about allowing Jim, at seven, to go live with his father. It was hard, she reminded me several times, being a divorced, single mother of three, with "no money, no work background, no education, nothing." She scraped by doing "whatever kind of work I could get."

Despite his faults, Joyce maintained that James Nichols Sr. had "a lot of personality, a lot of charm." But, she confided, his will was strong and he made every effort to control his children's lives—trying to tell them "what to do and what to think." In contrast, she insisted: "I wanted them to have their own opinions—to really *believe* in something and not just take an idea from someone else. . . . No follow-the-leader. I wanted them to be independent."

I asked Joyce how she got to be so independent. "I don't know. It was just me. I think I came into the world wondering why."

A month after this conversation, I am in Muscle Shoals with Nick and Reba. I meet with Pat, who still calls it home. She often weeps as she speaks with me of their childhood. And Nick, too, back in his hometown, is overwhelmed with childhood recollections. I ask Nick more about his mother, and he responds: "With all the bad stuff with my mom, I was her baby. There were some good things. . . . I remember her reading to me. It's one of my best memories."

I had wanted to see Nick's hometown with him—guessing that it would force some tucked-away memories, and luckily, a larger reason for this visit serendipitously emerged: Muscle Shoals became the centerpiece of Nick's if-it's-Tuesday-this-must-be-Alabama publicity tour for his new book, *Earth to Sky: Among Africa's Elephants, A Species in Crisis.*

This deep breath in Muscle Shoals would allow Nick to celebrate with childhood and college friends, and to take me on a memory-lane drive-by so I could see for myself where he grew up, and gain a sense of certain particulars of his youth. The eight-city book tour, organized by Nick's close friend Darlene Anderson, was conceived with advocacy in mind: at each stop, Nick gives a talk about the plight of African elephants and the blood-ivory trade. He is a stirring speaker: books are sold, and hopefully awareness is raised—all very much thanks to Anderson's initiative.

A slender woman with long dark hair streaked with gray, fine features, and a crisp voice, Darlene Anderson is forceful and thoughtful, but impatient with fools. Based primarily in Cincinnati, she and her husband, Jeff Anderson, a real-estate developer with the solid build of a former pro-football player, are generous supporters of conservation efforts. But their philanthropy is hardly limited to writing checks: both are ready to leap into the action of their causes. At one memorable point in the early 1980s, Darlene volunteered to "courier" bongo embryos from the Los Angeles Zoo to the Cincinnati Zoo (cradled in her armpits to assure the necessary climate control) so they could be implanted into an eland, as part of Dr. Betsy Dresser's Center for Reproduction of Endangered Wildlife's project on interspecies embryo transfers. On the same day—as Darlene was in LA getting ready for that trip—a last-minute transport glitch arose at the Cincinnati Zoo's high-profile welcome event for a new koala, part of the zoo's annual gala. Jeff Anderson was enlisted to help, and he himself chauffeured the very wide-awake koala in the backseat of his Rolls Royce Corniche convertible, top-down, to the red-carpet event.

Such stories animate lunch with the Andersons and other friends in Florence, Alabama, one of the quartet of towns—along with Muscle Shoals, Sheffield, and Tuscumbia—that comprise the larger metropolitan area known as The Shoals. The clinging heat of an Alabama Indian summer has given way to a cool, bright mid-October day as we lunch at Trowbridge's—a Florence fixture since 1918.

This no-frills ice-cream and sandwich bar—with a whiteboard menu hanging above a linoleum counter lined with a dozen tall, pistachio-green counter-chairs—was a favored spot for Nick and Reba and many of their friends who, in the mid- to late 1970s, overlapped at the University of North Alabama (UNA), just up the street.

UNA is Alabama's oldest public four-year university. Its campus is an architectural mishmash of eras and styles—three buildings predate the Civil War—and in general, the university's charm coheres around expansive lawns and pretty pathways. Nick's time here was intermittent: he first enrolled at UNA in 1970, leaving after a semester to attend the University of Montevallo, about 145 miles south of Muscle Shoals, where he stayed for three semesters before being drafted into the U.S. Army. Ultimately he returned to UNA for another two years, and it was from here that he received his BA in 1978.

With us at Trowbridge's is a coterie of some of Nick's oldest friends. Shannon Wells is a photographer who works for UNA; under her charge, the university is hosting this weekend's book signing, lecture, and general fêting of its alumnus. Don Cash has traveled from Austin, where he works as a videographer for Texas Parks and Wildlife. And Frankie Frost, who photographs for a local paper in California's Marin County, has lovingly made the journey from the West Coast with his son Tyler. Nobody is being mushy about it, but it's clear that this reunion matters. At Trowbridge's, the talk eventually turns to what Nick was like back in the day, as a student at UNA.

Shannon Wells was twenty-three when she started at college, and already a single mother of three children. With Nick, she felt an instant kinship: like her, he had seen more of the world and was a few years older than most of the other students, given his three years in the army. She recalls that Nick was always passionate about photography, always inventive, and his drive to achieve was very clear.

Frankie Frost remembers the first time he saw Nick's photographs: "He had an eleven-by-fourteen Kodak box full of prints. He opened the lid, and it was like a scene out of *Raiders of the Lost Ark*. It's like this light appeared: they were the most beautiful photographs—of people, of caves—I had ever seen."

Wells smiles, remembering that it wasn't only Nick's photographs that were compelling: "He would turn heads, because he was tall and good-looking. He always had a *smooth* aura about him, with a silky voice and a kind of sly smile—like he knew a secret about you."

After lunch, cheerful and sated, Nick, Reba, and I leave the restaurant to begin our tour through the town and its surroundings. Several factories—Ford, Union Carbide, and Reynolds aluminum, among others—were based in the largely blue-collar area when Nick was growing up. The environmental consequences of their polluting continue to this day, correlating with high rates of cancer, prevalent respiratory issues, and more. These plants and companies were also unionized, and as the 1970s progressed, high union costs were a factor in employment cutbacks. By the early 1980s, the area was desolate, desperately trying to recover from crushing unemployment. Some people escaped; others, trapped in poverty and misery, turned to alcohol or other momentary fixes.

More recently, however, Muscle Shoals has experienced periods of renewal, as new companies have moved in, improving the school system, and expanding the middle class. It has been a tumultuous stretch of decades, but the town now seems to be reviving.

For a man who has successfully navigated his way through uncharted jungle in the Congo, Nick has a surprisingly lousy sense of direction. As he drives us around the area, we rely heavily on our phones' GPS systems. Still, he is an assiduous tour guide: he shows us the site of his first school, Gilbert Elementary, in Florence, as well as almost every house he lived in as a child. Joyce moved the family seven times. Nick once asked his mother about this. "She said she was 'restless.' Instead of constantly rearranging the furniture—which she also did—we moved." The longest they ever lived in the same house was two years, 1963 to 1964, in Muscle Shoals, when Nick was in fifth and sixth grades at Highland Park Elementary School.

It wasn't until he entered Muscle Shoals High School that Nick encountered his first real mentor, an art teacher named Jean Schulman. He has stayed in touch with her over the years, and still refers to her with deep respect as "Mrs. Schulman." I had an opportunity to speak with Mrs. Schulman in Charlottesville in 2013. Plainly, she is enormously proud of her former student, and when I asked why she thought her class had made such an impact on him, she considered for a moment before pointing out that art classes were a novelty at that time in Muscle Shoals:

> No art had ever been taught in Muscle Shoals High School. *Ever.* Almost all the people who lived in Muscle Shoals were blue-collar workers, and most of the students I taught had never been out of the Muscle Shoals area. . . .

> Something that I think influenced Nick is that I am really a *design* teacher. I believe in design. If you know design, you can go in any direction. We also did life drawing, and I gave the students still-life assignments, and assignments that would entice them to fantasize—"Your assignment is to draw this plant, and make it into an animal."

Nick credits Mrs. Schulman with first introducing him to the possibilities of visual thinking: "You taught me to see," he once told her. Inscribed on one of several photographs by Nick that hang in his teacher's home are the words: "To the mother of all my work."

A couple of hours into our excursion through Nick's youth, we pause to stretch our legs at the top of the steep Whippoorwill Cliffs, and peer down at the Tennessee River meandering peacefully, far below. Nick tells Reba and me that he remembers leaping into the river from here with his friends—but when he sees our horrified expressions, he laughs and confesses that he actually jumped from a much lower point. (This is a pattern I'll learn to recognize as our conversations proceed: Nick catches his own exaggerations as they trip off his tongue—ultimately favoring fact, after first offering up the embellished account, as if to get it out of his system.)

As we cruise the backroads, Nick is fully warmed to talking about his youth. It's clear that despite the troubling aspects of his childhood, he still feels connected to that time and this place. Many of his stories involve Little League pals Steve Lawler (whose eyesight was so terrible he was nicknamed "Stevie Wonder"), Gary Traffanstedt (called "Fuzzy"), and Wallace Weddington (known simply as "Bubba"). Donald and Ronald Phillips, fraternal twins at times referred to as the "evil twins," also make several appearances in Nick's reminiscences.

And then there are the girls, including a bevy of cheerleaders (as we drive, he points out where each of them lived). At this point, we are winding through the streets of Muscle Shoals, and Nick wants us to see a particular tree that holds significance for him: as a teenager he had spent nearly an entire day hiding in its branches after being "abandoned" by Teena Crabb, the girl who gave him his first kiss. "I kissed her when we played spin the bottle, and then she went steady with a football player. I was devastated." A pause. "She was probably a foot taller than me."

From the 1965 Muscle Shoals High School yearbook: seventh-grade class officers, including Teena Crabb (far left) and Nick (upper right)

After a while of circling, the tree remains elusive, so Nick—who has spoken with Teena no more than a handful of times since high school—asks me to track her down on the phone. "Her married name is Teena Noles. Dial 411," he commands, "and ask for Teena Noles. Muscle Shoals, Alabama." Once connected, he takes the phone. The singsong drawl kicks in immediately. "Teena? Hey—it's Mike Nichols." He laughs warmly. "Yeah—before you hang up on me!—where did you used to live? I'm giving a tour of places I lived, and I can't remember, and . . . Lewis Street! Cool!" Before hanging up, he reminds Teena of his UNA book event that evening—hoping she plans to be there. Grinning at Reba and me, he chortles: "She says she's getting her outfit together right now." Sure enough, a few minutes later, "There's the tree": a big and healthy maple with perfectly spaced limbs that still beckon.

Around a couple of corners: "There's the Baptist church. . . . That's where all the girls were 'saved.'" Nick recalls that once their souls had been safely cleansed and their sins washed away, his friends marched over to his house and announced to his mother: "We want to save Mike!'" Joyce chased them out of the yard, hollering.

"I did not bring up my children with religion," Joyce had told me. Her decision to forego religious education was, she admitted, an unusual one in the Bible Belt—but Joyce was disillusioned with what she saw as the greed, ostentation, and divisiveness of the church. "It did not work for me to teach my children religion," she said, "because I could not accept it for myself—the selfishness—and that religion has caused so many wars and so much pain."

When I met with Joyce at her home, she and I leafed through some of Nick's old yearbooks. Images dating back to his elementary school days revived her memories. Joyce shook her head, recalling her youngest child's remarkably lively imagination:

> He made up a lot of stories when he was little—things that he *wanted* to be true, he would imagine to be true. He'd disappear into the woods, and there his fantasies were his reality. And he was always bringing all kinds of critters into the house, including the neighbor's dog. He did not get into trouble . . . he could talk his way out of anything. Still can!

Nick's sister, Pat, confirms that as a kid he was amazingly convincing: he could get people to do or believe anything, no matter how outrageous. He was very funny, and she also remembers him as being something of a showoff. During an elementary school performance, Pat tells me, "while all the other kids were singing and doing what they were supposed to do, he started doing the Twist and twirling a hat. . . . He just did his thing—because he hadn't been given a speaking part."

Pat saw all this as compensation for a lack of maternal attention. Her own mode of coping with their mother, and with the poverty of those days, was to pretend that everything was all right. She says that Nick's "way of dealing was his fantasy life. Before he *truly* went somewhere else, he went somewhere else."

Nick agrees: "I was always off on some adventure—real or in my head, it kind of didn't matter. And I got addicted to the outdoors growing up in Alabama, because we'd go to the woods all the time. . . . The woods saved me." Nick's natural survival instincts, honed by his family life, led him to seek safe havens. He was clearly receptive to people and ideas, wanderings and wonderings that offered respite from the bleakness and uncertainties of home.

On visits to his father and first stepmother, Nick discovered a mesmerizing vehicle for quick mental getaways in the pages of an illustrated magazine about wild animals and faraway lands and peoples. "My escape from my dad's anger, when I was at his house, was to look at *National Geographic*. My stepmother had a full collection. I would just sit on the floor and go around the world."

Along with his forays into the woods and into the pages of *National Geographic*, Nick often took refuge in the home of his best friend, Stevie Lawler. Although he was a couple of years older than Nick, from the time Stevie was eleven and Nick was nine, they were almost inseparable. Stevie's older brother, Chuck, tells me that the entire Lawler clan embraced Nick as part of the family. Chuck Lawler remembers Nick as a shy boy, and attributes his quietness to a tough home life (common knowledge in the small community). But he laughs, recalling that together Stevie and Nick could be remarkably aggravating, as only younger brothers can be.

To Chuck, who coached the boys' Little League baseball team, Nick's determination was clear early on, even when—especially when—he made mistakes: Nick was hard on himself, and rarely made the same error twice. At the same time, he and Stevie couldn't resist playing pranks in the field. With no apparent shame, Nick remembers invoking his nearsighted friend's nickname, "Stevie Wonder," in order to terrify the other team's batters when Stevie was pitching. "He has *no idea* where the ball is going!" Nick would warn the other team, a mix of pity and foreboding in his tone. "You've really got to protect your life here." It was on the baseball field that the name "Nick" began to stick—partly to differentiate him from several other "Mikes" but also because, Nick notes, "Southerners *always* have nicknames."

Nick can't imagine his childhood without the Lawlers. The generosity and kindness demonstrated by the Lawler parents—not only to him and to their own children, but to each other—was unknown in Nick's family. The Lawlers were a lifeline for Nick, and Stevie his constant companion. "Everything," says Chuck, "that Nick and Stevie wanted to do, they wanted to do together."

As they matured, the two boys remained close. Stevie went off to the University of Montevallo, and Nick transferred there from UNA, entering in the spring of 1971. Like many of their peers, Nick and Stevie were sampling from an array of drugs—generally favoring LSD and marijuana. For Stevie, this eventually evolved into a long and lethal addiction to Dilaudid—an illegally obtained opioid pain medication. Over the years that followed, Nick did all he could to help his friend, from hiring Stevie to work on his photo-assignments to trying—again and again—to help him get clean: "I would ask Stevie to come to wherever I was living and dry him out, and he would become strong again." But the ravages of off-and-on addiction, Nick believes, were ultimately too much for Stevie, whose heart stopped beating at the age of forty-two. He wasn't using at the time, but the damage to his system had been done. He died on his mother's couch in Muscle Shoals.

"I loved him," Nick says. "He is my best friend forever."

It was while Nick and Stevie were together at Montevallo that Nick, an art major, took a photography 101 class—his first serious exposure to the medium—and found himself suddenly and irreversibly hooked. "The moment I developed my first picture, that was it. . . . I started telling everyone that I was going to be a photographer. I didn't even have a camera—I had borrowed one for the class! I started carrying it with me everywhere, shooting everything. I started to look at books, at magazines. I started paying attention."

Nick had a college loan, and was making up for the shortfall in tuition by selling pot and LSD. His grades were good enough, he was popular, and he reveled in the dorm experience—it was his first time away from home and its tribulations. As on many college campuses in 1971, conversation often revolved around music—especially the Grateful Dead, the Beatles, and the Rolling Stones. Alliances to bands were fiercely debated. Nick listened to all of them, but the Stones spoke most directly to him. He had gone to hear them at Auburn University in 1969 and his mind had been utterly blown by Mick Jagger's charisma and sass: "They were about revolution!" One of the college bands adopted Nick as an occasional front man. "I wasn't a musician," he admits, "but I wanted to *be* Mick Jagger. I couldn't sing. I was just enthusiastic and jumped around onstage!" At Montevallo, he also met a curvaceous sorority girl named Patricia Pennington, and was smitten; soon enough they were a couple. He had, as he puts it, "*got love.*"

Nick was happy. The weight of the negative aspects of his childhood had lifted, and his world was expanding in every sense. But all at once, in his third semester at Montevallo, it came crashing down: Nick was drafted into the U.S. Army in the spring of 1972. As a college student, he could have taken a deferment had he filled out the necessary paperwork, but—with youthful magical thinking—he simply believed his number would never come up. "I thought," he recalls, "that it wouldn't happen to me. Which was really stupid."

He weighed his options. "I didn't want to go to war. I didn't want to kill." He considered claiming conscientious-objector status—but knew that was a difficult route, particularly in conservative Southern communities. "'What are you going to do when those Communists come over the hill and they're raping your mother?'"—he could hear the question at the draft board, or in his hometown. Furthermore, it was by then clear to everyone that the Vietnam War was drawing to a close—and indeed, just months later, in 1973, a ceasefire agreement was signed, the draft ended, and remaining U.S. troops were brought home. When drafted, Nick understood that the army he would enter would be a postwar force. Given that, his choice was either to sign up for two years in the infantry, or to volunteer for a three-year commitment in which he could select his job and perhaps, he thought, learn something. Despite having taken only one photography class, Nick was certain about what he wanted to do, and self-confident enough to consider signing on for an extra year in order to work as a photographer.

Ultimately though, it might be said that Nick's decision to join as a three-year volunteer was made by the Rolling Stones:

Nick and Patti Pennington's wedding, Falling Rock Falls, Montevallo, Alabama, 1972. Malcolm Steiner (in hat) officiated; Steve Lawler (right) served as best man. Photograph by Clay Nordan

As I'm agonizing over this decision of two or three years, I find out that the Stones are going to play two concerts in Alabama that spring. . . . They were going to play in Mobile on June 27—which was my report date—and then in Tuscaloosa on the 28th. If I gave up an extra year of my life, I could get an extension until late fall and go see the Stones. It was not an option to miss that concert. . . . So I signed on the dotted line, for 365 days of extra service.

Nick went to both concerts—and has no regrets: "To this day, nobody can produce energy like the Stones. 'You Can't Always Get What You Want.' It was magical, like we were all soaring through the air to Mick Taylor's guitar."

That fall, Nick began his three-year military commitment. But before leaving for Fort Campbell, he married his college sweetheart, Patti, in a classic flower-child wedding at Falling Rock Falls, in Montevallo, with Steve Lawler as best man. Patti's friend Nita Threet sang "Stand By Your Man," and Nick's friend Don Tinsley sang the Rolling Stones song "Dear Doctor," about a guy being afraid to get married, and the bride eventually running off with the groom's cousin.

Not long after, Nick got on the bus from Muscle Shoals to boot camp in Fort Knox, Kentucky. There, his shoulder-length hair was shaved off ("I felt like Samson, becoming powerless"), and he was assigned an olive-green uniform. Before leaving Alabama, he had had the presence of mind to carefully replace the tobacco in a couple of packs of menthol Kools with marijuana—a precaution that would make him "a very popular guy at Fort Knox."

After basic training, he was transferred to Fort Campbell, along the Kentucky-Tennessee border, with an assignment to work in the photography lab for the next three years. It was at the base that Nick began to learn his craft. The first two years at Fort Campbell, he hid out in the darkroom, developing film and learning—often by his and others' mistakes—the importance of exposure time and other darkroom techniques. He was eager to perfect his technical skills, so when he wasn't developing other people's negatives, he was photographing, and developing and printing his own.

Throughout his boyhood, when not intoxicated by the possibilities of Mars, Nick often fantasized about the local caves around Muscle Shoals: their deceptively unremarkable entryways, their promise of grand otherworldliness. Now at Fort Campbell, longing to extricate from the daily regimentation and restrictiveness of the army base, whenever he had a chance—even for an afternoon—Nick began to explore some of Kentucky's many caves. At first, his excursions were simply short escapes from the military grind, but they soon became something of an obsession, as well as a challenge. He was susceptible to every open-sesame, anything that felt liberating. The caves represented a confluence of all he had sought in his childhood reveries. But this was real.

Eventually he discovered, two hours from Fort Campbell, meetings of the Nashville Grotto of the National Speleological Society, where avid cavers gathered to show slides of their expeditions: "That's what got me. I was immediately challenged by photographing in darkness." It turned out that the tools with which to take this on were right there at the army base, in the form of huge old, Weegee-like flashbulbs capable of illuminating gigantic spaces.

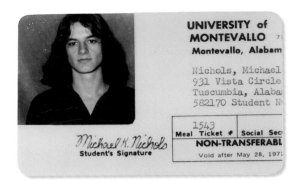

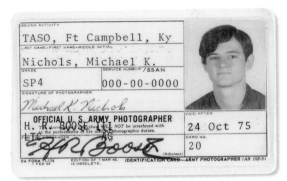

ABOVE: Nick's University of Montevallo ID, 1971; BELOW: Nick's military ID, 1975 (with altered Social Security Number)

Often, he was accompanied on his cave expeditions by his army buddy Steve Shirey, whom Nick recalls as "the bad boy in my unit, absolutely fearless." By contrast, Nick himself instinctively understood the necessity of fear: "I was always more controlled—which is, I think, the reason I'm still alive. I'm not an adrenaline junkie by any stretch. I'm alive because I've been careful."

Nick's marriage to Patti did not survive Nick's army duty. "Stand By Your Man" turned out not to be her forte. "Patti just completely destroyed me," says Nick. "The day I got out of the army, in October 1975, was the day I finished it with Patti. I didn't even cry that day."

After his three years of military service, Nick re-enrolled at UNA in the spring semester of 1976, now with support from the GI Bill. Over the following two years, his friendships with Shannon Wells, Don Cash, Frankie Frost, Dave Stueber, Mike McCracken, and many others were formed. His photographic bonafides also continued to build: he became the chief photographer for the UNA student newspaper, and from late 1975 through 1976 he worked at Florence's *Times-Daily* as a nighttime film processor; he also worked Friday nights as a football photographer. Given the slower films then available, it was difficult to work in the stadium's lighting, and this experience furthered his understanding of how to make compelling images in less than optimal conditions.

Rusty Cone, the *Times-Daily*'s leading photojournalist, was in charge of assigning stories to the younger shooters. Early on, eager to prove himself, Nick went to cover a community square dance, and lit his shots not in the conventional way, from above, but by bouncing the light off the floor. ("I thought it was more creative. The dancers, of course, appeared like ghouls.") He also took to heart Cone's advice about framing—"'Make sure they're tight; never waste part of your frame'"—and adhered to it so closely that in some early assignments the tops and bottoms of his subjects' heads are missing. He continued to learn from his mistakes, while never playing it safe.

Nick credits a breakthrough in his understanding of the power of photography to a conference in September 1976 at the University of Maryland, where the Pulitzer Prize–winning photojournalist Eddie Adams spoke. Adams's indelible 1968 photograph of a Vietcong prisoner being executed on a Saigon street was still very fresh in the public mind, with the war only three years in the past. Adams and his work astonished Nick: "I just didn't know—even though by that point I'd seen *Look* and *Life* and various camera magazines, and of course *National Geographic*—I just didn't know that what I was seeing was about photographing events, telling stories."

Nick realized then, he had to learn to be a storyteller through his images.

"Not nude."

Those were the first words Reba Peck uttered to Nick Nichols in October 1976. Although he admits that, after the debacle with Patti Pennington, he rebounded by smothering every girl he met upon his return to UNA with charm and attention, there was something very different about this beautiful young art student. His friends told him not to bother trying to win her heart; she was unattainable, she was shy. And she was engaged. But Nick couldn't resist. He would gaze dreamily at her through the window of her campus art studio, across the courtyard from UNA's photography department. He found ways to cross paths with her on campus— although she never returned his hopeful smiles. Finally, one evening, he confronted her directly, and asked if she would model for him. She did—with clothes on (well, at first). Nick was besotted. Their love affair began.

Nick's photographs of Reba from that time reveal a stunning, high-cheekboned, long-haired, modish young woman. Her recollection of their meeting parallels Nick's but doesn't match it precisely:

> Nick says he saw me first, but I sort of noticed him from afar, looking out the window from my painting studio. But I was very shy; I was always walking with my head down, and I never made eye contact.

Reba Peck, 1976

When we did meet . . . I fell in love within a couple of days. By the end of that first week, I had to break off my engagement with my high school sweetheart . . . I was so in love with Nick. And it felt like such a *pure* kind of love.

Reba attended a campus show of Nick's cave photographs and was astonished. What interested her was "his kind of adventurousness. I wanted to tap into that. I really didn't want an ordinary life."

Today Reba remains a beauty—her features now softened somewhat, her style now more gypsy than mod, with layers of textures, colors, and lengths. She is an independent, strong, and serene spirit who still listens to her instincts, as she did in 1976 when she broke off a comfortable, parent-sanctioned relationship that had been in place since high school for a dream of a life far more expansive and unpredictable than she had yet known. The decades since have proven her decision to be the right one. And they have only strengthened the bond between Nick and Reba.

After a passionate courtship with his new love, Nick arranged to meet the next individual who would remarkably alter his world: photojournalist Charles Moore.

Alabama-born, represented by the Black Star agency, Moore had worked for Alabama newspapers, and then later at *Life* magazine. He is probably best known for his in-depth work on the civil rights movement; he made national-mindset-shifting images of events such as the 1958 arrest of Martin Luther King Jr. in Montgomery (Moore was the only photographer present), and covered marches, demonstrations, and riots in Birmingham in 1963 and Selma in 1965.[2] He also photographed the Ku Klux Klan in North Carolina in 1965. Unlike many photojournalists reporting the civil rights movement, Moore was from the South, working for Montgomery newspapers—a geographic credential, as Nick notes, that gives his images a particular authenticity and empathy. This, along with his commitment to staying with the story as it unfolded, helped gain Moore both tips and access.

Moore visited UNA in the spring of 1977 and Nick admits that he "swarmed him." The older photographer recognized Nick's potential and soon enough was offering a mentor's advice. After Nick's graduation from UNA, Moore dissuaded him from enrolling in a master's journalism program (Nick had been accepted at the S. I. Newhouse School at Syracuse University), inviting him instead to come to San Francisco and work as his assistant. The only way to learn anything about photography, Moore insisted, was by *doing it*. So in the summer of 1978, after his graduation, Nick packed up his car and drove west, with his college friend Mike McCracken photographing the entire time.

Reba had graduated from UNA in the spring of 1977, and was now working toward a master's degree in studio art at North Texas University in Denton: "I needed to go to Texas and do my thing. Even though in my heart, I knew our relationship was real, I was still a little afraid." The separation tormented the new lovers—Nick remembers it, in visceral rock and roll terms, as the summer of the Rolling Stones' "Miss You."

And their time apart grew longer. Moore so appreciated Nick's work that when the summer ended he asked him to stay on as his full-time assistant. That fall, he invited Nick to New York to assist with a job, also intending to introduce him to Howard Chapnick, the longtime director of the Black Star

to Nick,
Thank you for helping to save the beautiful rainforests and great & beautiful animals of those forests & jungles.

Charles Moore

Martin Luther King Jr. being arrested in Montgomery, Alabama, 1958. Photograph (inscribed to Nick) by Charles Moore/Getty Images

agency. Nick, who had never been to New York—had never even flown in an airplane—was thrilled at the opportunity to show his work to Chapnick.

Chapnick was very impressed by Nick's cave images, and arranged an introduction to the New York editors of *Geo* magazine. Originally launched in Germany in 1976, *Geo* was an illustrated publication that had been enjoying a very successful run, and was now poised to begin publishing a U.S. edition. *Geo*'s U.S. slogan was "A New View of Our World." As Chapnick suspected, *Geo*'s editors were eager to put together a reliable team of photographers in the States who were hungry enough to take any assignment; he envisioned that Nick would be an excellent match.

Nick had been in love with *National Geographic* since his boyhood, and had been submitting photographs to the magazine since he was a teenager. His work had been regularly rejected (as had his application to work for *National Geographic* as an intern). He was understandably nervous about meeting with the *Geo* editors. He had only his cave photographs to show—most of them made while he was in the army. But with Chapnick's support, he hoped that *Geo* might take him seriously.

His appointment was set for 5 p.m. at the magazine's offices in midtown Manhattan, where he would meet picture editors Steve Ettlinger and Elisabeth Biondi. The young photographer bundled together his cameras and a carousel of carefully selected slides and hailed a taxi. Perhaps it was rush hour, or perhaps his Alabama accent tempted an unscrupulous New York taxi driver . . . but at 5:15 the car was still inching its way around the city. Panicking, and sensing that he was going in circles, Nick leapt out of the taxi and ran the rest of the way to *Geo*. There, he met first with Ettlinger, who recalls that Nick was "so enthusiastic, and just kept talking"; he brought Nick in to meet the magazine's executive editor Thomas Hoepker. In a sequence of events that Biondi describes as "quite amazing," Hoepker on the spot gave Nick an assignment for more cave photographs.

"I was on Cloud 9," remembers Nick. *"I'm going to do the caves."* He proposed a story on a cave known as the Fantastic Pit in northwest Georgia—where no one had photographed before.

Giddy with the prospect of this first assignment, Nick left the office and realized suddenly that he was missing something: his cameras. "I'd left them in the fucking taxi!" In his panic to get to his appointment, he had flown out of the car without them. Howard Chapnick calmed the tearful young man with an offer of an advance on the fee Nick would make doing his story. With that, Nick would buy his first Canon camera. Ever since, he has used a Canon for almost every project.

That night, from his hotel in New York, Nick wrote a letter to Reba: "Hot damn I got it . . . can you believe it!!!!" And he outlined for her exactly how he would proceed in terms of assistants, a writer, and the complicated technics of working in the massive cave. He had been given three weeks to realize the assignment.

Nick continued working with Moore that fall, and would assist him between his own assignments for years to come: "Charles had a great influence on me, and I feel like I owe my life to him in some ways."

Nick began shooting the caving story in fall 1978, and *Geo* published it in June 1979.[3] Everything was moving forward happily—except that Reba was so far away, and that was agonizing for both of them. "I just couldn't stand it," Nick says. Finally, "I told her: 'I'm coming to get you.'" And so around Christmas 1978, Reba quit school, and she and Nick gathered her belongings from Denton and drove to San Francisco. They didn't tell Reba's parents or Joyce until they had made it to California. "It was really hard for my parents," says Reba. Nick wishes they had been able to handle it differently but knows that the Pecks would never have approved of their plan. "The only way they eventually got over it," he acknowledges, "was when they saw that I was never, ever going to leave her. We didn't get married until around 2007, but we count our anniversary as Halloween 1976."

By January 1, 1979, Nick and Reba were in San Francisco. They arrived with $100 with which to start their new life. (Their first meal in San Francisco, vividly recalled, was at a hotdog stand called the Doggie Diner.) Nick would be working as Moore's assistant, and Reba soon got a job in a frame shop. They moved into an apartment in the Union Street district that had previously been inhabited by a friend of Moore's. Only because they didn't have to lay out the first and last month's rent were they able to afford it.

But they were rich in optimism, love, ideas, and ambition. "I had no idea how I was going to get to where I wanted to be," remembers Nick. "I couldn't formulate it. All I knew was that I was going to be the Mick Jagger of photography."

Nick in the Grand Canyon, 1978. Photograph by Mike McCracken

NICK DANGER

Warmup Pit, Ellison's Cave, Georgia, 1978

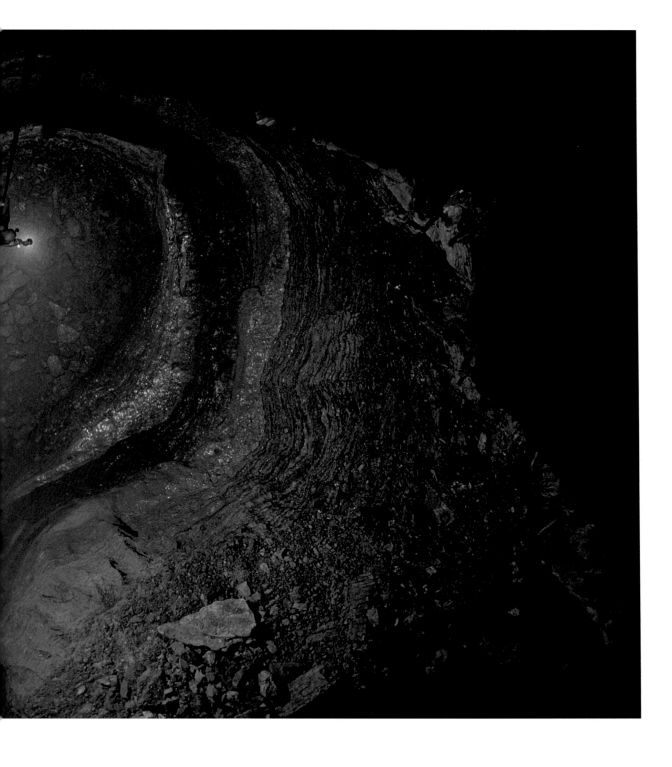

Tim Cahill: "Menaced by lizards in Indonesia, cuffed by a gorilla in Africa, stung by poisonous caterpillars in the world's deepest caves—it's the adventures of . . . Nick Danger: Boy Photographer!"

"Tim Cahill," Nick says glowingly, "was my hero. He was my favorite writer as a young man—I had read him in *Rolling Stone*. He was irreverent and hilarious." When Nick moved to San Francisco in the summer of 1978, one of the first things he did was seek out Cahill, then an editor at *Outside* magazine, to show him his pictures. It was the beginning of a beautiful friendship. The first of their many collaborations would not take place, however, until more than a year later.

As I walk to Cahill's home in Livingston, Montana, in October 2012, the Yellowstone River shimmers in the early-morning light. The jagged mountain range known as the Crazies is silhouetted against the bluest sky. Cahill, in his late sixties at this point, is built solidly and moves fluidly; he told me he had been hiking regularly in preparation for a forthcoming trek to the Mount Everest Base Camp. I was reminded that much of this writer's life has been spent in precarious spaces and with assorted wild creatures—including, of course, Nick.

Together we pored through stacks of photographs and other souvenirs from the many adventure stories that he and Nick created. From their first meeting, Cahill remembers equally Nick's enthusiasm and his photographs, and his own excitement at the prospect of working together. Although Cahill could not be the writer on the *Geo* caves story, as Nick had hoped (Cahill had just finished a caving piece for *Outside* magazine), they agreed to join forces at a later date.

The writer U.S. *Geo* assigned for Nick's first assignment was Mitchell J. Shields. The story, "The Lure of the Abyss," was in motion, and Nick began photographing the cavernous Fantastic Pit, in Ellison's Cave, near the Georgia-Tennessee border.[1] When they first met, Nick initially struck Shields as laid-back and boyish—not necessarily the sort of person who could pull off a complicated operation like photographing the deepest pit in the continental United States. But then Shields himself had never before done any caving, and by his own admission was clueless. Nick was patient as they worked together, and it became clear to Shields that Nick, along with being kind, "knows what the risk factors are, and has thought about them, and has planned everything out." But, he adds: "Nick *is* willing to do almost anything to get a good shot, including putting himself physically in harm's way." Still, Nick does not operate capriciously in the field. He comes prepared; he trusts his instincts. Although his subjects and stories demonstrate that he is by no means risk-averse, there is no risk for risk's sake.

In Nick's recollection: "Mitchell became part of our team. He was erudite, very learned—and had absolutely no business ever going in a cave!—but we taught him how to cave." Nonetheless, the writer's inexperience led to a mishap that could have been fatal. As Shields wrote in the article:

> All around me, the earth had frozen in a scream of creation. Boulders thrust up at impossible angles. Large sheets of rock were delicately striated with smooth, parallel grooves; it was as if a stream of water had been arrested and solidified. I had stumbled on a landscape more alien

than any I had seen. Somewhere I'd read that a man who has been in caves would be more at home on the surface of the moon than anywhere else, and now I understood why. It was hard to avoid watching, fascinated, as rock strata flowed by. Growing careless, I craned my neck sidewise to get a better view; that is when the loose hair sticking from under my miner's hat twined with the rope and ran into the workings of my rappel rack, leaving me terrified and spinning slowly in midair. . . . Slowly, I begin to saw my head back and forth until strands of hair and scalp tear free—at first in small, scattered amounts, then in large, painful chunks as my head finally rips clear.[2]

Shields's experience in this otherworldly space changed him—after writing "The Lure of the Abyss" he became a caver.

To round out the team, Nick brought in old friends. Hanging in the opening photograph of the published story is Steve Lawler; also with them was Steve Shirey, who had accompanied Nick on caving expeditions when they were both in the army. Lawler and Shirey had become close friends—through their mutual affection for Nick, their addiction to the rush of such adventures and, more forebodingly, their "addiction to dangerous drugs." Nick recalls that when not caving, "they were by then shooting up all the time," although while at work, they were focused and "all in."

From Nick's previous experiences in caves, he knew precisely how he wanted to create the images for *Geo*:

So there's two ropes and people hanging on them, and I have to light up this completely black world—you see nothing. If you're going to photograph in a cave, you've got to carry a camera that you could drive nails with. . . . I carried a very primitive manual camera called a Nikonos. It's an underwater camera that you could literally drop off a building. Of course this was way before digital. You couldn't frame precisely; you focused by distance. It had no light meter. It had no technology in it at all. It was just a box that you could put film in, with a lens on it that was waterproof. We were photographing waterfalls. Everything had to be able to get *really* wet and muddy. And the way I wanted to light things up—a normal electronic flash would have been destroyed by all that moisture and water. So I was using flashbulbs, which put out a tremendous amount of light, much more light than these giant studio strobes.

These huge flashbulbs had been salvaged from the storerooms of the Fort Campbell base; knowing they were to be trashed, Nick took them when his military service ended. He compares his use of the bulbs to Mathew Brady's use of flash powder: quick, white explosions of light. After asking the cavers to turn off their headlamps,

I would say: "I'll open the lens, and then you flash." Then we'd repeat. So I'm *painting in* the image as the climbers go down the rope to the bottom of the pit. . . . I realized that if you have this black world, you can fill in pieces of it with light. So I started understanding flash. Or really, understanding light.

Essentially, Nick opened the aperture so that the film was exposed, and when one of the cavers—generally Shirey or Lawler—flashed on cue, that part of the photograph was created. So the overall image evolved through multiple exposures over a period of time.

Shields tells me: "It seemed, maybe because Nick had to think about making pictures in a black cave, that he understood . . . the physics of photography—how it worked. And this informed everything about the way he made his photographs."

Nick wanted to understand light and darkness in all conditions, as well as how to mix flash and ambient light. In the late 1970s, in order to publish his work in magazines, it also was imperative that he use slide (transparency) film, which limited his range:

> The black shadows in my work are byproducts of transparency film—which was industry standard. What I did, and other color photographers using transparency film did, was to build a look out of the characteristics of the film—in my case, Kodachrome. I became interested in the intensity of the color—like Paul Simon sings—and the contrast, and what I could focus on to get some motion, to get that edge.

> So my aesthetic was built on a combination of Kodachrome and flash.

"The Lure of the Abyss" and other early projects laid the groundwork for Nick's lifelong methodology and inquiry. These stories focused on utterly elemental, mysterious environments that are intrinsically awe-inspiring. While working on them, Nick's inventive experimentation with and finessing of lighting became an ongoing preoccupation—although for him technology has always been only a vehicle toward realizing a vision.

Still, in projects where darkness is both adversary and partner—working with a medium that is all about light—one needs more than luck or divine intervention (although Nick seems to have had his share of both). There is of course the basic need for literal illumination. But the artistry resides in the achievement of metaphorical illumination, which must be perceived by the artist, captured and rendered.

Nick needs the viewer to experience through his images the emotional intensity that he felt. If he was fearful, he wants your hair to stand on end. If he was elated, he wants your very being to tremble rhapsodically. He finds boundless wonder in all that is wild: he needs that wonder to be yours, too.

All this is hard enough to accomplish in any circumstance. In the pre-digital era, Nick grappled with technological challenges of photographing in extreme and physically restrictive situations, and he clearly found the process electrifying.

Toward the close of "The Lure of the Abyss," Shields writes:

> For the first time in my life I was aware of having not one but two horizons, above and below ground. My feet beat drum tones on the earth. Quivers of information rode up my legs, my thighs, through the conduit of the spine and into my brain. Existence did not end at the ground as it had before but spun down in a full circle to envelop the open spaces

Fantastic Pit, Ellison's Cave, 1986

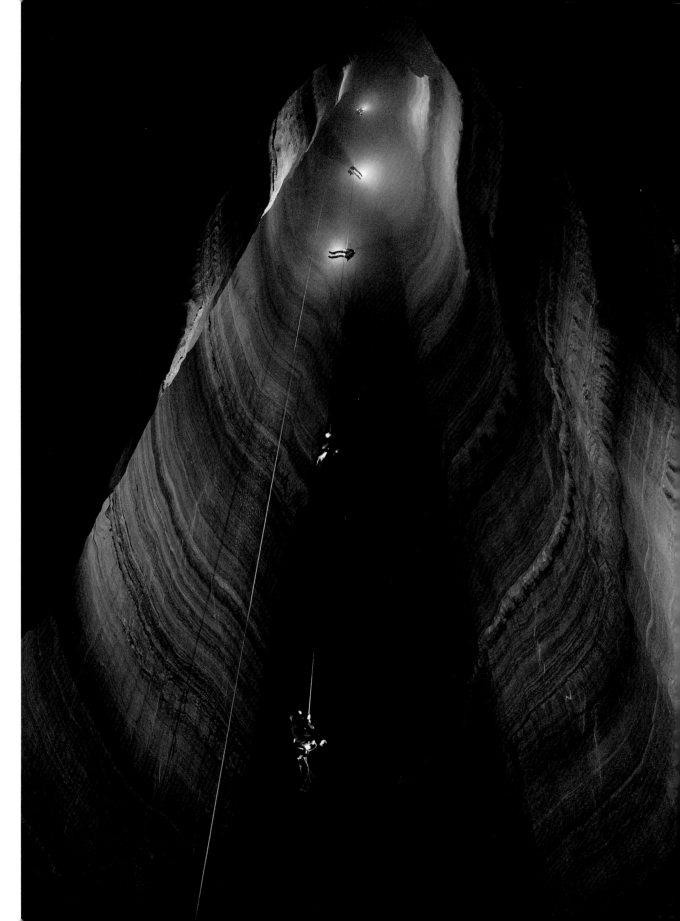

The Lure
of the
Abyss

Dangling precariously from thin nylon ropes, daring cavers lower themselves hundreds of feet into the inky-black recesses of Georgia's Fantastic Pit—the deepest natural shaft in America. Though it is a dangerous sport, thousands of people are addicted to the excitement of caving.

Inside Georgia's "Fantastic Pit"

High above the floor of 510-foot-deep Fantastic Pit, Steve Lawler takes a midair breather during his ascent to the surface after spending 12 hours at the bottom of the pit.

74 GEO

ABOVE: *Geo*, June 1979: "The Lure of the Abyss" (showing Steve Lawler); OPPOSITE: Mark Stock in the "Glub Glubs crawlway," Ellison's Cave, 1978

beneath me. I was made silent by contemplation of the years during which I had halved my world, knowing it only up, never down.[3]

The article provided a sublime and yet very concrete transition from Nick's childhood escapes into his expansive interior life, to real and quixotic possibilities right here on Earth.

Nick understood early on that people like seeing photographs about their passions. Cavers are fascinated by his photographs because they reveal their own world in a way they themselves haven't seen it. Showing an otherwise inaccessible subject—a colossal cave, a giant redwood in an old-growth forest, lions at night, a tigress with her cubs—in its visual entirety to those obsessed with it is a tactic Nick has come to rely on. He also understands the efficacy of captivating the collective imagination with stories of exploration and adventure, labors (in the Herculean sense), and possibility. He recognizes that such stories may function as foils for a conservation-driven subtext. It's not a process of bait and switch, but rather of seduction. He gets our fantasies of discovering magical worlds, of traveling through time, of communicating with wild animals. He engages our wanderlusts.

"The Lure of the Abyss," published in June 1979, made manifest Nick's extraordinary talents. As Shields said to me: "Nick hit it out of the ballpark—people had not seen photographs like that before." *Geo* gave the story twenty pages, including a stunning vertical foldout showing—for the first time with any clarity—the staggering 440-foot "Incredible Pit" as Larry "Smoky" Caldwell rappelled down.

But not everything ended well. Steve Lawler and Steve Shirey had started smuggling marijuana out of Colombia. On one run, toward the end of their work on the cave story, recalls Nick—his voice suddenly hoarse and dropping an octave, "the plane Steve Shirey was flying, which had most likely been booby-trapped over a drug debt, experienced total electrical failure." Shirey's plane crashed—after he managed to stay in the air just long enough to avoid a heavily populated area. As thrilled as Nick was with the success of his first story, Shirey's death was darkly destabilizing.

It was no surprise that the magazine's editors should ask Nick what he wanted to work on next. "I said, well, as a child I read a book by Sir Arthur Conan Doyle—*The Lost World*. I want to go there." Nick still has his fifty-cent 1965 paperback copy of the book, which he carried with him to that *Geo* meeting. Among the underlined passages is one in which Doyle's fearless protagonist, Professor Challenger, expounds on the continued existence of prehistoric animals:

> What is the result? Why, the ordinary laws of nature are suspended. The various checks which influence the struggle for existence in the world at large are all neutralized or altered. Creatures survive which would otherwise disappear.[4]

Nick was bewitched by Doyle's myth of a world lost in time and space, where Jurassic beasts survived and reigned. Banking on the clout he had earned with "The Lure of the Abyss," he proposed the

story—which would entail traveling to the *tepui* plateaux of Venezuela—adding: "Tim Cahill is the journalist I want to work with."

Wickedly funny, self-effacing, and able to fluently render the most intense, absurd, and terrifying circumstances through his richly detailed cliffhanger tales, Cahill was made for *Geo*'s "Lost World" article. And it was the start of a high-spirited collaboration between the photographer and the writer, who would team up repeatedly over the course of more than ten years. "With Tim, it's hand-in-hand, always," Nick told me. "I'm a character in the stories, and in all the things that go wrong."

Cahill puts it this way:

> It was always a big back-and-forth. We just went out and figured it out. Nick and I also shared a sense of humor and a sense of wonder at the natural world. He was actually more fun to work with than most people. But we weren't liable to discuss our work philosophically. A lot of it was just humor and anticipation. We generally laughed a lot, and were able to make fun of each other, too—which is what guys do on trips. And Nick was not out to illustrate my stories. He didn't know what I was going to write. I'd watch him work, and I'd see what he was interested in. Wow, I can work off that, because I know that photograph is going to be terrific.

The photographs from Nick and Cahill's first "improbable adventure" (as it was billed by *Geo*[5]) depict a kind of dreamscape, as alien to most readers as many of Nick's cave images were. Made

on Venezuela's Mount Roraima over the course of about two months, some of these images are infused with subaqueous tones that seem almost to ooze off the page. Nick chose to use the higher-speed Ektachrome film for this work, instead of his usual, much slower, Kodachrome transparency film. The resulting graininess—enhanced by the unceasing rain and mist on the high Venezuelan plateau—resulted in photographs that are more atmospheric than detailed. ("I seem to always make it as difficult as possible," says Nick. "Let's go in the rainy season! I knew it would be more beautiful.") These images are not about giving shape to darkness; they are about ever-fluid tonalities. Nothing in them feels fixed.

It was here—with the daily challenge of making a fire and staying warm and dry at night—that Nick first understood the innumerable benefits of working with indigenous people who are attuned to their environment and equipped with the skills to live in it. Their guide, a local Indian named

OPPOSITE: Nick's copy of Arthur Conan Doyle's *The Lost World*; ABOVE: Mount Roraima, Venezuela, 1979

Feliciano, described by Tim as "barely over five feet tall, but he was broad in the chest and shoulders, a powerful-looking man," led them to the perilous waters of Cuquenán, which he reluctantly crossed with them, before taking them through the jungle and up Mount Roraima.

Scale and the elements, the desire to reveal the living, breathing *whole* of a thing—intimately and with precision—have been persistent challenges for Nick. Venezuela's Angel Falls, more than three thousand feet high, was a phenomenon to be reckoned with. When researching his *Geo* story, Nick saw Robert Madden's photograph of Angel Falls with a small plane in front of it, published in *National Geographic* in August 1976. "Bob's use of scale to get that waterfall really caught me. I went out and did that kind of picture, using scale, although mine was very different. But the idea came from Bob Madden."

With the goal of conveying the scope of the falls photographically, Nick hired two planes: he flew in one, and the other was piloted by a man known as "El Tigre." Cahill later described that pilot's insane genius in *Image* magazine:

> El Tigre said he was the best bush pilot in the world and that, with Nick in the other plane, he, El Tigre, would fly so close to the wall of Angel Falls that his wing would kiss the pink of the rock. It would be the best picture in the world. El Tigre was, I should add, heroically drunk. . . . The photo Nick took seems an unremarkable bit of brilliance until you look

very closely and see the fly speck of El Tigre's plane against the wall. When you see that, the entire photo explodes with perspective.[6]

To provide a fuller context, Nick and Cahill drew not just from Professor Challenger's account, but from other tales and mythologies associated with the region—from El Dorado's lost gold to the fugitive known as "Papillon." The claustrophobic jungle itself became a central character. "I am frightened by the jungle," writes Cahill in his *Geo* piece. "I am frightened by the sickly sweet odors, by the moist darkness, by the dank fecundity. I am frightened by the chaos: green things lash about in slow motion, choke off lesser plants, rise toward the sun like those subconscious horrors that sometimes bubble up into the conscious mind."[7]

What would draw a writer or a photographer to such a potentially nightmarish place? Why face such risks? Cahill considers the question and then tells me:

> Early on in my career, some of the stories I did were truly dangerous. You had to train for them and do them properly. And I found that I enjoyed that. I enjoyed the spike of adrenaline that you got in doing these stories. . . . I'm kind of a lazy writer, but when your life is at stake, then research is scintillating. . . . You are focused on it. There are no outside things impinging on you. You are there. . . . Now, some people can get to that state of focus sitting crosslegged in an empty room. Others of us need a harder bump. We're born two drinks short of par. So that's the way I came to think of the risk thing—as my own jocky version of an Eastern meditative state.

Nick recalls Cahill—who swam competitively in college—challenging locals to a swimming contest in a pool of water near Angel Falls. "Everybody thought: 'Oh, we can beat this out-of-shape guy!' And then Tim would go three times across the pool without a breath." "Venezuela: Exploring a Lost World" was published in March 1980 with a cover photograph of Cahill swimming underwater. "It was my first cover," laughs Nick, "and came out of just a foolin'-around picture."

It wasn't long before Nick heard again from *Geo*. The magazine's editors had sent Mitchell Shields and photographer John Blaustein to do a story on the Indus River, which originates in the Tibetan Plateau and flows south into Pakistan. The journey itself was organized by the adventure-travel company Sobek, which would propose such expeditions to magazines like *Geo* or *National Geographic*—and the magazines, in turn, would fund the trips. This Indus descent was part of a series of rafting expeditions made up of explorers who wanted to accomplish the first descents of rivers all over the world—and *Geo* was keenly interested in adventure stories as part of its editorial mix. Just days after his arrival in Pakistan for the scout trip, Blaustein contracted dysentery and was unable even to begin shooting. *Geo* photo-editor Alice Rose George called Nick in the hopes that he could take over the job. He immediately said yes, although he admits he had some misgivings. "I couldn't swim well, and I'd never been in that kind of boat. . . . The river is cold, and it drops like a rocket—it was just *death*. Until that trip, I didn't know how dangerous rivers could be."

One member of the Indus team was John Kramer, a geoscientist and seasoned river-runner, whom Nick remembers as calmly staring down the intimidatingly paralyzing rapids—"focused, very Zen"—when the rest of the crew was petrified. "I remember wishing I was more like him." Nick recalls at one point being flipped head over heels into the water while photographing, and then being

Angel Falls, Gran Sabana, Venezuela, 1979

quickly pulled back into the boat by Kramer. For his part, Kramer describes Nick as "very flexible—he looked like a ragdoll in a way, with relaxed limbs." He also recalls Nick's zealous engrossment: "When he was shooting, he was very in the moment. There was this abandonment of his physical needs. . . . He was going after something on a higher level than just physical reality."

Working in a politically volatile area like Pakistan has its complications, among them the suspicions of the local people with regard to this group of strangers. To help mitigate the lack of trust, Shields recalls:

> Nick took a Polaroid camera with him. He was photographing people along the river sometimes, and he could give the people he met immediate gratification by giving them a Polaroid. Then he would explain that other pictures, still in the other camera, would be in a magazine in about six or eight months. We were in the mountains—very far away from media. This was both smart and kind.

At the end of the voyage, Nick was worried that he didn't have enough solid images to make a proper *Geo* story. Many of the photographs had been made working in hazardous conditions, "with me holding onto the boat with one hand, and holding the camera in the other." Furthermore, there was a visual annoyance in many of the images: Sobek. Nick describes Richard Bangs, who ran the Sobek company, as the "P. T. Barnum of that world." He was a publicity hound—for which Nick, who "wanted purity," at the time had no tolerance. (In hindsight, he understands Bangs's behavior as a business-survival strategy.) The words SOBEK GEO were "poorly painted" on every piece of equipment and other paraphernalia—there seemed to be no way to avoid them, which Nick found truly vexing. "This ruined nearly every picture I took." That may be a bit of hyperbole, but certainly the presence of a logo screams branding, which tarnished the integrity of the images in Nick's mind—making them feel more like advertisements than like reportage.

Nick ended up photographing four Sobek-sponsored river expeditions: the Indus, the Zambezi (in southeastern Africa), the Wahgi (in New Guinea), and the Alas (in Indonesia). After the Indus, he moved on to the Zambezi River, which runs through eastern Angola, along the borders of Namibia, Botswana, and then along the border between Zambia and Zimbabwe en route to the Indian Ocean. Zimbabwe in the 1980s was undergoing a series of violent uprisings and governmental shifts. Nick recalls that the banks of the river were thought to have been hijacked by landmines. Some of the ex-soldiers from Zimbabwe's recent civil wars accompanied them—hired, Nick believes, by Bangs—both to examine the beach for explosives, and to deter crocodiles.

Photographically, there was another adversary: the equatorial sun. "Equatorial sun is there, and then it's gone," explains Nick. "You don't get late-afternoon light; you don't get early-morning light. It comes up fast and zoom, it's hot. And on the river, it's a really harsh light."

The Zambezi River trip was followed by an expedition to the Wahgi (meaning "eater of men")—a river whose full length had never before been explored or documented. During this New Guinea trip, Nick found himself in the company of a team of BBC filmmakers, thanks to Bangs (who would later produce and host a number of TV shows about adventure travel for American Public Television). This was Nick's first exposure to a very different kind of documentary coverage. He was dismayed by what he saw as the showmanship and fabrications of the filmmakers: it ran counter to everything he believes his photography should be. "It was all about performing. You've got to have characters, so they found a woman who had ridden a white horse all over New Guinea and she became the on-camera 'talent.' I was appalled at how they made it up as they went."

But the television team didn't last long in the water. Nick grins as he says: "The river took over. It kicked our asses. We lost the BBC early on, as their boat flipped over and the whole crew almost drowned. They were like: 'We're not getting in those boats again.' And after that, they either filmed from a helicopter or from the shore."

Nick and John Kramer came up with a working setup to safely shoot in the turbulent waters: the camera was firmly mounted to the boat, protected in an ammo can; the lens pressed against the glass of the can so clarity was not lost and everything stayed waterproof. Finally, the can was wrapped in thick foam so that if the boat flipped over, nobody would be terribly injured if tossed against it.

On the whole, Nick wasn't greatly pleased with his work for the river projects, believing "everything felt more about sports than exploring a wild river." And ultimately, only two of the four river-expedition stories were published. *Geo* printed the Indus article, "Riding the Torrent," in August 1980,[8] and the Wahgi story, "Rafting the 'Eater of Men,'" in February 1984.[9] Still, some of the images are unquestionably riveting. In the opening two shots of "Riding the Torrent," the raft rips through the Indus's perilous, plunging rapids—boulders jutting out and threatening its every move, and John Yost's expression is euphoric as he races his boat toward the viewer. In "Rafting the 'Eater of Men,'" the Wahgi is equally merciless, as evinced in Nick's shot of John Kramer careening after a runaway raft, or the opening image showing Richard Bangs finessing his way down the rapids; the BBC helicopter hovering in the background, providing a sense of scale, flying chillingly close to the rising landscape in a wash of white water.

Nick did not fail in these assignments: he made a number of extremely strong images. But he did not make strong *stories*, which is, I believe, why they feel like great sports photographs, and less like vivid chronicles of two expeditions, or an expression of wildness. As Nick's work has evolved over the years, what distinguishes it in part from that of other photographers working in the wild is its narrative strength and evocative character portrayals—its storytelling capacity. His photographs are exalted by what Henri Cartier-Bresson famously dubbed "decisive moments," but they are not dependent upon them. Nick's early adventure images, while often spectacular, are all about adrenaline and, one might say, conquest. As he moved away from adventure assignments, his sensibility would become more nuanced. His own voice—beyond his endearing willingness to say "yes!"—was expanding and maturing with each story. Soon, it would burn intensely through his images.

The river stories were a kind of photographic bootcamp for Nick: a physical, psychological, technical, and conceptual training ground. He began to consider narrative and how to depict the complexity of a subject, ideas that he would continue to flesh out decades later.

At *Geo*, Nick was earning a reputation as a valuable photographer who would gamely agree to nearly any assignment, no matter how far afield, no matter how impromptu, and who would deliver

John Yost, Indus River, Karakoram Range, Pakistan, 1979

the goods. In 1979 he was asked to fill in for a photographer who had bailed on an article with the working title "Bush Pilots of Africa." Nick accepted immediately, although he admits that the idea seemed hapless from the start (beginning with the worrisome title, which implied that it was possible to generalize about the entire continent of Africa).

Furthermore, no real research had been done for the project and there was no solid game plan in place. Nick traveled to Egypt to meet the assigned writer, whom he found languishing and penniless at the Cairo Hilton, having gambled away all his expense money.

In retrospect, it provided a vital lesson in how not to realize a story. He quickly understood that *Geo*'s concept for this assignment was more about broad-stroke illustration of a stereotype than about the complex, sometimes lethal country-specific realities. The idea had been thrown together too quickly, and he was forced to wing it. I suspect he grasped that he, the story, and his photographs would have benefited from being more informed. He began to see the advantage of having control over how a story is conceived—not only photographically, but in all its aspects, from the idea to the preparation to the selection of the writer to the ultimate execution.

Nick is controlling. This is no surprise at all, given the precarious nature of his childhood: at an early age he developed a need to keep everything together, to be entirely self-reliant. With his photography, he is a perfectionist, which means he must have a plan, as well as a baseline comprehension of the issues and context. Only then can he work more intuitively—which allowed his cave and "Lost World" stories to sing. The debacle of the bush pilots story may also have shown Nick the journalistic necessity of fully trusting what he experienced in the field, over his own or his editors' preconceptions. A perspective grounded in fact and enhanced by serendipity would result in far more complex and evocative photographs. But to understand this, he confesses, "I needed some age on me."

And he was maturing rapidly. As he traveled from country to country in Africa,

> I was just trying to make pictures, but they didn't mean anything. Also, in some of the countries where I was working, I had to get official permission to photograph. So I had to deal with a certain amount of corruption. It was an incredible lesson. Nothing was clear, straightforward, or obvious. And I didn't know how to *create* pictures—I didn't yet know how to find them between the seams.

It was not about inventing what wasn't there, but rather about how to recognize, and then convey, what was. He studied the geography of Africa, learning about what distinguishes each country. Moreover, while Nick had experienced a dynamic and energizing "marriage" of words and images working with the likes of Tim Cahill and Mitchell Shields, the writer assigned to the bush pilots story was a washout, and Nick eventually gave up on him: "I want a real relationship with the writer," he states today, "or to work alone."

Much about the bush pilots story was problematic—and *Geo* never ran it—but there was one moment that, for Nick, changed everything. He had been in Kenya photographing the Flying Doctors: a group of physicians who traveled East Africa in bush planes, addressing medical emergencies as they arose. A few days before Christmas 1979, he boarded a plane from Nairobi to Goma, in Zaire (now the Democratic Republic of Congo, or DRC). He was following the trail of "a real bush pilot I'd heard about living in Kinshasa" (who turned out to be a mercenary from Texas). As the single-engine Cessna glided over the volcanoes—the Virunga Mountain Range—that unite the DRC, Uganda, and Rwanda, the pilot gestured downward and said to Nick: "That's where that crazy American woman lives alone with the gorillas."

Dian Fossey. "I'm like, *goddam*!" recalls Nick. Maybe, he thinks—getting all cosmic—that was why he was there, working on this ill-begotten story about bush pilots. "As a teenager I'd seen stories about her in *National Geographic*. Here I was, busting my ass, being lonely over the holidays, and coming back with only a few good pictures and a story that made no sense and would never be published. But . . . I've traveled in Africa, and I've flown over those volcanoes." To Nick, his path was clear: when the editors at U.S. *Geo* asked him what he'd like to do next, he said, "in a heartbeat, 'I want to photograph the gorillas Dian Fossey works with.'"

"*Geo* loved Nick," reminisced photo-editor Alice Rose George recently. "We would support his story ideas almost always. He made it so easy. He worked incredibly hard, arranged pretty much everything by himself, and he wasn't ever a prima donna." This affection for Nick crossed oceans: Ruth Eichhorn was working as a photo-editor at German *Geo* when Nick visited the Hamburg offices in 1980, at the time of his first assignment for that edition of the magazine. For a story about ferry pilots, he'd been commissioned to fly from the Mooney aircraft factory in Kerrville, Texas, to Hamburg the long way—in a single-engine plane, which required many stops. After that, Eichhorn recalls, "Nick would realize many stories for the German and French editions of *Geo*," as well as the U.S. edition.

Photo-editor Christiane Breustedt worked in the same office. She had been dazzled by Nick's cave work and by the "Lost World" article. She recalls:

> I was sitting at the big light table at the *Geo* photo desk in Hamburg; from that spot, I could look all the way down the hallway. Next thing I remember is the particular walk of the young man coming toward me. He seemed to be floating on a highwire. Sleek and elastic. I remember him standing in front of me, saying: "I'm Nick Nichols," in that lilting, blues-like tone. For a brief moment I thought he should have a guitar slung over his shoulder instead of a camera.

In Breustedt, Nick found a likeminded and engaged ally. They discussed his desire to go to Rwanda and photograph Fossey's mountain gorillas, both of them seeing that they must get *Geo* readers worldwide to recognize the imminent danger of these primates' possible extinction. It took Nick more than a year to convince U.S. *Geo* to take on the gorilla story, partly because of *National Geographic*'s extensive and recent coverage of Fossey's work,[10] but in 1981, Thomas Hoepker, U.S. *Geo*'s executive editor, ultimately agreed. Nick began to make it happen.[11]

But this wasn't the only primate project Nick had in the works: he and Reba were expecting their first child. In early April, he sent a preliminary story budget to Alice George, along with a letter that began: "Hello, we may have a baby here this weekend. I must say I'm sufficiently nervous." By the end of the letter, in a postscript: "We had a baby boy at 12:40 Friday morning." Nick and Reba's first son, Ian, was born in the house they were renting in San Francisco.

Earlier in 1981, after *Geo* had committed to the gorillas story, Nick had contacted Alexander (Sandy) Harcourt, a gorilla researcher working with Fossey, about photographing some of the habituated gorillas in Fossey's study groups in Rwanda's Volcanoes National Park in the Virunga Mountain Range (which also includes Virunga National Park in the DRC and Uganda's Mgahinga Gorilla National Park). *Habituated* does not mean tame—they are still wild animals. It means that over time, they have become accustomed to and will tolerate human presence under specific conditions. To habituate a wild animal takes remarkable tenacity, patience, and will—especially if the animals have been hunted and have learned to fear humans. At this point, Harcourt was in charge of Fossey's Karisoke Research Center, as Fossey herself had taken a leave of absence and was working from Cornell University, where she was a visiting associate professor while writing *Gorillas in the Mist* (published in 1983). Nick introduced himself and his proposed project for *Geo*, writing to Harcourt: "We want to show the gorillas' environment, climb some of the volcanoes, deal with the Rwanda/Zaire social structures that have endangered the mountain gorilla. It seems to me that there is much more to this story than just the mountain gorilla. It's very complicated." Harcourt wrote back, saying that while he would be happy to cooperate with the *Geo* story, Nick would have to get Fossey's approval of the project.

Nick and Reba editing the Suriname *Geo* shoot in Alabama, 1978. Photograph by Shannon Wells

And so, on April 6, Nick composed a letter to Dian Fossey. (His own copy of the letter is stamped with the Rolling Stones tongue logo, along with a scribbled assurance to his editor, Steve Ettlinger, that the tongue was not on the copy of the letter sent to Fossey):

> I would like to go to Karisoke and work with some of the researchers. Also to climb Visoke several times. I hope to cover as many angles to the survival problem as possible. . . . I'm most concerned that you realize Tim Cahill and I are responsible journalists and in no way do we approach the gorillas as an object of sensationalism. I have an intense desire to help in any way I can. I also have no objections to working under restrictions.

The telegram he received in response from Fossey four days later, on April 10, was to the point:

PERMISSION EMPHATICALLY DENIED.

She followed it up the next day with a note reiterating her refusal, and in closing:

> Numerous people are on ego trips concerned with mountain gorilla conservation, a very popular pastime at present. On this end of the ocean such interest is called "Comic Book Conservation." It might be advisable if you did not add your name to the list.
> Yours truly/Dian Fossey/Project Coordinator/Karisoke Research Center

As Nick might say: them's fightin' words. And his response of April 16 made that plain:

> Dian,
>
> First I would thank you for your quick response to my letter. Again I will add that I have great respect for your work and regret that you have no respect for mine and my intentions.
>
> I must say that I can't rest my request with your denial. I feel that it is grossly short-sighted . . . your assumption that my and *Geo* magazine's interest is "comic-book conservation." We purposely waited until [*National*] *Geographic* published the recent "Gorilla" story so as not to conflict. Project Survival of the African Wildlife Leadership Foundation has made a desperate appeal for donations to help the Mountain Gorilla. An article in an international magazine such as *Geo* could only help this fundraising. A previous article in *Geo* on the shame of domestic dog fighting led to the passing of strict and enforceable laws in Ohio.
>
> Your letter has inspired me to push harder to do this report. I was not approaching Karisoke as a "tourist" as you implied, no more than you did fourteen years ago when you started. I'm a journalist and again I regret that you can't respect me for that. I feel that your work and other work at Karisoke is an important part of any story about the Mountain Gorilla. If you feel I'm jumping on some kind of bandwagon to help the Mountain Gorilla, you might be right but it is with the best of intentions. I wanted your input and help but if we must proceed without it we will.

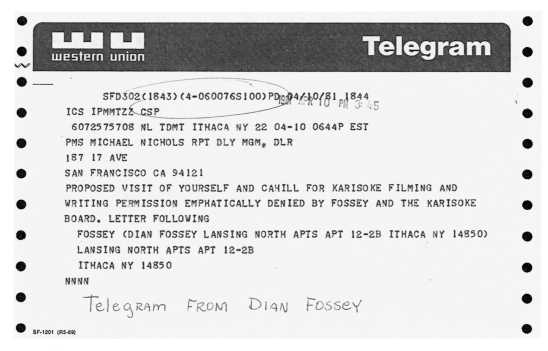

Telegram from Dian Fossey to Nick, April 10, 1981

I'm very aware that Karisoke is a scientifically oriented institution. My intention was to make a visit to Karisoke as part of a story on the Mountain Gorilla. As I stated to you and Sandy Harcourt—I was willing to visit under whatever restrictions were required so as not to disturb scientific research. I add that I don't see what place in scientific research there is for feeding young free-ranging Gorillas "Lifesavers" candy as pictured in the photograph of you with young Gorillas on page 504 of the April '81 issue of the *National Geographic* magazine.

I will continue my request through Dr. Eisenberg, *National Geographic*, and Project Survival of the AWLF.

With respect,
Nick Nichols

As Tim Cahill later observed: "'Permission emphatically denied' are probably not words one should use to working journalists. Two months after receiving Fossey's letter, Nick and I were in Rwanda." Still, the nature of her rejection made at least Cahill feel like "something the dog left on the lawn." Despite her denial of access, Cahill and Nick's respect for Fossey never wavered. In the article, "Love and Death in Gorilla Country," Cahill writes that they considered her a hero, with "a remarkable record of lonely courage and achievement."[12]

Today, more than thirty years after Fossey was hacked to death with a machete at Karisoke Research Center, on December 27, 1985, her murder case remains unsolved. Her unrelenting accusations against poachers for the slaying of mountain gorillas—many of which had been part of her study—as well as her rabid stance against tourism, have given rise to much speculation as to who might have been her killer. An early theory, that one of Fossey's own gorilla trackers murdered her, was never proven, as the man in question committed suicide (or was perhaps lynched) before he could be interrogated. Then an American doctoral student researching with Fossey was accused by Rwandan officials of her murder, but he learned of the forthcoming charges in time to flee the country. It subsequently became clear that everything the authorities alleged about that scenario had been fabricated.

Another theory, yet to be proven but believed by many, is that the guilty party is Protais Zigiranyirazo—the one-time governor of Rwanda's Ruhengeri Province (where Karisoke is based) and brother-in-law of assassinated Rwandan president Juvénal Habyarimana. Fossey was purportedly armed with evidence and ready to implicate Zigiranyirazo publicly for using the park to illegally traffic animals—including endangered species—and to smuggle gold and other precious natural resources. It is widely thought that he ordered her killing.

Zigiranyirazo was convicted in 2008 of crimes against humanity for his collaboration in the Rwandan genocide in 1994: it is believed that he was a primary instrument in the formation of the "death squads." He was sentenced to twenty years' imprisonment. In 2011 the International Crimes Tribunal for Rwanda overturned the verdict—because, it seems, of technicalities in the original trial—and Zigiranyirazo was acquitted and released. News of his recent whereabouts are scanty, but in 2009 the *Harvard Law Record* reported "Today, Mr. 'Z' is a free man."[13]

Fossey's fierce demeanor and mistrustfulness, although at times misguided, had a clear basis. Fortunately, other conservationists proved more welcoming to Nick and Cahill, and would later become crucial allies. After Fossey's rebuff, Nick wrote to British scientists Rosalind and Conrad Aveling, researchers with the newly founded Mountain Gorilla Project, also based in Rwanda. The Avelings were not surprised by Fossey's refusal, and wrote to Nick that they were eager to "help ensure a good article that will publicize the plight of mountain gorillas and the efforts being made to protect them and their habitat."

During the course of his work in Rwanda Nick came to experience, for the first time in depth, some of the intractable tangles of the conservation effort. The relationship between endangered species, endangered habitats, and local populations can be fraught. In Africa, the situation is further complicated by the fact that few black Africans were initially engaged in conservation, the local populations are often desperately poor, and the colonialist powers have been so pervasive and oppressive. Biologist and conservationist Craig Sholley, now with the African Wildlife Foundation, first studied mountain gorillas with Fossey at the Karisoke Research Center, and in the late 1980s directed the Mountain Gorilla Project. Sholley set the scene for me when we met in 2014:

> There's an evolution of how the world of conservation views wildlife. In the mid-twentieth century . . . wildlife was viewed in a very different manner: it was George and Joy Adamson's Kingdom of the Lion [*Note: the Adamsons became known popularly through the 1960 book* Born Free *and the 1966 film of the same title*] and Dian Fossey's Kingdom of the Gorillas. They had these little fiefdoms that were wild and wonderful and magical, but they were their own. The idea of engaging Africans in viewing wildlife as something magical or even as an asset that they could use—that didn't exist in the 1950s and the 1960s.

> When I was working at Karisoke, we relied very heavily on African trackers, who provided us with the knowledge to track on our own, and in many cases were the conduits through which we got to gorillas on a day-to-day basis. But one of Dian's rules was "When you go out and see the gorillas, the trackers can accompany you up to the point of contact. But don't let the gorillas see any African faces." So the Africans were never allowed to be with the gorillas or to watch them.

According to Sholley, Fossey's rationale for this was that, if the gorillas became accustomed to seeing black faces, it would provide African poachers with an opportunity to get close, and ultimately kill them. Sholley is quick to add that the idea was nonsense, noting that over the course of the past decades, it has been Africans who have served as the gorillas' chief protectors. "If it were not for those African men and women regularly risking their lives, the gorillas likely wouldn't exist today."

The African Wildlife Foundation (AWF) began in the early 1960s (originally known as the African Wildlife Leadership Foundation). Sholley tells me that the founders understood the importance of involving African professionals in their mission. "Unless you started to engage Africans in this whole idea of wildlife protection, the likelihood that there was a future for conservation and wildlife in Africa was nominal." AWF's first overall objective was to provide Africans with an opportunity to get masters and doctoral degrees in the realm of conservation.

The next step for the foundation was to strategize how best to ensure the long-term protection of the mountain gorillas. They were banking on the animals being their own best "spokesmen," says Sholley:

> Conservationists were looking at gorillas as a "magical" wild critter . . . their protection was going to be determined by providing them with an opportunity for being *ambassadors* for their species. Certain groups of gorillas would be habituated for tourist purposes. That would create an economic incentive that not only individuals living in the neighborhood but also national governments could buy into, because it was part of a long-term livelihood improvement plan for local communities and for countries like Rwanda, Uganda, and DRC.

But there were tragic obstacles to the success of their venture. Habitat loss, for example, was a major problem in Rwanda. In 1968, about 40 percent of the total park area was demolished—forests were cut—for plantations of pyrethrum, a daisylike flower that yields a natural insecticide. Then, just as the factories for its production were getting up and running in Rwanda, the development of low-cost synthetic pesticides caused the market for natural pyrethrum to collapse. Thus the Rwandans never benefited economically from the venture, and the gorillas suffered the loss of habitat, and yet more displacement. The devastation was compounded, Sholley says, by "a huge black market for gorilla parts as trophies, and gorilla infants as pets."

Back in 1959 to 1960, before his seminal work on the Serengeti lion, George B. Schaller, esteemed conservation scientist (and Sholley's hero), realized the first major study of the mountain gorilla (it was published in 1963 as *The Mountain Gorilla: Ecology and Behavior*).[14] Schaller later wrote of the period: "Poaching was the most serious immediate threat to gorillas. In the wake of the 1967 civil war in Zaire, hunters in large numbers entered the park to spear, shoot, and snare wildlife."[15]

In 1974 the Rwandan government increased the power of the guards in the Virungas. Eventually, conservationists Amy Vedder and William Weber of the New York Zoological Society would join forces with the Mountain Gorilla Project and other committed wildlife activists. Together, they would have a very positive impact on the future of the species by working with Rwanda's national parks system and office of tourism in the late 1970s. By the mid-1980s an ecotourism industry began to take hold throughout the country—perhaps most prominently in Virunga and the Volcanoes National Parks—an industry that relied on the health and well-being of the mountain gorillas, while providing economic incentives for local communities as well as for the government. The infusion of new income allowed for round-the-clock ranger patrols to guard against poaching—which not only preserved the animals, but served the best interests of the people and their communities. This pragmatic effort was supplemented by an awareness campaign that would have an important impact on public attitudes toward the forests and the gorillas in Rwanda.

Sholley:

> Dian was very against the idea of ecotourism, but as the Mountain Gorilla Project evolved, there was a realization that the tourism program was good from a conservation standpoint, because gorillas would be better protected, in part because of many unintended repercussions

that were positive for the community as well. We learned that conservation projects could be constructed in a manner that not only protects endangered species but also improves livelihoods for people who are willing to live with wildlife in their backyard.

Still, in the context of Rwanda's persistent conflicts since 1959—which ultimately exploded catastrophically in the 1994 genocide—and in the face of ongoing threats to the mountain gorillas, it is little wonder that Fossey was protective of their territory, and skeptical of even the most reasonable plans for ecotourism. Nick's determination allowed him to work around Fossey and complete his own project. And in retrospect, he is sympathetic to her adamant resolve—although he recognizes that she misjudged the impact on gorillas of intelligent ecotourism with clear, stringent, and enforced rules and regulations.

> People criticized her, often with good reasons. But she was a pioneer. She's up on a mountain, at ten thousand feet. She's freezing to death. She worked *so hard* to habituate these gorillas— and then they started being murdered. That's what turned her into a vigilante: her best friends were being killed by poachers, and Dian found the bodies.

Nick was ecstatic when conservationist George Schaller agreed to write for his very first book, *Gorilla: Struggle for Survival in the Virungas* (published by Aperture in 1989). About Fossey, Schaller said there:

> As the years passed, Dian Fossey became more and more involved in what she called "active conservation"; that is, she pursued poachers, burned poacher camps, herded illegal cattle out of the park, and in general became fiercely protective of her self-appointed charges. Her priority was correct: when the existence of a rare creature is threatened, a conservation effort becomes primary, science secondary. And the gorillas now needed all the help they could get.[16]

When Cahill and Nick arrived in Rwanda, the Avelings helped them, as promised. Conrad Aveling, one of the scientists who initiated the ecotourism program with the mountain gorillas, told Nick that he and Cahill could work with any of the gorilla groups that had been habituated to tourists, as long as they abided by the same rules that applied to visiting tourists. They would have one hour a day with the gorilla group; if either of them had a cold or any potentially contagious illness, he could not go to see them. And under no circumstances could they get closer to the animals than fifteen feet.

By this time, issues of habituation were understood differently than they had been when Dian Fossey (with gorillas), Jane Goodall (with chimpanzees), and Biruté Galdikas (with orangutans) had first begun their studies. Their methods were undeniably personal and, as Nick puts it, "a bit touchy-feely." Still, "these women were goddesses to me. As a kid, I'd fallen hook, line, and sinker for those *National Geographic* stories of the three beautiful women alone in the forests with the apes." The next generations of scientists learned to coddle less; no longer are great apes or big cats or any wild animal treated like beloved children; such behavior can make them vulnerable to poachers and to illness. Furthermore, as Nick attests, a gorilla who has been brought up not fearing humans can become dangerous: "I got hammered by some of these gorillas. They were now adults, and they threw me through the air because Dian had played with them on her lap." But, he adds,

Crater lake, Mount Visoke, Volcanoes National Park, Rwanda, 1981 if you are habituating gorillas or chimps, you have to get them to trust you. So it's really complicated. . . . Of course, if gorillas trust you, if the parents trust you, the kids—just like with chimps—are going to start coming over to you and they want to play! And are you going to tell them to go away after you've spent five years trying to get closer to them? Fuck no! They're going to end up in your lap!

Meanwhile, Fossey's colleague Sandy Harcourt had learned that Nick had come to Rwanda despite her offputting cable. At the time, Fossey was still in the United States. In her absence, Harcourt defiantly extended a warm welcome to Nick, inviting him to come to Karisoke.

Something deep had been altered in Nick: he had never been so on fire. Until this point, his work had been entirely about *photography*: how to make the most innovative, astonishing image; how to succeed, how to outdo; how to be the guy everyone turned to, whom they knew they could rely on. In Rwanda, Nick experienced a swell of emotion he could not account for, a sense of responsibility that transcended mere art, mere career:

> I started off in my life in photography just wanting to chase interesting images, but the gorillas changed all that. Everything that I do today comes from those mountain gorillas. I understood immediately that animals are individuals and have rights. This is when and where I find my soul.

That his soul could so organically align with his competitive desire to succeed and innovate—without compromise—bespeaks a confident, perhaps even messianic belief in his mission. But did he have the photographic chops to give voice to a nonhuman species in need? The challenge was to render what he was experiencing resonantly, with an interpretive edge that was respectful of his subjects and all their vulnerabilities. These struggles were compounded by the technical challenges of photographing in the jungle:

> It was so dark . . . I was using transparency film—Kodachrome. To make the colors rich and strong, you have to expose it perfectly. It's the opposite of working with negative film . . . with transparency film, you have to expose it perfectly—or throw it away. . . . So I'm with these gorillas, and they're black, and I'm thinking I should underexpose as a way to deal with the black creature in his dark habitat. Ninety percent of my first shoot came back unusable. . . . I went too far: I made the gorilla super black, so you couldn't see anything. But I was always experimenting, and I did get one picture that I love to this day, which is so mysterious and where the face is slightly blurred and the gorilla is looking at me through a dark bamboo forest.

Nick could have used a flash, which would have helped enormously, but "I didn't want to disturb the gorillas. They are very sensitive. The gorilla's demeanor is like a monk's. . . . Flash never felt intrusive to me—except with animals. I didn't want to upset them." This was Nick's first experience photographing animals. "I didn't know how to be a fly on the wall then," he admits. "Later I learned how to be, but not in those years."

Geo published Nick and Cahill's story "Gorilla Tactics" in December 1981. Other editions followed. Editor Christiane Breustedt recognized in Nick's photographs something unprecedented:

> I had seen pictures of gorillas before. But I strongly believe that Nick's portraits of these magnificent creatures changed wildlife photography forever. His pictures are a brilliant, baffling interplay of abstract and figurative interpretations of individuals and their biotope. A fascinating mixture of movement and calmness. Nick remained true to what we call photography, though pushing its boundaries to the limit. And that he does to this day.

That first trip to Rwanda to photograph the mountain gorillas was an epiphany for Nick—as a photographer and as a burgeoning activist for conservation.

Cahill observes: "You couldn't interact with those magnificent animals for over a month without becoming sensitive to their fate." Asked about his own motivations, and how he conveys his mission to his readers, Cahill responds:

> I have conservation imperatives that I feel very strongly about. But I think to write an argumentative essay about saving this particular piece of land or that particular animal is really a process of shaking your finger in the reader's face—and the reader doesn't want that. You want to make them fall in love with this place, this creature—and maybe go see it, or if not go to it, at least preserve it the way it is, so that they can still go to it in their fantasy. It's a "kinder, gentler" kind of conservation writing than the angry, argumentative writing which I find turns people off.

Cahill believes that Nick shares this conviction. His images tend to emphasize the extraordinary totality of the wild—not the human ravages upon it. "Maybe," says Cahill, "that's why we work well together, because we have the same conservation-oriented ideas, and the same sort of approach to how we convince people that something matters. What I am trying to do is quietly get together a conspiracy of caring."

As Nick puts it: "With the gorillas, I became a 'concerned photographer.' After that, it was about seducing the reader, with my photographs, into caring. I understood that the pictures could make a difference."

FOLLOWING SPREAD: Mrithi, silverback mountain gorilla, Virunga Mountains, Rwanda, 1981

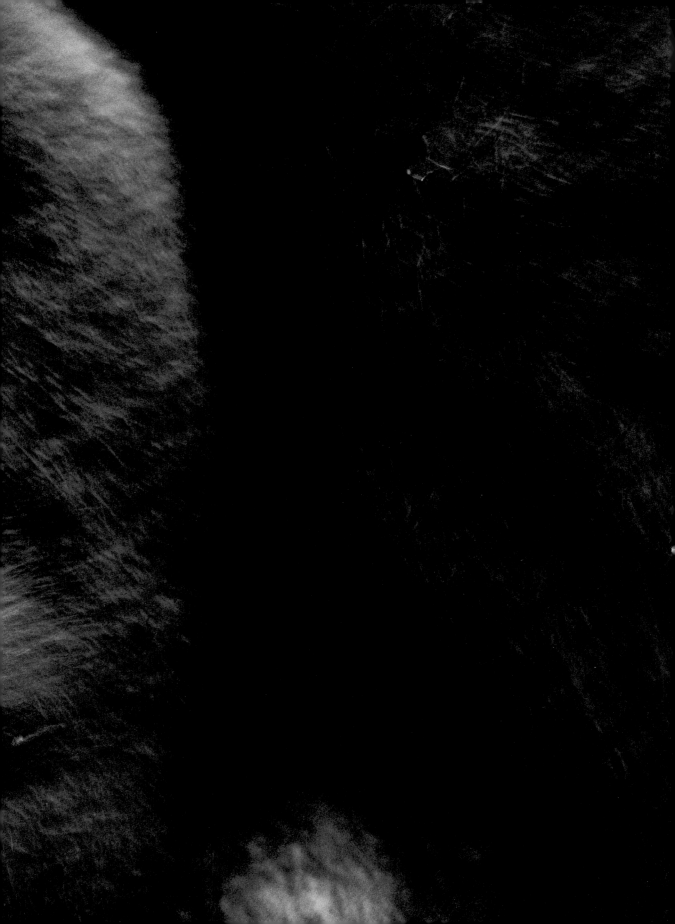

INDIANA JONES

Mount Thor, Auyuittuq National Park, Canada, 1982

t's like smoke signals," says Nick, laughing. "Smoke signals get to you that Magnum is interested. Nobody calls you—at least, not then. Philip [Jones Griffiths, president of Magnum Photos from 1980 to 1985] had put the word out: 'Come see us.'"

Magnum Photos, the cooperative photo-agency created in 1947 by Robert Capa, Henri Cartier-Bresson, George Rodger, and David "Chim" Seymour, was defined eloquently by Cartier-Bresson as "a community of thought, a shared human quality, a curiosity about what is going on in the world, a respect for what is going on and a desire to transcribe it visually."[1] For Nick and other photojournalists, membership in Magnum has long symbolized an apex of achievement, hard-won recognition by one's peers, and the potential to go further. As a cooperative, Magnum also represents, ideally, a kind of solidarity among its membership, whose sensibilities are remarkably diverse. One of the agency's senior photographers has characterized Magnum as "a community of divas." But it might be said that the arrogance is warranted: there is no denying the remarkable pool of talent in the cooperative. While some photographers have flowed in and out of Magnum—Mary Ellen Mark, James Nachtwey, Eugene Richards, and Sebastião Salgado, for example—others, once inducted, have remained members for the rest of their lives. At their most socially engaged, Magnum photographers share a dedication to addressing the world's formidable challenges, often propelled by a fervent drive to advocate for justice.

When Nick learned of Magnum's interest, in 1981, he was intrigued. He was still living in San Francisco, and although he was already a hardworking professional, he made a point of signing up for a workshop at SF Friends of Photography taught by Magnumites Mary Ellen Mark and Burk Uzzle. "I loved their work, but mostly I wanted to talk to them about Magnum." Both Mark and Uzzle had mixed feelings about the agency: Mark would take her leave that same year and Uzzle in 1983. Nonetheless, they encouraged Nick—saying: "But it can be really good for you." Nick, smiling: "That 'but' was all I needed to hear. I became a nominee in 1982."

As a student, Nick had studied the photographs of Magnum's founders and many others, and he was particularly jazzed by the work of his contemporaries at the agency—especially Gilles Peress, Eugene Richards, and Alex Webb. Welsh photojournalist Philip Jones Griffiths (who died in 2008) had made a profound impact on Nick with his seminal 1971 project *Vietnam Inc.*; he presided over the agency for five years with fierce single-mindedness. Nick notes: "He could sure be ruthless, especially when he was mad at someone, but it was Philip—the outspoken, brilliant Philip—who was the real conscience for me." Another important influence was Czech photographer Josef Koudelka. To Nick, "Josef was bigger than life. . . . He was *always* shooting. He never took assignments; he was constantly and only taking the pictures he believed in."

Nick had been working nonstop, primarily for *Geo*; the idea that he could ever have the liberty to turn down assignments in order to prioritize what compelled him, what he thought most mattered, was thrilling. He might have come to this realization without Magnum—and it took him some time to gain the clout and financial wherewithal to act on it. But he had been so hungry for assignments—gamely accepting any that came his way in order to prove himself, and always mindful of the crushing poverty of his childhood—that it came as a meaningful lesson that there could be a different, perhaps more fulfilling way to function.

"I believe in cooperatives," he says. "I believe that peer pressure can be helpful. We are all lone wolves, so it is nice to have a moment when you're sharing. I loved Magnum. Even when I hated it, I loved it."

But in the Magnum pantheon of photojournalists, Nick stood out in ways that were at times discomfiting for him:

> I was a little ashamed of being an "adventure photographer," and then later, a kind of wildlife photographer. I had always wanted to be a *journalist*. I loved the idea of reportage. So my challenge was doing that with the subjects that interested *me*. I'd started thinking that way with the gorillas, even before Magnum—but Magnum drove it home.
>
> Early on in the Magnum process, I showed some of my general assignment work to [Magnum member] Paul Fusco, who kind of knocked me out with a simple phrase: "Well, we don't care

Magnum annual meeting, 1992. Foreground, left to right: Josef Koudelka, Alex Webb, Peter Marlow, Nick (standing); background (seated): Paul Gauci, Magnum's business/office manager. Photograph by Paul Fusco/Magnum Photos

about any of that; that's what you do to make a living. We care about what *you care* about." That was a huge bell going off. . . . The best thing I got out of Magnum was arrogance—of vision, arrogance of editing.

As a Magnum nominee, Nick came in on the strength of the projects he had already done. For the next round, moving toward full membership, he would have to show new work.

I decided to go back to Alabama—to Muscle Shoals and Florence. That was in the post-Carter era: we had 20 percent unemployment; there was a tremendous amount of drug addiction—lots of prescription drugs that were really brain-killers.

So I did a group of pictures I called "My Hometown," playing off the Bruce Springsteen song. . . . I hadn't been back home since I ran away with Reba. In two months, I shot only fifty rolls of film. Each time I pressed the button it was incredibly painful. I was photographing my mom, who by then had married a guy my age who she'd met in detox, and who still had huge substance-abuse problems. Stevie Lawler was at his parents' home—where I had stayed so much as a child—shooting up Dilaudid: "hospital heroin." He was with a woman who was also a bit bent—I photographed them together after he'd shot up, and his eyes are so empty. . . . Everything about the project was so painful for me.

As he worked on this project—feeling "ripped apart"—Nick was in regular contact with Philip Jones Griffiths and his partner, photojournalist Donna Ferrato, who were based in New York. Ferrato recalls that during this period,

> Nick would make pilgrimages to our house. Philip really loved Nick, and believed in him. He admired his athleticism and bravery—"Nick Danger!"—and also saw him as a hardcore photojournalist. We were all, over the years, especially blown away by his pictures of animals, always. They are so tender and emotional, but not sweet. He gets into the heart and mind of animals better than anybody.

Nick understood that he was finding his own vision. He understood that Magnum photographers could be ferociously passionate and unflinching in their commitment and their work, that they were constantly reconsidering and debating storytelling, issues of text and image, of authorship, of "other," of the meaning of reportage, of what truly *mattered*—all this was exhilarating for him and instilled in him a sense of the agency of photography.

In his heart, he knew that he wanted his work eventually to land in the pages of *National Geographic*. "But they didn't want me then—I tried, and thank God for that! They would have eaten me up then, and would have had way too much influence on me. And I wouldn't have grown the way I needed to. I needed to be around all those great Magnum photographers who believe so much in the work they are doing."

Nick was realizing that his projects could accomplish more than just fulfilling his own personal aspirations. During his work with the gorillas, he had come to understand that photographs could serve as instruments of change. This notion was nurtured in the company of the Magnum group, and with feedback from figures like Griffiths, whose expectations of Magnum and its members were always exacting. Importantly, at Magnum, photographers are also expected to retain the copyright to their work—this is more than a pragmatic suggestion; it is a principal with ethical weight.

Magnum makes its potential members work for that status. After becoming a nominee, Nick was not immediately voted in as a full member; neither was Eli Reed, who had been nominated at the same time. (Nick later came to learn that this is standard operating procedure at Magnum, presumably to keep nominees on their toes. "They did the same thing to Salgado," he recalls. "It pissed all of us off.") Eventually he was voted in, first as an associate member in 1984, and then as a full member—with voting status—in 1987. The French magazine *Photo* took note, and in May 1984, in its special two-hundredth issue, featured a spread of his blurry gorilla photograph from Rwanda, with the headline: *"Missions impossibles: Indiana Jones vient d'entrer à Magnum"*—"Indiana Jones has just joined Magnum."[2] (For better or for worse, the "Indiana Jones of photography" moniker would stick with him for a long while.)

Even after being voted in as a full member, Nick remained an outlier of sorts, on the receiving end of what felt at times like withering belittlement. He was called everything from "the cave photographer" to "son of Vivitar" (because of his unprecedented use of flash). Occasionally he was taken to task by colleagues for his commitment to photographing in the *wild*, when the state of humanity was

Nick's mother, Joyce, with her husband Ron, Muscle Shoals, April 1985

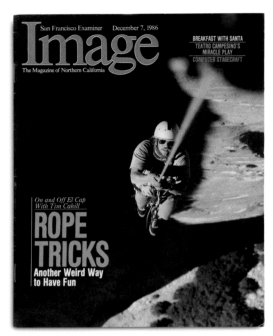

Cover of *San Francisco Examiner Image* magazine
(showing Tim Cahill), December 7, 1986: "Rope Tricks"

so desperate. Of course, he wouldn't argue with the necessity to bear witness on behalf of humans in dire circumstances—living in horrific conditions, besieged by conflict and its aftermath. But it seemed to him that nearly everyone at Magnum was fighting for the human cause; shouldn't someone stand up for the planet itself and its nonhuman inhabitants?

Over the years, conservationists, journalists, advocates, and others have more fully come to terms with the fact that human struggles with poverty and strife, health and sustainability, are all part of one ecosystem that we share with the forests we raze, the animals we poach or traffic, the natural resources we deplete, and the habitats we destroy. It is understood that our population density and displacement, our waste and carbon footprint, our migrations are inextricably intertwined with the life of the planet and with all other species. The human/nature divide has always been a false construct.

But for several of Nick's Magnum colleagues, deeply troubled by the human suffering they witnessed so closely, the idea of one of their own focusing on anything else may have seemed at best naïve and at worst heretical.

Despite the clarion call that had jolted him in Rwanda, and despite his immersion in more purposeful photography at Magnum, Nick continued throughout the 1980s to work in what he describes as "the genres of adventure photography, and then exotic essays . . . basically hedonistic adventures where white guys go out to conquer something." Magazines that prized the photo essay were still flourishing, and Nick was never without an assignment. The subjects of his stories ranged from faith healing (1982) to facing the Arctic's daunting Thor Peak (a 1983 article written by Mitchell Shields). Those pieces and many others were shot for U.S. *Geo*, where Elisabeth Biondi was now the director of photography. Biondi made a point of introducing Nick to editors at other publications that featured photo-reportage. "I thought a young, talented photographer should work for other magazines," she recalls, "as long as he offered his story ideas to us first." For *Rolling Stone*, Nick covered "Thailand's Home for Wayward Vets" (1984) and skateboarding (1987). And after U.S. *Geo* folded in the mid-1980s, he did a number of stories—including another written by Cahill on Balinese trance ceremonies (1989)—for *Geo*'s German edition.

For a *San Francisco Examiner Image* magazine piece, published in 1986, Nick climbed Yosemite's El Capitan, a few steps ahead of Tim Cahill so he could photograph the writer from above (they were tethered to the same rope, a problematic circumstance when, as Cahill later wrote, Nick announced:

"I'm sorry, but my bladder is going to bust. I mean it.")[3] For the *New York Times Magazine* in advance of the 1988 summer Olympics, Nick covered what he describes as China's government-sponsored "machine for creating athletes to win gold medals." The following year, *Southern Magazine*, where Shields was an editor, published Nick's "tacky tour of the South."

These stories were all done in the spirit of "Nick Danger" and "Indiana Jones." But Nick longed for the sense of exigency, of purpose, that he'd felt with the mountain gorillas in Rwanda.

And, while Nick was pleased to have been voted into Magnum, his pride was tempered by the knowledge that many top-notch photographers hadn't been invited to join the cooperative. He wanted to provide a less elite photography forum. He began organizing casual occasional slide shows at his and Reba's Berkeley loft. Many of the participants were seasoned professional photographers, but it was a decidedly open call.

> *Anybody* who came could show pictures. . . . Working photographers like George Steinmetz showed work; so did Ed Kashi, Frans Lanting, and Galen Rowell. But then, there was also work by the plumber, the doctor, the guy down the hall. . . . There were also lots of mountain and river guides—travelers catching up with each other and showing their latest adventure.

Slide shows were ingrained into Nick's process since his time in the army. In the 1970s, he had shared his images with cavers at the Nashville Grotto caving club, as well as with fellow soldiers at Fort Campbell eager to see his new work.

Nick and Reba's loft—a former mattress factory next to the headquarters of Fantasy Records—was perfect for screenings: about a hundred feet long and twenty feet wide, with concrete floors and a kitchen and sleeping space. Guests brought chairs and other potluck necessities, and settled in for a comfortable evening of projected images.

The slide-show gatherings soon became celebrated in the San Francisco–Berkeley photo community: more and more photographers and would-be photographers showed up. Steinmetz recalls the gatherings as "big, raucous parties—I think Nick was sometimes using them to edit his work when he felt just too close to it. Ian was really little and running around. It was this crazy, hippie atmosphere—a mini photographic Woodstock!" They were about sharing work, perhaps getting some feedback, smoking pot, and general goodwill. When eventually Nick and Reba moved to Charlottesville, Virginia, in 1990, they would continue the tradition in their new backyard. From 1992 to 2005, photographers would gather on warm summer evenings—over

Rolling Stone, September 26, 1985: "Fear of Frying"

ABOVE: Nick and Cahill at work on "Fear of Frying" for *Rolling Stone*, 1985; OPPOSITE: Cahill at the Darwin post office, Death Valley, California, 1985

Cajun food (jambalaya, rice and beans)—to project their work under the stars, on a screen and with equipment borrowed from *National Geographic*. The event came to be dubbed "Hotshots." It was in Virginia, recalls Nick, that "the evenings became something more. The sharing and community vibe really kicked in." And still later, that spirit of community would continue, on a larger scale, as these slide shows evolved into the independent LOOK3 photography festival.

Nick's early career as a photojournalist has been described by Steinmetz as "gonzo," that is, "where the experience of taking the picture was a central part of the story." One unquestionably gonzo project was a 1985 collaboration with Cahill for *Rolling Stone*. The seed was planted when Cahill came to San Francisco on a book tour and asked Nick to join him for a drink at the swanky Fairmont Hotel. That evening, Cahill proposed that the two of them walk from the lowest point in the continental United States to the highest—a trek of about 150 miles.

Nick recalls that he agreed enthusiastically—but quickly considered the conditions and specified that they would have to do the trip in the wintertime, "so it's not too hot and we won't die." He remembers Cahill nodding and parroting him: "You're *exactly* right. We'll do it in winter, so it's not too hot and we won't die."

But the best-laid plans don't always pan out. Cahill was late finishing his book *Buried Dreams: Inside the Mind of a Serial Killer* (on John Wayne Gacy), and the trip with Nick was delayed until the summer.

They were to start out in Death Valley's Badwater Basin, the lowest point in North America, at about 280 feet below sea level, and end up—about two weeks later—on the peak of Mount Whitney: at over 14,500 feet the highest summit in the contiguous United States.

As they set out from Badwater Basin, Nick recalls, they knew that they would have to hike at night and sleep during the day, when the temperatures could rise to 130 degrees.

> I say: "Tim, we've got to start on the full moon, or we'll die!" And he said: "Okay, we'll start on the full moon so we won't die, Nick." . . . So we start out at Death Valley—but so late in the moon cycle because of Tim being late, that we are *losing* the moonlight, and we have to walk with flashlights. But we are still going to walk at night because it's just so fucking hot. The water under Death Valley has these saltpans . . . you break through the mud, and it's *boiling* underneath. And the desert during the day is killer.

"We have always depended on the kindness of rangers." So opens Cahill's article, "Fear of Frying," published in *Rolling Stone* in September 1985.[4] Cahill describes a Death Valley National Park ranger's take on other adventurers who had attempted this particular expedition:

> Ninety percent of them, he said, quit the first day. He said it was psychological. Either that or poor planning.

> "We're pretty psychological," I pointed out.

Nick didn't reply. He was studying a copy of *Death Valley's Victims*, looking at the photos of desiccated corpses baking out on the valley floor.

"We're going to die," the Indiana Jones of photography said.

In fact, the Death Valley rangers they consulted thought that Nick and Cahill were crazy—but allowed them to undertake the trek provided someone along the way would keep an eye on them and report on their progress. Nick asked his old friend and comrade Frankie Frost to be that monitor: "He'd look for us with binoculars from high points every couple of days. He had a medical kit, and helped me bury water and food along the route ahead of the walk, so we didn't have to carry it."

Nick had carefully worked out a number of solutions to the challenge of survival in those sweltering daytime conditions. He made sure their tents were covered with space-blankets to block the sun—he tested the plan on a Death Valley golf course and calculated that the blankets would save them twenty degrees. ("And I'm thinking: that twenty degrees is going to save our lives!") But on their first day, they realized that on this front he had miscalculated. They set up their tents and settled in. Nick recalls:

> We're going to sleep out the day. We're right up against tumbleweed, so we're in a little bit of shade. But at about eleven in the morning, Tim says: "Nick—I think something's wrong with the plan. It's like 160 and then some in my tent." What had happened is, with my plan I had created an oven. The ground heats up from *underneath*. The idea of saving twenty degrees worked if there was grass underneath, but when you're on this baking pan . . . it totally fried us.

They broke down their tents and crawled into the holes in the tumbleweed, covering themselves as best they could and praying to get through the heat of the day. Only as the sun began to abate, in the late afternoon, did Nick say to himself: "We're going to live. But we both had set our shoes outside to dry. They'd been muddy and wet after walking all night. Tim's shoes were completely curled up—he couldn't even get his feet in them. He called them 'cruel shoes' after a Steve Martin bit, and ended up cutting out a whole part of his boots so his toes could stick out."

That night, they continued their hike, but as dawn approached, Nick was delirious. "I'd never been in that kind of heat. I was hallucinating like crazy. We had to get out of that flatland or we wouldn't survive. . . . It's getting close to dawn, and everything's red. And I have no fucking idea where the buried water is." In the end, they made it to a side canyon, where they were able to sit out the day—moving from one side to the other to remain in the shade.

As their trek took them out of Death Valley, Nick and Cahill passed through ghost towns and into nearly deserted areas, populated mostly with survivalists. "I had scouted all this," recounts Nick, "and I thought, it will be *great stuff* for Tim." They met a man along the way who firmly believed that his wife had been abducted in a spaceship. Nick thought "Cool!" and set a time for Cahill to interview him. (After speaking with the fellow, Cahill admonished Nick: "If you *ever* set up another interview for me, I will kill you.") They slept, undisturbed, for most of a day at an empty post office.

And after about two weeks, they were standing on top of Mount Whitney.

The opening image of "Fear of Frying" features a thermometer on a wire fence in the foreground, with a shimmery desert landscape—a mirage?—as a backdrop. Nick knew well that this was not so much a great photographic story as it was an adventure for him and Cahill. The writer would weave a wonderful tale from their exploits, and Nick would make a few good images. The story's rendering is classic Cahill: sharply observed, funny, compelling. The photographs are not Nick's strongest; they function as illustrations to this kooky spin on the genre of expedition photography. However, the experience of this trip further ingrained in him the necessary pacing and potential power of experiential storytelling. Subsequently, Nick would almost always be the narrator, his photographs providing the central voice.

The revelatory experience Nick had had with the mountain gorillas continued to resonate for him, and he longed to expand that project. In the mid-1980s, he had his chance. With editor Nan Richardson as a conduit, he went to see Michael E. Hoffman, the visionary publisher and executive director of Aperture Foundation. Hoffman, who could be dismissive with photographers whose work he believed was even remotely disingenuous—not "the real deal," as he would put it—immediately felt a great affinity for the young photographer and his project. He also believed strongly in its conservation agenda.

Nick remembers his first meeting with Hoffman, in his fifth-floor office of Aperture's East 23rd Street brownstone headquarters at the foot of Madison Avenue in New York:

> I went in literally with ten dark images, a dream, and a plan. There were three to four good gorilla pictures, and some other pictures I'd made in Rwanda. . . . And Michael basically said: "We'll do a book on the plight of the mountain gorilla. Go make the pictures." Dian Fossey by then had been murdered, and we knew a Hollywood film was being made about her, so we all thought it would sell. But all I could think about was: "I have Aperture! Michael Hoffman agreed to do my book!" I had been sanctioned. I was so encouraged, so determined. It changed my life. And Aperture's mission felt right.

In 1987, with Reba and their son Ian (now six), Nick started making two- and three-month trips to Rwanda. The three of them settled into a mud hut at the base of Mount Visoke. For nearly a year, Nick turned down almost every other assignment—"I just tried to put together packages of existing work with Magnum for them to resell—anything that would let me photograph gorillas for my book."

Ian had been attending a Montessori school down the block from their Berkeley loft. Now he went to school in the village of Bisoke, with some homeschooling on the side. Both parents remember their son drawing constantly during their time in Africa. Today, nearly thirty years later and around the same age his father was then, Ian resembles the young Nick so strongly—the intense, wide-set eyes, the chiseled features, the wavy, dark locks—that it's hard not to do a double take. He is thoughtful as he recalls those early days in the Virunga Mountains:

> Nick was always working, so I was in the village all day, left to my own devices. . . . I was the one little white kid in the village, and I remember the Rwandans being very kind and gentle with me. I was with a group of kids all day—and actually, *their* parents were also away working. So it was the older kids looking out for the younger kids. I only had good experiences there.

In a letter to his mother, Joyce, in Alabama, Nick described Ian's days:

> I have taken lots of pics of *Ian in Africa*, bathing in a bucket by the fire, school with Reba, Drawing, Drawing, Drawing, playing with chameleons (thought to be poison by the Africans), making things with Rwandan children all around. Hiking-whining-moaning exuberant—thru wild weird vegetation.

And Nick's extended gorilla project was progressing. As reported to Joyce:

> Work is going well. Through lots of walking and being wet and cold and hungry, I have taken some volcano landscapes of Biblical proportions. The light and character lend to the primal feeling here. When walking we all get the feeling of a primeval—beginning of the earth—environment.

Craig Sholley, at the time affiliated with the Mountain Gorilla Project, remembers Nick in that period as "a character with big dimensions" whose work ethic was hugely inspiring—"he just goes and goes and goes"—and also as someone who wanted to experience this part of Rwanda from the inside:

> Nick is a very culturally sensitive guy, and he wanted to fit in. He didn't want to be apart from the people who were a part of that landscape. He bought from the local markets and ate the same kind of food that everybody was eating, and he fraternized with the local folks. The whole Nichols family endeared themselves to the Rwandans living in the

OPPOSITE: Ian at seven and friend, Rwanda, 1988; ABOVE: Young boy, Virunga Range, Rwanda, 1981

area because they were part of the neighborhood. They weren't the "white folks"—the expatriates living on the hill in a grandiose house.

When Nick and Cahill had been in Rwanda six years earlier, they had benefited from the expertise of Mark Condiotti, another conservationist working with the Mountain Gorilla Project. Nick would go out day after day to photograph the same habituated group—family—of gorillas. His mannerisms, his acknowledgment of boundaries, would be key to his success, and to his safety. Condiotti had instructed them, when near the gorillas, to move gracefully and calmly, not to gesture abruptly, and never to look the animals in the eye or stare at them—which might be perceived as aggression. He also taught Cahill and Nick certain throat-clearing vocalizations that might help put the gorillas at ease.

These lessons in gorilla etiquette were to prove useful on his return trip with his family. Nick describes a particular silverback named Ziz, who helped him refine his manners:

> Ziz was the silverback of the study group at Karasoke. . . . I first met him on the *Geo* story
> in 1981. He was very aggressive and full of himself. When I came back, he had matured,
> and taken over the group. He had acquired females from all over the mountain. . . . There
> were somewhere close to thirty gorillas under his care. . . . And he was benign—as gorillas

become. The females won't stay with them if they're not fabulous, usually. He was the king.

Ziz would sit next to me. I never made moves to him; *he* would make moves to me. I was very well behaved. I didn't look him in the eye. I watched my body language . . . although a few times I made mistakes, because his kids would be getting too close to me, stealing my gloves. But I was into the school of "I'm not touching you; you can't touch me."

At one point, Nick learned that a pack of wild dogs was roaming Volcanoes National Park. Such dogs can pose a great threat to young gorillas—but Ziz clearly had the situation under control.

Ziz picked up a scent or saw something. He made some nonverbal gestures, and the other silverback males went to the perimeters. All the females gathered around Ziz, and he gathered the kids—there must have been ten under him—and he was just in that gorilla *strut*. I was blown away. That's what gorillas do . . . they protect their family, at all costs.

Ziz once walked up to me and looked me in the eye, and took a tree down, *ka-bam*! Just like that, as if to say: "See what I can do?" They've got these incredible muscles in their ass. I got it. I understood completely!

Nick made a powerful image of Ziz hooting. The animal's demeanor seems calm yet alert to his verdant environment, mildly disgruntled as it's raining—mountain gorillas generally don't enjoy being wet. In another photograph, Ziz is all teeth, perhaps after feasting on some bamboo. His paterfamilias stature is unmistakable. Evocative family portraits—of Ziz with his offspring rolling around his back, or of groups with nursing infants, or with frolicking juveniles—reveal the lives of the mountain gorilla with extraordinary intimacy, even tenderness.

When scientist George Schaller agreed to contribute an essay/firsthand account for Nick's Aperture book, *Gorilla: Struggle for Survival in the Virungas*, he had not spent time with Nick in the field. But he appreciated the project, reiterating that "gorillas need all the help they can get." Schaller recognizes that an embedded documentarian "can learn things, see things, that someone else either

OPPOSITE: Mountain gorilla; ABOVE: Ziz, silverback mountain gorilla. Both Volcanoes National Park, 1988

hasn't thought about or hasn't seen." He also notes that even the most "dispassionate" study is shaped by the perspective of the researcher framing the inquiry:

> Years ago, the first people that studied baboons were males. They chose to watch aggression in big male baboons, and they published papers stating that baboon society is run by males, and that it's a very aggressive society—that was based on what they saw. Then women started studying baboons, and they decided to study cooperation. They came up with a completely different perspective on baboon society. Now, these were all people who thought they were being completely objective. But the questions that guided their studies gave results that were quite different. Of course you want to be accurate. I'm simply suggesting that there are many ways to look.

Gorilla, published in 1989, reveals a perspective and approach that would become part of Nick's unique signature. He has never realized a project without exploring and understanding the context: the larger environment and its people. He immerses himself in whatever environment he is observing; his deftness in doing so distinguished him early on from other photographers of wildlife.

Photographer Steve Winter came to work as Nick's assistant in Berkeley in the 1980s. He had been studying Nick's photographs for some time. Working at a photography shop in San Francisco where Nick brought his films for processing, he'd become fascinated by his work:

> I wanted to find out more about what he was doing, so I started going to bookstores and looking at *Geo*. I was blown away! So . . . when he'd come back from trips, I'd log all his film for him, and then when it came back, I'd look at it and then put it back exactly the way it came in—all the slides returned in the proper way. This is how I got to know Nick before working for him as his assistant: I was looking at his pictures. I'd come into the store early if I knew Nick's film was back!

Winter, today well known himself for his tenacity and hard-won photographs—primarily of particularly evasive big cats—views Nick's journalistic approach to photographing the natural world as an antidote to the romanticizing sentimentality and anthropomorphism that are often the hallmarks of wildlife photography. Nick goes right in—close enough to experience the funky aroma of mountain gorillas, the paralyzing anxiety of being bluff-charged, the animals' percussive chest-thumpings. Close enough to perceive and reveal the nuances of the relationships among the gorillas in their respective groups. There is no exoticism in these images, nor anything remotely saccharine. Winter: "Nick shows the reality of the situation as a whole—the connectivity of our natural world and the people who live within it. . . . Animals don't live in a Shangri La. He photographs their world as it is—sometimes beautiful, sometimes full of death and destruction. It's not just about the animals—as if they don't live in a larger world. He tells us the *entire* story, really emotionally."

Although often epic in subject, his photographs consistently respect the importance of each individual. Ziz matters.

And, as Winter suggests, Nick has also never postulated a uniform, benign world where all creatures sidle up first to each other, and then to human beings in some peaceable-kingdom-meets-"Family of Man" extravaganza. What distinguishes Nick's work so profoundly is that, finally, someone is conveying animals with the purpose of revealing who they are, on their own terms—their *isness*—as much as is humanly possible.

Early in 1988, Nick, Reba, and Ian returned to the States. Nick went to New York to begin working with Nan Richardson at Aperture on the edit of the gorillas book, staying with Philip Jones Griffiths and Donna Ferrato.

Not long after, he became suddenly and very dangerously ill. Ferrato was terrified: Griffiths was traveling, and she was on her own with her young daughter Fanny, and with Nick, who seemed to be on the verge of death:

> He had blackwater fever, a kind of malaria. . . . He was emaciated and yellow and just *bones*.
> . . . He looked like a cadaver. He went to see Philip's doctor, who said . . . the only way to help him was to give him the antidote, and the only way to do that was to inject him in the ass! I said: "Oh, no, I couldn't!" I don't like needles at all.

Although in her groundbreaking documentation of domestic abuse, for example, Ferrato had witnessed terrifying physical and psychological violence, the "aggressiveness" of giving Nick a shot really shook her.[5] The doctor had her practice on grapefruits in his office.

> I had to stab him, plunge it in, then release it and pull it out. . . . He would just say: "Donna."
> But he was dying before my eyes. I had to give him these injections twice a day until Reba

Reba caring for Nick, sick with blackwater fever (falciparum malaria), New York, 1988. Photograph by Donna Ferrato

arrived—she took a red-eye from California immediately—thank God, so she could take over playing Florence Nightingale, and then get Nick home as soon as he was well enough. The hardest thing I have ever had to do was to give him those shots! . . . But really, he was dying.

Ferrato made a photograph of Reba embracing Nick the moment she arrived and saw him so very ill—a contemporary pietà charged with anguish and love. After a few days, Reba was able to take him home to Berkeley.

Not long after his return to California, as he was finishing up the gorilla book, Nick had a call from one of his original cave-exploring pals, Rick Bridges. Bridges was an Indiana caver Nick had met caving in Mexico with Ed Yarborough. (In the mid-1970s, Yarborough had introduced Nick to vertical caving—in pits.) Bridges told Nick they had found "the world's greatest cave," and that he had to come photograph it. Nick was reluctant—by this point he was "obsessed with other kinds of pictures." But his caving gear was still in the basement, and he listened to what Bridges, a caving pioneer, had to say. Apparently Bridges and others had been intrepidly searching for big caves. While exploring the well-known ninety-foot entrance pit of Lechuguilla Cave, in Carlsbad Caverns National Park, New Mexico, they suddenly realized, Nick recounts,

> that at the bottom of the pit, air was blowing ferociously and then sucking—blowing and sucking. When that's happening in a place with caves, you know there's something big down there. . . .
>
> So these cats—cavers are *obsessive*—start digging in secret—without park permits . . . and when they broke through, they immediately saw that they had found something spectacular. And, because they were real cavers and conservationists, they immediately put a tube in there with a door on it, so that it wouldn't let all that humidity out: all this incredibly beautifully stuff could dry up if the door was open. The cave had to live like it had always lived.
>
> They kept it a secret, and they just started sneaking in there and exploring and mapping. And they realized that it just went on and on and *on*. That's when they called me.

As U.S. *Geo* had by now folded, Nick contacted *Smithsonian*, which gave him three weeks to photograph the story—his first for the magazine. He had to assemble a strong, agile team that could carry in food as well as photographic equipment. And within this group, there had to be someone who knew the cave well. The cavers suggested a young man who'd been exploring with them: Neeld Messler. He was, as Nick remembers, "eighteen years old and strong as an ox."

Messler, who grew up in Colorado, has been caving since he was thirteen. Like many of Nick's long-term assistants in the field, he is healthy and handsomely open-faced, tall, slender, and athletic—not overtly muscular or stocky. "I met Nick in the middle of Lechuguilla's Apricot Pit," Messler recalls:

> Apricot Pit is a rift . . . rigged all the way down with rope systems. It might be a three- or four-hundred-foot drop. You're traversing the rift system at an angle. It's hard: it pulls at your energy all the time. I remember as I was exiting Apricot Pit, Nick Nichols was coming down,

so we met somewhere in the middle. He hadn't been in a cave for a long time. He was doing really well. The people who had been assigned to assist him were dying off. . . . They were *way* back, carrying these heavy loads and struggling.

When Nick invited Messler to join the team, he agreed immediately. He knows he was helpful to Nick, "because I was young, I wouldn't complain, and I would work hard. I was super-strong, and I could carry massive amounts of weight." It was the start of a long and close friendship, and the first of several expeditions Messler and Nick would undertake together.

Smithsonian published "A Labyrinth Called Lechuguilla" in November 1988, with Nick's photographs accompanied by David Roberts's words.[6] But Nick wasn't finished with Lechuguilla: he knew there was so much more to explore, to photograph, and he was determined to go back. As he had done many times before without success, he pitched an idea to *National Geographic*.

"I had one goal, and that was to work for *National Geographic*. I knew I needed that platform, that reach." He wanted to work on long assignments, and for his photographs to be seen in a forum that would allow their full power to come through. "I knew I had a message—but I wanted that message to be heard. I didn't want my photographs to be competing with ads like they were in almost every other magazine. I wanted real space, and real time, and real support."

Year after year, Steve Winter had assisted Nick in preparing a portfolio of images for *National Geographic*'s review. "I never saw anybody so intent on succeeding as when we would put a tray of slides together for *National Geographic* to consider," recollects Winter. " . . . We would put together the most killer tray that you could imagine. And the rejection was tough as hell . . . when he got that 'no' again, it was like somebody dying."

Nick had been trying to get his foot in the door at *National Geographic* from the time he was in college. One of his first rejections was particularly stinging: Bob Gilka, the magazine's director of photography at the time, wrote (as Nick recalls it) with a suggestion: "Why don't you choose another profession. Have you thought of being an attorney?" It is a testament to Nick's determination that he continued submitting work each year—he was told more than once, "We don't do adventure photography"—and later had the temerity to show his work to Gilka in person:

> He was intimidating. Plus he left the lights on, and my slides were all shown backward. . . .
> He also talked gruffly on the phone while my images were blazing by. He was a good and loyal
> man who took care of his thirty staff photographers and thirty-plus contract photographers as
> well as his support staff. He just did not believe in photographers as artists. He wanted good,
> solid carpenters. I was an outsider from the dreaded prima-donna group, Magnum, and what
> he definitely did not want were prima donnas.

National Geographic, at the time, was publishing for the most part conventionally documentary images. Nick's sensibility was ever-evolving, intentional, and interpretive, and he was developing an identifiable—although fluid—personal aesthetic. At the same time, as Nick's vision matured, he was moving away from "adventure photography." Even when adventure was part of the story process, it was no longer its raison d'être.

Especially after the conscience-shifting photographic coverage of the Vietnam War, there was in the United States a widespread renewed awareness of the potential agency of visual stories. Nick recalls that in November 1979, U.S. *Geo* published William Strode's photographic exposé on dogfighting in the United States, with text by Benno Kroll.[7]

> Nobody had ever seen anything like that in a magazine. The whole country got offended, but excited. . . . They made new laws in Ohio immediately. That forced *National Geographic* to start changing. . . . All that exotic stuff became less interesting. And the reportage could now be grittier.

With the evolution of *National Geographic*'s editorial approach, no longer did the emphasis seem to be primarily on dazzling exotica; lenses could be turned toward harder-hitting realities.

Rolling Stone was also taking on such stories: in February 1989 the magazine published "The Scorched Earth," Nick's visual essay on the burning of the Amazon rainforests, with text by Anthony DeCurtis.[8] Laurie Kratochvil, *Rolling Stone*'s photo editor at the time, remembers looking at Nick's images and thinking: "Wow, he really sees things differently—he goes beyond the story; he has his own opinion, he supplies a second source of information to the story. His pictures can stand on their own." Mostly, she liked the fact that "Nick surprised me, which is what I want when commissioning."

> I don't want to know what I'm going to get before I see it. I don't want to have a preconceived idea that a photographer simply illustrates. I want the photographer to bring me something new, to excite me. I gave a lot of freedom to photographers to do what they did. . . .

We are witnessing
an environmental
disaster of the first order:
The total destruction
of the planet's life-
sustaining rain forests

THE SCORCHED EARTH

Photographs by Michael Nichols

Rolling Stone, February 23, 1989: "The Scorched Earth"

I also really liked what Nick did with color. He was one of the first people to shoot in color for me and make it interesting. . . . His lighting and the color were odd and mysterious. His pictures have always had a lot of style, and incredible energy: they made me think, drew me in.

"We are witnessing," warns the text that opens "The Scorched Earth," "an environmental disaster of the first order: The total destruction of the planet's life-sustaining rain forests." These alarming words are overlayed on Nick's photograph, full-bleed across two pages, of an apocalyptic, smoky, landscape, with scrounging cows, smoldering fires, hazy light, all emanating through cool bluishness.

It may go without saying that, beginning as early as the 1930s, illustrated magazines featuring substantial photo essays served as vital and powerful media outlets around the world. Among the most visible were the *Berliner Illustrirte Zeitung*, *Life*, *Look*, *Paris Match*, *Picture Post*, *Stern*, *Vu*, and later *Rolling Stone*, *Time*, *Vanity Fair*, and others—as well as a slew of magazines connected to newspapers such as the *Daily Telegraph*, *El Mundo*, *Frankfurter Allgemeine Zeitung*, London's *Sunday Times*, the *New York Times*, and the *Philadelphia Inquirer*. By the mid- to late 1990s, many important editorial showcases for photojournalists were floundering, both as platforms for work and as sources of income. (And in just a few years, the advent of the Internet, digital photography, and the attendant revolution in image dissemination would of course deliver a new and unexpectedly severe blow to the old system.) Many print magazines have folded, and others have undergone myriad redesigns and conceptual changes. Subscription-driven *National Geographic* continues as a home for photoreportage, addressing subjects aligned with the magazine's mutable focus.

In the fall of 1988, Nick set up yet another appointment at *National Geographic*—this time, to show his work from Lechuguilla. He was hoping for an assignment that would allow him to keep photographing in the cave. By this point, Bob Gilka had retired; Nick met with Tom Kennedy, who served as director of photography, and his associate, Kent Kobersteen.

Kobersteen remembers that first meeting:

> I was really impressed with the quality of the photography, but even more . . . by Nick's determination, his intellect, and his desire to go much deeper with his work. . . . I think that's really what separates Nick from 99 percent of the other photographers around. It's aesthetics, certainly, but beyond that it is his willingness to work hard—which doesn't begin to describe it. Nick . . . is willing to work at a level that is as obsessive as a top professional athlete.

At the end of the meeting, they didn't say no. But they didn't say yes, either. Nick waited. And he sent "pleading" letters. And then he waited some more. Months later, in 1989, Nick finally achieved his dream: an assignment from *National Geographic* to return and continue photographing Lechuguilla— which was somewhat surprising, given that *Smithsonian* had published his story on the cave in 1988. But Nick knew, and had convinced Kennedy, Kobersteen, and others at the magazine, that there was a greater and more complex story to be told: "Caves again had opened the door, as they had with *Geo*, and even with Magnum in some ways. And with *National Geographic*, and Tom Kennedy—who had the courage to bring his new, out-of-the-box vision to the magazine, with important groundbreaking assignments—I knew I'd found my new home."

After giving him the assignment, Kobersteen challenged Nick "to make the kind of a picture that says to the viewer: 'I am in this dark place and all I can see is *part* of it'—which is a real photographic challenge." Nick photographed the cave for *National Geographic* in 1990. The opening spread of "Charting the Splendors of Lechuguilla Cave," the March 1991 cover story, with an essay by Tim Cahill, does precisely that.[9] The image is disorienting: like awakening from a vivid dream, and momentarily losing track of what's real, what's illusory. Vertiginous and vast, Lechuguilla dizzies; the caver in the foreground suggests scale but seems almost discarnate, more silhouette than matter. The light source is mystifying. Cahill later told me that the main questions with cave photography are:

> How do you shoot it? Do you shoot it as if there is light coming from one spot, when in fact there isn't? What about shadows? If you're putting your lights behind little pillars and stalagmites and stalactites, which way are the shadows going to fall? And should all the shadows fall the same as if there's natural light, or should the shadows fall against one another? Nick has all this in his head, and when you see his photographs, you can see that he has clearly thought about what light means, where it's coming from, and he seldom tries to emulate natural light—because it *isn't* natural in there.

Cahill portrays the cavescape as a kind of untouched wilderness in his *National Geographic* text. He quotes a National Park Service cave specialist named Ronal Kerbo: "Everywhere Lewis and Clark went, there were people. Exploring Lechuguilla is entirely different. No one's ever been in those virgin passages. It's Neil Armstrong stuff."

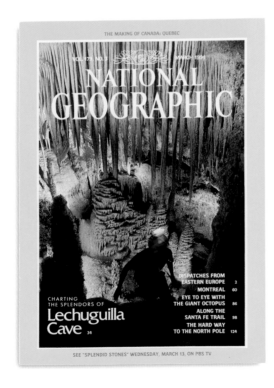

SEE "SPLENDID STONES" WEDNESDAY, MARCH 13, ON PBS TV

Good cavers, like other conservation-minded explorers, are fanatical about leaving no trace. Nick certainly had this in mind as he positioned his battery-charged lights—of all different sizes and levels of output—around the massive space. It was an additional challenge to the already daunting situation. For one thing: "It's total blackness. You can wave your hand back and forth and feel the air moving, but you can't see your hand. I don't even know if anything is *there*." Apart from light from the cavers' headlamps, which gave him clues about where they were, Nick had to rely largely on guesswork, and on small Polaroid test images. With the help of those, "I start making adjustments. I make tons of tiny Polaroids and that's how I begin to see and figure out the image. Each photograph is a major production."

The caving team this time was led by Neeld Messler—the young man Nick had worked with

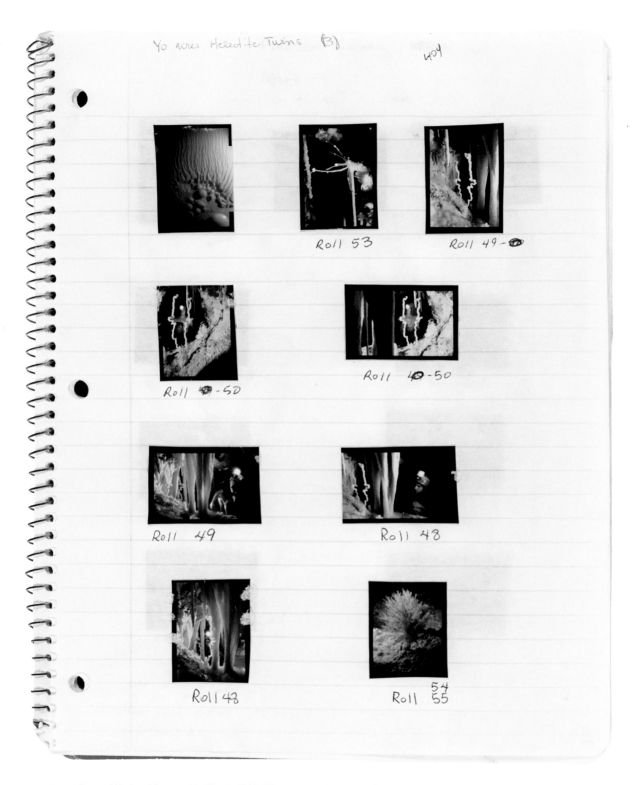

OPPOSITE: Cover of *National Geographic*, March 1991: "Charting the Splendors of Lechuguilla Cave"; ABOVE: Page from Nick's notebook, showing Polaroid test shots of Lechuguilla Cave, Carlsbad Caverns National Park, New Mexico, 1990

ABOVE: Nick and Reba with Ian and his newborn brother, Eli, 1989. Photograph by Paul Fusco/Magnum Photos.
FOLLOWING SPREAD: Temple of Dagon, Lechuguilla Cave, Carlsbad Caverns National Park, 1990

on the *Smithsonian* story. Like everyone on the team, Messler assisted on the photographs, which riveted him—but which, he recalls,

> took hours and hours . . . there were times where everybody on the crew was going crazy, asking: "When are we going to frickin' finish this shot?" Nick would say: "Two more frames, and we've got it." Then, I'm counting—and twenty or more frames later, he's still doing another one. We spent hours dialing in each photograph . . . and during all this, we're trying to minimize damage and impact. We all had to understand the balance between getting the photograph, and protecting the cave.

For the *National Geographic* story, the team worked over a period of months during 1990 in the cave, coming out at the end of each week for a day or two. After journeying deep underground, Nick notes, the outside world feels sensuously transformed: "You've made your way out of the cave, through the protective door the cavers put in, and now there's the ninety-foot entrance pit, and you feel so close—you're thinking, 'I just have to climb that rope'—and the sun is up there. . . . You could begin to smell the ozone or something: the earth smelled different. You know how the earth smells when there's been a lightning strike? It smelled like that." The cavers' sleep cycles became confused: "Because if you wake up at night and open your eyes, nothing happens"—it is utterly dark—"it completely messes you up." Further challenges were posed by the necessities of washing (with baby wipes), excretion (in plastic bags that were retained and hauled out of the cave at the end of the week), and hydration (Nick notes: "You can't possibly carry in enough drinking water for this work"; they ended up drinking from untested underground pools, which he now realizes was foolish). "But I was only thinking of the project. It was *National Geographic*, and it was my big break, and I was incredibly driven. I'm pushing, pushing, pushing."

After completing this first assignment with *National Geographic*, Nick and Reba decided to relocate to the East. Their second son, Eli, had been born in February 1989, and when Nick was not in the field, he wanted to be close to his family—and to the headquarters of *National Geographic* in Washington, DC. They decided on Charlottesville, about two hours' drive from DC: "I knew I couldn't service *Geographic* and the work I wanted to do for them and live in California."

Yes, Nick made the move east in 1990, having had only one assignment from *National Geographic*, and with no immediate guarantee of another. It was an unbridled leap of faith—willful, audaciously confident, even arrogant—that recalls his mother's terse summation of Nick's fantasy life as a child: "Things that he *wanted* to be true, he would imagine to be true." Happily, in this case, they were.

And given his family's financial needs, in 1995 he chose to leave Magnum. The percentage of Nick's income from his photography that was due to the agency was simply more than he could afford.

> I was doing everything I could to change the rules at Magnum to fit my particular situation. I was working all the time and we were living on what I made. Photography was my only source of income, and I had a young family. . . . I loved Magnum, but could not make it work, and I realized that I was trying to shift this cool-ass thing in a way that wasn't necessarily good for anyone else but me, so I left. But Magnum was really important for me. . . . I went from being an adventurer and photographer with nothing to say except something visual, to someone with a conscience, and with something to say.

Nick understood the strength and potential reach of his voice through photography. And now he had the bullhorn of *National Geographic*—one of the few visually driven magazines that could give him the wide-ranging support to photograph in a manner that was consistent with his convictions, over long periods, and to experiment with technology in service of the best possible image. Not to mention the pages—so many pages!—for his photographs.

Now, Nick became more convinced than ever that he really could "make noise for those who cannot make it for themselves."

BRUTAL KINSHIP

Chimpanzee, Monrovia Zoo, Liberia, 1989

Nick found himself at a crossroads.

It was early 1989. He had not yet received his coveted cave assignment from *National Geographic*, but he had plenty of work from other magazines—that wasn't the issue. Rather, the looming question was "Where am I going with my photography?" As an adventure photographer, he had begun to understand his athletic and psychological breaking points. Working in caves and with the mountain gorillas, Nick had considered lighting at its most elemental, and adapted into his methodology and mindset strict ethical imperatives, among them: never influence the situation being documented, and leave no footprint. At the same time, his experience with Magnum had solidified Nick's commitment to narrative, as well as to bearing witness in such a way that his photographs would speak for those who are otherwise unheard.

Moreover, he was about to publish his first book—one that he hoped would "make a difference." In the process of making the images for *Gorilla: Struggle for Survival in the Virungas*, Nick came to appreciate how critical it is that his work be informed by—yet not an illustration of—the relevant science and studies that helped to individuate each animal, each family he was photographing. Relating to his subject more personally could visually translate into the expressive, sometimes disconcerting, sometimes primeval intimacy he so aspires to. His vivid character studies of unique gorillas, their families and groups, combined with George Schaller's richly contextualizing essay, introduced a wide audience to these remarkable apes—their interpersonal dynamics, their sufferings, their daily lives and rituals, and the challenges to their survival.

Now in his late thirties, Nick was either going to devote himself fully to being the "concerned photographer" (a term he uses without irony), first inspired by the mountain gorillas, or risk becoming the caricature "Nick Danger." Whether or not he then fully understood it, he had to determine not only what kind of photographer he was going to be, but what kind of man.

Enter Jane Goodall.

Perhaps the world's most beloved animal-rights activist and scientist, Goodall has devoted more than five decades to researching Tanzania's Gombe chimpanzees; hers is the longest-running study of a large mammal ever conducted. In 1965, with the encouragement of anthropologist and paleontologist Louis Leakey, Goodall and her then-husband, Hugo van Lawick, started the Gombe Stream Research Center. Over the years, Gombe has functioned as a "living laboratory," where ethologists closely observe chimps and their behavior. In 1977 the not-for-profit Jane Goodall Institute (JGI) was founded, with three chief mandates:

> • *Improve global understanding and treatment of great apes through research, public education, and advocacy*

> • *Contribute to the preservation of great apes and their habitats by combining conservation with education and promotion of sustainable livelihoods in local communities*

Jane Goodall and Jou Jou, chimpanzee at Brazzaville Zoo, Republic of Congo, 1990

> • *Create a worldwide network of young people who have learned to care deeply for their human community, for all animals and for the environment, and who will take responsible action to care for them*

Nick had what he describes as a "come to Jesus" moment when Goodall entered his picture both literally and figuratively. The timing was ideal: she had recently had her own "come to Jesus" moment (again, Nick's words) after a November 1986 Chicago Academy of Sciences conference focusing on chimpanzee behavior and conservation issues. Evidence of widespread habitat destruction across Africa, illegal trade in chimpanzees for meat and entertainment, and the proliferation of chimps being used for medical research stunned Goodall. Demoralized by what was revealed, and acknowledging that her long-term study at Gombe could proceed without her constant physical presence (although she would continue to maintain it from afar)—Goodall became convinced that she must dedicate her time to advocating for chimpanzees. She writes that she came out of the conference "an activist, and since then I haven't stayed in the same place for more than three weeks."[1]

Nick notes: "That's when Jane became the Jane we know and love. It was then that it became a fight, *her* fight, and she decided to give her life to conservation, to saving chimps. She had clarified her own mission for herself, and it was well beyond being a primatologist."

The 1989 publication *Understanding Chimpanzees* collects many of the papers presented at the Chicago conference. In Goodall's foreword to the book, she is clear about the problems faced by chimpanzees. She begins by citing the research of primatologist Geza Teleki, who addressed the population status of wild chimpanzees, and the threats to their survival:

> I have lived in Africa for years, but even I am horrified by Geza Teleki's information regarding the situation of chimpanzee populations across the continent. He paints a picture of the future which is dismal, grim, and dark. The habitat of the chimpanzee in its native home is dwindling at a terrifying rate and, as yet, there are very few areas where the chimps are totally protected. . . .
>
> The wild population has been depleted across Africa not only by the destruction of the habitat and the explosive growth of the human population, but also by the demand from zoos, the entertainment industry, and biomedical labs. Even in captivity the possibility of establishing a self-sustaining population is grim. The best breeding mothers are those who were caught as infants in the wild. To capture the baby, hunters shoot the mother. You can imagine the trail of destruction that is left behind: females who died, infants who died in the forest, and infants who died during the transportation, having been wrenched from their mothers' bodies. . . .
>
> Unless something is done about captive breeding, the scientists engaged in medical research, particularly hepatitis and AIDS research, will undoubtedly want to obtain more chimpanzees from their natural habitat. This is going on today, even between countries where it is illegal both to export and import chimps. There are unscrupulous dealers who

OPPOSITE: Jane Goodall with chimpanzees Gremlin and Fifi, Gombe Stream National Park, Tanzania, 1995; ABOVE: Bill Wallauer and Nick, Gombe Stream National Park, 1995. Photograph by Ines Burger

manage, often by means of bribes, to get chimpanzees out, leaving a trail of dead, dying, and wounded individuals behind them.[2]

In 1989 Nick saw a National Geographic Television documentary directed by Wolfgang Bayer about the use of chimpanzees for medical experimentation, especially in the United States. "In terms of DNA," Nick says, "they are so like us—chimps differ from humans by a little over 1 percent." Titled *Brutal Kinship*, the film revealed that "there seemed to be no questioning of the ethics, the limits—no thinking about conservation." Nick immediately recognized an urgent imperative.[3]

Soon after, he met Geza Teleki, who had studied chimps in east Africa with Goodall at her Gombe research site, and who had delivered the paper that so galvanized Goodall in Chicago. Teleki (who died in 2014) had seen Nick's work on gorillas and implored him to help bring attention to the plight of chimpanzees. Nick's images could, he hoped, serve as a persuasive tool in the fight Teleki, Goodall, and other conservationists were waging. He offered to introduce Nick to Goodall.

Nick did not hesitate. After making the photographs for *Gorilla*, he explains, "I wanted to only do projects that mattered, and that could build on themselves—become books, or be in some way expanded. I began my own 'Brutal Kinship.'" German *Geo* agreed immediately to fund and publish the initial article in this long-term project.[4]

ABOVE: Adult female chimpanzee eating the head of a red colobus monkey; OPPOSITE: Chimpanzees hunting cooperatively. Both Tai Forest, Ivory Coast, 1991

Nick started out by following Goodall as she toured and advocated for the protection of chimps. In May and June of 1989, he traveled through west Africa, and in August he traveled to Tanzania to photograph at the Gombe Stream Research Center. There he encountered chimps, habituated to human presence, roaming free. He recalls:

> The chimps were so quick, I couldn't keep up with them! Chimpanzees take you from here to there, and then say: "Where ya been? It took us five minutes to get here—it took you three hours!" And there is nothing more demanding than Gombe Stream. You're racing through insane thickets with briars and steep slopes, running after somebody who is three feet tall, when you're six feet tall. Talk about chasing a photograph! What happens when he gets to a small tunnel? He keeps going, and you get hammered.

On subsequent trips, he had an affable and intelligent guide in Bill Wallauer, who has worked in Tanzania since the late 1980s, and at Gombe since 1992. Agile and built (as Nick points out) like a rugby player, Wallauer "was a family member—he could run with and become a chimpanzee. . . . He was also helpful identifying everyone, and predicting behavior—he has made the most real, the most intimate videos of the chimpanzees ever done anywhere."

At Gombe, each group of chimpanzees is designated by its own letter, so the G family includes Gremlin and Goblin; in the F family there is Flo, the mother of Fifi, and Fifi's sons Freud and Frodo, and so on. Nick quickly became familiar with the individual personalities of the chimps—some were docile and easygoing, while others were more taxing: Freud, he suggests, was "a nice guy, who would come sleep next to me," while "Frodo was kind of a psychopath."

When I spoke with Wallauer, he gamely defended Frodo:

> If Frodo's a bit of a thug, it's just his personality running into the fact that he was probably a little bit over-habituated in the early days, and so has no fear of humans. He's not a psychopath in my mind. I know his other personalities. It's true . . . Jane's been hit by him several times, and I've been thumped a lot by Frodo. But Frodo just uses his resources to show his might and power, and if someone happens to be standing in the way, you're going to get knocked down. Obviously if he wants to hurt us, we're gone. He's five times, six times my strength. He probably also earned some respect and clout by being brave enough to knock over these people who tower over him.

> Chimps are all bravado: they can be real prima donnas. They're the ultimate soccer players. . . . You know the soccer player that barely gets touched and then falls on the ground, writhing in agony? All you have to do if you're a big alpha male is just go by another chimp and whack him on the shoulder. Apoplexy! They just go nuts! They're really funny that

way. It doesn't take much for a high-ranking male to send everybody screaming. But they rarely hurt members of their own communities.

Nick would photograph chimpanzees periodically for the next six years, learning about and then documenting their individual natures and social habits, their family dynamics and modes of communication. He remained fixed on Goodall as well, who helped to guide his documentation of the seemingly limitless abuses chimpanzees have been forced to endure. He investigated the often horrific treatment of the animals in laboratories, in entertainment, and as house pets. The project was intense, at times crushing for him. In 1999 Aperture published *Brutal Kinship*, with photographs by Nick and a moving essay by Goodall, in which she poses the question:

> How should we relate to beings who look into the mirrors and see themselves as individuals, who mourn companions and may die of grief, who have a consciousness of "self"? Don't they deserve to be treated with the same sort of consideration we accord to other highly sensitive, conscious beings—ourselves?[5]

In *Brutal Kinship*, Nick applies an effective conceptual strategy that he seems to have understood from the beginning. He first shows viewers the most pristine and Edenic conditions, and then delivers a distressing and profound jolt with images of humans' assaults on the balanced systems of nature. It is a tactic: start with seduction to set off the impact of what follows. But there is nothing simple about the images or the message. Consider, for example, the scientists experimenting on chimpanzees with a view to finding cures for AIDS. Even people who deplore the slaughter of animals for bushmeat, cosmetics, or trophies, or their use as performers, pets, or props, will accept chimpanzees being offered up to biomedical research when it comes to life-threatening diseases, all the while insisting that these chimps have rights to some quality of life—when they are not being probed, stuck, or sliced open—beyond steel-barred solitary incarceration. There is no easy answer here.

Goodall considers each creature in her purview as an individual. She has also always perceived the advantage of photographs in reaching people. "How do we open blinded eyes, bring feeling to frozen hearts?" she asks in *Brutal Kinship*. "Perhaps with stories; stories about the chimpanzees in the wild, the fascination of their lives in the forest."[6] And Nick is a consummate visual storyteller.

I had the opportunity to speak with Goodall in 2012 (on April 22: Earth Day, as it happened). She was in New York to help to publicize Disney's just-released nature-documentary *Chimpanzee*. Of her collaborations with Nick, Goodall told me:

> I think Nick and I have the same mission, basically. We're both doing it because we want to help the subjects. Maybe overlaid on top of that, for me, is the science bit of it; for him, making great photographs.

> Nick is very calm to be around, compared with a lot of photographers who get all jumpy. . . . This is nice, especially with animals. And he's very intuitive . . . you either have that relationship with animals or you don't. Nick doesn't crowd the animals. He doesn't get

The chimpanzee Whiskey, chained in a garage, Bujumbura, Burundi, 1989

upset if they don't quite do what he hoped they would do. Patience is so important, and he is patient.

Right from the beginning of our work together, Nick has been very involved not only with conservation, but also with the use of chimps in labs, as am I. It's a double connection, really.

Goodall notes that the conditions in laboratories have improved greatly since she and Geza Teleki first got involved.

The biggest issue facing chimps now is the fact that they're vanishing in the wild. It's huge. Chimp numbers have dropped since 1960, when I began, from way over a million to fewer than three hundred thousand, in twenty-one countries.

The wild chimpanzee population is dropping, says Goodall, primarily because of "the bushmeat, trade, the commercial hunting of wild animals for food, and the loss of habitat." To give an idea of how dire the situation is for apes in general, and chimps in particular: in 2013, a report titled *Stolen Apes* was issued by the Great Apes Survival Partnership (GRASP), a United Nations initiative and alliance of governments, conservation organizations, research institutions, and private companies committed to ensuring the survival of great apes in Africa and Asia. Coauthored by GRASP's Nairobi-based program coordinator, Douglas Cress, *Stolen Apes* lists 643 documented cases of illegal smuggling of great apes out of Africa between 2005 and 2011—a figure that Cress characterizes as "the most conservative estimate."

GRASP's database tracks law enforcement's seizures and confiscations of apes that have been taken in Africa and Asia. Cress notes: "The fact that the trade is out there and heavy is beyond dispute."

"The primary destinations for illegally traded great apes are the Middle East and Asia," Cress says. "In the Middle East, most disappear into private menageries of the wealthy elite, and it is extremely difficult to track them from that point forward. The Middle East is also a transit point for . . . trade to Asia, primarily China, followed by Thailand." In Asia, a new middle-class population has prompted the creation of hundreds of new zoos, where many apes end up, often compelled to perform antics for the public.

Chimpanzees are among the most vulnerable, as Cress explains. Bonobos are rare—and so are less frequently captured, while gorillas are "notoriously fragile and die of the stress of capture, trade, and confiscation very easily."

Cress and I corresponded from fall 2015 into spring 2016. He told me that since the publication of *Stolen Apes*, forty more chimpanzees and seven gorillas had been seized while traffickers were attempting to smuggle them out of Africa. Cress provided what he termed an "equation of loss":

> Since apes are primarily trafficked live, and it's impossible to take a baby chimpanzee or gorilla from its family without killing the family, there is a standard "equation of loss" for every

OPPOSITE: Chimpanzee used for HIV study, LEMSIP Research Facility, New York, 1989; ABOVE: LEMSIP Research Facility, New York, 1989

seized ape: one live chimpanzee represents ten dead chimpanzees; one live gorilla represents four dead gorillas, and so on.

In addition, 132 gorilla and chimpanzee skulls were seized in Africa between May 2014 and autumn 2015. Cress said:

> The trophy market for dead ape parts is a largely new—and entirely illegal—phenomenon, and we're still trying to understand it. Nigeria is the destination for most skulls, although markets in Europe and the United States (primarily Texas) are big buyers.

Nick is infuriated by what he refers to as "the endangered-species loophole," which he explains thus:

> Wild caught or captive animals cannot legally leave Africa because they are endangered, yet anything can happen to them *within* certain African countries, as the rules are few and oversight is minimal. In many countries, there is desperate poverty and overwhelming corruption. Bribing happens regularly.

When Nick first met Goodall, in early 1989, she encouraged him to go to some of the most volatile areas of west Africa to address this and other horrors—especially as they pertained to chimpanzees.

She suggested that Nick travel with her son, Hugo Eric Louis van Lawick, better known as "Grub." Then in his early twenties, Grub was familiar with the field:

> I first met Nick just after I had dropped out of college, when I was about twenty-two. I had been investigating photographers working in Spain and the Canary Islands who made money from tourists by offering them the chance to get their pictures taken with chimpanzees—for a fee. My mum thought it would be a great idea for me to join up with Nick on his trip to west Africa. She told me I'd easily recognize him, as he had longish black hair, wore a headband, and looked like Rambo!

Nick had read about Grub from studying the work of his parents, Goodall and Hugo van Lawick.

> All I knew was that this was the famous "Grub the Bush Baby," and that he spoke great Swahili. Well, there is no Swahili spoken anywhere *near* west Africa. So we've taken a white African out of Tanzania, and put him with Alabama me in Liberia and Sierra Leone . . . where it's crazy and dangerous, there are no rules, no codes. But both of these countries had wild chimpanzees, as did the Tai Forest in Côte d'Ivoire—which had a special culture of chimps that Christophe Boesch had discovered—and Guinea. The chimps in these countries were being murdered summarily for food, or captured for the pet trade or to populate laboratories for biomedical research, and for the space program. . . .

OPPOSITE: Health-worker Jenneh Briggs with chimpanzees used for hepatitis B vaccine research, VILAB II, Liberia, 1989;
ABOVE: Caretaker Ludovic Rabasa with orphans, Tchimpounga Chimpanzee Rehabilitation Center, Pointe Noire, Republic of Congo, 1995

> Grub and I made a trip (there is strength in numbers), and we . . . basically stayed ahead of people who might kill us. . . . I would find out about someone smuggling and selling the chimps, make a picture as well as I could, and then we'd get out of there as fast as we could. All this trade we were witnessing was illegal, and people did *not* want me photographing.

Nick and Grub traveled to southeastern Guinea to see the Bossou group of wild chimpanzees who were being studied for their use of "metatools"—that is, they use one tool to improve upon another: say, cracking a hard nut by placing it on one rock and hitting it with another rock. Researcher Tetsuro Matsuzawa had used the natural isolation of the Bossou chimps—Nick describes the habitat as a "forest island" comprising two hills, and surrounded by deforested and cultivated land—to conduct a multiyear investigation that centered on tool use. And here, the villagers coexisted with the approximately nineteen chimps, and even tolerated their crop-raiding. However, as Nick recalls,

> when Grub and I got to Bossou, Matsuzawa was not there. Like many researchers, Matsuzawa only came for a few months each year—if at all. When we arrived, he had not been there doing his work for maybe even several years, and the chimps were no longer habituated. I could hear them, but never saw them, so no way could I make images. I tried with a tracker guide, but the chimps remained invisible.

It was also in the village of Bossou that Nick and Grub ran out of food. They had been buying their food as they went along, and by the time they reached Bossou, they had no more provisions. They asked if they might pay to have meals prepared for them in the village each night—although Nick was concerned about where exactly the food was coming from, and also about the quality of the water:

> We thought the safest thing to do was to buy a chicken every morning. We could *see* it being killed and cooked, and then we could eat it all through the day along with rice, and we could also eat bananas. It was for just three or four days. On the last day, though, the villagers said they had no more chicken . . . but they had something else they could feed us. Grub and I both tasted the soup, and then he pulled out bat wings . . . and neither of us ate anymore.

Three days later, Nick and Grub were in war-ravaged Liberia, at the VILAB II facility of the New York Blood Center, and Nick was photographing experiments being done on very young chimps—an American veterinarian was performing liver biopsies for hepatitis research. Nick then visited the so-called "Monkey Island"—actually a group of mangrove islets on Liberia's Little Bassa and Farmington Rivers—where retired chimps were relocated by VILAB after years of invasive, painful, and unrelenting experimentation. To his horror, he discovered "monster chimps. They're gigantic, they are understandably a bit crazy. And they're really scary."

At this point, Nick had not been feeling well for several days. Upon returning to his hotel at the Firestone Tire and Rubber Company's Liberian rubber plantation—he collapsed. Grub found him curled up on the floor of his room. He called the vet, and Nick was immediately taken to the Firestone Plantation Hospital, where an African doctor cared for him with the help of the veterinarian. But he got progressively worse. His fever spiked to 105 degrees, and he was going in and out of a comatose state. Tests indicated that he again had blackwater fever, also known as falciparum malaria—one of the deadliest malarias—in combination with typhoid fever. The typhoid had most likely come from something he ate or drank in Bossou (the bat soup is Nick's guess), while the malaria would have come from a mosquito bite sometime during the journey. He later learned that he also had hepatitis B, likely contracted from the needles in the hospital where he was being treated. Once contracted, hepatitis B remains in the body for life, dormant until triggered.

"So I'm dying," declares Nick.

> I remember I was trying to read *Bonfire of the Vanities*, going in and out of this coma. And it's so surreal. Grub is sitting and holding my hand by the bed. . . . And I remember the vet and the doctor arguing about giving me a drug called chloramphenicol, which is a super antibiotic—kills everything—but causes high instances of leukemia, so it's not used because of this wicked side-effect. The veterinarian was saying: "Give him the drug—if you don't, he's going to die anyway!" But the doctor was rightfully worried about my getting leukemia.

Nick has a hazy memory of hearing additional bits of this debate while drifting in and out of consciousness. Ultimately, the veterinarian convinced the doctor to administer the chloramphenicol, assuring her that Nick would die without it. "As soon as they stuck me with it, I was being cured. I knew it." In fact, the swiftness of his recovery was remarkable; in just a matter of days, he was working again.

Goodall first saw the chimpanzee who came to be known as Gregoire in 1990. He was starving and alone, confined to a bare cage at the Brazzaville Zoo, in the Republic of Congo. He had been there, imprisoned in these abusive conditions, since 1944. That encounter and subsequent caretaking of Gregoire were pivotal for Goodall, igniting her far-reaching desire to create rehabilitation sanctuaries for mistreated, displaced, and/or orphaned chimpanzees—victims of the bushmeat, pet, and entertainment trades, and of habitat destruction caused by logging and prospecting for oil and other natural resources. In 1992 Goodall convinced the Conoco oil company to build the Tchimpounga Chimpanzee Rehabilitation Center, established with the collaboration of the Congolese government, as a safe haven in Pointe Noire, Republic of Congo. Looking after chimpanzee victims has been at the heart of the Jane Goodall Institute, along with research, and insisting on better lives for chimps held captive in labs.

In the early 1990s, and again in 1995, Nick joined Goodall in Kinshasha (in the Democratic Republic of Congo, or DRC) and in Brazzaville.

The interaction between Goodall and Gregoire yielded two classic photographs, one of which eventually became Nick's cover image for the December 1995 issue of *National Geographic*, accompanying "Jane Goodall: Crusading for Chimps and Humans," a biographical story written by Peter Miller with photographs by Nick.[7] In this image, we find a standing Gregoire, intensely focused on grooming Goodall's hair, as she sits cross-legged in front of him. The mutual etiquette, trust, and affection are stirring. Nick notes that when photographing her, "never did Jane Goodall *make* a picture for me. She does what she does. It's best just to watch her."

The issues to which Goodall has committed her life—including the rescue and care of orphan animals—permeate Nick's own life's work. This, as well as efforts to reintroduce them into their natural habitats—to "rewild" them—are continuously examined in Nick's stories, whether about chimpanzees, elephants, gorillas, or other species. Again, the notion and definition of *wild* are called into question. Can an animal born in captivity and raised by humans ever be truly wild? Is it safe— both for the animal and for humans close to it—to release into the wild an animal that has been raised by humans and therefore has no fear of them? And can an animal reintroduced to the wild be accepted into a wild population of its species?

For some conservationists, the focus on orphans and sanctuaries is regarded as a misplacement of priorities, when funds are desperately needed, for example, for the preservation of habitat. Others have never perceived the two goals as mutually exclusive.

Bill Wallauer of the Gombe Stream Research Center explains that the reintroduction of chimpanzees is rarely successful, for a number of reasons:

> First, if they're reintroduced anywhere they might see humans—they're accustomed to humans . . . they don't fear them. So there's a danger to the humans. And there's a danger to

the chimps, because of possible disease transfer to them from humans.

The biggest reason, however, is that chimps are incredibly territorial and *any* new chimp from the outside is a bitter enemy, a deadly enemy. They patrol their ranges to keep outsiders away. So if you try to introduce a male chimp into another community, he will almost certainly be killed. And that's the way most mammals patrol their territories. They have to keep their resources safe. That's their food safety, that's their community safety. . . .

Equally, there is much we don't understand about the subtle behaviors and vocalizations of chimpanzees. Will a chimp from one community necessarily assimilate well into another? We may be inadvertently condemning a chimp to a life of being an outsider, so all alone, or possibly being attacked.

Wallauer notes also that relocating chimps to presumably viable, unpopulated habitat is deceptively complex. A habitat may seem very suitable, but if there are no chimps already there, there may well be a reason for it. "It is likely," he says, "that newly introduced chimps may meet the same fate of the chimps who once lived there. . . . It is an incredibly difficult and complicated process."

On the other hand, orphan gorilla introduction—while still fraught—has met with more success, and Nick would later photograph this process (published as the February 2000 cover story of *National Geographic*, "Orphan Gorillas: Fighting to Survive in the Wild," with text by Michael McRae).[8] Nick photographed eleven baby western lowland gorillas whose mothers had been killed for bushmeat. The young gorillas were first held captive and would have been illegally sold had they not been rescued by Projet Protection des Gorilles, a sanctuary program based in the Republic of Congo and Gabon, funded by the Aspinall Foundation. (The late John Aspinall was a zealous advocate for animals—a zoo owner who famously made his money as a gambler.) When war broke out in the Congo in 1997, a French aircraft was dispatched to evacuate both the expatriates and the orphaned gorillas, as well as Gregoire and other chimpanzees in the Brazzaville Zoo, moving them to Goodall's Tchimpounga sanctuary.

OPPOSITE: Jane Goodall and the chimpanzee Gregoire, Brazzaville Zoo, 1995; ABOVE: Monrovia Zoo, Liberia, 1989

Gregoire died at age sixty-six, in 2008; he had been Africa's oldest known living chimpanzee. After almost fifty torturous years, terrified in solitary confinement, he experienced restorative freedom and companionship in the sanctuary during the last ten-plus years of his life. For years, Gregoire and a female chimpanzee named Clara had apparently been inseparable. He was with her when he died.

Looking through stacks of Nick's photographs of the mountain gorillas in the wild, of the orphaned baby gorillas and their caretakers, of Gregoire's interactions with Goodall, of Frodo, Gremlin, and other wild chimpanzees, I begin to see in Nick's work a narrative of the rhythms of their lives, contextualized by an ever-shifting set of particulars. At the same time, he intently focuses on specific characters, and always there's a sense of parity with himself.

To achieve this level of intimacy, Nick insinuates himself, as discreetly as possible. Trusting instinct, he observes the complex weave of events, day after day and night after night, as they naturally occur. The habitats provide necessary context, and he begins to understand what behaviors are repeated, what interactions are regular, the causes of certain gestures, the times of day when they happen, and the nature of the light at those times. Watching the individual and group dynamics, Nick is able to suggest visually a sense of what might be driving the action he is witnessing. The way we might define these drives in human terms, of course, may not match

OPPOSITE: Caretaker Liz Pearson with orphan gorilla, Mpassa Reserve, Gabon, 1999; ABOVE: Orphan gorilla Bangha, Tchimpounga Chimpanzee Rehabilitation Center, Pointe Noire, Republic of Congo, 1999

what is going on in the animal's mind—there is no way for us to know. But there are recurring gesticulations, reactions, and responses that we might describe as indications of stress, alertness, territoriality, or protectiveness, for example. However, this is about characterizing behavior, as opposed to presuming knowledge of feelings or moods (if they translate into chimpanzee) such as love, happiness, or hate. While his evidence may be "anecdotal"—that is, based on observation but unquantifiable—Nick's close attention has revealed repeated and meaningful behaviors, many of which were previously unaccounted for, or were seen as one-offs. While one cannot make inferences about a species as a whole based on a single action, witnessing the repetition of behavior allows the observer—the scientist, photographer, writer—to suggest causalities.

An image is always subject to the viewer's preconceptions, prejudices, and state of mind. With animals, anthropomorphizing is probably a given—including about their emotional lives. If two chimps are seen together all the time, the presumption may be that they are friends. Ultimately, though, a photographic essay must also be the interpretation of a subject by a singular, engaging, and convincing vision. It must be charged with primal candor. There can be no doubt. There can be no comfort. It must transgress the bounds of intellect and compel the viewer to feel something—a communion of sorts. It is perhaps old fashioned, this desire to be moved, even shaken by art; it demands an audacious honesty on the part of the artist. This is about an image's power to depict

ABOVE: Nick with orphan gorilla, Gabon, 1999. Photograph by Steve Gullick. OPPOSITE: *National Geographic* covers, clockwise from top left: December 1995: "Jane Goodall"; March 1992: "A Curious Kinship: Apes and Humans"; February 2000: "Orphan Gorillas: Fighting to Survive in the Wild"; October 1995: "Mountain Gorillas of Africa: Threatened by War"

essential truths, and the viewer's capacity and willingness to experience them, to "go there." Before Nick, with very few exceptions, the wild was not evoked with such relentless, unblinking authenticity.

Nick's greatest lesson from Goodall is also what vitalizes his work—everything begins with and resonates from the individual: Gregoire, Frodo, and Gremlin. He knows the families of elephants in Kenya's Samburu: the matriarchs, the calves, the lone bulls. He knows the tigers Sita and Charger, the lionesses and cubs and males of the Vumbi and Barafu prides. He knows specific redwoods and sequoias. In all cases, the subject's distinctiveness is manifest in his images.

With such attention to differentiating detail, Nick works as a portraitist as well as a storyteller. His strongest projects have at least one protagonist. The storyline follows, radiating out to the family of animals, or interactions among animals (which may include humans) or their environments like concentric circles. This expansiveness takes into account the ravages of human famine, poverty, greed, conflict, and territorial clashes on these already fragile dynamics and ecosystems; it also provokes questions about humans, nature, and the nature of humans. All this distinguishes a Nick Nichols.

After Nick's chimpanzees story was published by German *Geo* in July 1991,[9] *National Geographic* assigned him "A Curious Kinship: Apes and Humans."[10] Along with new photographs, this project

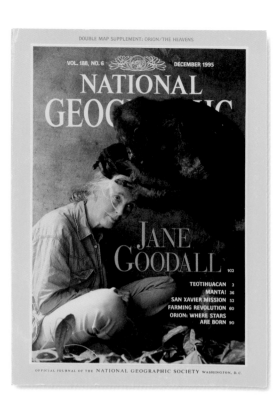

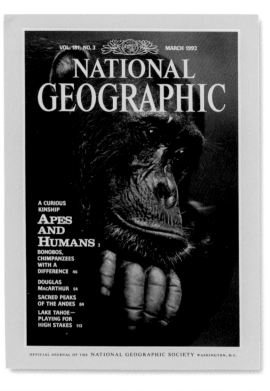

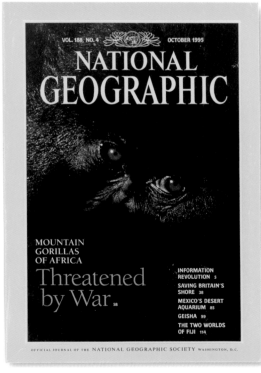

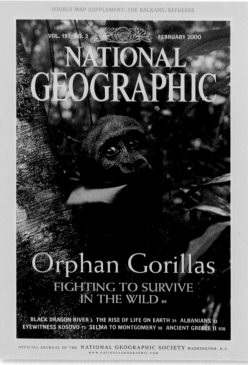

would comprise the best of his work on apes to date, including images previously published in *Geo*, and those that had never been published, such as pictures of orphan orangutans—part of Biruté Galdikas's study—that Nick had made near Jakarta. Other images of orangutans in Sumatra were also included. Like Goodall's and Fossey's work, Galdikas's research was originally facilitated by Louis Leakey. She was one of the first to attempt the rehabilitation and reintroduction of an ape back into the wild, and witnessing this helped Nick enormously, when he first photographed her study for *Life* magazine in 1984: he had access to the animals as well as opportunities for some extraordinary images of humans carrying habituated orangutans around and bottle-feeding them as part of the caretaking process.

Eugene Linden, who wrote the text for "A Curious Kinship," traveled with Nick in the Republic of Congo, the DRC, the Central African Republic (CAR), and elsewhere. He describes the process of working with Nick:

> He's hardcore, and knows what he wants to get. He wanted to photograph the bushmeat trade, so he wanted to go into a market. Africans were often either nervous or really angry when Westerners . . . pulled out cameras and started shooting. . . . Those in the bushmeat trade would not want their photographs taken. It was very nasty. You're in a market, and it's very close quarters, and you look for where you're going to go if things turn ugly—it could get really combustible. But Nick was quite used to that, and he has a good eye and ear for taking the temperature for where he can go, what he can do.

"A Curious Kinship" came out in March 1992, featuring Nick's photograph of Frodo on the cover.[11] With his second *National Geographic* cover story, Nick was now convinced of his future with the magazine. Mary Smith was assigned as his editor, because of her expertise with the subject matter. "She was Leakey's editor," Nick recalls, "and the editor for all of the great ape ladies—Dian, Biruté, and Jane."

Nick was thrilled that *National Geographic* published so much of his earlier work with Goodall, and gave him the opportunity to continue photographing her and the creatures and issues she holds dear. The ultimate manifestation of their collaboration would be the book *Brutal Kinship*.

And it was with that book that I first met Nick. Aperture had published *Gorilla: Struggle for Survival in the Virungas* in 1989, and I remember asking Aperture's executive director and publisher, Michael Hoffman, why we had not done anything with Nick since. Hoffman suggested I go to Charlottesville and meet him: "You'll enjoy it. And I'm sure there's a project." So sometime in around 1997, I paid Nick and Reba a visit. Nick and I spent a day going through photographs at his studio—of chimps in the wild in the Tai Forest of the Ivory Coast (part of Christophe Boesch's study), in Tanzania's Mahale Mountains (part of Toshisada Nishida's study), and of course in Gombe.

Sometime during that first afternoon, Nick more or less narrated what would later become the book iteration of *Brutal Kinship*, alternating between humor and sadness, anecdotes and advocacy.

Freedom and wildness were juxtaposed with captivity and all that implies. Sanctuaries seemingly offered some respite from abuse and danger.

The experience of looking at the images, and later sequencing them for the book, was gut wrenching. In my time as an editor, I had worked on many projects that evinced the endless capacity of humans to behave cruelly and manipulatively toward other humans—and I wasn't inured to the effects of such images. My faith in the inherent empathy and goodness of human nature was already shaky. Nick's images revealed humans' egocentric, savage, and mercenary inclinations and actions toward animals, toward nature.

The images representing experimentation and the exploitation of these animals for entertainment and as pets are often claustrophobic and always upsetting. Chimps peer out from behind bars, or through the tiniest opening in a cage. There are stone-faced hunters and chimp traders, and pet chimpanzees kept in chains (baby chimps get bigger, and difficult to control). There are photographs of Southwest Institute technicians in San Antonio, Texas, removing chimps from the bleakest imprisonment in order to be experimented on for hepatitis B studies, and of breeding compounds for biomedical research with all the warmth of correctional facilities.

The pathos Nick achieves in *Brutal Kinship* is deep and complex; the sense of violation is overwhelming. We see chimps forced to behave in ways that are profoundly degrading: animals are dressed in tutus; "Mr. Jiggs" is made to wear a black tie and suspenders, and to kiss the hand of a diner at the New Jersey Fireman's Ball. Mr. Jiggs was actually a female chimpanzee; she was caught in the African wild, and her mother was killed during her capture (this is almost always the case with young chimps). Her trainer invented a remote-control electric-shock device to control her behavior. There is Christopher, a baby chimp performing with an elephant in some Florida roadside attraction. He is regularly disciplined by harsh commands and beatings when he does not obey. Christopher, had he been left in the wild, would still have been nursing.

In *Brutal Kinship*, Nick shows us performances and backstage moments, focusing on movement, expression, and context—we learn the backstories through extended captions. The impact is devastating. The book also includes

Chimpanzee Susie and trainer Dan Westfall,
Palm Springs, California, 1991

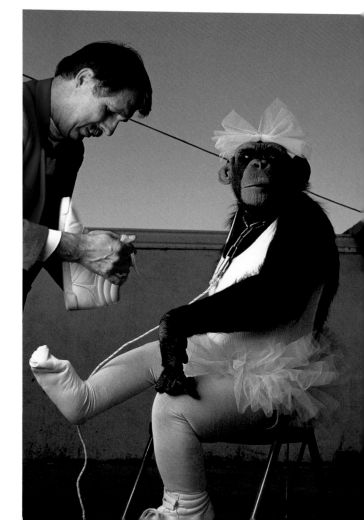

1960s images from NASA and the U.S. Air Force that were found at a museum devoted to aeronautical medicine at the Brooks Air Force Base in San Antonio. Fortuitously, Nick had "rescued" these images when they were about to be trashed. The photographs—many of which bring to mind the laboratories of H. G. Wells's evil Doctor Moreau—depict how chimps were conscripted as surrogates in the development of the space program, and the horrors they endured as various invasive procedures were repeatedly performed on them.

A number of the chimps Nick photographed in 1989 at VILAB II, the Liberian facility operated by the New York Blood Center (NYBC), were killed during the second wave of a civil war that began in 1992. Some were shot; others died of starvation or dehydration when it was impossible to reach them because of ongoing fighting and occupation. Eventually, when the violence began to subside, emergency care had to be administered to save those chimpanzees who were still alive.

Around the same time that the VILAB II research program started up, an important new policy began to gain traction: the 1973 treaty of the Convention on International Trade in Endangered Species of Wild Fauna and Flora—better known as CITES. An international agreement that countries enter into voluntarily, CITES grew out of a 1963 resolution adopted during a meeting of the World Conservation Union. Representatives from eighty countries agreed on the final treaty. The aim of CITES is to ensure that international trade in wild animals and plants does not threaten the survival of the species in the wild. It accords varying degrees of protection to more than thirty-five thousand species, based on their endangered status. *All* great apes are included on its "most endangered" list. CITES specifies that it is illegal (with extremely rare exceptions) to hunt, kill, eat, own, sell, trade, or traffic in chimpanzees, gorillas, bonobos, or orangutans. The only way to transport apes legally across national borders is with import and export permits issued by CITES. If an ape is moved without proper permits, it is to be seized by the country of import, and reported through the CITES annual seizure databases. (In the United States, the legislation that enables the provisions set up by CITES to be enforced is the Endangered Species Act signed into law by President Richard Nixon in 1973.) Nevertheless, such an agreement does not ensure their humane treatment.

Between 2005 and 2015, the NYBC chimpanzees were reportedly receiving substandard care and insufficient quantities of food. In March 2015, after the NYBC abandoned their approximately sixty-five surviving charges in Liberia by withdrawing all funding, the Liberian Institute took responsibility for these chimpanzees—the chimps Nick had encountered on "Monkey Island." The food supply slowly diminished, and the water systems broke down (there is no freshwater on the islands). The Liberian government did not have the ongoing resources to cover the chimps' care, so the Humane Society of the United States (HSUS), along with like-minded organizations and individuals worldwide, together raised almost $300,000 that went toward food, necessary emergency care, and alleviation of the more dire conditions left by the NYBC when it renounced its responsibilities. According to journalist James Gorman of the *New York Times*, the people hired to care for the chimpanzees had been doing so for more than three months without remuneration. In his May 28, 2015, article on this situation, Gorman quotes Victoria O'Neill, a spokeswoman for the NYBC, claiming that the center "never had any obligation for care for the chimps, contractual or otherwise."[12]

We are brought back to humans' ethical responsibilities and the rights, if any, of animals—in this case, animals who were torn from the wild, from their families, and have sacrificed their lives for our benefit.

HSUS and its partners subsequently helped to establish Liberia Chimpanzee Rescue (LCR), both to permanently care for the chimpanzees left by NYBC to die, and to develop a chimpanzee sanctuary in Liberia. LCR will also support law enforcement, confronting all the egregious activities discussed in *Brutal Kinship*. LCR's consulting director is Jenny A. Z. Desmond, whose husband, Dr. Jim S. Desmond, is the organization's veterinary and technical advisor—both are conservationists. When Jenny and I were put in touch, thanks to the Jane Goodall Institute, she sent me a photograph of one of the Liberian chimpanzee caregivers featured in *Brutal Kinship*, Jenneh Briggs. Briggs, who has been working with chimpanzees for twenty years, is one of the caregivers the Desmonds immediately hired back when they started receiving confiscated orphans in November 2015. The chimps' ages range from six months to over four years, and, according to Jenny Desmond, they require round-the-clock care: "This means that the infants are physically sleeping with us overnight as they would have with their natural mothers in the wild. There are many, many others needing rescue right now."

Other situations have evolved for the better since Nick's and Goodall's *Brutal Kinship* project. In June 2013 the U.S. National Institutes of Health announced that it was significantly reducing the use of chimpanzees in agency-supported biomedical research, and on June 16, 2015, the U.S. Fish and Wildlife Service officially designated captive chimpanzees as endangered. Five months later, in November 2015, Francis S. Collins, director of the NIH, announced a revision in the Institutes' policy regarding chimps and medical research.

> I have reassessed the need to maintain chimpanzees for biomedical research and decided that effective immediately, NIH will no longer maintain a colony of 50 chimpanzees for future research. All NIH-owned chimpanzees that reside outside of the Federal Sanctuary System . . . are now eligible for retirement. Relocation of the chimpanzees to the Federal Sanctuary System will be conducted as space is available and on a timescale that will allow for optimal transition of each individual chimpanzee with careful consideration of their welfare, including their health and social grouping.[13]

That captive chimpanzees may no longer be used in biomedical research in the United States (one of the last "first world" countries to permit it) is on the one hand a victory for many advocates of the great apes—but for others, it has created a potentially insurmountable problem. For example, a current threat to the wild ape population is disease. Peter Walsh lectures at Cambridge University on primate ecology; for many years, Dr. Walsh has been attempting to address the spread of Ebola in Africa's great ape population. As he observed in the *New York Times* (September 27, 2015): "The Ebola virus has in recent decades killed perhaps one-third of the world's gorilla population and an untold number of chimpanzees."[14]

Walsh is working to develop an oral vaccine to save the wild apes in Africa from further devastation by Ebola. One of his many challenges is the recent change in the captive animals' status on the Endangered Species Act listing. Walsh needs to test his vaccine on captive apes—it must first be proven safe and effective in a captive population—in order for him to be allowed to deploy it in a wild population of endangered gorillas and chimpanzees. One solution, he proposes, is to test the vaccine on chimpanzees that were once in laboratories, and are now in sanctuaries in the United States. As he has said: "Chimps can live fifty years or more so this would provide a study population for literally decades." But many facilities capable of overseeing this testing in the United States are loath to do so—even if sanctioned by the U.S. Department of Fish and Wildlife. Another option is to do the testing in Africa, where the U.S. Endangered Species Act does not apply—but the sanctuaries there are not yet capable of this kind of biomedical research.

Ironically, if this testing does *not* happen, the consequences for wild great apes may be dire. As Nick observes: "Testing was completely allowed when needed to fight diseases harmful to *us*, but not allowed now, when the apes could be used to fight disease harmful to *them*."

Is it ethical to force chimpanzees in captivity to undergo testing to help their relatives in the wild? Is a healthy wild population worth their suffering? Nick tells me that he has asked himself: "Is an ape that does not know the wild really an ape?" Ultimately, he feels certain that scientists could "utilize chimpanzees in sanctuaries to test Walsh's oral vaccine, and if they are rewarded, and honored, and treated well, they will be just fine. This life of being experimented on is all they know. And saving the wild ape population is critical."

Today, more than twenty-five years after Nick began the *Brutal Kinship* project, the ethical considerations of testing and conservation have clearly not become any easier. Has the world changed in such a way—given habitat destruction, climate change, and subsequent species migrations, and greater human population density—that each circumstance has to be considered on a case-by-case basis? Many conservationists believe that the Endangered Species Act is the most important official mandate protecting the wild ever enacted. Yet they fear it lacks an "ecological pragmatism," and that it does not take into account the entire ecosystem, which must include humans and our assaults on the natural world. Others see this inclusion as a kind of acquiescence, and believe that considering the human-altered landscape as a factor of nature undermines the very concept of nature and ultimately of conservation.

Nick has grown to understand that, because humans often resent what they perceive as a heavy governmental hand, the inclusion of a species on the endangered list does not always serve the animals it seeks to protect. At the same time, he recognizes that such protection has saved many species from extinction. For conservationists, the act of balancing the interests of government, local populations, land and resource management, and species and habitats they wish to protect, is precarious. Throw in the notion of an ideal—of a pristine wild, with indigenous species flourishing—and a just equilibrium is even more elusive.

And what happens in a man-made "wild?" Zoos are complicated in both theory and practice. Many undertake excellent conservation and research, overseen by principled scientists who have devoted their lives to wild animals, and who have a profound understanding of what is being lost. Over recent decades, many zoos in the United States have been reconfigured and reconceptualized from the cage-lined peepshows they once were, and are now designed to provide a kind of home, or habitat, for the resident animals. Most zookeepers look after their charges with care. Baby animals are born, the sick are tended to, and human children visiting zoos may emerge from these confines with a lifelong fascination for wildlife.

And yet zoos are also troubling because the resident animals are so far removed from the wild. Although some credit zoos for adding to the population of otherwise nearly extinct species, Nick says:

> I don't believe that captive animals play a role in stopping extinction other than in the literal sense. I believe that zoo animals work as ambassadors, but can never be *wild*, as they are born and bred in captivity—this is the same with cloning and other current science. My feeling is that real conservation is about protecting the land that these endangered species need in order to survive in the wild. Captive animals are not "saving" anything. Use them to show why we need to save habitat, why we need to save their wild relatives. But they are not replacements.

Zoos do objectify animals. In his 1977 essay "Why Look at Animals?" cultural critic John Berger discusses the colonialist origins of zoos:

> In the nineteenth century, public zoos were an endorsement of modern colonial power. The capturing of the animals was a symbolic representation of the conquest of all distant and exotic lands. "Explorers" proved their patriotism by sending home a tiger or an elephant. The gift of an exotic animal to the metropolitan zoo became a token in subservient diplomatic relations.[15]

He goes on to liken zoos, in their civic function, to museums:

> In principle, each cage is a frame around the animal inside it. Visitors visit the zoo to look at animals. They proceed from cage to cage, not unlike visitors in an art gallery who stop in front of one painting, and then move on to the next or the one after next. Yet in the zoo the view is always wrong. . . . However you look at these animals, even if the animal is up against the bars, less than a foot from you, looking outwards in the public direction, *you are looking at something that has been rendered absolutely marginal.*[16]

In the early 1990s Nick set out to cover the evolution of zoos in the United States for *National Geographic*. While it was not hard for him to distinguish between this form of "benign" captivity and the imprisonment he'd witnessed working on the darker parts of *Brutal Kinship*, the contrast between observing chimpanzees and gorillas in zoos, after having experienced them in the wild, was almost unbearable for him. Still, "zoos have a higher visitation rate than almost anything we do," observes Nick. "They influence how we perceive nature, so in that way can achieve so much."

National Geographic's "New Zoos" was published in July 1993.[17] Nick followed it in 1996 with a story for *Smithsonian* on the National Zoo,[18] and ten years later with "Panda, Inc.," on captive pandas, for *National Geographic*.[19] In all three stories, the photographs managed to render a sense of the observer as well as the observed—turning the dynamic of visiting, of being in a zoo, back on the viewer. According to Nick, the animal knows that it is not free, not in its true habitat. "The fakery" of the zoo environments, he contends, "is for the people." Therefore, in his zoo photographs, he tended to construct complicated lighting—making a portrait of the captive animal, while removing all illusion of "natural habitat" rather than intensifying it. His images suggest the theatricality and artfulness of habitat design.

Appalling ethical breaches are committed by certain wildlife photographers, who have been known to photograph captive animals and then misrepresent them as wild. With his zoo images, Nick perhaps was subconsciously emphasizing the full disclosure he so unwaveringly insists on. The credibility of the photographer's project is contingent upon fair and accurate reporting. This is especially important for a photojournalist like Nick who is positioning his photographs as potential tools for advocacy—grounded deeply in truth. This is the larger mission at the heart of *Brutal Kinship*—and of almost every project that follows.

For the 1992 article "A Curious Kinship: Apes and Humans," Nick had expanded upon his work with the Rwandan mountain gorillas. He would not return to Rwanda until after the bloodbath—the genocide that took place in Rwanda in 1994 and all but destroyed the country. That horror unfolded rapidly: in the space of about one hundred days, some eight hundred thousand to a million Tutsis and moderate Hutus were exterminated by Hutu extremists with unprecedented murderous barbarity. As hundreds of thousands of men, women, and children were being

OPPOSITE: Wild-caught Sumatran tiger in captive-breeding program, Taman Safari Park, Indonesia, 1997; ABOVE: Giant panda, National Zoo, Washington, DC, 2006

massacred—sometimes by their neighbors, their coworkers, or betrayed while seeking refuge in churches—most of the world turned a blind eye to the genocide and its consequences. Millions of refugees fled the country, often escaping through the Virunga mountain range.

When the Tutsi rebels eventually gained power, the Hutu killers—or *génocidaires*—themselves fled Rwanda, often through the Virungas as well. They set up camps, trees were cut for firewood, and animals were hunted and slaughtered. The *génocidaires* also left landmines in their wake, causing more heinous deaths, and further destroying the forests and its inhabitants.

George Schaller speaks of the toll on both humans and animals in the postscript to the 2010 edition of his book *The Year of the Gorilla* (first published in 1964), which chronicles his years observing mountain gorillas in the Virungas. Of the Rwandan genocide he writes: "While humankind indulged in an orgy of violence, the apes could only endure silently, waiting in their forest home for everlasting peace."[20]

When Nick returned to Rwanda, he felt that he needed to try to find friends who had assisted him—Tutsis, Hutus, Twa tribesmen, and others who were his neighbors when he lived in the country with his family in 1987. And he wanted to track the mountain gorillas, whose fate had always been so precarious, and who were now perhaps more threatened than ever. The same animals that had become emblematic of the potential success of ecotourism in Rwanda suffered collaterally during the humans' massacre.

Nick wanted to shed light on the aftermath of the genocide and its impact on conservation. He knew that if he was going to have any true sense of what had befallen the mountain gorillas, he needed to work with someone who understood their behavior and social structure profoundly, and who had firsthand knowledge of the Rwandan gorilla groups from the Fossey days—someone with impeccable intuition and sensitivity. He contacted Craig Sholley, onetime director of the Mountain Gorilla Project, who had turned that responsibility over to the Rwandan National Park Authority in the late 1980s. Although Nick and Sholley had never worked together in the field, they respected each other and clearly shared a love for Rwanda and the gorillas. Nick reached out to Sholley to see if he might work with him as a guide and colleague on the story, which would take them through Rwanda, Uganda, and the DRC, through lava fields and into refugee camps. Sholley remembers:

> My first reaction to Nick's call was: "No, I can't do this. This is much too close to my heart. It will tear me apart, to see what this country that I love is like in the aftermath of the horrors that just occurred." In the end, I decided that . . . this is a story that needs to be told . . . from a people standpoint and from a gorilla standpoint, from a wildlife-conservation standpoint.

They visited refugee camps—sprawling tent cities built in the mud—where they searched for and eventually encountered old friends and colleagues. They also learned of many losses.

Photographically, Nick felt he made a breakthrough with the mountain gorillas on this 1995 trip because of Sholley's presence.

> All that time before when I'd been photographing mountain gorillas, I never actually had a guide. I just was there with one of Dian's trackers or one of the park rangers—who were great, but they would step away and I would spend the time with the gorillas. But I didn't really know enough about the mountain gorillas to make great pictures. With Craig, he would say: "You know, I think they're going to walk this way in a few minutes," and he would tell me about the groups, the particular silverbacks. It was personal. Craig gave me the courage to sit right down in their path. And I also saw gorillas I knew, who I'd photographed as kids.

National Geographic published this story relatively quickly: Nick and Sholley worked together for two months in early 1995, and the story—with written contributions by George Schaller ("Gentle Gorillas, Turbulent Times")[21] and Paul F. Salopek ("Gorillas and Humans: An Uneasy Truce.")[22]— was published in October of the same year. The magazine's cover image is of two sorrowful (so they appear to me), unblinking gorilla eyes—the remaining features are hardly discernible. The story's lead lines move us quickly to an important underlying question:

> Among the last of its kind, a young gorilla peers from its leafy refuge in Rwanda—a nation bloodied by ethnic slaughter. Conservationists fear that Rwanda's instability could endanger the gorilla's survival. Others ask: How should the plight of the world's rarest ape be weighed against more than 500,000 human dead?

While Nick's photographs are principally of the gorillas, some images also focus on a devastated people, on displaced and orphaned children, and on a war-scarred landscape.

In 2014, I wrote to the office of General Roméo Dallaire, the Canadian humanitarian and activist who was in charge of the United Nations peacekeeping mission in Rwanda, whose warnings, and then urgent pleas for assistance, before and during the genocide were almost universally ignored. Dallaire is the author of the 2004 book *Shake Hands with the Devil: The Failure of Humanity in Rwanda.*[23] In my letter to the general, I asked about the impact of the genocide on the mountain gorillas, framing my query—for better or for worse—in terms of collateral damage. I received a response from David G. Hyman, Dallaire's personal secretary:

> Dear Melissa,
>
> Your very kind message has been forwarded to General Dallaire.
>
> However I have to tell you that he has told me that he was beyond appalled that during the height of the massacre the West appeared to be more concerned with the fate of the great apes than for the hundreds of thousands of men, women and children that were being hacked to death at check points and in their homes. It was almost as if the humans were considered collateral damage, as you put it. It was bizarre, governments didn't wish to be involved in

Fidele Nshogoza, gorilla tracker, Volcanoes National Park, 1995

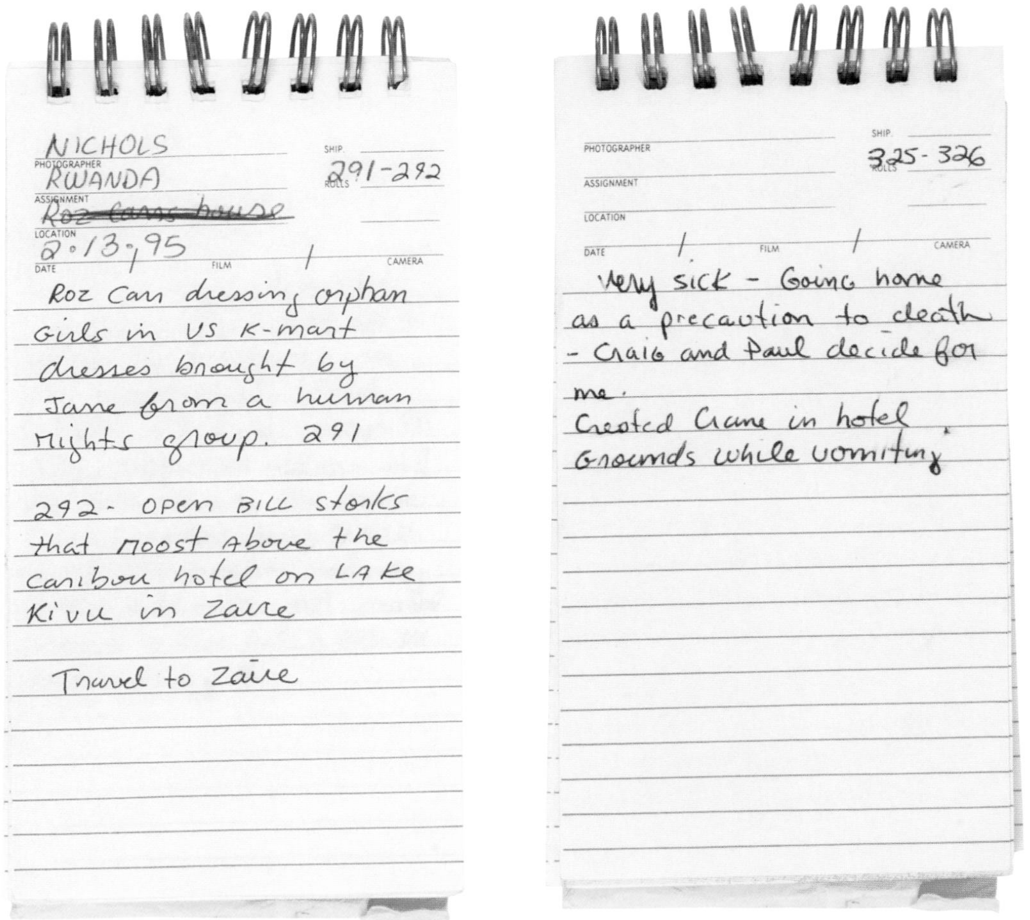

NICHOLS
PHOTOGRAPHER
RWANDA
ASSIGNMENT
~~Roz eans house~~
LOCATION
2·13·95
DATE   FILM   /   CAMERA
SHIP
291-292
ROLLS

Roz Carr dressing orphan
Girls in US K-mart
dresses brought by
Jane from a human
rights group. 291

292- OPEN BILL storks
that roost Above the
caribou hotel on LAKe
Kivu in Zaire

Travel to Zaire

PHOTOGRAPHER
ASSIGNMENT
LOCATION
DATE   /   FILM   /   CAMERA
SHIP
3·25- 326
ROLLS

Very sick - Going home
as a precaution to death
- Craig and Paul decide for
me.
Created Crane in hotel
Grounds while vomiting.

preventing the killings yet private citizens were appealing to their governments and NGOs to save the apes. How was it we knew and cared more about the killing of the gorillas but not of the humans?

It is appalling that these amazing creatures, apes for trophies and particularly elephants and tigers are being harvested for ivory and traditional Chinese medicine. In view of this, I'm not sure that the genocide had any effect, other than attenuating the poaching as the poaching continues to this day. How very sad.

In 1994 Dallaire's dismay grew exponentially as his repeated appeals for help for those being massacred were dismissed—or worse: some governments in last gasp attempts to secure neocolonial power, provided aid to the murderous Hutu extremists. That concern was expressed for the apes while the human slaughter was disregarded seemed inconceivable. That the human carnage was not immediately and globally recognized and addressed was and remains unconscionable—compounding the nightmare.

"We are all Rwandans," a Rwandan friend tells me when I ask about President Paul Kagame's National Unity and Reconciliation Commission, and whether he believes the mandated forgiveness between the Hutu and Tutsi people is truly possible. Is it possible to forgive the killer of your father, your husband, your brother; the rapist of your mother, your wife, your sister?

This gesture of forgiveness has generously been extended to the West as well, despite the disgraceful indifference we exhibited.

I traveled to Rwanda in 2014, twenty years after the genocide. The country's capital city, Kigali, is home to the Kigali Genocide Memorial. There, the country's bloody history of colonialism and factional war is recounted candidly—as are the more recent atrocities—both visually and through oral histories. The story is agonizing to consider, impossible to come to terms with. It is also, in some ways, difficult to envision, given the lushness and sense of peacefulness in Rwanda today.

Kigali is a sun-drenched and graceful city. I arrive on the last Saturday of the month—the designated "cleaning day" in Kigali, during which everyone participates together in the city's care. Even in

THE MOUNTAIN GORILLAS OF AFRICA

A Fragile Home Threatened by War

Among the last of its kind, a young gorilla peers from its leafy refuge in Rwanda—a nation bloodied by ethnic slaughter. Conservationists fear that Rwanda's instability could endanger the gorillas' survival. Others ask: How should the plight of the world's rarest ape be weighed against more than 500,000 human dead?

PHOTOGRAPHS BY MICHAEL NICHOLS

58

OPPOSITE: Nick's notes for *National Geographic* captions, Rwanda, 1995; ABOVE: *National Geographic*, October 1995: "The Mountain Gorillas of Africa: A Fragile Home Threatened by War"

its most impoverished neighborhoods—the disparity of wealth is pronounced—the city appears to sparkle with a sense of civic and communal pride.

Leaving Kigali, I ride with Yasin Hamdan, a gracious and articulate guide for an ecotourism group, who will work with me over the next few days. We drive up the ever-inclining, serpentine road of infinite fragrances—made more delicious and verdant by intermittent rains—toward the northern city of Ruhengeri. Days after my arrival in Rwanda, I am trekking more than ten thousand feet above sea level, up Mount Karisimbi in the Virunga's Volcanoes National Park (which borders Virunga National Park in the DRC and Uganda's Mgahinga Gorilla National Park) to visit the Susa gorillas—one of the oldest and largest groups (boasting three silverbacks) of observed habituated gorillas.

As I climb over the rocky and slippery terrain through the dense growth and prickly nettles, I can't help wondering: who passed through here, what happened here on this ground, during the genocide? Emblazoned in my brain are photographer Gilles Peress's harrowing images of the victims of the killings, so incisively sequenced in his 1995 book *The Silence*.[24] I hear echoes of Philip Gourevitch's excruciating accounts in his 1998 book *We Wish to Inform You That Tomorrow We Will Be Killed with Our Families*.[25] Dismembered bodies. Cadavers rotting, belongings strewn nearby. The skeletons of children. "Those dead Rwandans will be with me forever, I expect," he writes—and as I walk I feel: yes, the dead Rwandans are here, too, in this forest.

All of a sudden the gorillas make their presence known—the little ones tumbling over each other, beating their chests like the grownups, nonchalantly checking out our group of eight. With devoted tenderness, a mother fastidiously grooms her infant as he luxuriates on her belly. The silverbacks, low-key, preside; their musky scent intoxicates. This blissful moment of bamboo-filtered sunlight feels like the purest state of grace. The horrors, the unnerving sense of despair and soullessness, it is all so irreconcilable with the immediate, vital present.

I know, too, that seemingly interminable human conflicts still persist in the region at large. George Schaller, when we spoke in 2012, lamented the ongoing turmoil. He had recently learned that three guards had been murdered in the Virungas by rebel soldiers.

> Here you've got these poorly paid guards, and they love the gorillas, and they may be the only reason there are any gorillas left. And they've lost maybe thirty guards over the years to all this war. When I was in Rwanda in early 2009 . . . four armies were fighting each other. So the poor people and the poor gorillas are still in great danger.

This danger was rendered profoundly in an August 2007 *Newsweek* story on the Virungas and the mountain gorillas besieged by ongoing conflict in the DRC.[26] That story includes South African photojournalist Brent Stirton's images of the silverback Senkwekwe, one of seven mountain gorillas who were slain execution-style in Virunga National Park over a two-month period. As journalist Sharon Begley reported:

> Authorities doubt the killers are poachers, since the gorillas' bodies were left behind and an infant—who could bring thousands of dollars from a collector—was found clinging to its dead mother. . . . The brutality and senselessness of the crime had conservation experts concerned

that the most dangerous animal in the world had found yet another excuse to slaughter the creatures with whom we share the planet.

Stirton's poignant and haunting portrait of the six-hundred-pound alpha-male mountain gorilla on the opening spread inspires chills. This spectacular creature is being carried by disconsolate Congolese guards and porters and park rangers in a solemn procession out of the park. The image—suggestive of depictions of Christ's descent from the Cross—speaks to the respect and trust between the mountain gorillas and the African guards, many of whom, as Schaller has reminded us, have lost their lives while protecting the animals.

Nick was deeply moved by Stirton's picture—which he calls a "powerful crossover photograph—both a conflict and a conservation image." It inspired him to reach out to the South African photographer and to encourage him to work with *National Geographic*. Stirton takes it further:

> When I first met Nick—after that photograph was published in *Newsweek* he tracked me down—I really woke up to the fact that I had greater responsibilities as a photojournalist. I had always been interested in photographing human conflict and its consequences, but Nick showed me how interconnected these issues are with conservation.
>
> My work is all about the problems associated with those animals Nick photographs. His work is a reminder of why I should keep focusing on these problems—I can't look at his work and then abdicate responsibility.

Newsweek, August 6, 2007: "Cry of the Wild." Photograph by Brent Stirton

Stirton had earlier worked in the Virungas, photographing fighting between "a special forces group of conservation rangers and FDLR [Democratic Forces for the Liberation of Rwanda], the Interhamwe Hutu fundamentalist group behind the Rwandan genocide. All of the hardcore *génocidaires* fled into what was Zaire [now the DRC] and Virunga National Park in 1994 to escape reprisals." Although the worst of the blood battle is long over, Stirton echoes Schaller, making it clear that things are by no means safe in the Virungas. He outlines some of the ongoing challenges:

> This area is totally destabilized since the Rwandan genocide. When the conflict was resolved, the vast majority of refugees went back into Rwanda, [but] the most murderous Hutus were not allowed to come back by Paul Kagame's government. They were hunted, and so they have settled throughout Virunga National Park, as a military force. They are an insurgency—an illegal occupier in the park—and they've been doing everything they can to maximize what they can get out of this park. They have no conservation values, so they make charcoal illegally, they kill animals, they eat bushmeat, and they attack on a regular basis the rangers trying to protect the park, the gorillas, and other wildlife. And they exploit all the mineral wealth inside this park. They are a well-armed force inside Virunga, now going on two generations.

Stirton points out that these insurgents are not the only group exploiting the park. There are "at least eleven paramilitary groups," he declares, as well as the Congolese Army.

Describing the conditions confronted in 2016 by the world's largest primate, the Grauer's gorilla—whose habitat is primarily the eastern forests of the DRC—science writer Rachel Nuwer reports that "populations have plummeted 77 percent over the last 20 years, with fewer than 3,800 of the animals remaining."[27] As with the mountain gorillas, the Rwandan genocide, subsequent destabilization, and then civil war have led to the precipitous decline of this eastern lowland gorilla's numbers. Nuwer continues:

> From 1996 to 2003, that conflict cost the lives of an estimated five million people, and also brought the formation of more armed groups, 69 of which continue to operate in the eastern part of the country. Bushmeat feeds many of them, and gorillas, which can weigh up to 400 pounds, prove easy and worthwhile targets. To finance their efforts, many armed groups have also set up artisanal mining sites, nearly all illegal.[28]

"The bottom line," Stirton admonishes, "is that the gorillas in the region are severely under threat because of groups fighting, and also competing for resources—and this includes groups sponsored by Rwanda." The park rangers, as well, remain constantly at risk. In the July 2016 issue of *National Geographic*, Robert Draper wrote: "Attempts by rangers to drive [locally formed militias called Mai-Mai] out have led to deadly reprisals. This past March two rangers were executed in the Virunga's central sector, driving up the death toll of park rangers to 152 since 1996." There was also an attempt on the life of Emmanuel de Merode, director of Virunga National Park, in 2014.[29]

FOLLOWING SPREAD: Mountain gorillas, Volcanoes National Park, Rwanda, 1995

Clearly, vigilance is key, despite the revitalization of Kigali, the building of schools, the extension of clean water and reliable energy into the poorest villages, and other positive developments in Rwanda—due in part to intelligent, considered, and sustainable ecotourism that helps the people and their communities, and the gorillas and their habitats. Penalizing poachers for their criminal behavior, and then rehabilitating and educating them about the potential benefits of coexisting with wildlife are crucial steps. Although, as poverty drives people to poach animals, there must be income alternatives that are legal and nonlethal, or the cruelty will continue.

As Schaller writes in *The Year of the Gorilla*:

> It is difficult to reconcile the congenial nature of gorilla society with the brutality of my own species. The travails of the gorillas emphasize a basic lesson in conservation: if we treasure something and wish to retain it, not just for the next fifty years but for centuries, we can never falter in our commitment; not for a moment can we turn our backs, or we may lose it. The fact that the gorillas have endured during these violent years fills me with optimism and hope. I know that the world must do all it can to assure the gorillas their right of survival, to treat them with respect, compassion, and devotion, and to retain the trust that they have so generously given to humankind.[30]

SITA AND CHARGER

The tiger Charger (camera-trap photograph),
Bandhavgarh National Park, India, 1996

"There is no creature on Earth who will make your hair stand on end like a wild tiger," says Nick. "They are magnificent."

Wild tigers are the first predatory animals Nick photographed, and determining the ideal approach was initially confounding. He began in late 1995 with a two-month scouting trip to central India, where much of their natural habitat has evolved into protected national parks that restrict tourists to certain areas at designated times of day. Although accustomed to seeing humans, the tigers are not in any way "tame." Also, during the annual monsoon season in this part of India, the parks may become more or less inaccessible to visitors, sometimes even to park rangers, for many months. All the animals thus go through a kind of cyclical rehabituation process each year. The tigers here are wild—solitary, territorial, nocturnal hunters.

Nick viscerally conjures the tigers' awe-inspiring presence: "When a tiger walks, the whole forest talks. If you get tuned in, you can hear it. The monkeys are saying: *He's walking*; the birds are saying: *He's walking*. Each makes a singular alarm call for the tiger."

Nick had learned in the early 1990s that *National Geographic* wanted to do a story on tigers. Even though he almost always proposed his own ideas, he wanted this one. Because other projects precluded tackling the tigers story for another three or four years, he asked the magazine's editors to hold off on the piece until he was ready. They agreed.

During his coverage of new zoos, Nick had seen seemingly endless funds allocated to conservation efforts and breeding projects with captive tigers—an attempt to help save a species whose numbers are rapidly dwindling. Nick, however, believes that the only *real* tiger is a wild tiger. From his perspective, if the species is going to continue to exist, conservation must be weighted in favor of the wild tiger. Hoping to do a project similar to his work on chimpanzees—contrasting images of wild and captive animals—he would document the species in zoos, living as pets, and working in entertainment, demonstrating that while big-cat owners may, in their way, love and cherish their animals, they still diminish the wild cat to a domesticated shadow of its former self. When cornered or otherwise provoked, its tiger-ness may reemerge from deep within, but otherwise what remains is a broken creature. Nick wanted to balance his work on captive tigers with a long-term engagement with wild tigers.

For this project, he was in the field about thirteen months altogether, including visits to Russia, Indonesia, and Thailand. Again, *National Geographic* offered him the time and resources needed to go deep into the story.

Nick focused his work on wild tigers in India. Over two years, he made five trips in all (of six to twelve weeks each) to the 268 square miles of jungle then comprising central India's Bandhavgarh National Park, in Madhya Pradesh. The park also offered topographical and seasonal variations: a dry season of muted tones as well as a brief period of saturated greens after the monsoons.

Mother tiger at Sriracha tiger farm, which breeds tigers for the bone, pelt, and organ trade, Thailand, 1997

Nick recognized that the tigers' survival here derived, paradoxically, from their historic value as trophies:

> The tigers' stronghold is in one of the most populated places on Earth. It seems almost impossible that India would have wild tigers—yet it does. But they wouldn't be there if Indian maharajas hadn't liked shooting them. They set aside land in India for these tigers to live on so they could hunt them for fun—not in a sporting way whatsoever—and almost every piece of that land now is a national park that has tigers in it. They have survived this long because wealthy people liked hunting them.

The bizarre codependent relationship between legal trophy- or "sport"-hunting and conservation, and the implications of wildlife habitats abutting dense human populations, are tensions that would continue to amplify Nick's stories. The presence of humans—whether violent or benign, rich or impoverished—must be fully and sensitively considered for any hope of peaceful coexistence and long-term ecological balance. Geoffrey C. Ward is the author of the 1993 book *Tiger-Wallahs: Encounters with the Men Who Tried to Save the Greatest of the Great Cats*,[1] and contributed the text for Nick's 1998 book *The Year of the Tiger*.[2] He also wrote the article accompanying Nick's cover story on tigers in the December 1997 *National Geographic*, "Making Room for Wild Tigers."[3] In his text, Ward refers to

ABOVE: Siegfried and Roy with white tiger cub, Las Vegas, 1997; OPPOSITE: Tourists at Sriracha tiger farm, 1997

"alarming drops in the world tiger populations" and outlines the challenges, first in broad strokes, of "how to preserve wild cats in wild lands as farms and cities eat away at habitat." But recognizing the reality of living with predators, Ward acknowledges:

> Asians living with tigers must regard them pragmatically. Farming villages on the fringe of tiger territories lose livestock—and human lives—to tiger attacks, and villagers fight back.[4]

A more immediate threat to the tigers are poachers, who collect bones, organs, and other body parts—all in frighteningly high demand because of their supposed value in traditional Chinese medicine and as aphrodisiacs. In "Making Room for Wild Tigers," Ward writes of these specious assumptions:

> Tiger bone, like all mammal bone, is essentially phosphorus, calcium, and iron, and no scientific proof of its benefits exists. Investigations show that some bone products contain mercury and arsenic, added to convince users of their potency by producing a sensation.

While working on his tiger project, Nick conferred regularly with Ward and spent time in the field with him. He told me that Nick is "tireless—I mean, *indefatigable*." Ward suffered from polio as a child; "It's a little hard for me to get around," he says. In the jungle, he was struck that Nick—although clearly so unwaveringly driven to work—helped him on and off elephants and in and out of jeeps "without the slightest hesitation or annoyance or anything else." Mostly, he remembers their mutual fascination for two particular tigers living in Bandhavgarh National Park. "We knew the cast," recalls Ward. "We were both interested in Charger and the prolific tigress Sita."

Ward had first encountered Sita in 1986. When he returned to Bandhavgarh ten years later, she was almost sixteen—old for a tiger—and had recently been seen mating again. This would be her sixth litter. Regal and aloof, Sita was the stunning Bengal who reigned in the park. "There are other tigresses," says Nick, "but Sita was unique. She was so frustratingly smart and elusive. No matter what I did, she always seemed to have the upper hand. She did what she wanted to do. If I followed her, it was only because she let me."

The jungle's dominant male tiger was aptly nicknamed Charger. Nick's son Eli learned firsthand how the tiger got his name when, in December 1997, Nick took his family to India for six weeks, after he had completed the story. The first close call with Charger happened during the family's first outing: the tiger "charged" the passenger side of their open jeep, making contact with the tire next to Eli. Although he was only seven at the time, Eli can still envision that moment. A few days later, as Nick, Reba, and the boys mounted two elephants in search of Sita or Charger, there was even more drama:

> I was on the elephant with my dad and the mahout [the "driver" and handler of the elephant]. We were going through a meadow, and we came upon this pig carcass. We must have gotten between the dead pig and Charger, because within seconds Charger just came straight up to the elephant—he *jumped* on the elephant—I mean it was really up close and personal! The elephant

Looking for tigers, Bandhavgarh National Park, 1996. Photograph by Roy Toft

reared up, and we were barely holding on. Charger was hanging on this elephant for a good five or ten seconds, and then the elephant finally shook him off, and started chasing him. It all happened so fast.

Although a terrifying moment for the little boy at the time, today Eli remembers being impressed by Charger's prowess.

With each story, Nick always tried to find a way to include his family—typically, once he had more or less finished shooting. Their father was not as present in their daily lives as most dads, but Ian and Eli recognize how lucky they were to have had so many remarkable adventures growing up. It also helped them understand their father's work. Even now, as he and I speak while looking at one of the project's signature photographs—of Charger, about to be airborne—Eli's voice drops in a kind of hushed reverence, and then he just gazes at the picture and smiles.

In that image, Charger's back paws barely touch the rocks as he pushes off from a cliff, weight forward, body outstretched, taut, muscular, front paws seemingly relaxed, his gaze bright and directed upward. The supple grace of the animal's thrust over the void and his propulsive power are extraordinary: the image practically drips adrenaline.

With Sita and Charger, Nick once again had charismatic protagonists, along with information on their family histories and predilections. His tiger portraits—the results of strategic timing, exasperating trial and error, and gifts of serendipity—are deliciously chilling. His love affair with Sita and Charger began with the tantalizing possibility of proximity to subjects admired with awe from afar, and then progressed swiftly from courtship to romance to something akin to stalking. As he worked, Nick was possessed—by a hunger to *know* Charger, to *know* Sita, and to discover or orchestrate situations in which they would reveal themselves in some essential way. There is no sentimentality in these images, not even in the portraits of Sita and her cubs—which doesn't mean your heart won't swell looking at them. Indeed, the presence of the cubs helps to advance Nick's underlying narrative: Sita's interactions with them provide evidence of her intensity of purpose. It is Sita's biological imperative to keep them safe from potential predators—including humans on foot—and teach them how to survive on their own, honing their own predatory, self-perpetuating, and territorial instincts. To Nick, this is *tigerness*.

Working with these apex predators, Nick quickly came to understand that a variety of image-making approaches would be needed to create the intimacy, energy, and edge that he strives for. First, he utilized the camera trap—an indispensable tool when working with tigers. A camera trap is a camouflaged and weatherproof "remote" camera (the photographer is neither holding it nor necessarily anywhere close by) with a shutter triggered by the movement of an animal as it crosses an infrared beam that is invisible to the animal. He had used these traps before with a degree of success, in the Congo—but in India, with tigers, he took the process to an unprecedented level. It was no longer simply about making a record of an animal passing a particular point on a trail; Nick now began making camera-trap images that were painstakingly conceived, composed, and lit. Positioning the camera traps, and then configuring the lighting for the optimum results, is a labor-intensive, precarious act of faith requiring enormous patience, thought, and time. The process is inverted: proceeding according to the tiger's previously observed behavior, the photographer composes the image without a subject, setting the stage for behavior that *might* occur. Nick studies animals' routines, movements, and preferred pathways, and with that knowledge places the camera, hoping that a dance might happen at this spot as it did at least once before.

Unlike telephoto photography—in which the camera is situated at a distance from the subject—the close-up images that an innovatively set-up camera trap with a wide-angle lens can achieve more faithfully reflect Nick's sensibility as a photographer. His ingenious strategies offered him exceptional proximity to these animals, which sometimes come so close to the camera that their breath fogs the lens. Critically, Nick learned how to set up the camera trap so as not to stress or endanger the animal (or anyone on his team). But that technique was learned only after some frightening and humbling mishaps.

The traps were an important vehicle for achieving Nick's vision in the tiger story, but he also had ideas for how he himself might get close to the animals. Almost every morning, just before dawn, Nick and his team would travel through the park on elephants, who can navigate the terrain and are rarely vulnerable to tigers. Tigers do not fear elephants, nor do they view them as prey. But they will charge one if provoked—for example, if the elephant inadvertently comes between a tiger and its kill, or a tigress and her cubs. The elephant Nick selected to ride each morning had to meet certain requirements. He did not wish to tower over any tigers—as that would determine the angle of his photographs—so older, fully grown elephants were too tall. The younger and smaller ones at first seemed right, and would allow for a more level vantage point, but according to Nick: "They were too squirrelly, just dancing all the time."

They all seemed to *love* looking for tigers. Even more than wild elephants, domesticated elephants need stimulation. Finally I settled on a medium-sized elephant who really seemed to enjoy the work. There were plenty of times, when we got into tough terrain, that the elephants would crawl on their knees with us on these huge seats strapped to their backs.

Domesticating elephants is an Indian tradition that some (such as elephant specialist Dhriti K. Lahiri Choudhury), based on readings of cave paintings, have dated to 6000 BCE. And currently, in Bandhavgarh for example, domesticated elephants born in captivity are typically cared for by the mahouts who drive them, generally with tourists astride, through the park. As the elephants provide their livelihood, the mahouts presumably nurture the animals, bathing them twice a day and making sure they are well fed.

However, when Nick traveled to Kaziranga in India's state of Assam (a major stronghold for the one-horned rhinoceros), he witnessed the "breaking" of what he's almost certain were wild baby elephants, captured for the purpose of domestication. He describes an ugly process:

> Their legs are tied, and they are basically brainwashed into submission, generally by deprivation. In order to survive, the elephant eventually gives in and becomes domesticated.

Nick knew the elephants he was utilizing for the tiger project had never lived in the wild and had been bred for domestication; still, seeing this distressed him greatly. However, those trained elephants were crucial to his work, and there really was no way to move safely through the jungle while on the trail of tigers *except* on the back of an elephant. Nick also knows that, for the most part, the mahouts care greatly and warmly for their elephants. Again, layered ethical questions are raised: is it justifiable to sacrifice one animal's wildness in order to study another species? Or should we perhaps consider the question in terms of the overall local ecosystem, in a kind of cost-benefit analysis: the elephant's wildness is sacrificed to tourism, which helps keep this part of India economically healthy and the mahouts employed, and therefore perhaps ultimately serves to protect elephants from being killed for their tusks—ivory.

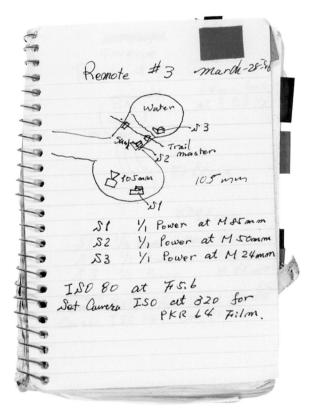

This sort of ethical relativism is paralleled in the justification for sacrificing captive chimpanzees for the benefit of their counterparts in the wild, or even the counterintuitive acceptance of trophy and

OPPOSITE: Page from Nick's notebook, India, March 28, 1996; ABOVE: Setting up camera trap: Roy Toft is at right with camera; Butch Lama is holding the rope. Bandhavgarh National Park, 1996

nonsubsistence hunting and population culling as components of a larger conservation equation. These may be regarded, at least by some conservationists, as lesser evils—pragmatic compromises for the greater good—but still, as actions or solutions, they must never slip in as unexamined givens.

At Bandhavgarh, Nick and crew would awaken at 3:30 each morning, have coffee, and be on their elephants by 4:30. Their goal was to track the tigers at the end of their nocturnal hunting forays, before dawn if possible. Nick's team was comprised of the elephants and their mahouts, Phool Singh and Kuttapaan; biologist Roy Toft; videographer Erin Harvey (during part of the spring 1997 trip); and their invaluable Nepalese guide in the field, Nanda S. J. B. Rana—a former game hunter who Nick asserts was "obsessed with the tigers of Bandhavgarh. He knew their habits as well as a human can. He really knew how to find tigers."

Constantly on high alert, the troop listened for the alarm calls that resonated throughout the jungle as the tigers moved, followed the scent of the animals' kills, and observed their "pugmarks" (footprints) and their territorial scratch marks on tree trunks, which were often accompanied by territorial scent marks. Tracking the tigers on the backs of elephants also enabled Nick to observe the cats' behavior from a perspective he otherwise might not have had, to learn about places they frequented and when, and the routes they took to get there. This research subsequently determined

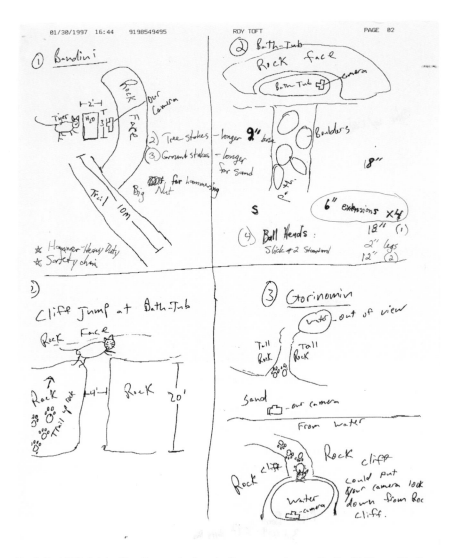

Roy Toft's 1996 sketch of locations and setups for tiger camera traps, reflecting Nick's specifications

the locations where he and Toft would install camera traps—which might remain in place for several months. Nick remembers:

> We just kept placing them. Any time I saw the tigers do anything that was cool, we would go and set up a camera trap. Most of them didn't yield, but some did, and that was my secret weapon. I saw that Charger went to a particular watering hole. To get to it, he had to walk along this cliff edge and jump over a big opening. When I saw him do it, I knew we had to put a camera trap there. We used ropes to climb the cliffs, and place the cameras. The camera sat there for three months—so many bad pictures, mostly of monkeys and some bats. There was only a single frame of a tiger, and another of a tiger's tail! But finally there was one—that

really Charger took of himself, on his own terms because of the way the camera traps work—and it is unbelievable. With camera traps, it's all about a perfect setup, and time.

Kenji Yamaguchi, *National Geographic*'s resident "camera engineer," often modified the cameras and also the flashes to perform in ways specific to the project's needs. The exigencies of shooting in India seven days a week, ninety days per trip, at times in 130-degree heat, requires, as Nick notes, careful fine-tuning and then some: "On a camera trap, the camera needs to keep *thinking* as the light and time of day change—lengthening or shortening the shutter speed. But this must stop at night or the exposure gets too long."

Nick called on many of the skills he had tested and refined in the caves: increasingly sophisticated flash and lighting work, as well as climbing up tricky ascents or down perilous drops to realize his setups. To assist him with all of this was Roy Toft, whom Nick had met when photographing the San Diego Wild Animal Park for the "New Zoos" story. Eventually Toft, who had his own photographic aspirations, quit his job at the zoo and asked Nick if he might need an assistant. Thirty-five at the time and ready to pick up and go, Toft was just in time for the tiger story.

Now a respected wildlife photographer in his own right, Toft's experience working with Nick was life changing: "Nick was the best mentor I could have." As we spoke, Toft relived some of Nick's "over-the-top" methods in Bandhavgarh:

> Nick does a lot of really dark imagery, in an often dark environment. He was doing crazy slow-shutter speed pans, painting with light. . . . His mind always went to lighting something—a kind of studio lighting in the field, working with a soft box on a cue and a small flash, or with a large flash—the type normally used in a studio. . . . I never saw him take a picture with the flash actually *on* the camera. Nick was figuring out how to expose a multiple three-, four-, or five-flash setup, to mix with ambient light, in a remote system when you're not there. We had a large, 4-by-5 classic Polaroid in the field, just to see what our lighting was doing. It made for incredible rawness and enthralling storytelling.

But there were also many practical challenges to contend with, as Toft points out. For example, if using film with thirty-six exposures, "one group of monkeys can waste your entire roll with a camera trap." In the heat of the day, when the tigers were sleeping, Toft and Nick would move through the jungle checking all the remote cameras: "Are they working, do we need to replace film, batteries. . . ? And we were always making sure not to surprise a sleeping tiger in the process, so I'm banging sticks and making a lot of noise."

Nick notes that the flash did not seem to disturb the very confident tiger—"Certainly not Charger."

Toft tells me that working with Nick in the field was very intense: "We would never hold back. It was always 'What's the next level?' 'How can I get more edge?' 'How can I be more intimate?'"

One way to get closer was to make use of "hides" or "blinds"—safe, camouflaged hiding spots, at times elevated—from which Nick could photograph the animals. He spent sixteen days, six hours a day, in one particular hide made of tall grass draped over a bamboo frame. He'd go there in the early afternoon, and stay until after dark, at which point Nanda Rana (or Butch Lama, a Nepalese tiger guide who worked with Rana) would fetch Nick via a public road outside the park. They would exchange whistles as Rana or Lama approached Nick's hide, in this way communicating that the coast was clear—that is, there was no sign of a tiger close by. Then they would all head back to camp: a one-time maharajah's hunting camp and reserve just outside the park gate.

Because it wasn't feasible to take the elephants out after dark, working from hides allowed Nick unprecedented access to the tigers at night, as they hunted. Using a telephoto lens, he made an eerie, pink-purple-hued image of a tiger known as Bachhi, Sita's daughter, in the foreground, seemingly unaware of a deer some distance behind her—a dynamism that lends the image an intriguing frisson. Using a bit of flash, he captured the tiger's eyes, "burning bright." On another night, Charger dropped by unannounced as part of his evening rounds, his vocalizations sonorous and petrifying. "Charger came right to my hide, which was on the ground. He stood at the opening where my telephoto lens was set up. He was *so* close. I backed into the corner—I think I went into a fetal position. I was terrified! He turned and *sprayed* the hide": an unsubtle reminder of Charger's dominance.

Erin Harvey (son of Nick's close friend, photographer David Alan Harvey) was twenty-five years old when he joined Nick and his team in India. Tall and strong, Harvey had apparently endless endurance and stamina. He was a few years out of film school and, reflects Nick, "extremely meticulous and hardheaded to the max. Erin always had scenes and camera angles playing in his head."

Harvey filmed the daily life of the team as the project unfolded. His footage conveys a number of stories behind the stories, shedding light not only on the intricacy of the camera-trap setups, but also

on the amazing—and sometimes ridiculous—features of the working process. They were especially determined to catch the tigers in the watering hole. In one clip, we see Nick and Toft mimicking tiger behavior on site—leaping, crouching, and enacting other feline gestures—as they try to predict what the camera traps might be orchestrated to reveal. At another point, they dubiously wade into the favored watering hole, murky and laced with monkey pee. Says Nick:

> Erin placed his video camera traps masterfully. He realized: "Okay, not only do I have to have the angle of the tiger lying in the pool, but I have to have the angle of the cameras." . . . He's got a camera pointed at the cameras, he's got one pointed at how the tiger enters the pool. He's got one on the trail approaching it. And then, every time Roy checked the camera traps, Erin would also follow him, filming. Erin created a sequence by the way he placed all his cameras, and then followed Roy.

Harvey managed to position three video camera traps at the watering hole where Nick had earlier captured a wonderful image of Bachhi, her front legs outstretched to each side, paws resting tranquilly on the rocks. Harvey set them up so that if one infrared beam was triggered, all three cameras would start recording. The result, states Nick, is "one of the great sequences of wildlife filmmaking."

OPPOSITE: The tiger Bachhi and deer, Bandhavgarh National Park, 1996; ABOVE: Nick's notes for *National Geographic* captions, India, March 28, 1996

It is certainly one of the most humorous as well. We first see Charger's handsome face, as he saunters into the frame from the right. Approaching the rocks defining the pool's contours, he turns to the side and pauses in a downward-facing-dog crouch, then carefully inches his way toward the water, which he taps appraisingly with his front left paw before taking a little drink. He then backs out over the rocks, only to turn around so that he may look away from the watering hole, cautiously steadying himself, his sprawling body hugging the rocks. His mass, his muscles, his weight are sharply sculptural as he aligns and realigns himself with the demands of his short yet potentially tricky backward descent into the pool. There, very tentatively, he places his left back paw into the water, while his front legs extend, bracing on the rocks. Finally, he lowers himself fully into his bath, his head alone remaining above water. For a moment, he closes his eyes in apparent contentment.

As the cameras were rolling remotely, Nick, Harvey, Toft, and the others had no idea what was being captured on video. Harvey and Toft—chaperoned by one of Nanda Rana's young guides (the team was not permitted to move through the park unaccompanied)—were on a routine inspection of the camera setups, including the watering hole. As Harvey tells it:

> I'm going with Roy to check on the camera traps like we do every few days, and that is when we see some markings, some tiger tracks, as we are approaching. So we are very excited and hopeful, because for the first time, we are finally seeing some evidence that the tiger has traveled toward the watering hole. But there were still a few hundred yards more to go, including a climb up a cliff, to get to there. When we finally did, we saw a bunch of freshly splashed water all around the edge, and that's when we were sure something big had just been in there!

Toward the end of the tiger's cool soak, the film reveals Toft and the guide, with deliberate noisiness, approaching the watering hole, and discovering more indications of the tiger's presence.

Hearing them, Charger's eyes open wide, ears suddenly erect, and for a moment he seems to consider his options. Finally, his powerful body springs out of the water—and quickly out of the frame. Harvey's

edit of the footage ends back at their camp, in Nick's tent. He and Toft tell Nick they *think* they've got something on film—but even Harvey doesn't yet know. Not trusting his own poker face, he'd chosen not to look ahead of time—wanting to "film their genuine reactions to it," if indeed they'd managed to get the tiger. *"Tiger?"* Nick bursts out, grinning. And then laughing: "Where's the video, dude?!"

Sita was a very different story. As Nick intensified his focus on her, he came to understand more and more about the particulars of her behavior—especially when it came to her cubs. Rana deduced that Sita had recently had a litter; the sire was a very large tiger, a rival for Charger's territory and role as the dominant male. Sita was in hiding in the mountains—not venturing down to the lowlands where there was water and hunting was easier. The only explanation for

ABOVE: Nick at Bandhavgarh National Park, 1996. Photograph by Roy Toft. OPPOSITE: The tiger Bachhi (camera-trap photograph), Bandhavgarh National Park, 1996

keeping this distance was that she was protecting her cubs from Charger. A male tiger will often kill its rival's cubs.

The larger story Nick wanted to tell for *National Geographic* was about wildness, and that story hinged on capturing a powerful image of a tigress with her cubs, one he would go to any lengths to get.[5] On the trail of Sita, he and his team trekked into the hills on the backs of elephants. Once they had a sense of her whereabouts, they progressed on foot. When they confirmed the location of her lair—a deep hole at the base of a group of massive boulders—Nick came up with a plan:

> I'm going to put a camera trap on that den. I was thinking, camera traps are benign—which was kind of stupid, because they make noise—especially back then, there's the triggering device, and all kinds of wires . . . and this is her *house*, where she's hiding her babies. . . . We can't see them, but we hear them squeaking. But I say: "Okay, we're going to lower ourselves down into the hole when we know Sita's not there. . . . We'll bother the cubs for about an hour, putting the camera trap up, and then we'll go away, and they'll be fine." That was my rationale.

Toft narrates how, with hearts thumping, they dropped themselves down through the boulders, into Sita's den. He and Nick then commenced the camera and flash set-up process (which in reality almost always took more than an hour—in this case, three). The equipment needed to be screwed into trees and rocks, and entirely camouflaged, with all wires buried. All the while, Sita's presence was palpable.

She was *somewhere* aboveground, nearby, watching, and if she felt that she or her cubs were threatened, she could lunge at any moment. At one point, the mahouts, on the lookout, began shouting with an urgency that panicked Toft and Nick—was Sita approaching? As they scrambled out of the pit, Toft recalls: "Nick slipped and skewered himself on a tree spike that we had put in the tree to hold the flash." It was a false alarm, but Nick was now injured. Nonetheless, they resumed their work, and when they had finished, with great self-satisfaction, the team departed.

The following day they returned to the den with almost giddy anticipation, only to find "total destruction!" as Nick recalls. "Sita had systematically destroyed everything. All the wires, all the flashes. There are no pictures because she destroyed the flashes first." Worst of all, she had moved her cubs.

Toft and Nick were simultaneously astonished by Sita's rebuke (as they saw it) and filled with self-recrimination. Their ethical convictions dictated that their presence should never impact the wild situations they were photographing—and here they had forced Sita to move her cubs, perhaps making them more vulnerable. How much more impact could they have made?

And yet—rather than dissuading them—Nick and the team were consumed by the desire to get the picture they craved. Rana told them that if they didn't find Sita's new hiding place for her cubs then and there, they never would. The group continued on foot. "We're still driven like crazy," Nick confesses. "It was like a mob mentality. We *wanted* that photograph."

As the team picked their way into a bamboo thicket, a flash of orange burst forth. Nick:

Nick (camera-trap photograph), Bandhavgarh National Park, 1996

There is nothing, *nothing* scarier than an angry tiger. Sita came at us like fire. . . . I was trampled. I was hurt, I was in shock, my clothes were torn, I'm bleeding. . . . But it wasn't Sita who trampled me—it was the mahouts, Phool Singh and Kuttapaan, who ran over me, running away from her. She didn't touch me. . . . If she'd gone after me, she would have killed me. Nanda Rana threw a rock and screamed at her. He didn't run. I didn't run. You are never supposed to run. And then she went away. If she'd wanted us dead, we'd be dead. But she went back to her cubs.

This interaction with Sita changed Nick fundamentally. If his experience with the mountain gorillas was an epiphany, Sita provided the next critical lesson regarding the photographer's relationship to his subject. Yes, it was a lesson about behaving with integrity in the field—even if it means not getting what you want. Equally important, it taught Nick to respect animals on their own terms, and never to put his needs above their well-being.

After Sita's charge, Nick admonished himself: "Game over. What the fuck was I thinking?"

That changed my approach to photography. She taught me the ultimate lesson—and she didn't touch me! I saw her ears go back, her body tense, those stripes, that roar . . . her terrifying anger. . . . And I said: "We are leaving her alone. We are never again going to follow this cat in any aggressive manner." My lust got the best of me. . . . I've never done that kind of intervention since.

Nick left India in late May 1996, as the monsoon season was approaching.

Although Sita had remained evasive, he had some exceptional images of Charger. And he planned to return about five months later for more.

Steve Winter has spent much of his life, according to Nick, as a photographer "chasing the impossible with elusive, shy cats. He never gives up." Winter, who has done powerful projects on tigers, snow leopards, and jaguars, among other animals, attributes his own tenacity and ethical standards to Nick, who was an early mentor:

It was Nick who said that photographers in the natural world must treat their subjects the way a documentary photographer, a photojournalist, treats his or her human subject. He understood that without ethics being part of our conversation, we, our photographs, would have no credibility. . . . Nick is a photojournalist. That's what I wanted to be, too. He is not a "wildlife photographer." Wildlife is his subject.

As with photojournalists, working ethically in the field is an imperative for conservationists who devote their lives to a specific species—operating both as scientists and as advocates. Panthera is a global nonprofit organization devoted to saving big wild cats and their habitats. I had the opportunity to speak with Panthera scientists Luke Hunter (president and chief conservation officer) and Alan Rabinowitz (CEO and cofounder, with chairman Thomas S. Kaplan). Although Hunter and Rabinowitz have themselves never worked with Nick in the field, their paths have crossed repeatedly. I wanted to better understand the delicate balance between observation and intervention from their perspective: When are lines fungible? When is the scientist or the photographer influencing the animal's behavior, even if inadvertently? What are the ethical boundaries and issues with, for instance, flying low over herds of animals, or with placing cameras in presumably active dens for the sake of a photograph? What about "baiting"—that is, coaxing animals with food or other offerings?

Hunter and Rabinowitz are very aware of the role photography and other media play in their conservation work. Rabinowitz draws two hard lines immediately; both have to do with integrity of process and honesty of representation:

> Some well-known photographers will do anything without thinking about the consequences or the morality—and with no larger, meaningful reason. . . . I once saw a photographer trying to get photographs of a flying lizard. He had captured a whole bunch of them, and was flinging them off trees. Of course, a lot were dropping to the ground and dying until he got that photograph of one flying. . . . There is no gray area here. No excuse for this kind of behavior. Nor is there any excuse for representing a photograph of an animal taken in captivity as having been made in the wild. And I have seen this kind of dishonesty a lot.

The second ethical mandate in both journalism and scientific research is *full disclosure*—without which accomplishments in both fields can have no credibility. Hunter:

> From the scientific standard, you declare everything you did and everything that happened. . . . For example, if you do long-term projects where you are sedating and collaring animals (as Craig Packer has of lions, and we have of leopards and snow leopards) some animals may die as a result of your intervention. It may be a very small percentage, but we feel we should disclose that: here are the reasons why an animal died under sedation. We're very careful, but everyone has to understand, with an intervention like that, there is a risk.

Rabinowitz:

> But it should be disclosed, and this is an issue. The whole premise of good science is to disclose everything, so that somebody can reproduce exactly what you did to get the same results. And also, so we don't keep on reinventing the wheel.

I heard similar sentiments from William (Bill) Allen, who served as *National Geographic*'s editor-in-chief from 1995 through 2004: "Disclose," Allen states unhesitatingly. "One must never mislead a reader in any way." Allen has an interesting take on camera traps: "In some ways, camera traps are the paparazzi of wildlife photography. And some people might smile and argue that photos taken at public banquets are similar to photographing 'baited' subjects."

Baiting comes into play with legal nonsubsistence and trophy hunting, as well as with subsistence hunting—why should photographers and scientists avoid a strategy that is clearly so effective? Luke Hunter points out that regularly baiting animals risks making them dependent on humans for their food, or at the very least, can make them more acclimated to human intervention, and therefore more vulnerable to people who want to kill them. Furthermore, baiting can cause bad relations with human communities near an animal's habitat—if a big cat is lured out of hiding by a researcher (or photographer), it may lead other cats to begin relying on humans to provide for them, which in turn may result in domestic cows and goats being killed by the wild animals. "I'm not saying that baiting will fundamentally change behavior," Hunter continues. "In most cases, I think if you're careful, it probably won't. But it is an issue."

And Rabinowitz cautions: "I think if you bait regularly, you *can* actually change an animal's behavior, and . . . this is a problem. If it's a one-off thing, I think differently about that. It depends upon the larger goal."

Rabinowitz and Hunter, like all the scientists I've spoken with, constantly ask themselves whether what they stand to achieve with their work in the field is worth the potential negative impact on the animals and their habitat. And they want photographers to ask themselves the same questions. Rabinowitz acknowledges that sometimes intrusion is worth its impact:

> There is flexibility, even with putting cameras in a den and trying to get a photograph, if you're doing it for the right reasons and there will be no injury to the animals. If you believe that getting a photograph of a mother and cubs which has never been seen before will really move people, and it's going to be used in a larger campaign that will help save snow leopards, okay. . . .
>
> Anything we can do which is done for the right reasons, and which we think we can use to leverage more money for their protection, more protected habitat, more emotion, or more changes in the local villages—for that, I'm willing to cross more of a line.
>
> But I would not be willing to put a camera in a den *just* to get a picture of a baby so that they can have another *ooh-aah* picture for the cover of *National Geographic*, and that's it. That, to me, is morally wrong. There must be a larger goal.

When I spoke with Rabinowitz and Hunter, it was more than a year and a half before National Geographic Society's September 2015 announcement that it had in effect sold its flagship magazine, among other assets, to 21st Century Fox. At the time of our conversation, in February 2014, both scientists were clear about their respect for National Geographic, while still wishing its commitment to conservation was more aggressive. As Rabinowitz put it:

> The world is a better place for having a magazine like *National Geographic*, whether it gives a conservation message or not. But the fact is that they *say* it's part of their mission to do conservation. They could have a huge impact, and should do more.

What exactly is the National Geographic Society's mission in the twenty-first century? The magazine, which for so long was suffused with a white man's "noble savage" exoticism, has clearly evolved, but into what? Why and for whom does National Geographic exist?

I posed this question of mission to Gary Knell about nine months after he became NGS's president and CEO in January 2014. Knell feels that the roles of the magazine and of National Geographic Society's many ancillary programs are less about lobbying for conservation and more about providing tools, and solid evidence, for others to do so:

Illumination is the word that I would use: that is the role of a journalist or a photographer, and to put some context into things that are happening around us. I think it is National Geographic's role to photograph the wildlife-trafficking trade, or the ocean coral-reef deterioration, or some pristine sea that is working as a park in the ocean—that's what we do here. I think it is someone else's job to really lobby and advocate. . . .

We did reboot the organization into this "Inspire, illuminate, and teach" . . . platform since I've been here . . . because the place was too siloed, and not connected. "Inspire, illuminate, and teach" is the role of National Geographic, and obviously people will do with it what they can. We hope that people are inspired by Nick's work, for example . . . enough to go *do* something about it. We're not just throwing stuff out there as something pretty to look at—it's not Muzak.

I asked two editors-in-chief of the magazine, Bill Allen and Chris Johns, for their views regarding *National Geographic*'s mission. Allen said that during his decade as editor-in-chief (starting in 1995):

We felt that our role was to bring aspects of the world to our readers that presented information beyond the ordinary aspects of a place or a subject. . . . We also tried to go beyond headlines; to look, for example, at the subject of global climate change by examining the evidence *on the*

ABOVE: *National Geographic,* December 1997: "Making Room for Wild Tigers"; OPPOSITE: Nick's notes for *National Geographic* captions, India, April 16, 1996

ground—the actual movement of species adapting to changes. This was a straight presentation of what was going on across the globe. The evidence leads to the inescapable conclusion that global climate change is real, and the nonpolitical creatures that inhabit the planet are indeed being affected. That is presenting evidence to all, without any political agenda.

Chris Johns started out as a newspaper photographer, and later turned to wildlife as his subject. He published many stories in *National Geographic* before taking over as the magazine's editor-in-chief in 2005. In April 2014 he left his position at the magazine and became chief content officer of the National Geographic Society. When Johns and I spoke—in April 2012 at the NGS offices in Washington, DC, and then again in February 2014—it was clear that he'd given *National Geographic* magazine's purpose a great deal of thought:

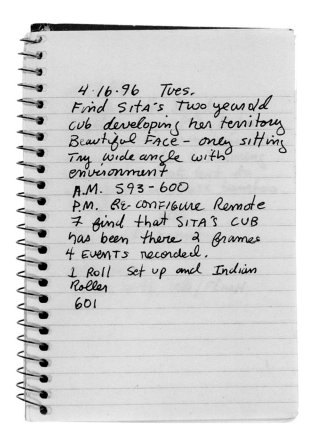

> To me, the tenets of journalism are: Do your very best to get at the truth. Although there are people who maybe won't believe what you believe is the truth. But it's to *convince* them. It's to be a messenger of thoughtfulness—really get people to stop and think. . . . I want *National Geographic* to be . . . the bridge-builder for all different kinds of people. If it's known as an "advocacy, conservation magazine" . . . I'm going to lose some readers. I like being in a big tent. I want to be the convener where people can come to elevate debates, and not be screaming at each other.

Like Gary Knell and Bill Allen, Johns believes that *National Geographic*'s most crucial role is in providing concrete evidence of what is taking place on the planet—evidence that may inspire action and serve as an instrument in efforts toward positive change. An editorial stance with a strictly conservation-oriented agenda will, Johns believes, polarize readers, and even alienate some of them. Alternatively, he insists:

> The magazine is very careful to use solid, *solid* science. It doesn't mean we're not going to go into areas that are political or controversial. Quite the contrary—we will. But we'll do it not through an advocacy role, but by saying: "Here's what's going on. Here are the facts." Advocacy is not part of the mission. But telling truths, exposing lies, is.

I believe in the power of a thoughtful voice. I also believe, though, there are a lot of neglected voices. . . . I believe in giving voice to thoughtful people with power, and giving voice to thoughtful people who have been disenfranchised . . . and I believe in giving voice to a landscape, or a male lion who is trying to keep his pride intact.

Beginning with his and Tim Cahill's notion of a "conspiracy of caring," Nick early on understood that the more emotionally gripping the image, the more convincingly it speaks for its subject and engages the viewer. He knows that the Bengal tigers, as seen through riveting storytelling, will be the best possible advocates for themselves, and for all wild tigers.

In November 1996, after the rains had come and gone, Nick and the team reconvened in India for the next shoot. He was looking forward to seeing Sita's cubs: they would be about eight months old by now, and perhaps more accessible. Nanda Rana and the mahouts, who had begun tracking her again once the roads were passable, knew that Sita was now situated much lower down the mountain. Nick and the team were on elephants looking for her, when all of a sudden, they heard squeaking, which gave them pause. Cubs? Phool Singh said: "They only squeak like that when they're really young and tiny." And then, a sighting of something they hadn't expected: "Little fluff balls!" exclaims Nick. "Sita had *new* cubs."

The previous litter had been killed, most likely by Charger, who ultimately would not tolerate a rival's offspring. This new litter was Charger's own, so Sita, while still very protective, did not fear him as she had before—and in fact allowed him to visit, if he kept his distance. Nick and the team watched her from their perches on the elephants for a very long time. Nick hardly dared hope that this was the moment he had been waiting for. He was also committed to not harassing her, to not being aggressive:

She was very relaxed. . . . At some point that day, we could sense that she was going to move. I don't know if I'm in the right position, but I'm not going to move the elephant and in any way disturb Sita. And then, one by one, she got her little babies and moved them to another hole in another rock, crossing our path!

Nick's photograph of that moment shows a resolute Sita carrying an utterly submissive cub in her mouth. The tigress's exquisite markings highlight her golden eyes as she gingerly transports the tiny animal, paws dangling, face barely discernible amid the mesh of stripes and whiskers. Sita dazzles, calm, graceful—the iconic wild tigress. And with this image, we can see very clearly that this dynamic, this pure wildness, is elemental to the perpetuation of the species.

Nick remains convinced that Sita was fully in charge of this photograph, and all others made of—or avoided by—her. He notes, with deep admiration:

So who *never, ever* appeared in a camera-trap photo? Sita! She would come up to that invisible beam near the watering hole—hah, "invisible!"—and walk around it. We could identify her tracks: she'd stop right in front of the beam, and then go around it. . . . *Not one photograph* of her in there. She was Sita. She was transcendent.

Destruction at the hand of man is not reserved for apes, or elephants, or rhinos: the mighty predators are at risk, too. The scourge of poaching is only getting worse, as prices on the black market for tiger parts keep going up—especially as tigers get rarer (because of the poaching). John Goodrich, senior director of Panthera's tiger program, told me in 2016 that "tigers are easy to trap, snare, and poison for anyone who knows just a little about interpreting the signs tigers leave behind."

The International Union for Conservation of Nature's "Red List of Threatened Species" evaluates the global conservation status of at-risk mammals. By the end of 2016 there were about 3,900 wild tigers left in the world. China and Southeast Asia are the chief culprits in the black market, with "traditional Chinese medicine the primary black market driver." As Goodrich explains: "The biggest market is for traditional Chinese medicine, in China and Vietnam. However, there is no proven efficacy—absolutely *none*—to the medicinal use of tiger parts." "China banned the use of tiger bone in 1993 and removed it from the list of approved medicines," Sharon Guynup reminds us in her 2014 National Geographic blog post, but the "manufacture and sale of tiger bone wine never stopped."[6]

At the same time, ascribing scientifically unsubstantiated magical healing powers to tiger parts undermines the very real benefits that may be achieved through traditional Chinese medicine as practiced by skilled individuals.

Although not drawing as large a market as traditional Chinese medicine, "trophies are also a big thing as a sign of status and there is evidence to suggest markets for trophies in Russia, Japan, and Indonesia," says Goodrich. He acknowledges that, in certain controlled and legal circumstances, "trophy hunting may be a useful conservation tool when it generates funds and local support for conservation." However:

> Like some wealthy Chinese, some wealthy Russians are now looking for tiger skins to hang on their wall. As economies improve and the upper class increases, so does the demand for trophies. The U.S. is also a market for trophies of wild animals, though I am not aware of data pointing to the U.S. market for trophies currently pressuring wild tiger populations. There are other species though, especially lions and leopards in Africa, and wild sheep and goats in Asia, that U.S. trophy hunters prize—potentially contributing to the decline of certain species and the predators (for example snow leopards) that depend on them.

How do we get the traditional Chinese medicine practitioners utilizing tiger parts, or the wealthy elite worldwide that displays its riches at the expense of other animals, to reconsider? How do we get them to understand that the poaching their practices and desires set into motion has so many other lethal implications beyond the murder of animals? As Goodrich says:

> Yes, this is a poaching issue, but the illegal wildlife trade is an international problem tied to other illegal markets, such as human trafficking; it's tied to terrorism; it's tied to drugs and arms trafficking. It's not just somebody *else*'s problem.

If people stop valuing big cats and other endangered species for their skins, tusks, horns, penises, and so on, the poaching will end. How do we somehow convince those who create the grisly demand to instead become part of the solution?

FOLLOWING SPREAD: Sita and cub, Bandhavgarh National Park, 1996

THE LAST PLACE ON

J. Michael Fay on the Megatransect,
Minkébé Forest, Gabon, 2000

EARTH

on't come."

That was the gist of the response from every scientist Nick initially reached out to—in Gabon, Cameroon, and the Central African Republic (CAR), among other West and Central African countries—inquiring about photographing wild western lowland gorillas.

Because they are persistently hunted—this is the species most often captured for zoos, or killed for bushmeat (hence the large orphan population)—these gorillas were skittish and not at all habituated. The scientists trying to study them didn't want Nick to waste his time or theirs. There was no way he would be able to photograph the lowland gorillas: he'd just end up getting in the way of their efforts to habituate and study these elusive creatures, so different from the mountain gorillas of the Virungas.

This was a bit too reminiscent of Dian Fossey's rebuff, and it had pretty much the same effect: Nick was now more determined than ever to pursue the challenge. Lowland gorillas had been imaged only rarely, but he knew he had to include them as part of his work for his forthcoming *National Geographic* story "A Curious Kinship: Apes and Humans" (March 1992).

Vexed, he turned to his editor at *National Geographic*, Mary Smith. Nick remembers her saying without hesitation: "There's only one man. There's this wild man who is as tough as nails. . . . If anybody can show you lowland gorillas, it's going to be him."

Enter Mike Fay.

Bespectacled, wavy-haired, intense, fanatical, verbally unsparing, sharp-tempered, yet infinitely full of wonder, ecologist-conservationist-botanist J. Michael Fay would become one of the most significant figures in Nick's life. And Fay—the man Nick now refers to as his "brother from another mother"—was indeed an expert in the subject; his PhD research had been on western lowland gorillas, after a life-altering tour of duty as a Peace Corps volunteer based in the CAR.

Rampant logging is one of many incursions into the previously lush and fertile central African forests that have made this species especially vulnerable to hunters. Their consequent fear of humans, from whom they seek protection in the remaining thick forests, has made them extremely difficult to observe with any consistency. To learn about them without being intrusive, Fay had devised a strategy of trailing the gorillas inconspicuously, at a polite five-minutes' distance, as they moved through the forest, collecting data from their nests, their scat, and anything else in their wake. He enlisted the help of an exceptional tracker named Mbutu Clement, part of the local Bambendjellé community. Nick recalls Fay describing Clement as his "forest guru"; he would eventually accompany both of them on several treks.

In 1990 Nick traveled to the CAR, where he first met Fay and Clement in the village of Bayanga, in the country's southwestern Dzanga-Sangha region. This was pretty much the end of the road in the

Mike Fay, Sangha River, Central African Republic, 1990

CAR, and the point of departure for Fay's camp, reached by boat, down the Sangha River. From there they traveled together into the forests of Dzanga-Sangha.

Fay has described that initial team-up with Nick in the opus they coauthored many years later, *The Last Place on Earth*.[1] It seems that even though Fay had figured out how to be in the gorillas' vicinity—they no longer tended to run from him—challenges persisted. He likens making contact with the wild western lowland gorillas to "going into combat, because the silverbacks there were bad-asses. . . . They would sometimes come freight-training right up to just a meter away, stopping with a strut, slapping the ground, pinning you down with their eyes and their size."

Nick was apparently undaunted, and that impressed Fay, who writes:

> I focused on Nick, he on gorillas. . . . For him, this was not about getting a photograph he had to get. This was a lifelong dream, and here he was living it. There was a clear and direct connection between him and the animal through the camera. . . . When he finally re-emerged from his trance, I noticed for the first time that Nick is kind of cockeyed from having an eyepiece stuck to his face for the better part of his life. He was beat up, he had a ripped knee, nostrils full of sweat bees, and a neck full of itchy forest detritus, but he was the happiest man on the planet.[2]

Nick, too, recognized a kindred spirit in Fay. "We immediately were *simpatico*," he says, noting that Fay was already a furious activist for wildlife. While in the Peace Corps, Fay had formed a friendship with Richard Ruggiero, who is (as of this writing) Chief of the Division of International Conservation for the U.S. Fish and Wildlife Service. Ruggiero has collaborated with Fay over the years on various projects—including a major conservation effort on behalf of the dwindling population of African elephants. Ruggiero's understanding of Fay is based on a lifetime of parallel obsessions, and on the fact that they shared a mentor in the form of a onetime-professional-game-hunter-turned-conservationist named Jean Laboureur.

I spoke with Ruggiero in Washington, DC, where he described working alongside Fay as Peace Corps volunteers in the CAR:

> There we were, in the early '80s, in what was one of the most magnificent national parks in Africa at the time [the Manovo-Gounda St. Floris National Park, near the Chad border] and which has now been completely destroyed and turned into a rebel stronghold in the northern Central African Republic.
>
> In the midst of ongoing civil war and fighting, we watched the complete destruction of nature happening right in front of us: from hundreds of rhinos to zero, and from ten thousand elephants to fifteen, or whatever was left there. We watched this spectacular, wanton destruction of nature, which twisted us into being the misanthropic, depressed, angry, militant, resolute, intractable pains in the ass that we've become (and that's on a good day). . . .
>
> So we're trying to figure this out, and Jean Laboureur comes along. He set up this whole park. He created it. . . . He was in his late sixties, and he was on this political mission because the park was going badly . . . so he came through and spent a week with Mike in the southern part of the park and a week with me in the northern part of the park, and we showed him the

Western lowland gorilla, Central African Republic, 1990

carcasses and the poaching. . . . Talk about extreme manifestations of suffering . . . he started his life in a concentration camp and then wound up watching Africa be destroyed. . . . Mike and I learned a lot from him at a very critical time in our professional development. We were so inspired by his greatness, and his vision, and his personality.

"When I meet Mike," says Nick, "he's deep into elephants—he's just trying to save everything." Fay was the conservation director for the World Wildlife Fund in the CAR; he would also begin a long affiliation with the Wildlife Conservation Society (WCS) in 1991. As Nick embarked on the next stages of his photographic life, this brilliant and maddening maverick was precisely the person he needed to know.

If Nick's collaboration with Tim Cahill was about seducing the reader into caring, his partnership with Fay—equally gonzo—took this to the point of consummation, inspiring the reader to act. Fay, for his part, immediately recognized how integral Nick's photographs could be to his conservation intentions. Nick says he thinks Fay was "totally attracted to my *anything's-possible-with-photography*. And also my ethics. He was used to photographers coming in and trying to manipulate the situation rather than just trying to *see* it—which takes time and patience. I'm quite willing to lay siege and not get a picture forever."

I first met Mike Fay in 2001, when I went to Washington, DC, to interview him for *Aperture* magazine.[3] Memorably, it was a chilly sunrise in December, in Rock Creek Park—tent-side. He was living in his pup tent while methodically exploring and collecting data in the park. (Fay cannot bear to sleep indoors.) As an interviewee—as in life—he is uncompromisingly in-the-present, and not particularly interested in thinking retrospectively. But in one of our later conversations, in 2012, he articulated his rapport with Nick:

> He's my best friend. . . . There are . . . other things too that are just kind of operational . . . when you're together and you're working. . . . We're basically on two different tracks, but those two tracks are combined in a way that serves both ends, and from that point of view, Nick has always contributed more than I have, to not just the relationship, but to the actual work. . . . He's kind of the maestro of the presentation, the melding of the team. . . . Nick is very organized. He's cutting-edge. He maintains human relationships in a much more thoughtful way than I do. And he has a lot of power because of that . . . his presence is power. . . . Nick applies that kind of personal energy to what we do together.

Likewise, in Fay—more at home in the wild than anywhere else—Nick found an ideal partner. Here was a visionary with whom the photographer could confidently position himself on the cusp between discovery and wonder, testimony and advocacy. Fay is ecologically prescient, and a warrior for his convictions. Their personality differences would serve them. Nick "right away understood that Mike's ego is huge like mine, but it's different. I'm a populist. And I want people to like me. He doesn't care. He just wants to make political change, for the sake of the planet."

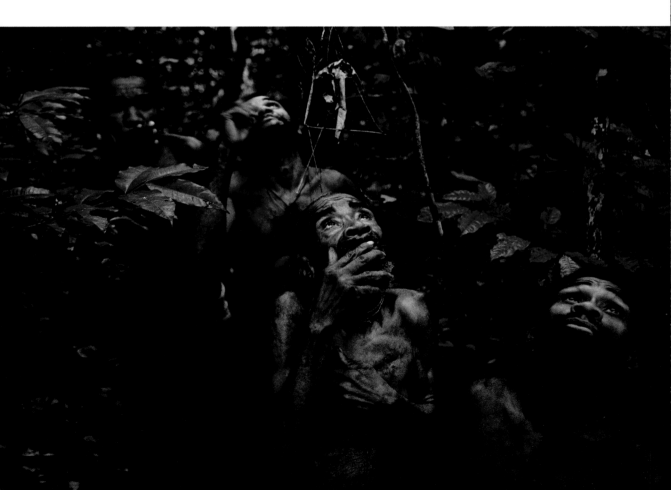

Photographer Brent Stirton has worked with both Nick and Fay, and is concerned with many of the same issues of conservation that obsess them. About the two men, Stirton muses: "At the heart of it, you're talking about two fundamentalists":

> Nick is certainly more flexible than Mike, and a much easier person to deal with—at least that is my experience—but he's as much a fundamentalist. And like Mike, he wants what he wants. They are both disciplined, and they both believe very strongly in conservation, and they are both pioneers. Nick understands the power of personality, the power of inclusion, the power of strategic alliance. He gets all that, and he casts it in a good ol' boy accent—which is bullshit, because Nick is so sharp. But it comes in a beautiful package.
>
> Mike has no package, no filter. He's a fundamentalist in the bush. . . .
>
> We must remain sensitive to the fact that various cultures operate from their own perspective, but that doesn't mean we should shy away from the facts. Respect for cultural values cannot supersede the fact that we are in a serious race for time when it comes to the threat of extinction. The local people are also not ignorant, and our job as journalists is to communicate not only to the audience through our publications, but also to communicate with people we're dealing with on the ground while making the story.
>
> There is often a degree of political correctness to public thinking that simply is naïve, and both Nick and Mike understand that. We don't have a lot of choices. What we're really trying to do—all of us concerned with conservation whether working as journalists or scientists or community organizers . . . is to keep things alive for a more enlightened time, and that's a leadership issue. Nick understands that. Mike understands that.

Despite their differences and quarrels, Nick and Fay are bound by their mutual respect and their unbridled passion for the wild—one that established its deep roots in the last place on Earth.

Nouabalé-Ndoki, in the northern part of the Republic of Congo, was, Mike Fay has written, "the kind of place that I had dreamed about my whole life: a huge wilderness beyond the reach of man."[4] By the late 1980s, Fay had pored over endless topographic maps of Nouabalé-Ndoki. They showed no signs of man: no villages, no roads. He was determined to decipher this enigmatic wilderness.

At that time, to venture to Ndoki ("sorcerer" in the Bantu language, Lingala) required flying first to Brazzaville, from there to Ouésso, and traveling seven hours upriver in a pirogue to the town of Bomassa, at the convergence point of Congo, the CAR, and Cameroon. Nouabalé-Ndoki is east of Bomassa, and naturally isolated by nearly impenetrable swamps. The lack of easy access was the area's best defense—thwarting what would otherwise have been a thriving bushmeat trade.

Fay first revealed the fact of Nouabalé-Ndoki—with its remarkably opulent and diverse, naturally protected population of animals and plants, and its intact ecosystem—to Nick and journalist Eugene Linden around 1990. At the time they were working on "A Curious Kinship: Apes and Humans" for *National Geographic*. Linden recalls being very interested in the Ndoki story, but wary

Bambendjellé men, Makao, Republic of Congo, 1994

of how such attention would affect this untouched place. "At first I didn't want to go," he tells me. "I felt—leave it alone. Nothing good is going to happen if Ndoki is featured on the cover of *Time* or whatever."

In fact, many conservationists—especially those devoted to chimpanzees—were virulently opposed to any intervention in Ndoki. It was such a rarefied situation. If indeed there existed, as was envisioned, populations of "naïve" chimpanzees—chimps who had never seen a human being—then perhaps they should never *have* to see one. Fay, however, was focused on his larger goal of permanently protecting the forest, and felt that it was only a matter of time before Ndoki was "discovered." Having previously witnessed avarice-driven assaults on forests and their inhabitants and natural resources, he could picture the inevitable pileup of slaughtered animals once the area was denuded, and access was less encumbered. The animals of Ndoki would not fear humans, never having been hunted by them. This lack of exposure to man would increase their vulnerability exponentially, if the paths to their habitat were invitingly cleared by loggers. Another likely consequence would be that human populations in the area would grow considerably, as hunters for bushmeat arrived and markets flourished. Any hope even for balance, let alone true protection, would be forever undermined.

Fay knew that the only way to save Ndoki was to be ahead of the curve, and to raise its profile by bringing attention to it. If the land was not transformed into a national park, and in this way at least somewhat protected, the forest would be eviscerated and destroyed. By October 1992, Fay had begun corresponding with Nick and his editor (and their matchmaker), Mary Smith, at *National Geographic* about arrangements for an initial Ndoki story. This dialogue ignited a collaborative investigation into this region that would continue for more than a decade. Fay was working with WCS in Brazzaville, and the *National Geographic* team could rely on WCS's infrastructure and the Bomassa base camp as a support system, when necessary, during the expedition.

William Graves, editor-in-chief of *National Geographic* from 1990 to 1994, did not initially approve the story on Ndoki, despite urgent arguments from Nick and Smith. In the meantime, the writer Linden had changed his mind about the coverage "because loggers were encroaching from the South, and it seemed that the only way to protect the place was to bring it to the world's attention." He went into Ndoki with Mike Fay, and wrote a cover story about it for *Time* magazine in 1992.[5] It was a powerful piece, and it would play an important role in the ultimate protection of Ndoki, but Nick felt that there was still significant work to be done visually in this forest. Mary Smith agreed, and finally managed to get Graves's okay.

In early 1993, Fay confirmed Nick's suggested team for their first Ndoki project together— Neeld Messler (of the Lechuguilla Cave story) and twenty-three-year-old Bryan Harvey (son of David Alan Harvey and brother of Erin Harvey, the videographer who would later film Charger, the wild tiger, bathing in India). Energetic, sandy-haired, with the sure-footed grace of the surfer he is, Bryan Harvey was an excellent addition to the group: a pilot who could double as a videographer. The team would make three eight- to fifteen-week expeditions. Montana wildlife biologist Douglas H. Chadwick was the writer assigned to the story. He would join them for three weeks on the initial trip.

Other details in the Nichols and Fay correspondence include discussions of schedule, the need for night goggles, and how they might assist Andrea Turkalo (Fay's wife at the time) with her ongoing work with forest elephants at the Dzanga Bai in the Dzanga-Ndoki National Park. Fay was particularly focused on the Dzanga *saline* (forest clearing). Nick wrote to him on January 23, 1993, about this popular gathering spot for elephants:

> I want to go there 1st for selfish reasons: all of this equipment and techniques I want to try are ideas that are not field tested. . . . The *saline* gives us that opportunity without taking such high physical and emotional losses if it doesn't work out. . . . I'm not thinking so much of photos of elephants using the *saline* but of elephants on the forest trails getting there. This is how we could test the remotes and tree platforms for viability. The high traffic makes our time well used. . . .

> I must admit the animal photos from the Ndoki intimidate me because we will be pioneers—I much prefer scientists putting in the years of groundwork to make my job as an artist possible. I do hope that I give as much as I take. . . .

> My experience warns me that this is going to be very tough and I do not want to put the indigenous people into a slot that I will have trouble with because of exhaustion. . . . I would like to make discoveries with you but it is very risky photographically. I need to lay siege on areas that you know are fruitful.

"My job as an artist" is a telling phrase. As much as Nick was and remains unequivocally committed to conservation, and is eager for his images and himself to be co-opted as tools for advocacy, ultimately he privileges the photograph. Bryan Harvey says respectfully of him: "He can be a bitch to work with sometimes because he's so focused on getting cool, unique, and impossible pictures. In the field, he's intense, and he wants what he wants."

The priority that Nick gives to a great photograph has provoked acute tension between him and Fay; this is clear in any discussion with either of them. Fay sometimes gets apoplectic with disbelief at Nick's favoring of his art. Fay cannot tolerate what he perceives as any deviation from the conservation imperative. "Conservation is hard," Fay says. "It's really difficult. So stopping at photography and saying, 'Well, it will have an impact but it's really about the *photography*' is not the way I could ever think." But he understands that Nick and his photography are inextricable from one another:

> Nick is an artist, and he is a genius at photography . . . when he wakes up in the morning, he doesn't think about conservation; he thinks about photography. . . . Every moment of every day is focused on these images. . . . It's all about becoming part of that landscape, and just having this relationship with whatever it is.

One could say that their approaches are not so different. Just as Fay gathers data, Nick collects and processes information by embedding and observing over long stretches of time. Fay brokers his data into direct relief for the situation. Nick brokers his images to far-reaching mass media—sharing potentially resonant messages to large numbers of potentially active recipients. Fay builds on his data, forming hypotheses, leading to results. Nick builds on his images to tell a nuanced and affecting story. In the end, Fay's achievements, and the reasons he has given his life over to the protection of vulnerable creatures and their habitats, are made palpable to large numbers of us through Nick's photographs, which help persuade readers and viewers that what Fay is doing matters. The message is clear: Attention must be paid. Action must be taken. Fay gets it strategically, even if he may not always appreciate it personally.

But Nick is not, has never been, interested in simply illustrating the science. And his populist inclinations—his belief that minds and hearts can be changed through awe and empathy—deter him from focusing only on humanity's violations of the natural world. Nick believes he must sometimes glorify what remains inviolate to express why we have to devote our resources toward its survival. And to keep people engaged, there must be storytelling—whether disquieting or radiant, tragic or ecstatic—always riveting. And it is about voice: first, the richness and clarity of his own, with which he can then convincingly give voice to his subjects.

While their personalities differ, many who have worked with both Nick and Fay find their similarities more striking. Kent Kobersteen was *National Geographic*'s associate director of photography at the time of the Ndoki story and went on to become the magazine's director of photography. His take

on the two men: "Nick and Mike both have blinders on, they are both obsessive, they both are get-the-hell-out-of-my-way-and-let-me-do-my-job. You put two people like that together and you end up with a story that's off the charts. . . . On the other hand, it is not without its conflicts, *because* they are both the same kind of people."

Ultimately, as Nick says, "our dance works. Mike's instincts are great. He always knows where there is the potential to see something. But he also is not going to sit in a tree for twenty days observing—and I'm the guy who will."

Pristine and extravagant, Ndoki erupts with wildlife: forest elephants, leopards, lowland gorillas, chimpanzees, parrots, bats, shrikes, and much more. But the challenges to photographing there are daunting—aesthetically, technically, and physically. It was during his initial 1993 expedition that Nick first began using camera traps and combining them with flash (this project preceded his work with wild tigers—Sita and Charger—by several years). In Ndoki the approach yielded only a single photograph Nick values—of a leopard, one of the most elusive creatures, and one that Nick felt was key to his story. "You can be looking directly at a leopard," says Nick, "and never see it. Your only chance is if something twitches."

In his eagerness to get this photograph, however, Nick committed an ethical breach that gnaws at him to this day. He had been told by Michel Courtois—a French hunter who, at the time, had been living there for more than twenty years, flagging mahogany for cutting—that the only way to entice a leopard was to use a dog as bait. The proposed method was horrific. Nick recalls: "What you had to do was take a dog out into the forest, put chili powder up his butt, tie him to a tree, and he'll squeal like crazy. Michel said that 'the leopard will come to kill the dog and then you can shoot the leopard.'" Needless to say, this is not a strategy that Nick would ever use. In the end, Nick decided on a marginally more humane solution: they got a dog from the closest village—some eighteen miles away—and built a small cage for it, to be lodged in the cavity at the base of a tree. The dog would be protected by the cage, but it would bark, and the noise would attract the leopard. They did not use chili powder.

The dog they were given by the villagers was, it turned out, missing one leg and had just had a litter of puppies. "It was a little bit cruel," admits Nick, "but not *insanely* cruel." Nonetheless, once the dog was in the cage and they had gone back to basecamp for the night, Nick and Messler were restless. They were not at all comfortable with what they'd done, and agreed that they'd go retrieve the dog in the morning. When they returned for her, however, she was gone. No sign of violence; nothing on the camera trap—but somehow the dog had escaped. Nick chuckles: "We return to the village and they say: 'Oh, she's back. She came home this morning.' She'd walked all those miles on the trail—that three-legged mom just wanted to nurse her pups!"

Things went no better with the next option offered by the villagers: a baby goat, which got out through a small hole in the cage and was sitting placidly beside it when they came for her in the morning. At this point, says Nick: "Neeld and I are: 'Okay—done. No more! Strike it up to really bad judgment.' Tell the story, be ashamed of what I tried, but learn from it." In the end, the enticement

Leopard (camera-trap photograph), Nouabalé-Ndoki National Park, Republic of Congo, 1993

that worked was male leopard urine, sent from the Henry Doorly Zoo in Omaha. "We put it on the trail, and that's what attracted the leopard. That's how I got the photograph."

Against the deep greens and browns of the tangled jungle backdrop, a luminous stalking leopard moves out of the frame, one eye still visible, staring intensely and directly at the camera.

Nick did own and learn from the experience: "I knew I had to do and be better, but it took a while. Now, other than making or using animal sounds to call an animal—I use natural, pre-existing bait. Water is great. And salt—like in the *saline*."

Ndoki's visual complexities could be overwhelming. If photographing the Virunga mountain gorillas against the inkiness of their habitat had allowed only minimal definition, Ndoki's enervating jungle, relentlessly humid, dense with organisms that live off the bodily fluids of others, took this challenge to a darker dimension.

"Reap the whirlwind," Bryan Harvey prophetically scribbled at age twenty-three, in an early entry in his own Ndoki journals. When we spoke more recently, he elaborated:

> Mike was like some kind of crazy general, marching across the forest. . . . Nick was trying to take pictures; Mike's on a completely different mission. Nick had to hunker down, make peace with the forest, and figure out how to photograph the gorillas and the chimps and everything, and meanwhile Mike was trying to march us to some latitude/longitude point in the middle of the forest. . . . Doug Chadwick, the writer, was really having a hard time. He had an allergy to bees and we'd get stung by bees all of the time. He had already used two of the three EpiPens *National Geographic* had given us, and he was worried about getting stung by another bee.

Although Chadwick was a committed outdoorsman, nothing in his past life had prepared him for the "claustrophobic hothouse" he encountered in Ndoki. (He confessed to me at one point that his experience in Ndoki was also colored by that fact that he was, as he put it, "stoned out of my mind on Larium"—an antimalaria drug. Nick so despised Larium's side effects—including tormenting nightmares—that at some point he just stopped taking it, preferring the risk of malaria over the drug.)

Chadwick, in a voice that meanders between panic and wonder, writes evocatively about his experience in the African jungle as like "being passed through the guts of the forest and being slowly digested." Among the many marauders in Ndoki are blood-hungry leeches and hordes of tiny, aggressive, stingless sweat bees, which crave salt and shroud any human's body in a full-on devouring of perspiration, no nook or cranny left unexplored. Bryan Harvey shot some skin-crawling footage— not for the squeamish—of Nick photographing with swarms of these bees obscuring his face and any other exposed skin, while Messler attempts futilely to fan them away.

William (Bill) Allen had become *National Geographic*'s editor-in-chief by the time "Ndoki: Last Place on Earth" was published in July 1995.[6] He marvels at Nick's drive, but recognizes that such purposefulness can have a flipside:

Nick, self-portrait, Goualougo Triangle, Republic of Congo, 2002

I wondered at times just how far Nick could push himself before his body detonated—but I never thought he would quit. As is true of many people with such strong wills that they are able to push themselves beyond what most of us would consider normal or smart, some can have moments of doubt that can cause them to retreat internally, perhaps to undesirable places.

Indeed, Nick has the capacity to shut down, spiraling into a bleak mind frame from a noxious mix of stress, fear of failing, and depression. This debilitating state could be exacerbated by the exhausting physical hurdles he encountered when photographing in extreme places.

Mike Fay is by all accounts both physically and mentally stoic, unflinching. He has little patience when Nick "goes dark." But whatever the challenges of these tropical forests, Nick, like Fay, ultimately feels happiest and most at peace in the wild—or as Nick says they both still call it, "the woods."

Chadwick recalls traveling in a pirogue upstream toward Ndoki to meet Nick and Fay, and finding them "perfectly at home, wearing shorts and sandals and kind of lounging on the riverbank in the middle of nowhere." For Chadwick, though, this river journey, like some previous ones he'd made in the region, conjured up Joseph Conrad's "heart of darkness":

> There's this point where the jungle closes in and there are little shacks alongside the river with gorilla and chimpanzee parts hanging from them for sale—arms and legs and all-too-familiar faces. My relatives, they are up for sale on the riverbank. . . .

ABOVE: Hunter with bushmeat, Motaba River, Republic of Congo, 1999; OPPOSITE: *National Geographic*, October 2000: first installment of Megatransect story

> In Ndoki, you could practically hear everything growing. And half the stuff there wants to devour you. I came away seeing nature in a different way—a lot more honestly. Ndoki replaced a lot of illusions with the reality of our being just one more species competing to keep going, to thrive.

As much as this Ndoki journey was about overcoming obstacles, both physical and psychological, it was exhilarating. Nick, with only the slightest hint of uncertainty, invokes Fay's mantra: "The forest is your friend." More difficult to subscribe to is Fay's notion that to cross a swamp you have to "become one with the swamp." A chief reason why this part of central Africa had remained largely untouched until this point is its seemingly impassable swamp areas. No hunter could go that deep into the bush and make it out the same day with his prey. Anything he might kill would rot by the time he had emerged from the forest. When passable, the swamps would require dogged will and time to navigate safely. Swaths of deep bog, animated by creepy-crawlies of all shapes and sizes, summon the cold sweat of childhood nightmares. It is wet, it is dark, and it is unknown. To Nick, "swamp walking requires part of the brain to let go—the bogeyman part."

Bryan Harvey remembers what their feet went through in the murkiness:

> Mike made us all wear these Teva sandals, so our feet got exposed to the air, and could dry out, as they could not in boots. . . . We were walking through all kinds of crazy wet,

sometimes bottomless stuff in the swamps. . . . Nick had really bad foot worms—his feet were all torn up . . . one would get under the surface of your skin, and then travel and die under your skin . . . and it would itch like crazy. But then there was this other worm that would get between your nails and your toes, and just start to grow. They were super, super painful. The [Bambendjellé] Pygmies knew how to dig those things out of your feet with a little splinter they'd make. That was a big part of the misery.

The most critical thing for the team was, in fact, self-maintenance. They needed to bathe to avoid skin rot, take care of their teeth, and wash their clothes. Wherever they camped, Nick, once finished with his evening ablutions, would log in his film from the day, write general captions for what he was seeing, maybe read some of a mystery novel he'd brought with him, and then go to sleep.

The thrilling essence of this time in Ndoki was that it crystalized for Nick his first true apprehension of pure *wild*. His central goal was to document *first contact* with the "naïve" chimpanzees of the area. He knew that if he could capture the wonder of that encounter, it would be a photograph that would, in his *Big Lebowski*–inspired parlance, "tie the room together."

En route to Likouala swamp—about halfway there—they stopped at a Goualougo clearing to make their camp. As they began to set up, they heard what Chadwick describes as piercing screams, and immediately headed in their direction. "Nearing the source, Mike signaled for us to crouch motionless."

BY DAVID QUAMMEN

PHOTOGRAPHS BY MICHAEL NICHOLS
NATIONAL GEOGRAPHIC PHOTOGRAPHER

MEGATRANSECT
ACROSS 1,200 MILES OF UNTAMED AFRICA ON FOOT

At 11:22 on the morning of September 20, 1999, J. Michael Fay strode away from a small outpost and into the forest in ▸

Plunging into the wild for science, J. Michael Fay of the Wildlife Conservation Society, at right, leads his survey party of Bambendjellé Pygmies through the Goualougo swamp of central Africa during his yearlong trek across the heart of the continent. His goal: to chronicle the region's still pristine forests. This is the first of three articles about the grueling journey.

Harvey has remarkable footage of Fay—alert, controlled, as naturalized as any nonindigenous creature could possibly be in the jungle—vocalizing what sounds like a shrill cat yowl: "I squeezed my nose," Fay later writes, "closed off my esophagus, pumped up my lungs, and let out two low, guttural bleats: '*Miiiiyaaaooouu, Miiiiyaaaooouu.*'"[7] He was attempting to imitate a bleating baby duiker (a small antelope)—a call that, Mbutu Clement had taught him, interests chimpanzees. Suddenly, his eyes darting about, Fay spotted one and, still calling, pointed the chimps out to Nick as, one by one, at first camouflaged by the foliage, they rushed in, screeching and gesticulating frenetically. And then, just as suddenly, the chimps stopped, apparently dumbfounded. Fay writes:

> They stared intently at these new primates they had discovered. You could see it in their eyes, asking: "What beast *is* this?" . . . It didn't take long for them to break out into a frantic series of pant-hoots. They were calling everybody else in to see this crazy thing they had found.[8]

Nick, of course, had his camera pressed to his eye and was shooting like mad. When we spoke, Chadwick recalled the moment too:

> It was a primate-to-primate meeting. Two tribes. Our group and what sounded like a couple dozen chimps, and I think we just sat and stared at each other and kind of danced around for three or four hours. The chimps would egg each other on, holding onto each other almost—touching each other for reinforcement—except for some of the young ones who would come a little closer.

OPPOSITE: Naïve chimpanzees, Goualougo Triangle, Republic of Congo, 2002; ABOVE: Naïve chimpanzees, Goualougo Triangle, Republic of Congo, 1993

Nick was photographing in this dim jungle light, using flash, trying to focus as he wiped sweat bees out of his eyes, nose, and ears. He has amazing concentration. What he went through for each picture is unimaginable. He was in his element. *Nobody* had done this, photographed this before, and he had the opportunity to show us things that we had never seen.

Nick's photographs convey the mutual awe of this primal interaction, the cheeky curiosity of the chimps, who may not trust these new bare-skinned apes, but certainly don't fear them.

Neeld Messler, lean and athletic, was an invaluable assistant to Nick here, as he had been in the caves. Messler would rig the trees and set up blinds in their crowns; this way, Nick could photograph animals in the *bais* (clearings), especially the aquatic lowland gorillas Fay had discovered at Mbeli Bai, east of Bomassa. From here, Nick made the first-ever images of this species of gorillas who feed in the water—as long as it's not over their head, as they can't swim.

The *bais* are made by forest elephants as they dig for minerals that supplement their diets. In Ndoki, these clearings are very popular congregating places for a range of animals. From the tree platform, during this first foray to Ndoki, Nick photographed them for nineteen days, dawn to

ABOVE: Neeld Messler, Ndoki, Republic of Congo, 1993; OPPOSITE: Bushmeat trade, Sangha River, Republic of Congo, 1994

sunset—equipped with lunch and snacks. Messler, meanwhile, spent his days replenishing their provisions, setting up and adjusting the camera traps, and taking care of everything else. He was so fast and agile, shinnying up trees or running through the forest—sometimes naked—that he became legendary among the locals. Tales circulated of him transforming magically into a duiker.

Fay, Messler, and Nick had all gone feral.

Nick: "You're shit-scared when you first start, but then you just block it out. It's all psychological. This is epic. We're savage—Mike, me, Neeld! We don't care about anything except doing it. Something happens."

As ever, Nick insisted on photographing the larger context of this place along with the wildlife—to render a sense of the people, the terrain, the scale of it all. He spent time with the Bambendjellé and other indigenous people, both in their communities and as part of the Ndoki team. The trek itself would come alive in the images of palpable experiences: the sweat, the physicality of taking a machete to the bush, cutting one's way with every step.

Nick also wanted to address the unchecked poaching taking place in the more accessible parts of the region and driving the ivory trade, as well as the bushmeat trade. Fay showed Nick illegal snaring and indiscriminate killing in Cameroon by local commercial hunters. Nick and Messler returned to this spot—although neither had an entry visa for Cameroon. The Dantesque scene they witnessed will forever remain in Messler's mind's eye. He recalls: "A bush pig was trapped in the snare, totally alive, squealing, trying to pull away. The hunters took their clubs and they beat him to death," after which, all bloodied, they tied the pig to a pole in order to transport him horizontally out of the forest, and then to sell as bushmeat. Messler's voice breaks up: "When the beating started, the pig kept crying. I personally shut down. I think I closed my eyes. Hearing it was the most horrific thing, ever."

Another important aspect of documenting Ndoki, Nick knew, was aerial photography, which could show the jungle's diversity from a perspective that might lend more texture. But it takes a specific kind of aircraft to do this: flying too high would be pointless, and flying low over the forest in a conventional single-engine plane is dangerous. Nick found an engineer named Phil Lockwood who had designed and built single-engine Ultralight airplanes, and who, providentially, was at work inventing a twin-engine Ultralight. With the help of funding from National Geographic, Lockwood designed the plane—the "Aircam"—adapting his concept in such a way that Nick would have an unobstructed view in front of the wing. There was also a rocket-propelled parachute on the top so that if *everything* failed, the whole plane could parachute down into the treetops. The prototype was built at Lockwood's home base in Florida and shipped to Brazzaville in five boxes.

Nick, self-portrait with "Aircam," flying over Mbeli Bai, Republic of Congo, 1994

On the second leg of the Ndoki project, in autumn 1993, Bryan Harvey traveled to the Republic of Congo's capital city to pick up those boxes. He was supposed to be joined there by Lockwood, who would train him to assemble and fly the plane. But the country was aflame with political turmoil; Harvey found himself in the middle of a civil war. He hunkered down in the WCS housing in Brazzaville, as bullets of the Ninja militia flew overhead, combating supporters of the country's recently elected president, Pascal Lissouba. The integrity of the vote in the Republic of Congo's new multiparty elections was being called into question, and the streets were exploding in violence.

Furthermore, the delivery of the Aircam was delayed in South Africa, a problem WCS had to deal with. That the Ndoki project was draining WCS's resources to an unforeseen extent would create serious friction between Nick and Fay.

Finally, during a relative lull, the Aircam boxes were delivered and the plane was assembled in Brazzaville. Lockwood decided that, as Harvey had no training in flying this very particular aircraft, he would fly it himself—with Fay onboard—the six hundred miles to Bomassa, a trip that would take several days. There was only one snag: no airstrip existed in Bomassa. Undaunted, Nick and his team gathered the locals and, with hoes and shovels—they did not have a bulldozer—cleared a runway. A cheering crowd welcomed the plane's landing in Bomassa, all smiles. Progress had come to their village in the form of a new landing strip. Nick dubbed it "Bomassa International."

Fay was pleased about the plane, as flying had become enormously useful to him in collecting data, and *National Geographic* had promised to donate the aircraft to Nouabalé-Ndoki National Park (jointly managed by WCS Congo and the government of Congo) after the story was completed. Unfortunately, as the plane was a prototype, there were glitches, especially with the landing gear, which in the end was too weak. It sustained damage almost immediately, during an especially hard landing in Bomassa, and was temporarily grounded. Further fouling Fay's mood, he received a note from *National Geographic* reneging on the promised donation of the plane. He was enraged.

Nick, meanwhile, was demoralized. They'd been away on the expedition's second leg for more than three months, and had not yet realized the aerials. The only light was that he, Messler, and Harvey were going home for Christmas, while the Aircam was being repaired. Their plan was to catch the once-a-week flight from Ouésso to Brazzaville, and then fly from Brazzaville home through Paris. As the three of them stood on the steamy tarmac in Ouésso, sticky with their own sweat, all they could think about was getting on that plane.

But for Nick and Messler it was not to be. Harvey had renewed his visa when he was in Brazzaville waiting for the Aircam, but Nick's and Messler's had apparently expired—as two gendarmes gruffly informed them before leading them off the tarmac. Harvey boarded the plane and looked out the window: "And I see them put Nick and Neeld in the back of an army-looking jeep and drive away." As Nick tells it, the gendarmes were drunk and vindictive. They were also no friends to Mike Fay—who had implicated their general as having an involvement with the ivory trade—and so by association, they were no friends to Nick and Messler.

The next two days were hell: Nick and Messler were stripped and thrown in jail in Ouésso. Word spread, and Congolese friends and colleagues visited and brought food but could do nothing to free them. When Harvey reached Brazzaville, he immediately got to work with WCS and National Geographic to get them out (further stressing WCS's resources—eventually yet another point of contention with Fay). Finally, the WCS appealed to the U.S. embassy in Brazzaville, and $5,000 later, a small airplane came for Nick and Messler in Ouésso.

And so Nick, Messler, and Harvey were all home over Christmas, and for the first months of 1994. Meanwhile Lockwood, back in Florida, finessed the plane's landing gear. The Aircam remained in Bomassa until Nick and his team eventually returned with the improved landing gear in the spring of 1994 to finish the story.

Fay, by this point, had gone stony cold. Perhaps too many things had gone wrong—maybe it was about the plane, or about what he perceived as Nick's irresponsible behavior and misuse of time and precious resources, or some conflation of everything that had, in his mind, unraveled. He wasn't speaking to Nick; nor would he allow the team to set foot in his camp. But, as Nick says: "I'm just as hardheaded as he is. I'm not giving up." He and Lockwood and the others set themselves up in tents near the Bomassa airstrip, from which they took trips up in the Aircam so Nick could make his aerials. All this without a word from Fay.

In March 1994, before Nick's return to Bomassa, Fay had delivered a coup de grace. He sent a fax to Kent Kobersteen at *National Geographic* that Nick now refers to drolly as "100 Things Nick Did Wrong." Over the course of eight pages, Fay listed fifty-three points—a litany of perceived missteps—involving Nick and his team. Kobersteen, to his great credit, maintained his professional equanimity, and judiciously tried to restore peace. It should be said that Nick concurred with some of Fay's points (the incident with the lapsed visas was one), but others he found ridiculous. Fay excoriated him for episodes that in fact they had either planned together, or that were Fay's own ideas. (Point 46: "damage control" after Nick's and Messler's time in Cameroon, making poaching images—a trip that had happened at Fay's prompting.) Nick was stunned, of course. But today, with the clarifying hindsight of more than twenty years, he resignedly says: "We're going to fall out at the end of every one of our projects. But Mike's amazing, and I love him like a brother. Even when I'm ready to kill him."

While Nick was on this initial Ndoki project, his editor at *National Geographic*, Mary Smith, decided to retire. She assigned Nick to editor Kathy Moran in late 1993. Nick was frankly skeptical: Moran was young and untried. "Baby on board," Moran jokes. But Nick soon learned that her Goldilocks curls and sweet manner belied a strong backbone and a rigorous editorial mind. Moran laughs as she recalls:

> Mary basically gave me all her natural-history stories—it was my big break. Nick's Ndoki, which at that point was still unfinished, was already the most expensive story that the magazine had ever produced. The very first thing we had to do was deal with the budget. . . . Nick didn't know that Bill [Graves] had brought me to the magazine, and he liked me. . . . I had to go ask him for another $60,000. This was at the end of 1993, and that was a monstrous amount of money, on *top* of how much had already been spent. I asked for the money, and we got it. Nick saw I could stand up for him and the story—the work.
>
> Nick and I then began at the beginning. I went through every single roll of film from Ndoki.

Nick found a true ally in Moran—and their collaboration and friendship would only deepen. Moran says that when Mary Smith "handed" her Nick, she in effect bestowed upon her "next to my family, simply the most important relationship of my life. Every time I'm with Nick, I get stretched in every possible way. I learn on multiple levels."

So much time, energy, thought, and money had gone into the Ndoki story. David Griffin was at the time working on design and layout at *National Geographic*. He had observed Nick working with other designers on the Lechuguilla Cave and "New Zoos" stories, and he had a strong feel for how this talented photographer operated, but Ndoki was their first project together. Griffin says: "He was razor-focused and smart as a whip in the layout room, explaining the story and working with editors and designers. Totally articulate, decisive: 'This picture needs to go here,' and 'This has to happen there.'" Griffin smiles. "But then, you'd watch him go all Alabaman and charming" when the moment demanded it, "and doing everything possible to get his way." Griffin initially called him on it, but says that Nick was "super sensitive, and told me I was making him feel badly. It freaked me out at first, because I thought he wasn't going to allow me to be honestly critical with him. But we got there." Griffin came to understand Nick's sensitivity, and says that Nick "had to understand that I'm not mean—just smart-alecky at times—but that I want the same excellence he does."

Although they would eventually bond—Moran and Griffin would later marry—the trio had some false starts before establishing their collaborative rhythm. Inadvertently, Moran and Griffin sent Nick storming out of the office after they burst out laughing in reaction to Nick's divulging something about his masturbatory habits—apparently as an antidote to a caption crisis. It would seem that Nick did not see the humor in his disclosure: Moran, donning her best Alabama drawl (as people do when invoking Nick), shares his dismay at their hysterics: *"Ah am just tryin' to be a human bee-an. Ah'm tryin' to share mah innermost feelin's with you, and you are makin' fun of me, and ah will never tell either one of you anythin' iver agin."*

Moran and Griffin later entreated, "Please don't be mad," and all was forgiven. Meanwhile, Moran is thinking, "Who *is* this guy?" Moran knows Nick well enough now to say: "With Nick, there is never, *ever* any self-censoring, to the point that I've said to him, 'Sometimes I just want to get a speed bump on your tongue!'"

In early August 1994, Moran, Griffin, and Nick presented the final show-and-tell of the Ndoki images and layout to the magazine's new editor-in-chief, Bill Allen.[9] It was a day Moran remembers well. She had celebrated her birthday into the early morning hours, and Nick and David Alan Harvey had had a late night at a Rolling Stones concert at Washington's RFK Stadium. Neither Nick nor Moran was in top form the morning of the presentation. Moran recalls making an aspirin run and, as she returned to the meeting, hearing Nick drawl confidently to Allen: "I think you'll find that the photos speak for themselves." To which Allen rejoined, somewhat coolly: "I think you'll find that I need a little information."

At that, Nick and Moran rallied. After this part of the presentation, they moved on to the main layout room to review design and cover ideas. Griffin had mocked up a particular cover that the "pre-team" had instantly rejected: the photograph was blurry—and *National Geographic* had never put a blurry image on its cover. It was tossed into the trash, but Moran pulled it out and put it on the wall with the other contenders. Minutes later, the executive team walked in, and Bill Allen chose it as the cover. (Years later, Moran would say to her husband: "I've always wondered what *idiot* put that cover mock-up into the garbage." Griffin fessed up: "*This* idiot.")

The cover image is of a forest elephant in Ndoki, just before dawn, braking after a mock-charge, her weight thrusting forward, splashing through the glistening water of a creek. For this image, to compensate for the low film speed of 100 ISO, Nick used flash to provide definition—the foreboding forest, trees faintly delineated in a spectrum of greens from which the elephant emerges, eyes catching the light of the flash, on fire. Her tusks, pinkish and sculptural, are set off by her trunk. Tail back, ears extended, she is sheer motion, a frame from a Muybridge study.

Nick tells me that the moment after he made this photograph, both he and the elephant fled—terrified—in opposite directions.

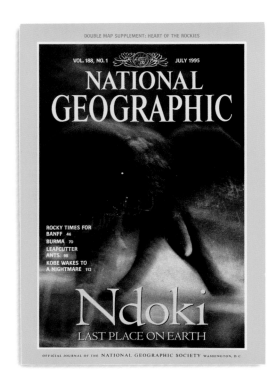

DOUBLE MAP SUPPLEMENT: HEART OF THE ROCKIES

VOL. 188, NO. 1   JULY 1995

NATIONAL GEOGRAPHIC

ROCKY TIMES FOR
BANFF 46
BURMA 70
LEAFCUTTER
ANTS. 98
KOBE WAKES TO
A NIGHTMARE 112

Ndoki
LAST PLACE ON EARTH

OFFICIAL JOURNAL OF THE NATIONAL GEOGRAPHIC SOCIETY WASHINGTON, D.C.

Moran believes that Nick effected a change in *National Geographic*'s aesthetic with his Ndoki photographs:

> With the Ndoki work . . . there's a kind of rawness. And in a way, it was a controversial set of pictures—especially for a magazine like *National Geographic*, with its very classic, straightforward, traditionally beautiful, almost romantic imagery. Nick's work was not that. The blurry elephant, the one-eyed leopard . . . not everyone was ready for that very different style of looking at the natural world. Nick came in and turned everything upside-down. I was with him when people would stop him and berate him for its starkness. . . . Nick was not giving us the "peaceable kingdom." He was giving us what *he* saw and experienced, and with *his* vision.

The work is in every way photoreportage: each of these images takes on a complex and layered series of truths. Which is likely what leads Jean-François Leroy to dub Nick a "street photographer in the jungle." And furthermore: "Nick is never boring." Leroy is the founding director of Visa pour l'Image, the annual festival dedicated to photojournalism in Perpignan, France, where Nick's work has been shown regularly. Perpignan is one of the places where Nick is extricated from the yellow rectangle of *National Geographic*; his reach is recognized as interpretive, wide-ranging, consonant with photojournalists who address human conflict.

In his capacity over the years as an unofficial mentor to other photographers and, beginning in 2008, as editor-at-large of photography at *National Geographic*, Nick has attempted to liberate photographers from generic categories, urging them to work with the impulse of storytelling, to build larger ideas with their photographs—encouraging them to establish a distinct sensibility and voice.

And he demands the same of himself.

By the time the Ndoki story was published in 1995, the Nouabalé-Ndoki National Park had been created. Fostered by the WCS and the Congolese government, with support from the United States Agency for International Development, the Global Environmental Facility, and the U.S. Fish and Wildlife Service, the park, established in December 1993, initially covered some 955,290 acres of pristine forest. Its existence is in large part due to the unflagging energies of Fay—at that time in his late

ABOVE: Cover of *National Geographic*, July 1995: "Ndoki: Last Place on Earth";
OPPOSITE: Charging elephant, Dzanga Bai, Central African Republic, 1993

thirties—and the Congolese wildlife biologist with the Ministry of Waters and Forests, Marcellin Agnagna.[10] Nouabalé-Ndoki National Park was headquartered near Bomassa—the closest village—where some years before, a camp had been set up by Fay and Richard Ruggiero.

When Fay discusses U.S. policy in Africa, he tends to speak about the environment in terms of resource management. He recognizes that he cannot end logging; he cannot end the bushmeat trade. So what can be done to make these practices, and their consequences within the ecosystems, less lethal, more sustainable? Turning the Nouabalé-Ndoki area into a protected park seemed the only way to stave off greed, at least for a while.

At the same time, Fay comprehends that those who are ransacking the land, poachers especially, are often operating from unfathomable destitution. Somebody is paying them—for elephant tusks, for bushmeat, for whatever the desired commodity. So until we can change the "demand" part of the equation, we must intervene with the "supply"—which in this case meant eliminating all hunting in Nouabalé-Ndoki, including the subsistence hunting of the forest communities. While some individuals naturally took issue with this, to allow subsistence hunting would create a loophole to be exploited: subsistence hunters would soon be co-opted into poaching, thus destroying a balanced ecosystem.

Fay is not a slow-burn sort of guy. When he perceives that people—whether representing governments or NGOs or businesses—out of laziness or corruption are not acting responsibly, he pounces.

Nick describes an example of Fay's full-frontal pragmatism, from 1996:

> When Mike was flying in his small plane between Brazzaville and Libreville, he kept flying over this one clearing on the edge of Odzala, and he kept spotting lots of dead elephants there. He let the conservationist in charge of that area know about the massive poaching. Mike had known him for a long time, but they clashed, as this conservationist tended to be more government-oriented in his methods, and Mike is all action.
>
> When Mike flew over it again and saw *more* dead elephants there, he decided, "Fuck this," and contacted some television people. They went in with him in a helicopter, and with the camera running, he showed them all the dead elephants.[11]
>
> Then Mike does another one of his classic moves. Through WCS, he hired the guys who were killing the elephants, and paid them *more* than what they were getting as poachers to instead guard the clearing. That stopped the killing immediately.

After the publication of the initial Ndoki article in *National Geographic*, Nick traveled for several stories—including his trips to India photographing Sita and Charger. All the time Fay was, according to Nick, "ferociously park-building."

After some bitter exchanges, Nick and Mike had more or less ceased communication. Nick: "Mike and I broke up." Fortunately, it didn't stick.

An unspoken rapprochement began in December 1997 when Nick, Fay, and Tim Cahill were invited to be keynote speakers at the "Zoos and Aquariums: Committing to Conservation" conference, hosted that year by Busch Gardens in Tampa.

Soon after this conference and the publication of the tigers story in December 1997, Nick received an e-mail with the subject line "Big Walk to the Congo from Mike Fay." As early as around 1989, Fay had developed what he termed "the *long walk* method of censusing a forest. We would identify the biggest contiguous, uninhabited blocks of green . . . and we would traverse them. It usually took weeks, and we recorded everything we saw along the way: wildlife, trees, human sign."[12] Eventually, Fay would call these long walks "transects."

His e-mail read, in part:

> Dear Nick,
> I am in the planning stages of a very long forest walk. It would take me from the Mokabi concession to the north to the Nouabalé-Ndoki National Park and Dzanga-Sangha all the way down through to Ouésso, over through the Odzala area to the escarpment, through the swamps of NW Congo, through the Minkébé, down through the Mingouli forest, through Lope and then on to Petit Louango. I figure that it will take me about a year. I will pick up supplies about every six weeks at some strategic location.
>
> The objective would be to document all that is left, via data collection, written accounts, pictures, and digital video. It will take us through not only all the most pristine and wild

places left in central Africa, excluding Zaire, but also through the last of the wild Pygmy lands, diamond camps run by Senegalese traders, logging concessions, isolated and weird Bantu villages, gold camps, conservation projects, oil fields, road building projects, safari hunting camps, elephant poaching camps and a lot of other wild and bizarre places. I think that when it is done it will provide one of the best data sets documenting the flora, fauna and human impact on the wildest places and in between. We plan on doing GPS all the way so we would have a constant track. At the same time it is going to be an adventure without parallel.

There is nobody else that is going to do this in the next couple of years and in 5 years you won't be able to. I figure that I am only going to have to cross around 5 roads. . . .

Anyway I was thinking about you of course. Do you think that National Geographic would be interested in the trip in general. If so in what way. I wouldn't want to bring people along with me the whole way. I want it to be more or less solo with about 4–5 Pygmies from Makao that I would bring the whole way to the coast with me if we can make it. . . .

Nick you are the only person that I know who could come close to making this big. . . .
See you,
Mike

The acrimony, whatever it had been, was over. Fay's "100 Things Nick Did Wrong" venting wasn't a divorce petition but an aria of complaint. The lives of the two men are entwined—through their histories, passions, friendship, a common sense of mission, and sheer drive and intelligence. Fay may be mercurial; Nick may get upset by a barb that strikes him as mean-spirited. Fay might wish Nick were tougher, that he'd "man-up"; Nick might wish for less drama, a kinder, gentler Fay. (Nick has his volatile moments too, and sometimes a stinging temper—especially with his sons and his assistants if he feels they are not listening to him—but his anger never owns him. It's like vomiting after food poisoning: once it's out of his system, it's gone.)

The concept Fay had outlined, which he would soon dub the "Megatransect" (having done shorter transects previously), was irresistible to Nick—as Fay had surely known it would be.

Ultimately their earlier exploration in Ndoki served as the springboard to this epic fifteen-month trek. Fay—again under the auspices of a WCS-NGS partnership—undertook the Megatransect with three contiguous teams of African men, across nearly two thousand miles of forest and swamp, from Bomassa to Makao in northeastern Congo to the Atlantic coast of Gabon. Nick would join up with the group at various points throughout Fay's journey.

From its earliest planning and preparation through the publication of the final Megatransect follow-up story, the project would wend its way through seven issues of *National Geographic*, and encompass ten years of their lives—culminating in the elegantly packaged publication titled *The Last Place on Earth*. This box holds two volumes: a large-format, horizontally bound collection of Nick's color photographs, lushly reproduced and with words from David Quammen and an afterword by Fay; and a smaller book, *Megatransect: Mike Fay's Journals*, which features excerpts and facsimile pages from Fay's journals, along with Nick's black-and-white images of Fay and the team.

By the time of his "Big Walk to the Congo" e-mail, Fay had attained his pilot's license. During the Republic of Congo's war years, he had flown regularly between Libreville, Gabon, and Brazzaville in a single-engine plane. From the air, he observed the forests with his botanist's eye, noting new growth, old growth, invasive trees, where there were roads and where there weren't. He understood that if he could make this walk, and collect data on everything, he would be building toward protecting more critical land. And land, as Fay had come to understand, is everything.

Although Fay wanted to work with Nick, and hoped for the support of *National Geographic*, it wasn't going to be an easy sell. As Nick says:

> Fay proposes the Megatransect to *National Geographic*. He's written a huge proposal that's as dense as stone, and nobody reads it. I thought it was an amazing idea, and said to everyone: "You don't need to read anything: it's a guy in shorts and sandals walking for a year or whatever through the wilderness with a team of Pygmies. It's totally grounded in conservation, as that's all Mike thinks about. It's not an adventure. It's a guy who will kill himself to find out what we need to do to protect these areas. What more do you need to know?"

Nick did have one caveat: "David Quammen was the only writer I wanted for the Megatransect." Nick was an avid reader of Quammen's "Natural Acts" pieces in *Outside* magazine, and "was a huge fan! It was just like with Tim [Cahill]—I knew I had to work with David." An original thinker and gripping essayist who focuses especially on science and nature, Quammen is masterful at translating the more esoteric aspects of science into laypeople's terms, eloquently and without condescension. Nick appreciates the balance he achieves: "He knows exactly where that line is to *hold* you. And even how to translate Mike Fay. He got it." Their work together on the Megatransect engendered more than fifteen years of inspired collaboration between Nick and Quammen—rooted in deep and mutual admiration, trust, and affection.

Kathy Moran recalls that it took about six months of discussion and cajoling before *National Geographic* editor-in-chief Bill Allen finally gave the go-ahead. They were all in a room with Allen—Nick, Quammen, Fay, Moran—and they laid out a map showing central and western Africa on Allen's coffee table. It was in that meeting, Nick says, that Mike Fay convinced everyone of the worth of this project. Allen, who had been "searching for a full explanation and plan," concurs, adding: "That meeting provided the answers as to why we should do the article and the importance of committing so much effort on everyone's part to producing it." Nick: "Mike literally walked across the map on the table and gave everyone a tour of what he wanted to do."

Quammen explains the plan:

> There were big areas of intact forest that were contiguous with one another. Each was defined by maybe a road, or a river or a railroad . . . but in the *middle* of each area that Mike planned to walk through, he thought there was nearly zero human impact. Mike wanted to understand, in each of these areas of forest, the abundance and diversity of animals and big trees and the presence or absence of human impact, and how that changed when one walked from an edge into the middle, and then approached another edge again. For instance, if you're on an edge and this is a road, then you wouldn't expect to find many elephants because they would have been poached or scared off by human presence. As you go into the

middle, you would expect to see more and more elephants. How far do you have to walk before you begin to see evidence of elephants? Then, as you come toward the outside of that area Mike had defined, toward a line of villages or another road, you'd expect the elephants to decline again. . . . Mike defined his route, to pass in and then out of the middle of all of the sections he selected—that's why it's a zigzag line—to get to the Atlantic Ocean.

He had already spent nearly twenty years [in this region], and he'd been flying his Cessna over the line he drew. He'd videoed the line. He'd studied the line. He just hadn't done it on the ground yet.

Now it was time for Fay to walk the line. The data he'd collect, the time-space measurements of everything, would allow him to understand, for example, precisely how deep into the forests animals had to go, or under what circumstances, what condition of forest did they need to live in, to be safe from human encroachment and poachers.

As a kind of scouting trip, Moran and Nick proposed a *National Geographic* story on orphan gorillas. During this visit to the Republic of Congo, in 1999, Nick would do a flyover with Fay of the Megatransect route. He would also create one of his most poignant portraits of an animal in the wild, of the western lowland silverback known as Ebobo.

Fay had known and been telling Nick about this animal for years; Ebobo was, as Nick says, "self-habituated," and had actually established—after a rocky start—a relatively friendly rapport with the village people of Bon Coin, near Bomassa. During Nick's 1999 trip, he and Fay waited for Ebobo where Fay anticipated he might make an appearance. Sure enough, he did. When, just as suddenly, Ebobo took off, Nick and Fay ended up trailing him into the bush—no flashlight, Fay barefoot, and Nick just barely able to grab his camera and film before the silverback disappeared. Nick says:

> He was pretty aggressive toward us when we started—he would display and then bark a little bit. But Mike knew this gorilla well enough to know that he wasn't going to charge. Eventually it's like he let us follow him; it felt like he *wanted* us to . . . he'd wait for us if we lagged behind. . . . He'd walk softly, listen for us, and then he'd walk on a little more, then he would look to see if we were still with him. He let me photograph him—and I was probably no more than ten feet away.

Nick and Fay made their way back to camp after dark with minimal stress, and high on the "euphoria of the day, and getting the photograph." Fay later wrote: "We made a pact that day to do the Megatransect across Africa, to convince the world to save as much as we possibly could."[13]

The portrait of Ebobo is in a heavy forest-palette of greens; the gorilla's striking face emerges through a scrim of brush, head slightly tilted, with an intense gaze that seems—at least in human terms—focused and wise.

Another surprisingly tender image from that day, in black and white, shows Fay and Ebobo locked in a stare-down of apparent mutual fascination and curiosity. Nick made it using his Leica with a 35-millimeter lens. It was the first time he had used the lightweight and unobtrusive Leica for an assignment. On the spot, he decided that when he returned to document the Megatransect, he would photograph Fay and

ABOVE: Mike Fay and the gorilla Ebobo; OPPOSITE: Ebobo. Both Nouabalé-Ndoki National Park, 1999

the team throughout in this way. It would allow him to walk with the monumental journey's protagonist more quietly and unencumbered—to be, he says, "the invisible photographer Cartier-Bresson talked about." (Others on the Megatransect team followed at a distance, carrying the rest of his equipment and all the additional necessities that were not being immediately utilized by Fay and Nick.) When walking with Fay, Nick focused only on Fay, so had no use for his Canon, which was reserved for wildlife. "The key to Mike is just to keep up. To bear witness. I never ask: 'Could you walk through that swamp again for me?' This is totally authentic—everything in real time." Nick suspected that the Leica would also allow him more intimacy while photographing Fay with his support team of Bambendjellé men.

This decision to document the *walking* of the Megatransect with the Leica—and primarily in black-and-white—while photographing the wildlife parts in color with his Canon, was a necessary strategy: "I could not do natural-history photography when doing Mike photography. It had to be one or the other, with absolute focus. Otherwise, both suffer." This would play out beautifully, as two distinct but interwoven stories took shape.

On September 20, 1999, Mike Fay, along with a young Congolese biologist assistant, Yves Constant Madzou, and a team of indigenous men, set out from Bomassa. Fay planned to pick his second team a hundred miles east, in the remote Motaba River village of Makao, because of particular forest skills possessed by Makao's Bambendjellé people. He also needed to start the official survey—the Megatransect—from the northeastern edge of this vast Congo basin forest block. This second team of twelve Bambendjellé men—with Mambeleme quickly earning the position of Fay's "point man"—would walk from Makao to the border of Gabon, over the course of eight months. In all, it would take 456 days to complete the expedition all the way to the Atlantic—led by Fay, the only one who, as Nick puts it, walked "door to door." The entire Megatransect was a continuous trek that would be featured over three issues of *National Geographic*.[14] With his new Bambendjellé team, Fay continued on the first leg of the "long walk" ("leg" meaning how the trek was broken up for the three magazine installments—not "Fay time") from Makao east to the Ndoki and Goualougo River confluence (the naïve chimp zone), and then southeast back to the Sangha River—traveling through the Pokola logging concession.

Nick would join Fay and the team for prearranged segments of the expedition, documenting the men as they cut the line of least resistance across enormous areas of swamp and tropical forest. Otherwise, he focused separately on the wildlife of the area. "I was documenting the glory we needed to save and protect," says Nick of his mandate. He walked with Fay "just enough to give the coverage a soul, a character." Otherwise, he believed—knowing Fay so well and understanding how he could best achieve his scientific goals—that Fay should mostly be left alone with his team. In fact, "anyone who *joined* the Megatransect was a burden and barely tolerated by Mike."

Fay's self-imposed directive was to collect data on *everything* in his visual purview—from scat to all forms of life, including indications of human presence, such as trash, graffiti, and evidence of hunting—while tracing his path with a GPS system (long before this technology was common).

The pace varied. Some passages of the Megatransect were extremely arduous—requiring bushwhacking or wading through swamps or climbing steep inclines—while others were on trails made smooth and passable, having been previously trampled by elephants. Gear and supplies were carried by the Bambendjellé men.

However, for Fay to realize what he had set out to achieve, he could not possibly walk with a group. There would be too much noise and too much disturbance—not conducive to experiencing and gathering accurate data on wildlife.

Fay's daily routine was (according to Nick): wake up, have coffee and oatmeal, and then, with just one of the men, take off into the woods. The rest of the team would wait two hours before they'd pack up and start walking. Nick describes trekking with Fay:

> You are walking and also spotting all the time, and almost never speaking. Mike is fully and only Megatransect. He's data-collecting, writing everything, filming everything . . . notebooks and a video camera. I would shadow Mike most of the time, every once in a while moving in front of him, which made him complain a lot—but I couldn't always work from behind.

Beginning with his Bambendjellé colleague Mbutu Clement, Fay had consistently relied on and learned from different groups of indigenous forest peoples—nomadic hunter-gatherers considered Africa's oldest human populations, and historically referred to as Pygmies. The Bambendjellé, who live in the deep forest, have knowledge, skills, and intuitions that were essential to the team's survival. Communication with the group was facilitated by Fay's fluency in French, Lingala, and Sango (spoken in the CAR and the Democratic Republic of Congo, as well as in parts of Chad).

When photographing in indigenous communities, Nick also used the Leica, but with color film. Again, it allowed him to be close yet relatively inconspicuous. To help deepen his cultural understanding, he reached out to American ethnomusicologist Louis Sarno, whom he had previously met with Andrea Turkalo, Fay, and Eugene Linden in the CAR while photographing lowland gorillas. Sarno first worked and lived with the Bayaka people in the 1980s, recording their songs— which were quickly disappearing—and helping to safeguard their culture and very existence.[15] By the late 1990s, he had been living among indigenous people for many years, and Nick knew that he had a profound knowledge of their art, culture, and polyphonic music, as well as how they had shaped the forest's ecology for generations. "When Louis made the effort to learn and speak their language . . . it opened up the playbook of gods and music," says Nick.

Certainly, Nick and Fay understood that the indigenous people have well-honed capabilities in the region's forests. They also knew that many of the communities of the area are plagued by alcoholism. (In fact, the team's drinking was something Fay had to contend with while on the Megatransect, but only when they reached a road or village, never while they were on the walk itself.) Nick appreciated

Bambendjellé man with smoke for gathering honey, Makao, Republic of Congo, 1994

the much fuller understanding Sarno helped to provide. "Louis showed me the brightness and range and smartness in the culture, beyond their forest skills."

Neeld Messler had been enlisted to assist Nick again on the Megatransect, but early into it, Nick correctly diagnosed that Messler had become infected with leishmaniasis, caused by flesh-eating protozoan parasites. He had contracted this after the first Ndoki story, while working with another photographer in Central America. Eventually Messler accepted that he was too sick to continue. ("Once you see the flesh holes," says Nick, "there's no continuing.") Ever responsible, the young assistant put off returning home until Nick had reached a juncture where he could alter his process, without suffering too greatly from the loss of Messler's prodigious range of skills. Messler would later rejoin the trek for a portion of the second leg, and his rope-work talents proved especially useful in the crossing of the Ivindo River at the Kongou waterfalls in eastern Gabon.

Working with Nick in other capacities was Tomo Nishihara, who had originally met Fay in Bomassa in 1991. Fay was establishing his WCS project at the time, and Nishihara was an independent researcher from Kyoto University who started off studying theories of human origins and evolution, and then moved on to apes. Nick says that Nishihara "worked nonstop, could eat and live off anything, and has a deep understanding of the geography and wildlife situation in Congo." Nishihara is a quiet man, who confided to me that he is happiest in the forest—that

OPPOSITE: Mike Fay and a Bambendjellé child on the Megatransect; ABOVE: Bambendjellé camp. Both Republic of Congo, 1999

when there, he wants to "kiss the ground." He credits Fay with his own quarter-century-long commitment to conservation.

Nishihara met Nick in Bomassa in 1998, and later that year he would stay with him and Reba in Charlottesville as they made final preparations before the Megatransect expedition got underway. (Nick refers to their house during that period as "Megatransect Central.") His formidable research credentials and ability to speak both Lingala and French made Nishihara a vital addition to the team. He signed on as logistics coordinator and as a scientific advisor to Nick—while at the same time helping to organize Nick's setups in advance of his arrival at a site, so that the animals might get habituated to the presence of a hide, for example. Nishihara also arranged food drops for Fay and the team, and procured and delivered supplies along the way. He explains how it all came together:

> Before the Megatransect was launched, Mike showed me a rough plan indicating approximately on which date he would need supplies, including food, at which GPS coordinate. I followed this original schedule, while we communicated by satellite phone regularly to confirm our appointment, to meet either in the middle of the forest or somewhere in the villages.
>
> All I needed to do was to arrange/purchase everything necessary and to find out how I could get them to each supply point—by boat, by car, or on foot. If I could not get there this way,

I arranged for the Cessna to drop off supplies from the air. I think we had twenty-six supply points in total. And we succeeded in getting everything to Mike's team correctly . . . in the middle of the forest at most of the supply points, almost always only thirty minutes' difference from what we had scheduled. It was a miracle!

Nick's work has had a very clear influence on the life of David Morgan, who was a zookeeper at Tampa's Busch Gardens when he saw Nick's 1993 "New Zoos" story in *National Geographic*. That, along with Nick's *Brutal Kinship* and his 1995 Ndoki story for the magazine, weighed in Morgan's decision to travel to central Africa to work with wildlife. He and Nick first met in 1999 in Nouabalé-Ndoki National Park's Mbeli Bai. Morgan had been collecting behavioral data on lowland gorillas, which developed into a larger ape study based in Goualougo, at the southern end of the park.

In late 1999, toward the end of his first leg of the Megatransect, after having photographed Fay for three weeks, Nick joined Morgan at his remote camp at Goualougo. He was eager to reconnect with naïve chimps, Morgan remembers. "Nick was up every day by 4:30," he says, "doing whatever it took."

Morgan tells me that his site at Goualougo is the first to use remote video cameras to study chimpanzee behavior: "This is a direct result of having worked with Nick. Nick saw immediately that the tool use of the chimps in Goualuogo was different from what he had experienced earlier in Gombe with Jane Goodall, and with Christophe Boesch's study in the Tai Forest. He said that I needed to document all behaviors to figure out why they are using these tools—and we needed to use video camera traps to do so."

When Nick was photographing in Goualougo in 1999, his son Ian was eighteen. He had been taking care of orphan lowland gorillas through John Aspinall's Projet Protection des Gorilles (PPG) in Gabon, working under Liz Pearson's direction. When civil war broke out in Congo, in 1997, Fay had collaborated with Aspinall and Jane Goodall in their bold rescue of gorillas and chimpanzees from the Brazzaville Zoo. Fay had become so compelled by these "amazing little creatures" in Congo, that he started a gorilla sanctuary in Gabon. At one point, he also gave refuge to orphaned baby gorillas in the backyard of his Libreville home. When they were older, he would release them into protected habitat in Gabon—from which gorillas had long ago disappeared, but which remained intact.

After his time volunteering for PPG, Ian Nichols traveled to Goualougo in November to December of 1999 to see Nick (as he often calls his father), and have a look at the naïve chimpanzees. They made their way on the winding forest trails of Goualougo.

Ian:

Nick said he'd been there tons of times, and knew the way, and didn't want to wait for the guides—so we went off on our own. And we ended up lost in the woods for, I think, two days.

In my pack, I had a one-man tent that we slept in. We burned my copy of *Pickwick Papers* to start a fire. We had two Clif bars. We had to drink out of puddles. And it was Thanksgiving!

I think Nick was a little freaked out. We were lucky we didn't die. Marcel Meguessa—the camp manager of Goualougo—knew we were lost since we had not shown up in camp. Along with the Pygmies, he formed a rapid response team and saved us by cutting large circle paths through the forest, and making arrows pointing the way to the main path.

Finally they hit a recognizable trail and made their way back. The "huge silver lining," says Ian, "was numerous encounters with curious chimpanzees in the canopy, who never ran from us, but watched as we crawled through the dense understory."

After Ian left, Nick stayed on in Goualougo to continue photographing. Morgan identified a fig tree that would soon bear fruit and was likely to attract hungry apes. They set up a blind one hundred feet off the ground, and Nick sat there, day after day after long, long day. . . . As anticipated, apes came to test the still unripe fruit, but for Nick, it also became increasingly clear that he was being hit by an illness. "Something was really wrong. . . . I started feeling sick and turning yellow. The hepatitis that I'd contracted in Guinea and Liberia years before while photographing *Brutal Kinship* had been dormant in my body for years—but suddenly it was blooming, big time."

Nick returned to the States. But after four months in the field, so much work and so much planning for the Megatransect, he was not about to stop altogether. He went to the National Geographic headquarters in Washington to meet with Kathy Moran and begin the edit of the first part of the story. He collapsed in her office.

"It seemed impossible at that moment that he would go back to Africa," recalls Moran. "I really think it was just sheer will. Nick was *not* going to walk away from the Megatransect."

Nick was ill for about four months, during which Moran was able to get special dispensation to remove his films from the National Geographic offices and bring them to his home in Charlottesville. She stayed with Nick and Reba two or three days a week, working with Nick for a few hours a day—as much as he could handle. Together, they slowly put together the story of the expedition's first leg.

While Nick was recuperating, Fay and his team were making their ten-week punishing journey through what Fay later dubbed the "Green Abyss." It was one of the most grueling passages of their long trek,

> with a thick understory cover of plants the Pygmies call *kokombe*, with big lanceolate leaves, forming thickets that in common parlance would be called *impenetrable*. . . . The going was unbelievably slow. . . . Some days, we moved only a few thousand meters forward after ten hours of cutting. Filaria flies trailed behind us in swarms, biting my tender legs. The sun was hot and water was hard to come by. Only weeks of cutting would release us. . . . It was as if we had been swallowed by turf that stood seven meters high, and we had to cut every blade of grass over several hundred kilometers to escape.[16]

As soon as Nick felt well enough, and against his doctor's orders, he went back to Africa. He would not immediately rejoin Fay—he was still too weak to undertake the walking challenges of the Megatransect. Instead he traveled to the Odzala National Park in Congo to focus on wildlife. While flying over the Megatransect route, he and Fay had spotted gorillas at Odzala's Lokoué Bai. Now, while photographing them for two months, he—in Kathy Moran's words—"basically healed, alone in the forest."

For this and the final part of the Megatransect, Nick enlisted the assistance of James Alred, who replaced Messler as his tree rigger, and John Brown III, a young man whose French is as excellent as his interpersonal and survival skills. Brown is also mechanically gifted, able to build and fix motors, construct platforms, and do whatever was needed, says Nick, "to keep things going." A former zookeeper at the Audubon Zoo in New Orleans, Brown had met Nick while he worked on the "New Zoos" story. Impressed by his energy, Nick was happy to make introductions for him in Africa. Brown first worked out of Bomassa, and then out of the logging site at Kabo for Fay and WCS. He then helped to build and set up the Gabon orphanage for lowland gorillas, while Fay was organizing the Megatransect.

At Lokoué Bai, Nick's plan was to spend every bit of daylight photographing from a ground-level hide that Tomo Nishihara would build some time before his arrival. Nick wanted the animals to be accustomed to the structure by the time he began working there. Nick also didn't want to

OPPOSITE: Lowland gorilla, Lokoué Bai, Odzala National Park, Republic of Congo, 2000; ABOVE: Lowland gorillas, Mbeli Bai, Nouabalé-Ndoki National Park, 1999

return to a distant basecamp every night; but to set up the whole team's camp closer to the *bai* would likely have kept the wildlife away, so Nick's outpost was about three miles away from the main camp, as far into the jungle and as close to the *bai* as possible. Twice a week, Brown and other members of the team made their way to Nick's campsite to check on him and bring food and other supplies. Occasionally—if, say, there was a platform to construct, which would take extra time— Brown would stay with Nick near the *bai*.

For Nick, this spot where he had pitched a little nylon tent was "gorilla Mecca." During his sixty days there, he counted more than 365 gorillas using this clearing (and researchers who came after him counted more than 500). There were many groups and solo silverbacks, but what particularly interested Nick were groups of young, extremely curious orphan gorillas that came to the clearing every day. "I saw all these kids, and no mothers, no silverbacks—which almost never happens," he says. "It was a natural *family* of orphans: wild orphaned juvenile gorillas who had somehow found each other." (It remains uncertain why so many of the mature gorillas had apparently died; retrospectively Nick guesses that there is a relationship between these deaths and the Ebola outbreak a few years later, in 2004, which killed 95 percent of the western lowland gorilla population in Odzala.)

Although Nick describes his time at Lokoué as "spiritual," there were frightening moments. More than once, forest elephants circled his tent at night, trumpeting and stomping about. On one "freakishly scary" occasion, a legion of aggressive army ants invaded his camp.

John Brown remembers:

> I go out to check on Nick, and he is freaking out because massive army ants had come to his camp in the middle of the night before, and had completely covered his tent. Then the army ants had started to drill a hole through the bottom of the tent. Fortunately, Nick had been able to cover it with duct tape just in time, and the tape seemed to keep them out—duct tape is the cure-all for everything!
>
> But the ants had completely covered his tent, and he was thinking: "Are they going to get in here and devour me?" You're not able to see anything, and you're not able to get out of your tent, because you don't know which way you are going to run. . . . These are killer ants. They are not like anything you know or have seen before. . . . He had actually started writing a letter to Reba saying, "I love you, this is how I died. . . ."

At the time, the extreme ant visitation felt interminable. After several hours, they marched on.

In the fading late afternoon light, Nick often found himself navigating groups of gorillas— on their way to where they'd build their nests for the night—crossing paths with him as he made his way back to his. Dusk is a time of much movement in the jungle, and Nick recalls one day:

> It was late afternoon and suddenly the clearing was full of gorillas. I was photographing and photographing. Then they left as it was getting dark, and they took the same trail to build their night nests that I took back to my tent. I'm thinking: "These thirty-five gorillas are going to be sleeping next to the trail or on it as I walk home in the dark."
>
> The way to get hurt by a gorilla is to surprise any member of the family—someone screams, and the silverback comes to take care of business. I had it figured out: I would just roll into a ball, and he'll realize I didn't do anything wrong, and probably leave me alone. But still, I was scared to death. So, I clapped and talked all the way back: "Hey, Mr. Gorilla, I'm here! Please don't kill me, Mr. Gorilla!" I just made a lot of noise. And I was fine. They were there, but let me slip by.

It took time for Nick to fully regain his strength. Days were spent watching and photographing the myriad animals that came to the clearing. Nights, in his tent, he read pulp fiction and wrote romantic "lovegrams" to Reba—missing her, asking about her own work, and about the boys: "Eli baseball news, Ian girl news." They were used to being apart for two to three months at a time, but this would be a stretch of six months: he missed his family terribly. In one April 2000 note to Reba, he wrote of his personal goals: "Pray that the animals will let me have vision. They have been holding back the access. I want to be an artist, not just a documentarian. I want to shake the world with my photos of this wild sanctuary."

Of course, there were many incidents when the animals did anything but hold back access. One morning, Nick and Brown were paddling downriver in a pirogue when they spotted an elephant by the riverbank, digging for salt. As they drew nearer, the elephant raised its head and started charging through the water. They back-paddled desperately, but the elephant continued. Fortunately, the force of his charge pushed them further away until, abruptly, he stopped. The elephant turned, climbed the bank, and sauntered into the jungle. Nick's photograph of that charge, mock or not, is thrilling. We see just the elephant's head above the water, ears flared widely, trunk and tusks roiling the surface into a wash of white, his power absolutely palpable.

In the summer of 2000, during the expedition's second leg (that is, the second installment for *National Geographic*), Nick was again photographing Fay—this time in Minkébé

This morning safari ants came. I held them off with BUG SPRAY but that only lasted long enough for me to barricade myself in my tent. As I write the ground around the tent is crackling and every surface I can see is seething. This may be my last Will and Testament. I think they know I'm in here. IF they decide to eat the tent I'm toast. I was joking but just this moment I became really scared they do seem to be eating the tent......

Page from Nick's Megatransect notebook, 2000

forest in northeastern Gabon. David Quammen—who would walk with Fay for about sixty days (four trips of two weeks each)—and Nishihara caught up with Nick, Fay, and the new Megatransect team. They arrived on July 7, via a Bell 412 helicopter, transporting necessary food supplies as well. Fay was 292 days into the trek. That night, they all camped at one of the granite inselbergs (rock hills) that rise so uniquely out of this forest.[17]

The highest inselberg—forty-five miles from the nearest village, with a splendid 360-degree view above the treetops—was the expedition's most remote location. Here, Nick's sublime photograph of Fay, seen from behind and to the side, offers the scientist's profile, defined by his ever-present wire-rimmed glasses. Thin, bearded, hunched with a rounded bare back, elbows and knees pulled in, he perches, staring into the vastness of adjacent hills. "Something happened to me on top of that lump of granite last night," Fay would write: "I have been to the mountaintop."[18]

The Megatransect's final stretch would take place in Gabon. Nick, now fully recovered from his illness, was excited to begin the last segment of the project. Readers of *National Geographic* were spellbound by the story unfolding in its pages. "By now, the world's imagination is captured," says Nick. "We're actually *in* a story that's playing out, and we're feeding it to the world."

Despite efforts on the part of both Fay and *National Geographic*, the Megatransect's Congolese team members were denied entry to Gabon. But even had their entry not been blocked, Fay "already knew he'd have to re-create the team," says Nick. They had suffered many illnesses, and some months earlier, in May, Mouko, a key member of Fay's original team, had become deathly sick—so sick he had to be carried by the other men. "The men were also so homesick," says Nick, "and with Mouko getting ill. . . ." As Fay himself wrote: "I need to ship these boys home. You can just tell they are haggard, totally worn out. No matter how good they were they are just going to go down one by one. I would love to keep my friends but I would be betraying them if I made them stay on any longer—it would be unjust."[19]

Mouko survived, and was ultimately flown back to his family in Congo. Soon after, Fay's Bakwele Bantu aide-de-camp, Jean Gouomoth (nicknamed Fafa), escorted the rest of the Bambendjellé men back to their homes (not the way they had come, but by what Nick describes as "overland using 'the path of least resistance,' which included motorboats and trucks").[20]

A new group of local villagers—some of them gold miners from agriculturalist tribes, others nomadic hunter-gatherers—had to be selected from Gabon. Among the new team were three men of the Baka tribe. Quammen writes that the youngest of them, Emile Bebe, had "good ears for wildlife and a strong machete arm."[21] That machete arm would prove to be particularly useful as they made their way through miles of bush and deep, dense swamps.

After their night at the inselberg, Nick and Brown, on their way to photograph wildlife on the Gabon coast, boarded the helicopter that had delivered Quammen the previous day, leaving him to walk with Fay for ten days in the Minkébé forest.

Quammen describes Minkébé as "ecologically rich but microbially menacing; many months earlier, as we had knelt over my map on the floor of an office at the National Geographic Society in Washington, this was where Fay had written 'Ebola region' in red ink."[22] Quammen goes on to say that this area, once teeming with all kinds of species, was now remarkably absent of both gorillas and chimpanzees—and speculates that the cause was three Ebola epidemics that scourged the area in the mid-1990s. A surrounding village, Mayibout, was especially devastated. Two of the seven Bantu men on Fay's new team, Thony M'Both and Sophiano Etouck, told sorrowful stories of losing friends and loved ones to Ebola. Then, as Quammen reports in *National Geographic*: "Thony said, 'You know, it was a peculiar thing. At the time Ebola struck our village, we also saw nearby in the forest a pile of thirteen dead gorillas.'"

Quammen's 2012 book *Spillover* traces the history and ecology of zoonotic diseases such as Ebola, AIDS, and SARS. There, in his discussion of Ebola, he says that Fay's team often craved a supper of wild meat, but that Fay "forbade hunting on conservation grounds—and during this stretch through Minkébé he had commanded his cook even more sternly: Do *not* feed us anything found dead on the ground."[23] Indeed, Fay admonished the team against *touching* any dead animal that they might come across.

Meanwhile, Nick and John Brown had set up camp on the southern end of the coastal reserve in Gabon. Nick would photograph for about three months, before rejoining the Megatransect team for the last sixty-five or so miles of the walk. Nick was enthralled by the bounty and the diversity of creatures—leopards, elephants, gorillas, reptiles, and more—roaming Gabon's coast. He and Brown found trails flattened by passing elephants (Nick calls them "elephant highways") on which they set up camera traps. It was more or less peaceful, except for the presence of one neighboring poacher, and a too-close encounter with a giant nesting crocodile. Nick's and Brown's voluble reaction to the predator provoked a charge by a surprised mama elephant they'd been camera-stalking. "A change-your-underwear moment," Brown told me, laughing.

In the fall of 2000, Quammen joined Nick, Brown, and Tomo Nishihara on the coast, and they traveled inland via river to rendezvous with Fay and the Gabonese team for the final two weeks of the Megatransect. Also present was Phil Allen, a National Geographic Television videographer

On the Mambili River, Odzala National Park, 2000

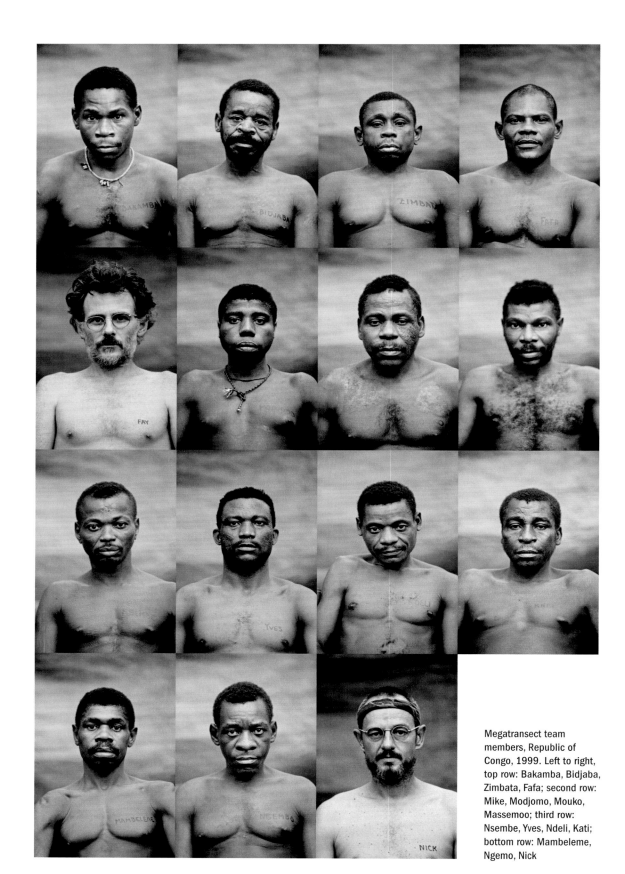

Megatransect team members, Republic of Congo, 1999. Left to right, top row: Bakamba, Bidjaba, Zimbata, Fafa; second row: Mike, Modjomo, Mouko, Massemoo; third row: Nsembe, Yves, Ndeli, Kati; bottom row: Mambeleme, Ngemo, Nick who filmed on two separate occasions during the Gabon part of the journey. The expedition had barely survived flooding October downpours, food shortages, and daunting terrain made doubly difficult by the rains. Maps had been faulty. Fay had contracted malaria and treated himself with Quinimax. Food drops arranged by Nishihara alleviated the hardship—but never for long.

In December, Day 453, they were just twenty miles from their final destination in Gabon, when Fay and the team encountered what Quammen refers to in his final essay on the Megatransect in *National Geographic* as a "blackwater sump"—a dark lake, swollen with rainwater.[24] Fay, who could not speculate about its depth or contents, preceded the group into the water, in the hope of figuring out a navigational approach. Quammen watched Fay as he waded in: "waist-deep, chest-deep, armpit-deep . . . then there was just a little head and two skinny arms vanishing into the thicket."[25] He was gone a long time. He might have called to them, but they could not hear him, and finally, after nearly an hour, the rest of the team—including Nick and Quammen—decided to follow Fay into the water.

They all made it across the lake—navigating a deep mesh of submerged vegetation—without incident. When they reached the other side, however, they discovered an incensed Fay, livid perhaps because they had taken the initiative to move forward into unknown and potentially dangerous waters without his okay. They had broken a crucial chain of command that was theoretically in place to keep everyone safe. And Fay was even more enraged—because, as Nick recalls, "the men had gotten some of the precious food supply wet . . . Mike's tantrum was all about survival." Fay harangued the team—"feckless," "incompetent," "childish," "insubordinate"—as if they had committed an act of willful defiance.

With only days left of the Megatransect, the men were utterly demoralized. There was talk of mutiny, or of simply giving up. Fay had less than zero patience for this, and succinctly snapped: "My mission is to get to the beach." Eventually, some grudgingly at first, they began walking once more—realizing also that they had no idea where they were, that only Fay could get them out of this dense forest.

For Quammen, however, the most vivid memory from that swim across the black lake is one of elation:

> We are swimming across this swampy black water. We don't know if there are crocodiles. We don't know how we are going to find our way through this tangle of mangroves to try to find land on the other side. Some of us have taken off our waterproof packs and filled them with as much air as possible, so we can push them in front of us like beach balls.

> I look up, and there's Nick dogpaddling along, and he's got his Leica pressed to his face, as Sophiano is dogpaddling along, coming out of the water and swinging his machete and cutting another mangrove root so we can keep swimming, and going under and we don't know if he's going to get stuck and never reappear . . . and then he comes porpoising up and he takes another swing with his machete. And there's Nick, still swimming along,

ABOVE: Mike Fay and the Megatransect team, Gabon, 2000; OPPOSITE: Sophiano Etouck, Megatransect, Gabon, 2000

and he's getting *everything*. It just thrilled me, watching him, and I thought: "Fuckin' A—yeah, Nick!"

We climbed out on the far side, and Nick was putting his film away, and checking his camera to be sure it was still dry and intact. It was an exhilarating moment to be his partner.

Quammen kept journals, making entries for each of his days on the Megatransect. In "Gabon: 12/5/00 Day 443 Megatransect trip 4" he wrote of asking Mike Fay: "How does he feel about the approaching end? Ambivalent & uncertain, MF admits. 'I'm certainly not rarin' to get out of the woods, at all. Not at all.'" In their final hours of walking, Quammen writes of the Megatransect team, "By 11 am, crossing now flooded forest, we can hear the roar of surf. Everyone feels the thrill of anticipation. . . . The canopy begins to thin, the trees are low and scrubby, & we can feel sea breeze. Hear the crash of waves on sand. . . ." Still, it was clear that Fay didn't want the trek to come to an end; he seemed to be basking in the forest, as if he was about to say goodbye to a loved one for the last time. It was impossible to imagine that after fifteen months it could end, just like that, with a single step.

Throughout the previous weeks, Nick had been thinking about how to depict the momentous finale of the Megatransect, "How do I make a picture of the last day?" He had already spent months working on Gabon's southwestern coast, and so understood it well. As ever, he did not want to influence the situation—something so monumental could easily feel forced or predictably sentimental when photographed.

Nick recalls that emerging from the forest onto the Atlantic beach was "like walking out of a cave into a blinding light. There was nothing in front of us but a big field, and the Atlantic Ocean. I'm shooting furiously. It doesn't matter what I feel: can I get what *Mike* feels on film in a way that will translate?"

None of the Baka men had ever seen the ocean, and they were not at all convinced by the notion of saltwater. Overwhelmed by the Atlantic, they incredulously began to take it all in—dabbling first with their toes before the braver souls ventured in to wade; others, more circumspect, dipped only their fingertips in the "miracle," to taste the salt.

Fay himself went right into the ocean. What happened next Nick considers the happiest of accidents. There were enough clouds to soften the shadows, although the day was bright. And when Fay came running back out of the water, wiping the salt off his face—his gesture so resembled praying. Behind him, Sophiano Etouck was doing an exuberant flip into the water, his legs in the air. "That juxtaposition," says Nick, "it's what photography—only still photography and that rectangle—can do."

Then, smiling and tearing up, Fay telephoned his parents: "I'm on the beach. Yes sir, just got here. This is the end of the line."

Quammen, closing the story of this most extraordinary "long walk," writes:

> At 12:39 p.m. on December 18, 2000, J. Michael Fay and his support team broke through the forest onto the beach at the Atlantic Ocean. "Wow," he said. "Wow." Then, matter-of-factly, "This is just where I wanted to come out." It was Day 456 of the 2,000-mile Megatransect.[26]

This dénouement of the Megatransect expedition was covered in the August 2001 issue of *National Geographic*, and would be followed by three more spin-off stories in subsequent issues: Mike Fay was just beginning. In the wake of the Megatransect, he (under the aegis of the Wildlife Conservation Society), and British zoologist Lee White, head of WCS's Gabon program at the time (now executive secretary of Gabon's Agence Nationale des Parcs Nationaux), crusaded relentlessly for the preservation of habitat and wildlife. In 2002, Fay and White together proposed to Gabon's President Omar Bongo Ondimba the concept of a country-wide network of protected parks—using Nick's images as an important part of their conservation arsenal. Bongo was apparently transfixed by the Megatransect, by Nick's photographs, and eventually by Fay himself, along with what Fay describes as their "dog and pony show" about the parks. Together, all this revealed to the nation's stunned president a Gabon he had never known. Until then, he had perceived his country's spectacular wildlife—its creatures and forests—only as resources to be cut down, dug up, or slaughtered, preferably at a sizable profit. In August 2002, President Bongo, to the evident astonishment of his own cabinet, set aside about 11,300 square miles throughout Gabon to be turned into protected national parks. In all, thirteen parks were created in a country that previously had none. The areas were chosen based on Fay's and WCS's recommendations regarding critical, highly vulnerable land that needed protection from prospectors and poachers. Soon after, U.S. Secretary of State Colin Powell committed $53 million for the Congo Basin Forest Partnership, which brings together businesses, government, and conservation.[27] David Quammen reported on the creation of the parks in Gabon in *National Geographic*'s September 2003 issue. There he writes:

> After decades of heavy reliance on petroleum and timber industries, Mr. Bongo said, "We are left with little oil in the ground, a fragmented forest, dwindling income, and a burden of debt." The next growth sector of his nation's economy, he vowed, would be "one based on enjoying, not extracting, natural resources."[28]

Increasing the amount of protected land comprising Nouabalé-Ndoki National Park never ceased being the goal of many conservationists, thanks in part to Fay's persistence, Nick's photographs, the writings of Linden, Chadwick, and Quammen, and the research of David Morgan. Still, there was one individual who could further intensify and drive the activism already in place. In the wake of the Megatransect, Nick and Fay brought Jane Goodall to see the naïve chimpanzees at the Goualougo Triangle. By then Morgan and his wife, Crickette Sanz, had started Goualougo Triangle Ape Project—an evolution of Morgan's original study—against great odds, as loggers and

Mike Fay, Atlantic coast of Gabon, 2000

other exploiters continued to creep closer and closer.[29] Nouabalé-Ndoki National Park had been created, but it did not yet include the Goualougo Triangle in its protection.

"Jane Goodall in the Wild"—a feel-good follow-up to the Megatransect stories—was published in *National Geographic* in April 2003, with photographs by Nick and text by Quammen.[30] Its purpose was pure advocacy—and as hoped, it helped fuel several more years of lobbying for the park. The full-court press marshaled several conservation organizations, the local logging company, and the Congolese government—and it worked. In 2012 the protected area of Nouabalé-Ndoki was increased by nearly a hundred thousand acres, to 1,054,646. The park now includes the pristine Goualougo Triangle—the jewel, the soul of Ndoki.

As of this writing, however, elephant poaching and illegal hunting for bushmeat still plague Nouabalé-Ndoki. As Fay had predicted and feared, more and better roads have facilitated access, allowing increased exploitation. According to Morgan and Nishihara (who is currently based in Makao with WCS Congo), logging has increased, as have mining, palm plantations, and the proliferation of dams constructed without the benefit of any environmental studies. And the region's human population has grown exponentially, increasing the bushmeat consumption and forest destruction.

At the same time, the sprawling exploitation of land also threatens the already poor and marginalized forest communities, which may one day disappear altogether. Nishihara adds, specifically about Makao,

ABOVE: *National Geographic* stories, April 2003: "Jane Goodall in the Wild"; September 2003: "Saving Africa's Eden"; OPPOSITE: Writer David Quammen, Megatransect, Day 455, Gabon, 2000

that it "is one of the places where the situations have completely changed since our age of Megatransect. No more forest around, lots of poaching, Pygmies becoming city boys, lots of logging roads and trucks." All this in turn makes the habitat and its wildlife more vulnerable, despite its designation as "protected."

Still, Morgan and Nishihara continue the fight and remain hopeful. Nick believes that "the parks and reserves that came out of the 'long walk' have proved to be boundaries that at least have a chance to stand forever." Along these lines, Morgan and Nishihara are not necessarily advocating for an increased quantity of protected land; rather, they are looking for ways for the protection that is supposedly already in place to function, in the face of much corruption. The park's guards must be more effective; there must be more checkpoints. Alternative food projects need to be established to help feed the local communities, in order to reduce, and eventually end, hunting wildlife for bushmeat.

The final *National Geographic* story that evolved out of the Megatransect was "Land of the Surfing Hippos," featuring Gabon's newly formed coastal Loango National Park and its diverse population of wildlife.[31] It was written by Fay, who was advancing conservation efforts on the coast—training guards and rangers to help protect against poaching and illegal commercial fishing, while also bringing people together (including Nick's son Ian) to help clean up the Atlantic beach area.

For this story, Nick lived on the Gabonese coast for about six months in 2003, along with Reba, Eli (being homeschooled), and Ian (taking a semester off from the University of Virginia).

Fay was there, of course, as was Sophiano Etouck. Bryan Harvey also came for a few weeks to work on a National Geographic Television film, and Fay's love, Jane Sievert, Managing Photo Editor at Patagonia, and her daughter Melia visited as well.

Nick was assisted in Gabon by Nathan Williamson—the start of a ten-plus-year collaboration that has greatly benefited both. Nick has always looked for intelligent assistants who can keep up with him—actually, who can surpass him in strength—and are quick, careful, honest, and game. That they share his conservation ethos and respect for the wild is, in theory, a given, even if they need to learn some details in practice. When he was working so often in French-speaking Africa, it helped if they could speak French. Williamson learned.

Williamson, from rural West Virginia, studied anthropology in college, then traveled to Bolivia on a Fulbright scholarship to do an economic analysis of sustainable forestry projects. Somewhere along the line, he saw the Megatransect story—and was riveted: "The whole package: the science that Mike was doing, and really strong photography. I'm like: 'That's the *god* of photography right there.' So I went to find Nick."

Nick has great respect and fondness for Williamson and considers him "one of the most self-sufficient people I've ever met." During their initial conversation, Nick learned that Williamson and his brother had been living in a cabin they'd rewired—"and they could live on *nothing*—dumpster-diving to get all the food they needed. And he knew how to fix everything. This is exactly the kind of assistant I need." But here's what sealed the deal: "After we'd finished speaking, Nathan left. Then, a few minutes later, he came back and said: 'I would swim through lava to work for you.' Well, hot damn—he just got a job! I always want people who are willing to do what I would do."

For the work in Gabon, Nick also hired Frederic Tassé, a French-Canadian mountain climber whose sociability and kindness had earned him the nickname "Soleil" (or Sun). Tassé is strong and ready for anything. Once in Loango, he assembled the houseboat—its foundation, a factory pontoon boat—where Nick and Reba sometimes slept, and which served as the project's base. They moved it only in calm waters, and as it had only a cabin cover, they set up tents on the roof and deck.

The team established and provisioned its various beach camps using the two all-terrain vehicles (ATVs) Fay and Nick had agreed to bring, with the understanding that they were, as always, committed to making a minimal impact upon the environment. To avoid creating permanent tracks or roads, they would travel only in tidal sand. As always, they would erase any trace of their camps. All the gear was packed in a forty-foot-long container and shipped from the States.

Issues connected to the use and availability of the ATVs—and many other perceived affronts—sparked sporadic bickering between Nick and Fay. At one point, rationality disappeared altogether. Nick was at the basecamp cooking beans, carefully following a favorite Cajun recipe, when Fay came along and blithely tossed a handful of mushrooms into the pot. This culinary improvisation was, Nick says, "the *antithesis* of what should happen! I just went fucking nuts!"

The tension and ill feeling between the two men had been on a low boil for some time. One of the provocations is almost funny: Nick and Reba were in the process of renovating an old farmhouse they'd bought in 1999 in Sugar Hollow, in Virginia's Blue Ridge Mountains—a rural, unspoiled spot enveloped by woods and gentle hills. Thinking they'd like to have, and might structurally need, big beams in the farmhouse, it occurred to Nick to reclaim some of the vast amount of wood—logged mahogany—that washes up along the beaches in Gabon, and ship it home. He was in the process of researching whether it would be possible to export salvaged mahogany, and he and Fay agreed that Gabon's legal and organized sale of salvaged wood could be a great way to raise money for conservation. Well—Nick *thought* they had agreed. In fact, when Fay understood that Nick planned to use it in his own home, he made his disapproval known. Quammen remembers him saying something like: "Those logs were all cut in forests that should never have been cut. It's immoral to salvage those logs." It was toward the end of the Megatransect. Nick was walking in the forest, photographing behind Fay when, he says, "Mike started tying pieces of fabric to the trees on which he's written something along the lines of: 'This is the tree you're going to kill to build your house.'" (In the end Nick, flummoxed, didn't follow through with the wood-exporting plan.) Quammen says: "I love Mike and I admire him hugely, but Mike can be totally obnoxious. You would not want to work for him, and you would not want him to work for you. I was lucky enough that I spent a lot of intimate, arduous time with him, and I never had either of those relationships."

Quammen continues: "Mike Fay is absolutely committed to conservation. He would lay his life on the line to save an elephant, and he often has. Nick cares deeply about conservation, but even more deeply about his art." Together, they can do remarkable things. But like many other people who get very, very close as friends and collaborators, Quammen adds, "they get pissed at each other. They would hardly be on speaking terms for a period of time. Then they would cook up some other huge adventure, and they would be able to operate together the way nobody else could operate with them, and be this incredible team."

Quammen, making a Rolling Stones analogy, concludes:

> I call them the "Glimmer Twins." The Glimmer Twins is the label that was given to Keith Richards and Mick Jagger. . . . They are very close, and they create amazing things together. As Keith says (something like): "Mick is my brother, but he hasn't really been my *friend* for years." . . . They don't hang out in dressing rooms together anymore. They're over that. They do their work. . . . Mike and Nick remind me so much of Keith and Mick. During the Megatransect

in particular I viewed this relationship from what I think of (probably self-flatteringly) as the perspective of Charlie Watts.

Despite his modesty, Quammen's essays expertly and insightfully "shine a light," interdependently building on each other as he narrates all the moving parts of this epic expedition.

Nick's photographs along the Gabon coast transport us, yet again, to a marvelous world of captivating creatures—especially his images of the surfing hippos. He needed to convey the miracle of them in order first to realize great photographs, and second to help inspire the support for conservation. Nick was also compelled to show the daily life of the ecosystem. We needed to comprehend the elemental interplay of ocean, beach, lagoons, forest, and animal trails; the sea mammals and those on land; predators and prey; the ebbs and flows of the tide.

Bryan Harvey remembers the process of working among the hippopotamuses—with their scarily agape, exaggerated, almost cartoonlike jaws—their mouths open so wide as to appear vertical. The animals made a daily trek from lagoon to ocean, and Nick's team had to keep up with them.

> Nick, Nathan, and I went and set up this quick camp—minimal gear, and enough food to last us for six days. We knew this little lagoon that the hippos would be at during the day. . . . Then they'd leave the lagoon, and go several miles into the ocean, down the beach— swimming in the ocean—and then get out to enter a field and eat some grass they liked. We wanted to photograph all of this. And then come back to the lagoon with them at dawn.

Mike Fay giving Eli Nichols a haircut, with Reba and Ian, Gabon, 2004

ABOVE: Orphan mandrill, Ivindo River, Gabon, 2000; OPPOSITE: Mandrill, Lope National Park, Gabon, 2000

We had to figure out where to camp downwind, so they wouldn't smell us. . . . There were times where we completely missed them—or we'd see them when it was just too dark to photograph . . . it was so frustrating! . . . During the days, we would also try to get shots of them once they were in the lagoon—and they didn't like it. I got charged a couple of times by this huge one. They open their mouths and they come right at you. . . . He's up to his chest in the water. We're behind the tree. We're trying to *be* a tree . . . . to sneak the lens around the tree. . . . We did not want to disturb them . . . when we just got too close, they let us know.

Nick and the team placed camera traps behind mangroves that brushed up against the forest, buffering the string of lagoons. They worked along wide trails made by elephants—who wisely discern where to walk in order to avoid tidal or rain-related flooding. So the cameras remained dry, and yielded some telling images of patrolling leopards and elephants. In a particularly luminous image from an earlier shoot there, an elephant walks before a radiant sunset of pink to purple hues, the grass bathed in gold, highlighting the lower part of the animal.

It was not easy to get the timing right with the hippos; they tended to wander back from the ocean to the lagoon very early in the morning. Nick woke up at four a.m. every day, working in darkness, getting ready for the hoped-for but never guaranteed moment when surf, light, hippo, and photographer might align for the perfect image.

The moment came near the very end of Nick's stay on the coast. An oceanscape in the deep-blue first light of day: we see just the top of the hippo's head; everything below is submerged. The eyes are laser-focused straight ahead, ears erect, against the backdrop of a spectacular cresting wave, foam cascading to one side. It's almost impossible to reconcile this sense of the animal's weightlessness with the formidable mass of the hippopotamus, exposed once he has emerged from the water.

Bill Allen is deeply proud of *National Geographic*'s role in the Megatransect: "Virtually everything that Mike and Nick saw, experienced, photographed, and then brought back was new information on this part of Africa." Allen follows this by saying that the Megatransect was "the most difficult fieldwork of any assignment that was undertaken during my time as editor-in-chief . . . and arguably far longer."

The creation of national parks in central Africa seems like a splendid climax to the Megatransect expedition. One would like to believe that now—critical land is protected, and the parks' inhabitants may flourish, unthreatened by man. Sadly this is not at all the case.

From 2014 to 2016, Nathan Williamson split his time between Gabon and Virginia—where he lives with his wife and two children (not far from Nick and Reba in Sugar Hollow). In Gabon, he trailed Mike Fay, filming him, his work, and wildlife for a documentary he plans to make. In the years since the Megatransect, Williamson says, "the Congo Basin has been decimated." Of particular concern

are the forest elephants—the population of which is shockingly low, and decreasing at an alarming rate, as elephant poaching rages throughout the country. While the current Gabonese government generally values its natural resources and parks, the problems are profound, corruption is a cancer, and the economic stakes are high. Fay, says Williamson, "is struggling to make viable the system of parks he inspired—yet to this day they remain fragile, with some largely dysfunctional."

It was mostly due to Fay's willfulness that the parks were first created. But he became so disheartened and disgusted by the endemic corruption and exploitation of resources that, in 2004, he left Gabon. He returned in 2010, at the request of President Ali Bongo Ondimba (son of former president Omar Bongo—whose tenure ended with his death in 2009), with the promise that they could make it work. Bongo needed Fay's credibility, ingenuity, and clout as a conservationist.

This time, Fay lasted only six months. The cast was still too unscrupulous to accomplish anything other than to replace almost half of the park wardens—whom Fay dismissed as venal and worthless. He returned to the United States. He was also severely ill at the time, most likely with the parasitic disease schistosomiasis, which he ultimately self-diagnosed and self-medicated, after being unsuccessfully tested and variously treated in a Seattle hospital. He called Nick—they had not been in touch for months—and began his slow recovery at Nick and Reba's. Upon his arrival, as Nick recalls, "Mike curled up like a dying dog" on their porch's concrete floor, "barely able to speak."

OPPOSITE: Forest elephant (camera-trap photograph), Atlantic coast, Gabon, 2000; ABOVE: Baby crocodile, Loango National Park, Gabon, 2003; FOLLOWING SPREAD: Surfing hippopotamus, Loango National Park, 2003

Once he had recuperated, Fay returned to Gabon, again at the president's pleading. As of this writing, he remains there, along with Lee White, working incessantly, involving the Gabonese in the ongoing fight to protect inviolably their country's valuable lands, coastal waters, natural resources, and wildlife.

Preferring *not* to be indispensable in Gabon, Fay is creating, mentoring, and directing a young Gabonese team, preparing them to someday lead the charge. Their understanding of the issues, their integrity, and their willingness to act—often against the status quo and sometimes against the authorities—are vital to the mission.

To endure, the parks need to be sustainable—and this is in large part dependent upon their being first wanted, and then managed by, an engaged populace that celebrates them as its heritage and ultimately its wealth. The park's success relies on the Gabonese seeing that there is great value in keeping existing forested landscapes, coastlines, and waters unsullied, and the wildlife populations and their habitats thriving. Of course, this coexistence cannot be one-sided: part of the equation means protecting arable land, crops, and livestock that are needed for humans to flourish.

The challenges are many, but resolvable when it is understood that the survival of people cannot come at the expense of the natural world—that protecting the natural world is in fact beneficial to people. When these ideas are acknowledged, the will of the people may at last be on the side of wild.

PEACE, L☮VE, AND

From Point Sublime, Grand Canyon
National Park, Arizona, 2005

PH☮T☮GRAPHY

n the Congo and Gabon, Nick had rendered landscapes and elusive wildlife that had rarely, if ever, been photographed. Both in Ndoki and then on the Megatransect, he had encountered—thanks to Mike Fay—naïve animals and species of flora and fauna that had never before been identified or codified. As *National Geographic*'s editor-in-chief at the time, Bill Allen, put it, "not since the celebrated journey of Livingston" had such a team ventured as deeply into such remote and untrodden areas.

Nick's next projects for the magazine could not have been more different. He was to photograph the highly habituated gelada baboons of the Ethiopian Highlands: "I'm pretty sure this assignment was an intervention on Kathy [Moran]'s part—to get me out of the jungle, and working on a fabulous and unique creature that is relatively easy to see and track." After his time in the Simien Mountains—the story was published in the November 2002 *National Geographic* (with text by Virginia Morell)[1]—Nick took on another World Heritage site, this one so familiar and so documented that it is almost a visual cliché: the Grand Canyon. Nick hoped to reveal one of North America's most visited sites in an original way that would rival, or at least not mirror, the images that already exist in the collective mind's eye.

The photographs, published as *National Geographic*'s January 2006 cover story (with Nick pictured on the cover, atop Toroweap Overlook, in a photograph by his assistant John Burcham), do not entirely meet that challenge.[2] The images are glorious, but they are ultimately more about the place itself than about a singular way of seeing a subject so tethered by preconceptions that must somehow be shattered. The project does not have the interpretive edge of so much of Nick's other work, which characteristically takes us far beyond documentation. Furthermore, the Grand Canyon photographs lack the narrative or protagonist components

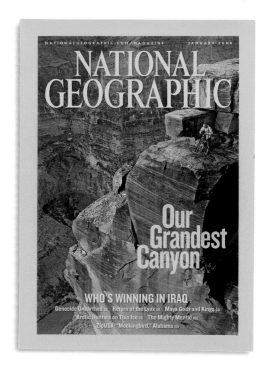

essential to his most extraordinary and revelatory work. This was Nick's first time photographing something that was already entirely familiar to his viewers, and it required a pushback kind of innovation. Perhaps he needed a foil, or a filter through which to tell the story from a unique perspective. Instead, the images resonate more like a series of contemplations.

Still, Nick's Grand Canyon work did serve as a breakthrough in other ways. Apart from his cave images (made more than a decade earlier), this was one of the only projects in which Nick was *not* photographing something fleeting, moving, advancing, or retreating—nor was he himself in constant motion. There is a kind of stillness in the Grand Canyon images, for both photographer and subject. Time itself seems to be one of the central concerns here—not just in terms of its capture or duration, but in relation to space. Nick considered ways to juxtapose the notion of immediacy with that of eternity:

OPPOSITE: Cover of *National Geographic* (showing Nick), January 2006: "Our Grandest Canyon." Photograph by John Burcham. ABOVE: Bachelor male gelada baboons, Simien Mountains, Ethiopia, 2002

Lightning became a way to talk about time—about history, and also the moment. The Grand Canyon is millions of years old—it's almost impossible to fully comprehend it—but a bolt of lightning lasts a split second. You have this ancient place, but the moon, the snow, and the lightning—all those are transient. I got that idea of transience stuck in my head. I didn't intellectualize it, I just said: "If I am doing the Grand Canyon, I am doing it in a snowstorm, by moonlight, or with lightning—so I am speaking to the specific moment in time." I was also really conscious of the relationship between fleeting time and frozen geologic time, and the concept that something frozen in time is affected by something that moves constantly in time.

This concept had begun to take shape for Nick as early as 1978, during a cross-country road trip he made with his University of North Alabama pal Mike McCracken—it was the first time Nick saw the Grand Canyon. As they were exploring the Southwest, Nick learned of Walter De Maria's spectacular Land Art project *The Lightning Field*, located in western New Mexico. Four hundred stainless-steel poles are precisely arranged in a grid of a mile by a kilometer, conceived as a nuanced and elemental dance of ever-shifting perspectives, tonalities, and vanishing points. The poles partner with sunlight, waxing and waning in intensity especially at dawn and dusk. (Although there are occasions when lightning literally strikes—spectacularly—the work's title is best interpreted more symbolically, cosmically.) Unfortunately, Nick and his friend weren't able to visit the site, which had been installed the previous year and to this day requires advance planning and reservations. Still, the idea of lightning not just as an active visual component of a landscape, but one that could momentarily alter and redefine the landscape, stayed with him. It was reinforced two years later, when he saw John Cliett's 1979 image of *The Lightning Field* published on the April 1980 cover of *Artforum* magazine.[3] In that photograph, a brilliant streak of lightning branches off into glowing filigree as it arcs downward, before broadening into a ghostly swirl of white light. The poles and the surrounding brush are visible in a subdued glow. Cliett's image lingered referentially as Nick first began to conjure notions of lighting, flash, and the alchemy of combining man-made with natural light. "It really influenced me," says Nick. "I saw immediately that marrying tech, vision, different light sources, and Earth subject matter could lead to the highest level of photography. . . . It took a great photograph to translate De Maria's vision to two dimensions, and make it available to the world."

Since the time of his cave work, Nick has "painted with light." At the Grand Canyon, he and Burcham decided to photograph from the high north rim of the canyon once summer arrived and thunderstorms erupted regularly. He allowed the "medium"—the lightning bolts themselves—to be the message. Lightning rarely lasts long enough to be seen and photographed. To create his image, Nick utilized a device called a "lightning trigger": it functions as a sort of camera trap for both heat and stroke lightning, including flashes beyond the camera's field of view. Once the trigger senses the lightning, it activates the camera's shutter release.

One image is particularly evocative. Two glistening tendrils of light—initially unseen through opaque clouds, but then exhaled, emerging through a wispier scrim—zigzag forward, brushing the rock in the foreground with light. The canyon's forms in the middle ground are lit by a break in the distant clouds, with their striated palette and markings and sculptural tiers distinguishing them and lending depth. The canyon's lineaments are revealed uniquely in this moment of illumination that shapes both time and space.

Here, for the first time, Nick was photographing with a digital camera—while not yet forsaking his film camera—so that he might begin to glean a nuanced understanding of their differences and learn how to get precisely what he wanted digitally. As it was a landscape project, using two cameras did not complicate his process. After years of working in lightless caves and dark jungles, he began to comprehend how much a digital camera could facilitate making a subject visible with just the slightest ambient light—or even without it. The algorithms of film speed, exposure time, and so on became the *camera*'s responsibility, practically speaking. One still needs to consider and understand light, of course; Nick has never relied on the technology as anything but a tool, and he always uses a light meter. Still, as he continued to use the digital camera in future projects, it began to liberate him. Flash and additional light sources now were needed only to further his vision—not as technical requirements. But this happened later. In the Grand Canyon, what first struck him using the digital camera was just how much it could register, and like most photographers, he so appreciated "being able to see what was captured instantly."

But digital photography has also introduced a new set of possibilities in terms of manipulation and enhancement of imagery—and these possibilities raise questions of documentary integrity and ethics. Nick is very clear about where he stands:

I think about the raw digital file as I thought about processing a negative. And your ethics come from *there*. The raw processor has evolved to the point that your file is pretty close to what your eye actually saw. But there's so much possibility to manipulate—which I never do. I never manipulate pixels. I just don't want to. I'm going to try to get the picture to be as interesting as possible, but not ever go into a realm of invention. My whole thing in my work is that it's *not* fantasy—that what you see in my photographs is what really happened.

Amazing shit can happen. Don't kill it by making it up!

"Truth" is crucial to Nick's photographs in terms of the information they convey, the credibility of his storytelling—allowing that any documentary photograph still represents a set of choices made by the photographer. To work otherwise, without disclosing the fact of one's manipulation, would be, for Nick, as deceitful as photographing captured animals and misrepresenting them as wild. "With wild," says Nick, "there must be no misrepresentation. I have no respect for anyone who fakes wild."

Nick's relations with *National Geographic* were undergoing a change around the time he was shooting the Grand Canyon. His friend and colleague Chris Johns was named editor-in-chief of the magazine in January 2005, and one of the first things Nick did with Johns was to renegotiate his contract.

The contractual vicissitudes of media photographers are complicated. Nick had started out in 1992 as a contract photographer for *National Geographic*, retaining the copyright on all his images. In 1996 the magazine bestowed on him a somewhat dubious honor by designating him "staff photographer"—a salaried position with benefits (all good), but with one big hitch: *National Geographic* would own his copyright. If Magnum had taught Nick anything pragmatic, it was never, ever, to forfeit your copyright. Nick attempted to negotiate a modified staff-photographer contract that would allow him to retain the rights, but in the end *National Geographic* was intractable. Nick acquiesced. It was 1995, he was already deep into the planning of the tiger project, and he wasn't going to risk that. Still, he felt as if he had sold a part of his soul.

Nearly ten years later, with Johns at the helm, Nick renegotiated his contract retroactively. He now shares his copyright with *National Geographic* on all stories. In 2008 he was named *National Geographic*'s editor-at-large for photography. Meaning? According to David Griffin, who has held several creative positions over the years at National Geographic, including four years as director of photography for the magazine, and then two years as executive editor of E-Publishing at National Geographic Society: "Nick being named editor-at-large for photography—it just meant he couldn't be told what to do. We officialized that role."

National Geographic knew what it had with Nick: a remarkably energetic, focused, and talented photographer who would go to amazing lengths to realize his vision and to tell an original and gripping story. And with that understanding, they extended him virtually free rein. As Griffin says:

Nick's deal with the *Geographic* on the surface is fucking nuts! At some point, he was cranking out stories. But then they became more complex, and took years—consuming more resources in the process. That you spend an incredible amount of money for a guy who produces one or two stories every three or four years, and you can't at all ask him to do a story you may want him to do . . . well, to a manager, it would seem crazy.

But the fact is Nick does so much for *National Geographic*, and the work is brilliant. And the stories rate off the charts. It's all worth it.

In what Griffin calls "the battleground of shrinking media"—including the rapid decline of print magazines—National Geographic Society had to reassess many of its longstanding arrangements with photographers. When Griffin was the magazine's director of photography, anticipating the new realities of budgets and readership, he advised *National Geographic*'s staff photographers to "make yourselves valuable to the company—*beyond* your photography." Nick, he says, took his words to heart, helping out on many fronts: "And the thing is, it's real. . . . He was an incredible ally to me—working with Chris Johns, building lines with Tim Kelly [president of NGS at the time], helping me with advice on photographers. . . ."

"My attraction to particular photographers," says Nick, "has always been about how they see, and if they stay with a subject—*own* it in some way." I asked Nick about his generation of photographers (defined broadly by Nick to include some who are much younger than he is) associated with *National Geographic*: Who possesses an original or wakeup-call storytelling sensibility? Which projects have legs in terms of the depth of the photographers' commitment to their subjects? Which stories are the most eloquent—fueled by an inspired voice and vision, powerfully rendered? Which are born of a considered concept that may also transcend the specificity of the story, with larger reach?

Nick is drawn, he says, to the way David Alan Harvey "works with humanity." As someone committed to the idea of a photographer's unique vision, he admires Jodi Cobb's "insightful and revelatory work—that only she could make—on Saudi women, twenty-first-century slavery, love, beauty, and geishas." He enjoys the consummate storytelling of Ed Kashi and Gerd Ludwig, who have long faced challenges of working in places of tumult: Kashi in the Middle East, and Ludwig in the former Soviet Union and today's Russia. Along these lines, he admires Lynsey Addario's reportage—for both *National Geographic* and the *New York Times Magazine*—on "the effects of war and human suffering, which climaxed with an incredible body of work on Afghan women during and after the Taliban regime." He loves the emotionality and intensity of Maggie Steber's work, especially in Haiti—"She was so *in it*," he says. "Like Susan [Meiselas] in Nicaragua." Nick also greatly respects and believes in Brent Stirton's revealing and tough stories on conservation. He deeply appreciates George Steinmetz, whom he describes as "smart and analytical," and he admires Vince Musi's abilities as a photographic problem solver who brings a comprehensive knowledge of the history of the medium to his work. He mentions Carolyn Drake, Kitra Cahana, Erika Larsen, Amy Toensing, and Stephanie Sinclair: "All are very different, but share fierce independence and a sovereignty of vision as they cover—with so much sensitivity—the human condition."

Nick strongly supports Christian Ziegler, who is building a large body of work on rainforests, and Paul Nicklen, a marine biologist who covers the planet's coldest regions and oceans (and who, Nick says, "broke out" with an extraordinary series on leopard seals). Brian Skerry works in protected ocean habitats: "He was the first to really use underwater photography to address the issues—like the overfishing of bluefin tuna—and still make really interesting photographs," says Nick. He talks of Max Aquellera-Hellweg's "quirky images of science that are in no way cliché." The ability to visually convey a narrative is key to the work's impact, and Nick believes that David Doubilet's remarkable underwater images are always compelling in this way. He continues to admire Steve Winter's "obsession with big cats. . . . He got himself in the door of *National Geographic* with impossible projects: a cat you can never see—the jaguar. And then a cat that you can *really* never see: the snow leopard. . . . He's tenacious."

The artist in Nick is also compelled by formal qualities in work—and he looks at other photographers' innovations and evolution with interest. He says:

> Composition matters a lot to me. Lynn Johnson, for example . . . has started using a square format in her storytelling. I've never been able to do that, to see in a square. It's too formal for me and leaves out the serendipity that I always want to see. I want to see an accident in the background. I need that extra part of the frame, the rectangle part—to show something happening that is not central to the content of what you're seeing. But Lynn's images are so exquisite, it doesn't matter. She's probably the *National Geographic* photographer whose work has grown on me the most. She figured something out.

Although at times feeling branded by the larger photography world because of the famous yellow rectangle, mostly Nick has been proud of the work he and his *National Geographic* colleagues have accomplished. As always, he appreciates being part of something larger. He believes in community and the dialogue and generosity it may engender. As David Griffin puts it: "He's always had that 'Kumbaya' thing. It's part of his nature."

Nick's "Kumbaya" inclinations were peaking: as he contemplated time, space, and light at the Grand Canyon, he was also brainstorming about peace, love, and photography.

In early 2006, soon after the Grand Canyon piece was published, I had a call from him—his voice effusive with his own "Muscle Shoals sound." Nick had an idea he was excited about: a photography festival. The notion had evolved organically, starting with the caving show-and-tells, and then the open-call slideshows during his Berkeley loft days in 1984; it then migrated east with an event he titled "Hotshots Halloween," which, starting in 1992, took place at his home in downtown Charlottesville. When Nick and his family moved to Sugar Hollow in 1999, the event came along with them—it took place right in his backyard.

On the phone, he said to me that he wanted to do something bigger, but with the same "vibe" (the word has two syllables when he says it: "vah-eeb"). People were so geographically scattered, he said, and our lives had become so virtual—images were everywhere, disembodied from their makers and often from their context. People e-mailed but didn't necessarily even talk on the phone, let alone hang out. The photography community needed to feel like a *community*. We needed to pay tribute to its legends who were still living. We needed each other. We needed a three-day festival.

It was cool. It was important. It was *tribal*. It would be fun.

ABOVE: Vince Musi and Nick, LOOK3, 2013. (Projected: Nick's photograph of Hildur and consort, Serengeti National Park, 2012.) Photograph by David Griffin. OPPOSITE: Sylvia Plachy, LOOK3, 2009. Photograph by Eve Styles

Nick hoped to assemble a curatorial advisory group. It's almost impossible to say no to Nick, and I didn't. (He had me at "vibe.") Neither did festival cofounders Jon Golden, David Griffin, Will Kerner, and Jessica Nagle. Nor did designer Yolanda Cuomo, photographer Vince Musi, or *New York Times Magazine* director of photography Kathy Ryan. As Musi puts it: "With Nick there's a kind of Pied Piper thing." It's hard to resist.[4]

The curatorial advisory board first met as a group on October 21, 2006. We walked through the charming, human-scale city of Charlottesville—home to the University of Virginia and Thomas Jefferson's Monticello. We looked at potential sides of buildings and any unclaimed outdoor walls. One would become our "free speech" wall, hosting a body of work addressing social justice. We looked at the trees bisecting the downtown mall—a row of them would serve as the annual home for a range of environmental projects, transformed into banners and featuring images of birds, apes, and myriad other creatures. We looked at galleries and other spaces that might be co-opted for weeklong or monthlong exhibitions of the featured photographers. We gushed over the impressive, recently restored Paramount Theater, built in 1931, where we envisaged the work of the festival's headline photographers being projected as they were interviewed onstage. The idea of these conversations grew out of Nick's years of working with Vince Musi and David Griffin on the National Geographic Seminars. At the Paramount, we'd see discussions meander in often unexpected directions—occasionally, but rarely, going south. Influences and photographic processes would be addressed. As would politics. And sex. Always, the images of the photographer being interviewed would be scrolling behind—a spectacular backdrop of content and context.

Then there was the more direct reincarnation of Nick's backyard slideshows. Friday and Saturday nights during the festival would feature projections held in the capacious covered amphitheater known as the Pavilion, at the east end of Charlottesville's distinctive pedestrian mall, which runs the length of the city's downtown. These curated projections would include projects by about forty photographers each night—from unknown to widely celebrated. Throughout the festival, the car-free mall would organically choreograph lovely chance meetings between photographers, editors, curators, students, teachers, and enthusiasts of all generations, deepening its warmth and camaraderie—its *vah-eeb*.

The event would emulate, in feel, photography and art festivals in Europe's smaller cities and towns, where everyone serendipitously runs into everyone else—such as Visa pour l'Image, the annual photojournalism extravaganza in Perpignan, France, the brainchild of impresario Jean-François Leroy, a close friend of Nick's.

After our first board meeting, Yolanda Cuomo, Kathy Ryan, and I drove together to Richmond, to catch a flight back to New York. The "Festival of the Photograph" still needed a name with panache. While in the car, we played verbally and visually (Cuomo was sketching our ideas during the entire ride) with words that resonated with photography, as well as with the notion of a three-day festival that would feature three main artists. We were so consumed that we missed the exit for the airport—and almost our flight—but by the time we got there, we had a consensus: "LOOK3." We telephoned Nick, who was with the rest of the team. It was unanimous: LOOK3, followed by "Festival of the Photograph"—to bring it home to the medium. And we couldn't resist adding Nick's Woodstocky tagline: "Three days of peace, love, and photography."

A festival was born.

For the first iteration of LOOK3, in June 2007, Andrew Owen, a Charlottesville native, was the festival's manager—the *only* paid staff member. Eventually Lisa Draine took over that role, while Owen served as managing director through 2013. Jenna Pirog first met Nick when she was twenty-four years old and working for Kathy Moran at *National Geographic*; eventually she left to work for Nick—dividing her time between managing his Sugar Hollow studio and working as LOOK3's full-time producer in Charlottesville.[5] She, too, continued through 2013. "Nick is a perfectionist," she says, "and I never wanted to let him down." Pirog observes, though, that Nick can be so focused on what he wants and what he feels should happen that he "doesn't always acknowledge the people in the background. There were times where it felt like—for all of us—'This is Nick's world, and we just all live in it.' His presence is large, and what he is doing is so important. He is often the most interesting person in the room."

For Nick, LOOK3 was a vehicle through which he could, in a sense, transcend "Nick's world" and give back to a community that had offered him so much. He recognized that *National Geographic* had granted him the time and resources to immerse himself in dream projects that were then published in the magazine essentially as he wished. Nick understood the uniqueness of his circumstances and good fortune: he had been able to support his family as a photojournalist. He wanted to honor both his colleagues and the medium of photography itself. Especially, he wanted to excite younger generations with the breadth and possibilities of the medium, in the way that Charles Moore, Mary Ellen Mark, and Philip Jones Griffiths had excited and mentored him.

OPPOSITE: Mary Ellen Mark photographing, Charlottesville High School prom, LOOK3, 2008; ABOVE: Vince Musi, Deborah Willis (seated), and Carrie Mae Weems (right), LOOK3, 2013. (Projected: still from Weems's *Lincoln, Lonnie and Me—A Story in 5 Parts*, 2012.) Photograph by Glenn Baeske

This commitment has been especially evident in the summers of 2010 and 2014, when LOOK3 has made way for the less formal "LOOKbetween." Andrew Owen's invention, LOOKbetween takes place every fourth June (when LOOK3 takes a year off), and provides young and emerging photographers with a unique confluence of workshopping and mentoring, showing and telling. About seventy photographers from all over the world are invited to attend, nominated because of their exceptional promise by professionals in the field. Owen notes that the inspiration for LOOKbetween came from his belief that emerging photographers need "a festival for themselves." With this in mind, he says:

> We moved the festival out of downtown Charlottesville and held it on a farm. We told everyone to bring a tent and camp. The badges were rubber cow tags. We converted barn stalls into workshop rooms. . . . A bluegrass band played during dinner and later, around the campfire. Daytime programming was for group discussion of critical issues. And evening programming was two nights of projections where each artist showed three to five minutes of new work. I think everyone left really on fire.

With LOOK3 and LOOKbetween, Nick knew we had to create a social space, to reaffirm the sense of community—and for this, too, Visa pour l'Image, with its intimate, comfortable atmosphere, was a role model. Nick regularly refers to LOOK3 as the "redneck Perpignan." It's a characterization Leroy enjoys immensely, and he attends almost every year.

ABOVE: Sally Mann (left) interviewing Nan Goldin, LOOK3, 2011. (Projected: Goldin's *Picnic on the Esplanade, Boston*, 1973.) Photograph by Jon Golden. OPPOSITE: Josef Koudelka responding to an audience question from Donna Ferrato, LOOK3, 2013. (Projected: Koudelka's *Czechoslovakia [Strážnice]*, 1966.) Photograph by Dennis Dimick. FOLLOWING SPREAD: LOOKbetween gathering at Deep Rock Farm, near Charlottesville, 2010. Photograph by Martin Gisborne

LOOK3 has also been a way for Nick to connect with some of the photographers whose work he greatly admires—men and women from Magnum and from *National Geographic*, but also from the larger world of photography and all the diversity of vision it embraces.

The first LOOK3, in 2007, featured William Albert Allard, Sally Mann, and Eugene Richards.[6] They were welcomed onstage by Vince Musi, who quickly became the master of ceremonies for the festival. His sonorous voice, relaxed yet dynamic stage presence, and richly informed introductions for the featured artists have made him a festival linchpin. Nick has also grown to depend on Musi as his consigliere—especially when overwhelmed.

As will almost certainly happen with any small, not-for-profit entity with a passionately identified purpose, LOOK3 has experienced a range of challenges, from the obvious—funding—to the more existential. The photographic landscape is very different from what it was in 2007—largely due to the evolving world of social media, and the fact that the vast majority of us are now rarely without a camera. This has provoked identity crises for many organizations dedicated to the medium of photography and its dissemination.

"We shape our tools, and then our tools shape us" (words generally attributed to Marshall McLuhan). Whatever shape LOOK3 takes in the future, it is paramount that the festival keep its soulful, backyard core: bringing together our community, as well as celebrating its practitioners and their work.

FAMILY TIES

At the David Sheldrick Wildlife Trust (DSWT) orphanage,
Nairobi National Park, Kenya, 2010

When dire threats to wildlife demand immediate intervention for the protection of habitat and species, how do we consider the potential impact upon a populace? How is this negotiated, and by whom? What is quantifiable? These concerns came into sharp focus shortly after the Megatransect, when Gabon established thirteen national parks, covering 11 percent of its land.

Some *National Geographic* readers took issue with the creation of the parks, and with the magazine's role—its advocacy—in that process. These critics believed that there had not been sufficient input from the Gabonese people, and that such autocratic action (as they perceived it) undermines any hope for a people's right to self-determination.[1]

These arguments were underscored by the fact that before his death, Gabon's President Omar Bongo Ondimba was denounced by many for alleged human-rights abuses, as well as for misuse and embezzlement of public funds and resources for his personal benefit, while doing very little to lift his people out of poverty. To make alliances with potentially unscrupulous leaders—knowing of their oppressiveness and/or avarice—in order to achieve laudable goals gives rise to myriad questions. It is hardly unprecedented for passionate, forward-thinking activists to engage with corrupt officials to advance otherwise unimpeachable agendas. What particulars permit the ends to justify the means? Moral relativism is slippery at best: how does one work within the circumstances in the moment, even when aspiring to an ideal?

On the other hand, if an expert like Mike Fay—who possesses compelling data and the means to disseminate it, and who will lobby tirelessly for (and usually receive) the necessary funds from the United States and other governments, along with NGOs—does not advocate for wildlife and all that it needs to thrive, who will? Had he not enlisted the cooperation of Bongo—whatever Bongo's motivations—Gabon's parks would not have been created, nor would the corresponding employment and ecotourism opportunities. It is certain that the wildlife of the region would be considerably worse off without them. Is there any probability that the Gabonese people would be better off without them? History hints that, in all likelihood, the acres now designated as parkland would otherwise have been harvested, primarily to the advantage of the timber companies and corrupt leadership, while simultaneously setting off a toxic chain of events: habitat is destroyed; wild animals are more accessible and therefore more vulnerable to poaching; natural resources are exploited.

What Fay proposed to Bongo had the double appeal of being economically pragmatic—the parks would bring money into the country, and provide employment to Gabonese—as well as ecologically sound. And there is nothing hit-and-run about Fay's advocacy. He commits himself entirely, for the duration. Indeed, as of this writing, Mike Fay continues to live, work, and fight for his convictions in Gabon.

That said, standing up for wildlife should not be in conflict with the needs of local people. A variety of approaches are being explored and deployed to accomplish a sustainable, balanced, and mutually beneficial relationship. These include creating conservation-driven ecotourism—conceived intelligently—and incentivizing communities to live alongside *wild*, including predators, by rewarding these human neighbors for the animals' longevity. The goal is to help communities to benefit from their natural resources, while respecting and not depleting them.

Mike Fay was thinking along these lines when he returned to Gabon in 2012. His intention, as he told me in retrospect, was "to make quantum leaps. It's warfare, and the military is now engaged to protect natural resources." But it is not only about land or wildlife: "It's about nation-building and setting national policy. There is a moral imperative."

Now working with Omar Bongo's son, Ali Bongo Ondimba (who assumed the presidency after his father's death), along with Lee White and WCS, Fay would soon establish several programs in Gabon. Critical among these is a "Presidential marine conservation" project known as Gabon Bleu. This initiative helped lead to the 2014 creation of a network of ten new marine areas, or parks, covering more than eighteen thousand square miles. One of the goals of Gabon Bleu, which strives to sustainably manage Gabon's coastal and oceanic waters, is to help protect the large numbers of leatherback turtle nesting sites, humpback and other whales, dolphins, and sharks, among other sea dwellers. This should begin to foster sustainable and economically meaningful ecotourism. It is also intended to improve the country's industrial and artisanal fisheries and fishery cooperatives, both for sustainability and food security. Gabon's waters have been overfished, and populations of depleted species must be replenished. Given the often unchecked offshore gas and oil production and exploration, Gabon Bleu is also in place to help ensure that extraction operations are ecologically safe and utilizing best practices.

In February 2013 I made a pilgrimage to see Fay in Gabon. Fay basically wakes up each morning and considers and plans his day—what must be accomplished? If something on his agenda strikes him as unimportant or not terribly interesting, whether he'll bother with it is a bit of a crapshoot. For sure, my visit was neither necessary nor interesting to Fay, who probably viewed it, at best, as a time-suck. Despite this, and with only a modicum of crankiness, he honored his commitment to see me (surprising many people who know him—I think some of them may have been placing bets), while orchestrating the most experiential visit I might have imagined. But Mike Fay has always been a stand-up guy with me. If he said he'd be there, he'd be there. I was counting on that this trip, as I'd first counted on it at dawn in Rock Creek Park in 2001. I was not disappointed, and gamely jumped into his learning-by-doing approach to my time in Gabon.

On two separate days, I found myself with part of Fay's Gabon Bleu team of young Gabonese men interested in conservation, including Koumba Kombila of the Agence Nationale des Parcs Nationaux. Kombila—persuasive, intelligent, and patient—clearly loves his country and understands and shares Fay's determination to work toward its ecological health. We patrolled the waters near Libreville in a small, beat-up motorboat (a newer model was on its way) under a parching sun, on the lookout for Gabonese fishermen either operating without a license or taking in more fish than permitted. The bottom line, said Kombila, is to respect the fish, respect the waters. During this process, the team would inform the locals who were fishing illegally—often families with young children who (my boat-mates informed me) should have been in school—about respecting laws which, because of limited resources, exist to protect them.

They want the fishermen to understand that catch limits don't arise from bureaucratic arbitrariness, but are there to protect *their own* best interests. At the same time, the Gabon Bleu team understands that a long-term view may be a challenge for those supporting their families hand-to-mouth. The true adversaries—the foreign, especially Chinese, trawlers overfishing the ocean—are also being taken on successfully by Gabon Bleu.

Later during my ten-day stay in Gabon, Fay let me join him on a "flyover" of the large Wonga Wongué Presidential Reserve, about an hour and a half south of Libreville, and where he planned to spend the night and catch up with his colleagues based there. We flew in a Cessna 182 belonging to WCS, a light, single-engine four-seater that would satisfy anyone's bird-envy. A flyover is no joyride (well actually, it kind of is). Dexterously spiraling and taking the occasional steep dip, our young German pilot, Dietrich Ian Lafferty, facilitated Fay's voracious spotting and counting and photographing of fauna and flora as we flew. During the twenty-four hours at Wonga Wongué, Fay was updated on any wildlife concerns and happenings, all the while continuing to collect data on everything from pressure drops after a storm to the quantity of animals he was seeing, tallied by species.

Seen from the air, the landscape was a gently undulating savanna of tall grass and patches of forest, partly denuded by logging and burning. Because of these human assaults, the forests' contours are sharply delineated, dark green, lush, and peppered with red-tufted trees.

There were elephants roaming below us—many elephants. The primary conservation goal of the Presidential Reserve has been to protect this population from poachers. And, unlike in so many other elephant habitats on the planet, the effort here seems to be working. In December 2015, Nathan Williamson, living part-time in Gabon, told me that the Presidential Reserve had just celebrated a full year without finding a single poached elephant. "Elephants are bouncing back here in a big way," he said—hastening to add: "We are the exception to the rule."

But some residents of the country at large have grown resentful of the elephants—or more precisely, what they view as President Bongo's privileging of wildlife over his citizens, often at the humans' expense. In Gabon's highly contested presidential election on August 31, 2016, Ali Bongo Ondimba was declared the winner again after a disputed vote that resulted in immediate demands for a recount, and days of rioting.[2] A few days before the election, it was reported that some voters "planned to sit out the vote in protest, repeating a common refrain that can be heard in the forests and on city streets alike: Let the elephants vote for him instead." The unrest has apparently forced Bongo to commit to addressing the needs of his citizens, which will include protecting their crops from elephants, but presumably doing so in a way that will not undermine his unique achievements in conservation.[3]

I asked Fay whether he considers the notion of justice when he thinks about conservation. He responded with characteristic terseness: "There is no justice, only those who fight for what is right." *Justice*, it seems, is a relative term.

The fight for what is right would become even more acute in Nick and Fay's project that followed *The Last Place on Earth*. It began—as is often the case with Fay—with a view from above. After the fifteen-month Megatransect, Fay considered what his next expedition would be—landing on the idea of a "Megaflyover." With funding from the National Geographic Society and WCS, he took off in June 2004, in a Cessna 182 that had been especially outfitted for his needs. With pilot Peter Ragg, Fay did a six-month, twenty-one-country, low-flying aerial survey of the African continent, as always collecting endless data, including more than ninety thousand photographs (cameras were programmed to automatically take pictures every twenty seconds). He wanted both to understand and to document the human footprint on some major and extremely diverse ecoregions.[4]

As anticipated, Fay found that "humans have penetrated very deeply into every single ecosystem in Africa" that was documented, and that there are many areas where "soils and vegetation and water systems are being exhausted." That said, Fay also concluded that for the most part, the human footprint appeared lighter throughout Africa than, for example, in the United States, Europe, or China—saying: "It looks to me like [Africans] are really thinking about their relationship with the land."[5] With this information, Fay would then approach the United States Congress, World Bank, United Nations, EU, and other key players, imploring them to emphasize natural-resource management in their development strategies and foreign policies. The idea was to figure out where the human demand upon natural resources already surpassed the land's ability to supply. Strategically, this would inform both where emergency action must be taken and where it was possible to engage natural-resource management more proactively.

During the Megaflyover, Fay made a discovery. After surveying Zakouma in southern Chad, he wrote an exultant e-mail: "Nick, I've found an incredible paradise." With his note, Fay included a photograph of an impossibly massive herd of elephants, gathered in a circle.

To Nick it seemed unreal: "That's what we dream of when we talk about elephants in Africa—elephants as far as the eye can see. I'm thinking: 'Wow—he's found the lost Africa!'"

Again, whatever chill might have lingered since their last collaboration—the surfing hippos story—dissipated. Nick, assisted by Nathan Williamson, joined Fay in Zakouma in 2006. The following year, he spent months at zoologist Iain Douglas-Hamilton's Save the Elephants research facility in the Samburu National Reserve in northern Kenya. And later, in 2010, he would go on to work with Angela Sheldrick and her husband, Robert Carr-Hartley, at the David Sheldrick Wildlife Trust's orphan elephant nursery in Nairobi, and at related sites in Kenya. After years of photographing forest elephants primarily, he'd committed himself to broader coverage of the species—hoping to look at specific populations of Africa's savanna elephants as well. (He would ultimately compile a selection of his work as *Earth to Sky: Among Africa's Elephants, A Species in Crisis*, published by Aperture in 2013.)

Chad's Zakouma National Park was created in 1963. By the time Fay alerted Nick to the area's exceptional ecosystem, the Zakouma conservation project—assisting both the park and the area at large—had had the support of extensive EU funding for more than fifteen years. An estimated 3,600 elephants lived in Zakouma National Park in 2002—just a couple of years before Fay's flyover. The census is conducted inside the park and just outside its borders during the dry season, when all the elephants in the region are concentrated there, because the park is the only place where they can find water. A natural "bowl" in the desert, during the rainy season Zakouma National Park collects and stores water in its rivers, and its lowest points get submerged. It becomes the elephants' sanctuary and stronghold during the dry season, because there is always water and therefore food. They forage better outside the park's boundaries during the overwhelming rainy season. Few people live outside the park's periphery, which is patrolled by guards paid with conservation resources. Nevertheless, outside the park's borders is *not* "protected" land; cattle and human settlements are permitted.

For Nick, the park's river—which provides quenching puddles even during the most arid periods— became a natural bait spot. He and Williamson set up elaborate flash systems and camera traps, using simple Canon digital cameras with interchangeable lenses. Williamson explains:

> The key is placement and angle, and we used the wide-angle lens to include the landscape as well. But you need some reason for the animal to put up with the gear, because—being incredibly intelligent—they know it's there. You are not fooling them, ever. So you want to find a place that they desperately need to be, or they'll just avoid the cameras, or really mess with them. Sometimes they get really curious if they see themselves reflected in the lens—and they stay for a while, triggering lots of self-portraits.

By the time Nick came to Zakouma in 2006, he had made the full switch to digital, using his Canon 5D and Canon 1D cameras. This would be the last project to be so visually inflected by his unique use of flash. (Six years later, when photographing the nocturnal Serengeti lions, he would truly grasp the digital camera's technical potential: the flexibility inherent in the raw files. He would be free to think less about "how to paint with light" and more about "how digital lets me stretch the dark.") But now,

OPPOSITE: Crocodile (camera-trap photograph). ABOVE: Serval cat (camera-trap photograph). Both Zakouma National Park, Chad, 2006

in the unsparing desert sun of Zakouma, he used the flash to finesse texture, luminosity, scale, and depth of field, imbuing some of his images with a painterly light, as in those of elephants drinking in a moonlit dusk.

In Zakouma National Park, along with an abundance of elephants, Nick, Fay, and Williamson saw a vast array of birds, many types of cats—from servals to lions—and plenty of fish, contained in the river's puddles. Beyond the camera traps, Nick flew more than forty hours in the no-frills Zenair Ultralight with the park's chief technical director, Luis Arranz. At the same time, Fay was flying his Cessna, collecting data and making videos. He would let Nick know where he spotted groups of elephants, and Arranz and Nick would follow, primarily so that Nick could make aerial shots. At one point, Arranz was forced to make a hazardous landing—after first *stopping* the plane in midair by flying into the wind—when they found themselves heading straight for a storm directly over their airstrip and home base. Arranz's maneuver allowed them to land gently, and stop without careening through rough terrain. Nick was severely shaken, but Arranz insisted that he fly the very next day. ("There's a lot of sense to that getting-back-in-the-saddle thing," admits Nick.)

Often Nick and Fay would work from the vantage of a culvert bridge, making photographs and shooting video, respectively. They had different theories about the optimal approach here: Nick thought it best to be camouflaged so the elephants wouldn't see him when they came to drink. Fay rejected the idea of camouflage, instead sitting out in the open, strategizing that it is better to make himself obvious to these wise animals. Nick is not sure which of them is correct (but notes that Fay's visibility made his own camouflaging pointless).

It was only one of many squabbles along the way. As ever in the Nichols and Fay dynamic, there was a period during this project when they ceased speaking, communicating only through Williamson—an unenviable role for the young assistant.

Nick and Williamson spent about four months working with Fay in Zakouma, beginning in March 2006. Fay's initial purpose was to observe the elephants as the seasons transformed from dry to rainy—when and how the animals left the protected park, and whether they left in big groups, more inclusive than just family, or instead converged as clans later, outside its borders.

Charles Siebert has written eloquently about the social life of elephants, and the intense role family and friends play in their existence:

> Any wild elephant group is, in essence, one large and highly sensitive organism. Young elephants are raised within a matriarchal family of doting female caregivers, beginning with the birth mother and then branching out to include sisters, cousins, aunts, grandmothers, and established friends. These bonds endure over a life span that can be as long as 70 years. Young elephants stay

close to their mothers and extended family members—males until they are about 14, females for life. When a calf is threatened or harmed, all the other elephants comfort and protect it.[6]

He goes on to describe the complexity and range of their communication—the vocalizations and calls conveyed at different frequencies, some of which can be heard by other elephants more than a mile a way. They are clearly sentient animals, and indeed, Siebert says: "The long-accrued anecdotal evidence of the elephant's extraordinary intelligence is being borne out by science. Studies show that structures in the elephant brain are strikingly similar to those in humans." MRI scans of an elephant's brain, and the presence of the neurons known as spindle cells, suggest a relationship to the human brain in terms of memory, processing emotions, self-awareness, empathy, and social awareness.[7]

In Zakouma, one way to understand their social patterns, especially as the elephants left the park, was to monitor their movement by fitting selected elephants with radio-tracking collars. Another was surveillance: looking down from the Cessna, Fay and his team would count, not just elephants but all the animals they saw, by species—giving him a sense of the health of the ecosystem at large. But most important, as Fay has written, was to understand "how vulnerable the elephants are to poaching during the four to five months they're outside the park."[8]

Even though there was poaching outside the park, where the elephants migrated for food during Zakouma's rainy season, within its borders they had been relatively safe. Still, they were always fearful, given the brutality they had experienced or witnessed especially beyond its boundaries, although precisely how or if they understood the moment they had crossed this abstract line between park and peril is unknowable. Luis Arranz says, in *Earth to Sky*:

> One of the things that affects me most is when you see a group of elephants, and as soon as they smell you they start to run. Some of the females come back to try to protect their young, but you can see the fear in all of them. They're animals that wouldn't have to be afraid of anything in nature, but after several centuries of being hunted in such a way, they have this panic inside them.[9]

Sadly, this evident inner panic would soon reflect an even more extreme and nightmarish reality. One day, as Nick and Arranz were flying, looking for big groups of elephants—Nick was exhilarated photographing this elephant paradise—they spotted a carcass from the air. They landed, and went out with the park's guards to investigate. The elephant had been shot by a poacher—with an AK-47 or M-14 rifle—and it had happened *inside* the park.

Literally before their eyes, the once comparatively protected Zakouma National Park and the immediately surrounding area were transformed into a paradise lost. The promise of thousands of elephants safely flourishing, the article they had planned about an Edenic haven for elephants, all turned crushingly dark. "The situation changed suddenly and horribly, and so the story became about the poaching," remembers Nick. "We're in it, so we don't see it yet, but this is the start of the next and most serious ivory crisis. This is blood ivory. Mike became a maniac and would go out on horseback, on patrol with the guards."

How had this happened? In April 2006 there was a failed coup d'état in Chad, when forces attempted to overthrow President Idriss Déby Itno. Suddenly the park was filled with rebels. Poachers, counting on everyone's preoccupation with the coup, took advantage of the chaos to infiltrate the park.

Elephants, Zakouma National Park, 2006

On April 11, Arranz received a report that eighty Chadian military vehicles were moving south, twenty-five miles east of the park. They had, Fay learned, been sent to intercept rebels moving north toward the capital, N'Djamena. On the same day they heard of the onslaught of rebel forces, Arranz found that one of the pools of water had been poisoned, apparently by poachers. Fay reported that "nine civets, a lioness, two hyenas, five raptors, and hundreds of doves had died from drinking the water." The lioness had two cubs, now orphans. "Without their mother"—wrote Fay in the March 2007 *National Geographic* cover story, "Ivory Wars: Last Stand in Zakouma"—"they were now members of the living dead."[10]

Later, Fay discovered the massive carcass of a bull elephant. He describes the scene in "Ivory Wars":

> I lifted the bull's ear. Lines of bright red blood bubbled and streamed from his lips, pooling in the dust. His skin was checkered with wrinkles. The base of his trunk was as thick as a man's torso. Deep fissures ran like rivers through the soles of his feet; in those lines, I could trace every step he had taken during his thirty years of life. This elephant's ancestors had survived centuries of raiding by the armies of Arab and African sultans from the north in search of slaves and ivory. He had lived through civil war and droughts, only to be killed today for a few pounds of ivory to satisfy human vanity in some distant land. There were tender blades of grass in his mouth. He and his friends had been peacefully roaming in the shaded forest, snapping branches filled with sweet gum. Then, the first gunshot exploded. He bolted, too late. Horses overtook him. Again and again, bullets pummeled his body. We counted eight

OPPOSITE: Park guards on patrol. ABOVE: Elephant-collaring team. Both Zakouma National Park, 2006

small holes in his head. Bullets had penetrated the thick skin and lodged in muscle, bone, and brain before he fell. We heard forty-eight shots before we found him.[11]

As the tumult continued, Fay proceeded with his initial project of collaring selected elephants with the purpose of tracking them and collecting data. By all accounts, wearing the collar does not influence their movement, and it seemed more critical than ever to learn where and when these elephants would be most vulnerable. Collaring is always risky, but the risk is especially grave when collaring a big animal like an elephant. There must be a clear, unequivocal sense that what may be learned from collaring the animal—the potential benefit to the larger elephant population—is worth the risk, and that there is no other, less invasive way to get this information.

One collared female, Annie, repeatedly circled out of the park and then back, for eighty-six days, covering 1,015 miles, only to be slaughtered by poachers. But Annie had served a valuable purpose: understanding her route helped Fay and his team eventually to protect the corridor she and other elephants took.

Given the strength of their family ties, the collaring process is particularly traumatic with elephants— for both the individual animal and the herd. Annie, it turned out, was the matriarch of a group of some five hundred elephants—all of them distressed when she was collared. Nick recalls: "Her little baby was standing next to her when she was darted. We created so much turmoil in her group—it

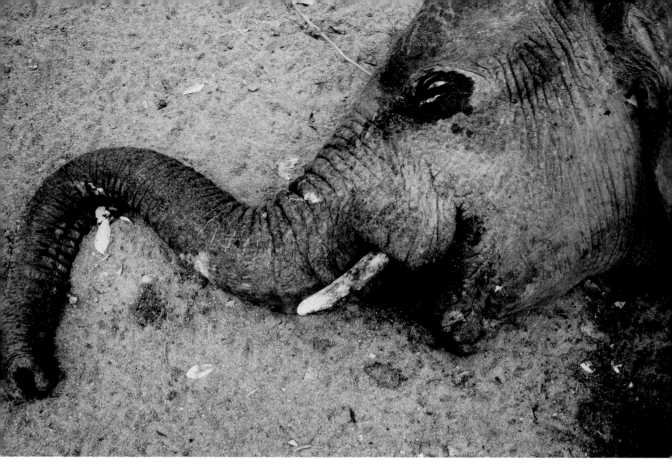

Young elephant, killed in Zakouma National Park, 2006

was horrible." To collar an elephant, it must first be tranquilized. Most often, this is achieved with tranquilizer darts generally shot by a highly experienced veterinarian who sneaks up on the elephant from downwind; as Nick says: "It feels like hunting, and is incredibly stressful for the families of the darted elephant, who witness everything." Once asleep, the elephant falls and may be collared. But it is possible that in the fall, or under sedation, the animal may stop breathing, and that his or her lungs will collapse. Therefore, it is critical to get the elephant standing up as soon as the collar is on. The attending veterinarian will move everyone out of the elephant's way, and then will administer a reversal drug—immediately moving to a safe place from which to observe the animal emerging from sedation, which happens almost instantly. If all goes well, the elephant will get up, and then try and get reoriented. The whole ordeal, once the elephant is darted, can take about thirty minutes.

But things can go terribly wrong, and that is indeed what occurred shortly after Annie was collared. One elephant, upon being darted, fell over and sustained an injury. "They could not get her up," Nick recalls. "And her family all came over. It was brutal. They had to put her down in front of her family. When that happened, Mike ended it. He said: 'We're done. I'm never doing this again. The collaring project is over.'"

Poachers want ivory—as much ivory as they can get—so they tend to target the largest elephants with the biggest tusks, usually the oldest members of the herd. When a large matriarch, such as

Annie, is killed, it affects the life of an entire family, an entire group of elephants. The leader, the teacher is gone. Poaching cripples and often destroys the entire family and societal structure of elephants, whose ties to each other are profound.

Also, according to Fay: "It screws with the gene pool seriously." Among other effects, tusks are getting smaller. When we spoke, he likened this to the depletion of resources in general, such as what happens to forests with logging: "If you go into a forest and you take out the biggest tree of every species, and then you go back in and you take the biggest ones that are left, and then you go back in and you take the biggest ones that are left again, and you hit it six times, you're basically in a forest of dwarves now. . . . They call it 'high-grading' . . . creaming off the best. . . . It's the same thing with elephants."

The elephant population in Zakouma National Park dropped from the 3,885 censused in 2006 to as low as about 400 just six years later, according to Arranz. The motivation behind this slaughter was economic. By 2013 a single large elephant tusk could be sold on the black market in Africa for $6,000, which is, as Nick points out in *Earth to Sky*, "enough to support an unskilled worker for ten years in some African countries."[12] Between 2010 and late 2014, the wholesale price of raw elephant tusks in Beijing, for example—China being the largest market—tripled, according to a Save the Elephants report.

The first global ivory ban went into effect in 1990 after the Convention on International Trade in Endangered Species of Wild Fauna and Flora (CITES) listed the African elephant as one of the world's most threatened animals. The ban was relatively effective until 1999. Then (according to Humane Society International), CITES succumbed to pressure from some African countries, and allowed an ostensibly one-off sale to Japan of 49.4 metric tons of stockpiled ivory from Botswana, Namibia, and Zimbabwe, with proceeds going to elephant conservation, and with the caveat that this ivory's provenance would be clearly indicated. This happened again in 2008, to the dismay of all those on the frontlines committed to protecting elephants. This time, CITES approved the sale of 102 metric tons of government stockpiled ivory to Japan and China, again with the caveat. But in both cases, the sale of legal ivory not only fed the market and increased the value of an elephant tusk, it has also served as a front for much larger trade in illegal ivory.

Resson Kantai Duff, the Nairobi-based Head of Awareness for Save the Elephants, told me: "Eventually, we must deal with all the international organized crime syndicates trafficking illegal ivory which operate just like drug or weapons traffickers, and are some of the people involved in the mass killings and civil unrest in the DRC or Central African Republic."

Brent Stirton and Bryan Christy's gripping investigative 2015 *National Geographic* cover story "Tracking Ivory" follows the trail of faux ivory elephant tusks, fabricated by taxidermist George Dante to pass as the real thing, and fitted with camouflaged GPS devices.[13] The false tusks were tracked as they were illegally trafficked throughout Africa. In his text, Christy reports bluntly:

> A booming Chinese middle class with an insatiable taste for ivory, crippling poverty in Africa, weak and corrupt law enforcement, and more ways than ever to kill an elephant have created a perfect storm. The result: Some 30,000 African elephants are slaughtered every year . . . and the pace of killing is not slowing. Most illegal ivory goes to China, where a pair of ivory chopsticks can bring more than a thousand dollars and carved tusks sell for hundreds of thousands of dollars.[14]

With regard to international ivory trafficking, in 2013 CITES named China, Kenya, Malaysia, the Philippines, Thailand, Uganda, Tanzania, and Vietnam all "countries 'of primary concern.'"[15]

Perhaps the most horrifying aspect of Christy's story—and there are many—are the connections among ivory trafficking, terrorists (such as the infamous warlord Joseph Kony, leader of the Ugandan Lord's Resistance Army), and the destabilization of African governments. As Christy reports, one of Kony's defectors, Dominic Ongwen, informed African Union forces that "Kony's plan is to obtain as much ivory as possible 'for his future survival should he not be able to overthrow the government of Uganda.'" According to Ongwen, Kony plans to establish ties to the Nigerian terrorist group Boko Haram—whose leader, Abubakar Shekau, is allied with ISIS, giving that Middle East terrorist group a foothold in west Africa. This investigation also looked at the Janjaweed of Sudan, responsible for the Darfur massacres, the Seleka in the Central African Republic, and the Democratic Forces for the Liberation of Rwanda rebels based in the Democratic Republic of Congo. Collectively these terror groups are responsible for the deaths of over two million people.

Luis Arranz (who answered my questions in his native Spanish) has worked in African parks for more than three decades. After his time as technical director at Zakouma, he moved on to direct the Garamba National Park in the DRC until mid-2014, and then did a brief stint in the Republic of Congo's Odzala National Park. As of 2017, he is with WWF managing the Dzanga-Sangha Protected Areas in CAR.

Arranz is not optimistic about the survival of wildlife, rhinoceroses and elephants in particular. Their future, he says, is *muy obscuro*—"very dark." He continues:

> I think most of the money that is "dedicated" to conservation goes to meetings, trips, dinners, great declarations, and long-term plans; what is really needed is work on the ground. No poacher will stop killing elephants because three hundred people got together in Australia to talk about the issue. Of

While poachers are slaughtering some of the last surviving central African elephants for their tusks, a refuge in Chad gives this endangered species armed protection—and a fighting chance. Conservationist J. MICHAEL FAY and photographer MICHAEL NICHOLS report from the front lines.

IVORY WARS

LAST STAND IN ZAKOUMA

54 NATIONAL GEOGRAPHIC • MARCH 2007

OPPOSITE: *National Geographic*, March 2007: "Ivory Wars: Last Stand in Zakouma"; ABOVE: Antipoaching team, Zakouma National Park, 2006

course, you have to have meetings, but keep it to a minimum, with only the necessary people. And then, *work* in the parks. . . . There is a race against the clock. There are still some parks in Africa that can be saved, but there is a lot of pressure on them . . . they could disappear in very little time.

The massacre of elephants continues in east Africa. In Tanzania alone, it has been reported, the elephant population dropped by over 65,000 between 2009 and 2015.[16] According to Tanzania's Ministry of Natural Resources and Tourism, Ruaha National Park and Rungwa Game Reserve have become a "slaughterhouse for elephants."

Arranz stresses the urgent need—while of course protecting wildlife and habitat in Tanzania and in Kenya—also to protect land in areas of human conflict, with lower human population densities, such as parks in Chad, Congo, and Gabon. If the conflicts cease, he notes, these protected areas may actually be able to recover. If there is healthy, intact habitat, there will be wildlife.

At the same time, he insists that more must be done *everywhere* to assist park guards in defending not just the wildlife in their charge, but their own lives as well, which are constantly at risk.

On September 18, 2012, Nick and others at *National Geographic* received an e-mail from Mike Fay letting them know that five park guards had been murdered in Zakouma. Accusations ricocheted in

ABOVE: Virtues family. OPPOSITE: Elephant enjoying a mud bath. Both Samburu National Reserve, Kenya, 2007

the ensuing chaos, which, wrote Fay, "if true to form in Africa will just cause the protection system to be compromised, thus allowing the poachers to kill more elephants." In response to events like this, Arranz insists on arming park guards—not always a popular position. The guards, who are being asked to risk their lives, are up against generally well-armed poachers. Arranz believes they must be given the tools to do their job both effectively and safely.

The rapid decline in numbers of Zakouma's elephants was frightening. Fay recalled in his e-mail the words of explorer William Stamps Cherry, who wrote in 1900: "There is no possible way of estimating the number of elephants in {Africa's} interior. It may be five hundred thousand, it may be a million. I think more likely millions." In stark contrast, Fay noted: "Now when we say elephants of Zakouma, we mean the last remaining herd (of just over 400 elephants . . . only a few males and a single baby.)"

Because of people like Fay and Arranz, however—and the courage and dedication of the park guards, and the attention elicited by articles such as "Ivory Wars"—from January 2013 to mid-2015 *no* elephants were poached in Zakouma. According to Arranz, the elephant population has in fact started to recover—at least in numbers. Christy reports that more than forty calves have been born; as of fall 2016, the herd has increased to 450 animals. Even so, in September 2015 poachers killed the mothers of two of the newborn calves: one died; the other is presumed dead. The park remains on high alert. Ongoing vigilance is critical.

Nick's work has consistently been revelatory, in the most literal sense. For the series of stories that would comprise *The Last Place on Earth*, he photographed as the odyssey unfolded, following the ever-changing ecosystems, terrains, and light, which allowed for a diversity of visual texture. That project, with its built-in plotline and an intensely dynamic protagonist in Mike Fay, was not about focusing on specific animals (other than Fay) or particular environmental features. With the Virunga mountain gorillas, the Gombe chimpanzees, and the Bandhavgarh tigers, Nick undertook a form of portraiture of individual animals in their environmental and social/family context, with their family histories—sometimes extensive—and long-term studies at his disposal. But he couldn't necessarily spend many hours a day with these animals: the animals' own activities, or the sometimes limited access permitted to them, precluded this.

On the other hand, photographing individual elephants and their families in conducive circumstances allowed for an intensity of observation over long periods each day, for many days in a row. This pacing took Nick's understanding, and thus his reportage, to new levels of intimacy and intricacy.

Still, the conditions had to be right. Until this point, Nick says, "I had never photographed elephants who were not afraid. . . . The forest elephants in Congo, and then the elephants in Chad . . . knew man as hunter. I'd get downwind of them, so I could sneak up on them for a photograph, but there was never the chance to peacefully and openly observe behavior."

It was in 2007, at Iain Douglas-Hamilton's elephant research camp in Samburu, northern Kenya, that Nick finally encountered elephants that as yet had no reason to fear man. He had met Douglas-Hamilton's

daughter Mara (known as "Dudu"), in Gabon, and had been intrigued by her promise: "You've got to come see the elephants where my family does its study. The elephants in Samburu are not afraid. You can get right next to them." Nick asked Chris Johns if *National Geographic* might publish a story on "happy elephants," and Johns agreed. It would be a welcome contrast to the horrors he had recently experienced and covered in Chad and the Republic of Congo.

With the Samburu elephants, Nick was able to take a concentric-circles approach, examining individual animals, family structures, and larger clans—all within a specific environment. This system afforded him a keen sense of the elephants' social dynamics, as well as a sense of their quotidian interactions and daily lives, constantly animated by dramas of their own making. Visually, this would enhance his compositional acuity, as he had ongoing access to repeated behaviors, gestures, formations, in a relatively predictable physical environment where the animals are wild, but habituated to human presence.

A natural geometry of nonlinear details, at times disjunctive, enlivens many of Nick's images from Samburu. Sometimes, there is a feral grace and self-possession in an animal's gesture—as seen in the photograph of a young male elephant reveling in mud. His position is nothing less than balletic: the bull's two forelegs are extended in front of him, his head and trunk tilted up in a parallel extension in the opposite direction, above his back leg. There is a magnificent sense of multidirectional alignment, and this is echoed in the larger composition, where we see other elephants, some lying down in their own yogalike poses, others with their backs to us—the landscape varying from mud to grasses and trees to a shapely hill in the distance. The dispersal of elements captured here, and in some of Nick's other more complex compositions, distinguish them from being simply illustrative documents of what's in front of him.

At their most provocative, Nick's photographs are more elliptical than documentary. They connote rather than denote. The spatial relationships between foreground and background, stillness and movement, what we see within the frame and what we are led to imagine outside its definition, are all in perpetual play.

Like the work of many of his peers—at Magnum, at National Geographic—Nick's images bear witness and tell stories. That said, he is not an "animal whisperer," nor is he interested in *becoming one* with his subjects. He has neither the presumptuousness nor the impudence to make such claims. But when he follows his intuition to go beyond the surface of his subjects, entering their world, abandoning his own ego in the process, the work blazes with a rawness, a transformative connection to something outside himself. Nick is not just depicting an elephant, but revealing its essence and individuality, and he achieves a resonant authenticity—on the animals' terms, we might say, rather than a vision filtered through a human perspective. This happens vividly with the elephants of Samburu, images that were first featured in "Family Ties," with a text by David Quammen, in *National Geographic*'s September 2008 issue.[17]

Iain Douglas-Hamilton was born in England in 1942, studied zoology at Oxford, and then as a young man moved to Tanzania, where he undertook the first important study of elephants' social structures and migration patterns. As Jane Goodall had with chimpanzees, Douglas-Hamilton focused on studying individual animals. In 1993, he founded Save the Elephants (STE), a conservation organization based in Nairobi. In 1997, he facilitated a study in Kenya's Samburu National Reserve that had been proposed and initiated by a young U.S. scientist, George Wittemyer. Wittemyer's

Maya Angelou and her daughter, both of the Poets family, greet Boone, an elderly bull, Samburu National Reserve, 2007

study focused on aspects of elephant social relationships. Douglas-Hamilton soon joined Wittemyer in Samburu, establishing the Save the Elephants research facility by the Ewaso Ngiro River.

STE has collected extensive data over the years through collaring—a practice Douglas-Hamilton has advanced despite the risks, and which he continues to develop. With the collars, he has focused on the land and travel corridors that elephants need to survive in Kenya (just as, in Zakouma, the elephant Annie provided Fay and his team with vital information about the routes of her herd before she was murdered).

Elephants need land, and they have to move. Douglas-Hamilton works with his colleagues in local communities to deduce how best to balance the needs of elephants with those of the human population. Elephants can alter the landscape advantageously by the way they travel through it, creating "highways" and forest clearings. If the elephants' habitat is too confined, however, and they do not have enough space to roam as they must, they may end up depleting and destroying their own habitat—for example stripping the bark off trees, which subsequently die. Furthermore, if the elephants' habitat does not provide enough food, they will also wreak havoc on agricultural areas—"crop-raiding," as it's commonly called—which negatively affects the lives and economies of the local communities.

STE is committed to expanding its network of "geo-fencing": an innovative, technologically driven tracking system that uses Safaricom cellphone SIM cards installed in GPS-GSM (Global System for Mobile communications) elephant collars. A virtual fence line is programmed into the tracking collar, which then sends a text alert message in "real time" to members of local communities when a collared elephant is too close

for comfort to humans attempting to live without conflict near wildlife. Concomitantly, STE is also building elephant-corridor routes—informed by the data collected from the GSM collars—along which elephants may move great distances safely between protected reserves. It is hoped that, together, the corridors and the geo-fencing will eventually facilitate the peaceful coexistence of elephants and humans in northern Kenya.

In the short term, while the technology continues to be perfected, the most immediate and effective approach is tangible fencing, and diligent, dedicated guards. The inhabitants of this part of Kenya are largely pastoralists who depend on grazing goats and cattle; the health of their grazing lands means the health of their finances. But the fence works both ways: it's not just about keeping elephants off grazing lands; a critical component of this strategy is the assurance that livestock will not graze on land that is reserved for wildlife, and that the carrying capacity of all the land will not be exceeded. Kenyans also recognize that elephants bring visitors and a tourism economy to Kenya. They are, in fact, the country's primary attraction, and (along with agriculture) a major revenue-generator.

Safari/trophy hunting, while illegal in Kenya, is permitted in most other African countries with large elephant populations. Soon after Nick's period in Samburu in 2007, however, the horror of blood ivory infiltrated Douglas-Hamilton's once murder-free elephant haven. Alarming numbers of elephants as well as rhinoceroses were slaughtered by poachers for their tusks and horns.

Douglas-Hamilton is soft-spoken and gracious, with tousled white hair and a broad smile. His research, concentrating closely on the familial interactions of elephants, would be Nick's entry point to this field, and later his focus. When I met with him, it became clear that this was one reason why Nick's time in Samburu was so fruitful. Another was that Douglas-Hamilton assigned him Daniel Lentipo, a young Samburu who had been a research assistant to George Wittemyer. Douglas-Hamilton told me:

> After a brief introduction from me, Nick quickly got sucked in and became part of the landscape. He was particularly receptive to the idea of working with local researchers. We gave Nick Daniel Lentipo from Samburu—one of our best on-the-ground, trained researchers—who knew each elephant individually, each elephant's life history. . . . Nick was able to look through his lens knowing the background of each animal. Daniel was with him nonstop, which was very valuable.

Each morning Nick would set off with Lentipo and Williamson (who was videotaping regularly, when not repairing any conceivable technical and other breakdown). They rented a Land Rover from Douglas-Hamilton's oldest daughter, Saba, a conservationist who works in television, presenting, narrating, and producing natural-history programming. Saba's vehicle was well-adapted to the savannas: open for 360-degree views, with a diesel engine that purrs more than revs (a calmer sound for the animals), and built with a short wheel base, helpful in negotiating the challenges of the often rocky or muddy surfaces, and the need for quick switchbacks, whether due to the crazed terrain or the sudden appearance of animals. The vehicle was also set up with a removable bump-out that allows a photographer or filmmaker to extend his or her reach. This was the first time Nick was photographing in a savanna environment and working for the most part *not* on foot. Counterintuitively, he found, shooting from the car allowed him to approach elephants more closely: accustomed to Land Rovers, they seemed less disturbed by them than by a pedestrian. And walking in the company of elephants generally requires precautions, about which Nick has serious misgivings:

Babylon, of the Biblical Towns family, with three generations of her descendants, Samburu National Reserve, 2007

I didn't want to be with a guy with a big-ass gun, which is what happens if you choose to walk. I didn't want any possibility that an animal would be shot because I had to be protected. All those years working and walking in central Africa, Mike Fay and I never had guns. We had big sticks. If you don't have a gun, you're going to have to use your brain. If you have a gun, it's too easy to use this missile. . . . You're smarter, more diligent, when you *don't* have the gun.

Lentipo knew every one of the elephants by name, and could identify them even from great distances. (For the most part, the names of the families had been devised by Wittemyer.) Lentipo would tell Nick: "That's Babylon, matriarch of the group known as the Biblical Towns. That's Babylon's daughter, and there's her granddaughter." He knew the ages, the familial relations, and the characteristics that distinguished the Biblical Towns from the First Ladies, the Royals, the American Indians, the Planets, the Virtues, the Spice Girls, the Winds—a few of the more than forty elephant families that coexist in the Samburu ecosystem. The names playfully designate the groups and the family ties, while identifying a subset of related individuals (recalling Jane Goodall's individuating system of giving chimpanzee family members names that begin with the same first letter: Frodo, Freud, and Fifi; Goblin and Gremlin, etc.).

Lentipo, an exceptional spotter, interpreted the elephants' behavior for Nick—behavior he could anticipate from miles away—enabling Nick to position himself strategically. As he had in Zakouma, Nick took advantage of the river meandering through the savanna, which lends physical contour as well as a destination to the elephants' movement.

Winds family, Samburu National Reserve, 2007

Lentipo's unique knowledge of each group's distinct habits, combined with the elemental pull of the river, allowed Nick and Williamson to focus on an individual herd over a period of many consecutive days. They'd wear the same clothes each day, never using deodorant (smell is a guiding sense for elephants), in order to habituate the animals sensorially to their presence. There were rules of etiquette to be learned, and Nick did not master them quickly. Eventually, however, he achieved the proximity he desired, primarily because the elephants, apparently judging him a kind of benign stalker, tended to ignore him and go about their business. That said, Nick never imposed himself in such a way as to influence their movement, never came between a mother and her calf, and constantly minded his manners. In *Earth to Sky*, Nick recalls:

> Upon encountering the elephants, we would park the car, allowing them room to decide what they wanted to do—feed, play, sleep. If I drove in among them too quickly, I would get the dreaded head-shake, which meant I'd been very rude. If I parked in a place where they wanted to be, we would find our car surrounded, elephants close in on all sides—snoring, grazing, passing methane, standing over their babies. Those moments of closeness were gifts from Samburu I will never forget.[18]

He focused on the bonds in the matriarchal structure of the elephants' families and clans, primarily the connections among mothers, daughters, sisters, and other female relatives. He watched how they affectionately rub noses in greeting, loll and play together—at times dizzyingly. He saw a clan gather around a dying elephant and stay with her until the end, and then return to her body for days after her death, clearly in a kind of mourning. He understood that bulls of a certain age leave the family structure but return now and then to visit. Some of his images show bulls during the rutting season, in musth—when testosterone levels and male aggression rise steeply.

For the first time, Nick was interacting with and photographing elephants who did not live in fear of humans. "All of a sudden," he says, "I was looking at elephants as a social documentarian."

In one image, a bull elephant cautiously slide-crawls down a muddy riverbank, following the group known as the Winds as they amble across the water ahead of him, led by their matriarch, Mistral. In another, the elephant Babylon leads the Biblical Towns herd—including tiny calves and a lame female named Babel; although she may slow their progress, Babylon never leaves Babel behind. We see the dramas of bulls mounting females in estrus. One photograph captures Mary Todd Lincoln of the First Ladies; she will have none of Leopold's advances toward her eight-year-old daughter. He is just too big. Elsewhere, elephants of all ages cross tusks and trunks in greeting and friendship.

Some photographs are made in the golden light of late afternoon, with its elongated shadows, in a wash of color. Others are taken in the cooler, white-gold glow of storm clouds; and still others in the pastels of dawn.

In the "Family Ties" article, David Quammen focuses, in his clear and engaging way, on the science and scientific logic behind the work of Douglas-Hamilton and Save the Elephants. But he is also sensitive to the uncanny values of Nick's modus operandi, which—although decidedly reliant upon intuition and emotion—often lead to insights that are as fully valid as those of any scientist studying animal behavior. Quammen calls it "Nick science":

> Nick would have a rough idea of the science, and a very good intuitive sense of what was going on. He watches animals and animal behavior very, very carefully. He thinks about what he is seeing, or what he is probably seeing. So he ends up with lots of ideas about what's going on—"Nick science"—and those ideas don't always agree with what the scientists think. (Sometimes they do, sometimes they don't.) But Nick's not there to illustrate what he calls "science-science," and his intuition brings him closer to those animals. We know that animals are not machines. Of course they have emotional lives. We don't necessarily know what these emotional lives are, but we can infer, and sometimes a great observer like Nick Nichols can infer just as well as a trained ethologist.

It is the confluence of data-driven, evidentiary science with "Nick science"—anecdotal evidence built on long-term observation of repeated behavior and other dynamics, character studies, and the narratives he subsequently weaves around his subjects—that liberates Nick's work from pure documentation, and imbues it with vitality, nuance, and edge.

When Nick photographs wildlife, because he is paying such close attention and everything is so fluid, there are times when he shoots in rapid succession (a practice facilitated by digital cameras). Williamson told me: "It isn't uncommon for Nick to take two thousand or more pictures in four to six hours of shooting." He anticipates a possible composition with details both fixed and in flux, and situates himself and his technology accordingly. But there remains, always, the unpredictable, the minutiae that distinguish every moment and will ultimately determine the most gripping image. This generally reveals itself during the editing process. Williamson says that in Samburu,

Nick took hundreds and hundreds of photographs. In many situations, it simply isn't possible to know which moment is the "decisive one." It is a myth that anyone really can. So you motor-drive your way through moments. Currently his cameras shoot fourteen pictures a second, for several seconds. That is a lot of moments. So later Nick will go through every image really carefully and look for micro differences in gesture, etcetera. He's an exceptional editor of his own work.

Nick also employed a "stick cam"—a camera on an extendable stick—in Samburu, and again later, with orphan elephants at the David Sheldrick Wildlife Trust in Nairobi. At the orphanage, Nick first tried various positions and angles, including lying down with his camera—but he soon became a plaything for the baby elephants to bump into, and could work more effectively sitting upright, using the stick cam and "pre-visualizing what the camera was seeing." The stick cam allowed him to lay the camera on the ground—without being on the ground himself, which would have been less than prudent while among Samburu's fully grown wild elephants.

Douglas-Hamilton and Lentipo taught Nick a great deal about elephant body language. In Williamson's footage, it is common to see Nick's hand raised in greeting—ultimately mirrored by the elephant raising his or her trunk, before the photo session gets underway. "I'm pretty sure the hand up is like the trunk up," says Nick: "it gives your scent to whomever you are greeting."

Daniel Lentipo met me at the landing strip when I arrived in Samburu in the fall of 2014. A slender, gentle young man who moves with pronounced calm, he had made the five-plus-hour drive from Loisaba in Laikipia, in north-central Kenya, to speak about his time with Nick seven years earlier. In Laikipia, Lentipo was then working as an elephant researcher and as a community-liaison officer. He was the first to individually identify and name the elephants there—about seven hundred so far.

After nine years with Save the Elephants, Lentipo had moved on to Loisaba in 2010, and during the intervening period had not been able to return to the reserve for a visit. As he drove me to the STE research facility, I could sense his eagerness—he was looking forward to seeing some of the elephants he had worked with and loved for so many years—as well as his apprehension; he knew about the massacres.

The route was rugged and rocky, with patches of brush and passages of brick-red clay earth. The STE site is marked with a discreet sign tucked behind a kopje. As we arrived, the sweet scent of jasmine overwhelmed our senses—until we were greeted by a welcoming party of frolicking baboons, some with newborns hugging their backs. The delight in their antics quickly dissipated at the sight of rows and rows of elephant skulls of all sizes, neatly lined up outside the reserve's main building. Elsewhere, used radio collars from poached elephants hung as if on a clothesline—all painful reminders. Samburu is no longer the idyllic elephant refuge that Nick, Williamson, Quammen, and Lentipo experienced; this is brutally evident.

Soon after our arrival, Lentipo and I got into a jeep with Jerenimo Lepirei, STE's research and outreach officer, to investigate the landscape so I might have a visual and sensory idea of what Nick's time here was like. We spot several unfazed elephant families, which made the wallop of what followed even more distressing.

Lentipo repeatedly asked Lepirei about favorite elephants he remembered—his excitement seemed to be allowing him to block out the tragic truth he knew generally, but not yet specifically. Lepirei gave him the deadly news each time in increasingly hushed tones—until finally, it was all Lepirei could do to whisper, yet again, "*poached*." Bonsai, Mahogany, and Ebony of the Hardwoods family, Bethlehem and Nazareth from the Biblical Towns, Goya and Titian from the Artists, Mercury from the Planets . . . all slaughtered.

For Lentipo, Lepirei might as well have been listing his family members. Distraught, he shook his head in disbelief at what he called the "sad revelations."

Those massacres seemed so implausible here, so incongruous with the placid beauty before us, where birdsong hung in the air, where the morning had burst into brightness and then transformed into an aching afternoon heat that sent many creatures in search of cover. But here, even the stillness breathes—life is palpably everywhere. Relief comes at last with the evening, which softens and cools. The landscape is animated once more by giraffes, gazelles, dik-diks, oryx, gerenuks—all types of antelopes, zebras, cheetahs, lions, impalas, and warthogs. Acacia trees camouflage peering owls, and iridescent birds swirl through the dusky sky.

Lentipo and I went out early the next morning, and encountered members of the Artists, the Hardwoods, and the Biblical Towns families. My hope was to replicate what a typical outing with Nick might have been like. Lentipo told me that, in the first couple of weeks of Nick's time here, he—Lentipo—was extremely nervous, as everyone at Samburu understood that Nick was a perfectionist whose photographs could be so meaningful to their efforts. Still, he says: "Nick told me to be free, and just tell him everything I knew about the families, the groups. Their names, who gave birth to which calves and in what year, their habits. And then we'd really look at their bonding."

In *Earth to Sky*, Nick describes the value of Lentipo's knowledge to his own work:

> I'm no "elephant whisperer." Elephants and humans are vastly different—but there were times when the gulf between us seemed very narrow. With the benefit of Daniel Lentipo's interpretation, I was able to document them with an intimacy I had only dreamed of. I opened myself up and looked hard without blinking for those months. Daniel and Save the Elephants provided family histories; each elephant became an individual with a past and present. Each simple photograph of an animal thus took on new weight, meaning, and narrative.[19]

A friendship developed among Lentipo and Nick and Williamson—"We worked very hard together as a close team for so long," says Lentipo. He invited them to his village to attend his brother's wedding; the Americans' presence at the traditional Samburu ceremony was particularly fascinating to the local children, who, Lentipo remembers, "followed them around everywhere."

Lentipo recalled the circumstances behind the making of a particular photograph of elephants sleeping. He and Williamson and Nick had been following the American Indians herd all day, and then into the moonlit night. Elephants can sleep standing up, but typically they will eventually lie down, presumably falling into a deeper sleep. Lentipo remembers that finally, around two in the morning, the family's matriarch, Navajo, lay down to sleep and the others followed suit—and the exhausted Lentipo did the same. Hours later, when he awoke, Nick was still photographing. The intensity of Nick's observation has remained with Lentipo ever since.

Bringing me up to date, Jerenimo Lepirei explained that community conservancies have been established to engage the local people in conservation, with the ultimate goal of creating and securing space for wildlife:

> Some, like the Nasuulu conservancy, were established when we had crises in that specific area. It was a way to respond to poaching issues as well as to bring peace among the community due to tribal conflicts. It was in 2013, during an alarming crisis, that we started an antipoaching campaign in the Samburu and Isiolo ecosystem. This had an impact, as we had a lot of dialogue with the community about the crises and how they might benefit from the wildlife. We were able to reform a few poachers, some who helped to serve as community scouts. When they join forces, they supply information about the poachers' strategies, which is very helpful.

These conservancies are putting aside land within their communities for habitat and are educating people about their ecosystems and conservation. As always, the more the local people recognize that they are benefiting, the better the situation for all. Lepirei says: "We found out that many of them think that they are not benefiting from the parks around them, so we kept reminding them of all the other benefits—like bursaries for the kids, job opportunities from the lodges, parks . . . ," along with safe grazing lands for their livestock.

Resson Kantai Duff of STE explains that one of the chief objectives of the conservancies—which occupy 10.6 percent of Kenya's land area—is security for all:

> The first employees of almost any conservancy are rangers, who not only look after the wildlife . . . they also look after the needs of the community. . . . They stop cattle rustling, and return the cattle to the rightful community. It creates an all-around approach where the people are happy and feel safe, so they want to expel poachers from their midst.

> And if life is not so desperate, it is not so easy for some organized criminal to convince some very poor boy to go kill an elephant. This is a great solution, when the conservancies work and people feel they are not alone, and part of a community.

During my time in Samburu, I spoke with David Daballen, head of field operations for STE. Our conversation began under the shade of a lovely acacia tree, but we quickly moved to avoid being pissed on by a monkey (Daballen: "That would *not* be okay"). We started again, now on a rocky perch by the riverbank—but were interrupted this time by the stealthy approach of a crocodile (from my perspective, even more *not* okay). Finally we settled on a bench farther away from the river, with nothing overhead. Tall and rather debonair, Daballen, who is of the Rendille people from north of Samburu, is an eloquent and thoughtful conversationalist. He spoke soberly of what had happened since Nick's time at Samburu. The elephant killings, he said, were "a catastrophe." No elephants should be the victims of poaching, but to Daballen it was particularly horrific, given that these animals lived in this ostensibly protected place and were thus so trusting of people. "The beautiful families that we all knew disintegrated." He told me that elephant matriarchs will do everything to defend their families: "They will not watch members of their families die. They are in the frontline of fire. And once a family loses its iconic matriarch unceremoniously, the family becomes nothing."

Daballen carefully parsed the economic tangle of supply and demand for blood ivory, explaining that, even though in 2014 Kenya imposed tougher punishments—longer prison sentences and higher fines— for poaching and wildlife trafficking, "killing poachers or jailing them won't work permanently— because there is always another poacher." And this is because there is always another person demanding ivory and willing to pay premium prices for it. Daballen proposes collaborating with like-minded people in the countries where ivory is in highest demand—most notably China. "The more Chinese who come here to understand the situation facing elephants, the better," he says. "If we simply accuse, it's a dead-end. Better to partner with them and ask them to be part of the solution."

An equally crucial aspect of the strategy is to continue working with the communities of people in African countries directly affected by the presence of wildlife—to create a balance that will make it clear that ensuring the animals' welfare is advantageous to *them*. Daballen says: "Now, if an elephant destroys their crops, if a lion eats their goats, they have no reason to want to protect them. . . . So we have to protect these animals in a way that accounts for the needs of both humans and wildlife." This should include viable migration corridors and the provision of enough land for the animals. As well, a significant portion of the parks' revenue must be distributed to the local communities—revenue that provides for schools and other necessities so often taken for granted. Daballen sees this as perhaps the most important aspect of STE's campaign: "The more the communities give land for wildlife, the better. But that can only happen if the communities have an incentive. . . . If they are being asked to set land aside for conservation they need to see value in this. If the local communities appreciate wildlife, then we are in a better position. If they don't, the animals are doomed."

Iain Douglas-Hamilton notes that Nick's visit took place in the final months of an idyllic time for elephants. In 2008, he says, "things swiftly deteriorated," and the next few years were disastrous. Today, Save the Elephants is addressing the reality of a new population of young elephants that have been orphaned by the slaughters of their mothers and family matriarchs. Douglas-Hamilton says:

> We have actually started looking at how these orphan groups survive, how a shattered family often tries to join up with another family. If an animal is completely on its own, it will try to court another family and join up with it. It may be rejected to begin with. But if they really, *really* try and they eventually get accepted, within a space of time, they become so totally integrated you cannot tell that they ever came from a separate family.

George Wittemyer—now an associate professor in conservation biology at Colorado State University, and the Scientific Director of STE—has, with a team of conservationists, been following ten orphan groups in the Samburu National Reserve. They have observed that some of the weaned orphans attach themselves to existing groups. Others choose to stay with what remains of their families, despite the loss of mothers and older relatives, and still others have formed makeshift new families. In each of these groups there is at least one collared animal, which allows the STE team to monitor activities. The studies are trying to gauge the stress levels of orphans compared with elephants from intact families (this is done by analyzing hormone data collected from elephant dung). They are asking whether orphans use the land differently and expend more energy than non-orphans. More generally, how do orphans make binding connections with other elephants? What role does blood-relatedness play? Ultimately, STE researchers are observing and collecting data on the orphans' social choices and their consequences—in terms of how they move through the landscape and their range, as well as their reproductive success and basic survival.

Understanding migratory patterns may also help to protect the elephants (as well as other wildlife) as Kenya continues to develop its infrastructure. More highways, railways, and an oil pipeline are in the works. These expansions, along with an ever-increasing human population, may have a severely negative impact on elephants and wildlife in general if their corridors are not understood and protected, and if alternative connective routes throughout the country are not conceived and built (such as the underpasses that were constructed under highways, currently to the advantage of all wildlife).[20]

Save the Elephants generally does not interfere with an elephant orphaned due to natural causes—but, as Daballen told me: "Once man has interfered, we tend to interfere." Douglas-Hamilton explains: "If we find a very, very young, isolated calf that's totally on its own and in need, we'll catch it and bring it in. And then we ring up Daphne."

"Daphne" is Daphne Sheldrick, a fourth-generation Kenyan, and founder—now chair—of the David Sheldrick Wildlife Trust (DSWT), based in Nairobi and in Kenya's Tsavo East National Park (in southeast Kenya). Author Charles Siebert once described the Sheldrick Trust (named for Daphne's late husband, David)[21] as "the world's most successful orphan-elephant rescue and rehabilitation center."[22]

Involved in establishing the trust's vision and direction since its founding, Angela Sheldrick (Daphne and David Sheldrick's daughter) has run the DSWT since about 2001, with great support from her husband, Robert Carr-Hartley (like Angela, a fourth-generation Kenyan). When they receive a call from STE or anyone else about an orphan at risk, they send an airplane anywhere in Kenya to aid in its rescue, then transport it to the orphan-elephant nursery on the edge of Kenya's Nairobi National Park. Here, the animal receives medical treatment, as well as vital milk. The "milk" is actually a formula that was perfected at the DSWT over a period of years, and is tailored specifically to each individual elephant; as the animal grows from infancy into childhood, the formula is modified, just as a mother's milk undergoes changes over time. Each milk-dependent orphan is cared for and bottle-fed (every three hours) by elephant keepers, who come from diverse tribes and locations throughout Kenya. These caretakers also sleep next to the baby elephants, walk with them each day, are essentially with them 24/7, rotating shifts with other keepers.

The young elephants are profoundly sensitive. In *Earth to Sky*, Nick writes:

> Each orphan sleeps with a different keeper every night; this is partly to prevent the elephants from becoming too attached to any particular human. (The rule was established after a hard lesson: years ago, after successfully bottle-raising her first infant elephant, Daphne had to leave the compound for a few days. The young elephant became disconsolate, would not eat, and quickly died.) The daily transition from one keeper to the next takes place only when the baby is contentedly full of milk and sleeping.[23]

Baby elephant Shukuru, DSWT orphanage, Nairobi National Park, 2010

The nursery's primary goal, and the reason for its remarkable long-term success, is to integrate the newly orphaned elephants with the older orphan elephants-in-residence as soon as it's physically safe to do so. An elephant nurtured and inculcated with a sense of family and community—so that it can bond with and learn from and teach other elephants—stands a far greater chance to coexist subsequently with wild elephants. The DSWT's ultimate conservation priority is "reintegrating orphans back into the wild herds of Tsavo" and it measures its success in part by the "many healthy wild-born calves from former-orphaned elephants raised in our care."[24] The Trust also educates local schoolchildren and other visitors at their Nairobi Orphan Nursery facility during the elephants' midday feeding and cooling mud bath. Here, young students meet the keepers, who teach them about the threats to Kenya's wild-elephant populations, and why these elephants have been orphaned and how they are cared for. When the orphans are about three years old, they are brought to Tsavo East National Park, where there are two rehabilitation centers.

David Sheldrick was the founding warden of Tsavo East, and this is where his daughter Angela grew up, learned about wildlife, and first started caring for orphaned animals. In Tsavo, the elephant keepers gradually begin to acclimate the still-young orphans to the bush during the day—at first walking with them, staying with them, and then bringing them back to the stables. Over time, the orphans learn to come back on their own, after which they are further weaned from people, becoming more accustomed to the wild. As they get older, they begin to walk away from the keepers

by themselves. Eventually, the orphan groups go out on their own and encounter groups of wild elephants. Still, they will usually return, by choice, each evening.

The re-integration process can take a very long time. Edwin Lusichi, of the Luiya tribe, was in his late twenties and working as head keeper of the Sheldrick Wildlife Trust's Nairobi Orphan Nursery when he, along with other keepers, assisted Nick during his two trips. In a perfect scenario, Lusichi told me, the young animals would interact closely with a herd of wild elephants, "becoming wild themselves, because the wild elephants train and teach them, and warn them against human beings." But this is the ideal; once relocated to Tsavo, it may take a group of orphan elephants five to ten years to decide to live in the wild. And even then, time and again, elephants who have been reintroduced to the wild have returned to the keepers if they are hurt—or sometimes to show off a newborn.

In the part of Tsavo known as Ithumba, the wild-elephant population was decimated by poaching decades ago. One collateral advantage of introducing the orphan-elephant population here is that, over time, it has attracted a new population of wild elephants to that section of the park. They seem to understand that now the habitat is safe—so the presence of the orphan elephants, in attracting wild elephants, ends up repopulating and rejuvenating a previously devastated landscape. Elephants prune and create trails in the scrubby brush, making it again accessible to herbivores. And once the herbivores return, so do lions and cheetahs, along with everything else necessary for a healthy ecosystem.

OPPOSITE AND ABOVE: Elephant keepers and their charges, DSWT orphanage, Nairobi National Park, 2010

But the human population is growing, too—disrupting elephant and other species' migratory routes and previously protected boundaries, and trespassing on what was for eons wildlife habitat. At the same time, various studies have reported that in Kenya, 70 percent of wildlife lives outside the protected reserves. To help mitigate the negative effects of this mutual encroachment, the Sheldrick Trust is now utilizing electric fencing as an added measure of protection. This is meant to ensure the safety of the large percentage of elephants living in or traveling outside the designated protected areas. These fences do not form enclosures; rather, they are barriers along the elephant corridors, erected at spots vulnerable to human-wildlife conflict. Hundreds of miles of linear fence-lines—in Tsavo, in an area of Nairobi National Park, and other strategic areas—have eased tensions between local communities and the animals: the elephants are encouraged to stay on the corridors, and crops of neighboring farms and grazing areas remain protected. An added benefit is that, especially at night, the fencing helps thwart poachers and others who may threaten wildlife. Moreover, communities profit economically when local villagers are hired to help build and maintain the fences. The bottom line: the elephants generate revenue, whether from fence-maintenance or ecotourism. Economic stability is truly at the center of the conservation issue.

The Sheldricks' lodge in Tsavo is solar-powered and imposes practically no footprint on the environment. They employ local people and, as in the Nairobi facility, village children are brought in to see the orphans in the hope that (unlike many of their parents) the children will grow to love and appreciate elephants rather than regarding them as a nuisance at best, and at worst as a source of quick cash for a would-be poacher.

Although Nick—who has photographed orphaned elephants, chimps, and gorillas—yearns for these animals to survive as wildly as possible, he believes that they themselves will never *be* wild: "Too much human presence in their lives—there is no *Born Free*."[25] Still, his time photographing at the Sheldricks' two nurseries convinced him of the long-term possibility for success in rereleasing an orphaned animal into the wild. But first, he says, "everything is about survival."

> As soon as the elephants come in, the humans are doing triage—keeping them alive. They don't put them with the other elephants physically, immediately—the little guys need to be stable, and less fearful—but the stalls have big openings between the wood, and their trunks talk and touch, and I just know the other elephants around the new guy are saying: "It's okay, it's going to be okay. We went through it, too, and it's friggin' horrible but these people are good, and you're with your kin."

In the wild, baby elephants often stand under their mothers, shielded from the sun or protected from the cold. Sometimes, when the mother strolls, her baby strolls beneath her—her protective presence is always nearby, and if there is any sign of trouble, the elephants will surround the calves. At the Sheldrick nursery, the presence of a familiar blanket can simulate this protective presence for orphan babies, and Nick believes that the blankets are nearly as important as milk. "The babies are very tactile," says Nick. "So in the stall, the blanket is hung over a rope, and the baby can stand by it and touch it all the time. And when they go out into the forest with the infants, the keepers have them wear the blankets—it's like a surrogate for the mother, and seems to be essential for reducing anxiety."

While photographing at the DSWT, Nick went out with the animals and the keepers day after day, habituating the elephants to his presence—working so close up that the animals would sometimes knock him over. Lusichi, who has seen other professional photographers come and go at the facility, told me that Nick was not at all like the others. For one thing: "He was soft and would do everything that we asked him." Lusichi also notes that "Nick never wanted to make a photograph that was not good for the elephant. Nick understands animals," he says, "so could work with us and the elephants well."

During my visit to the orphanage, I had the opportunity to accompany Lusichi and the other keepers on a morning walk with the elephants. The long-lashed baby animals ranged from one month to a little over two years old, the older ones just beginning to grow tusks. Their fragility was palpable. One keeper who has young children, and was walking with Ndotto—just over a month old at the time of my visit—told me: "It's just like having another child." Some were mischievous, others more circumspect, some pin-drop silent, others trumpeting insistently.

A couple of the littlest ones—their heads were about at my hip height—approached me. They checked me out from head to toe with their trunks, and one began blowing tangy-smelling warmth in my face. It was the most soulful, primal interaction I've ever experienced. Lusichi explained, "They are sharing," and told me that this was an exchange: etiquette dictated that I was to take hold of the elephant's trunk and blow gently into it. Intoxicated, I did, and the trust, the acceptance of my breath, our physical closeness was sublime.

Even with babies, trunks are deceptively strong. One youngster wrapped his around my lower arm, and with this firm grip tried to pull my hand toward his toothless mouth in play. I was smitten.

It occurred to me that the story "Orphans No More" (*National Geographic*, September 2011, with text by Charles Siebert) might in fact have been Nick's most challenging ever. Somehow he had to get an edge, avoid total *mush*, in the midst of all this genuine adorableness, innocence, and vulnerability, caked in red clay or secure in blankets or wearing custom-made bright-orange slickers. Not to mention conveying—without sentimentality—the beneficent tenderness and attentiveness of the keepers, in their bright-green smocks.

Clearly, Nick's images from the orphanage are not *tough*, but neither do they tug simplistically at our heartstrings. Yes, some images can make your knees buckle, melting you in the warmth of it all, but this is because they elicit an empathic response without drowning us in treacle or schmaltz. This project is one of the few opportunities Nick has had to show a positive relationship between humans and the wild. As with the orphan gorillas of central Africa, the humans are not trying to tame or domesticate the elephants. They have only one goal: to help these creatures return to the wild.

There is an anxiety resonating through some of Nick's images of the orphans with their keepers that explicitly reflects their daily struggle for survival. Ultimately, though, the photographs offer a sense of possibility, of hope, in the sheer teamwork depicted. This, perhaps, is Nick's edge in this body of work: the suggestion of *goodness*—not cloying, but real—evoked through intimate reportage. The images are charged with affection, and yet never lose sight of the potential for tragedy and loss, and the horrors that precipitated the animals' circumstances to begin with. The Sheldrick elephant orphanage is a genuine manifestation of what Siebert calls "interspecies empathy."[26] In Nick's images, that empathy is visually tangible.

I met with Angela Sheldrick and Rob Carr-Hartley at their very charming, somewhat rustic home, more or less next door to the Nairobi nursery and within Nairobi National Park. Angela's mother, Daphne, lives close by. We sat at a breakfast table in dappled morning sunlight, surrounded by family photographs and books—hints of lives richly lived. Before I can ask my first question, an orphaned hyrax, Rax, jumps audaciously onto the table to steal some toast. "Naughty!" says Angela—but beguiling. Soon after, Tickles the cat makes his presence known.

The morning is alive with activity. Sheldrick, a natural multitasker, simultaneously fields phone calls and reviews an extensive to-do list with Edwin Lusichi regarding the status of some elephants and their stalls. She is delighted to learn that Kiko, a giraffe they've recently taken in, is playing happily. Most important, an elephant calf will arrive at the orphanage that afternoon. It had fallen into a livestock well on the Namunyak conservancy in Samburu, and the Kenya Wildlife Service—with which the DSWT partners—requested the rescue. She makes myriad detailed arrangements, and then we adjourn to the living room.

Both Sheldrick and Carr-Hartley (who is rather more laid back than his wife) recall their time with Nick with tremendous warmth and respect. Since then, Carr-Hartley—whom Angela Sheldrick describes as Nick's "soulmate"—has continuously advised him, helping him navigate issues and projects in Tanzania especially, not to mention outfitting and customizing a "lion car" for Nick's future work on the Serengeti lions.

Sheldrick and Carr-Hartley inform me that the orphan project is only one of many meaningful initiatives realized by the DSWT in Kenya. It also sponsors antipoaching teams, an aerial-surveillance site in Tsavo, as well as a small army of veterinarians, including a group of "sky vets" who can fly in to reach elephants in remote areas. Other mobile veterinary units from the Kenyan Wildlife Service are equipped to operate in all sorts of field conditions. This program was inaugurated in Tsavo, and they continue to expand to other ecosystems. To date, they have saved over a thousand elephants. Like the researchers at Save the Elephants, they work with local communities whenever possible to "secure vast ecosystems for the future."

Carr-Hartley and Sheldrick are realists. As she put it to me:

> Sometimes communities destroy their land because of daily need, because of poverty. But once it's gone, they will be so much the worse off. Our approach has been to make public and private partnerships with government entities and NGOs.

> It's all about land. So many people, so little space. And without land, wildlife cannot survive.

At the same time, they are trying to engage with the "demand" side of blood ivory. We discussed the devastating implications of the CITES-approved 2008 sale of government-stockpiled ivory to Japan

OPPOSITE: Two-week-old elephant Wasin, DSWT orphanage, Nairobi National Park, 2010; ABOVE: Nick photographing at the DSWT's Nairobi nursery, 2010. Photograph by Reba Peck

and China. "We are a barometer on the ground," they told me, "and we felt the impact of that very misguided decision. . . . It was a disaster that was instantly felt."

China is the world's largest consumer of illegally poached ivory. The United States is second. In September 2015 Barack Obama and China's President Xi Jinping pledged together to end the global trade in ivory.[27] Their agreement to join forces and enact "nearly complete bans" on ivory import and export[28]—if enforced with the immediacy that this urgent situation demands ("and with *no* loopholes," adds Nick)—could mean the continuation of the species. If not, the African elephant may cease to exist.

Furthering its commitment, in June 2016, the U.S. Fish and Wildlife Service announced "a near-total ban on the commercial trade of African elephant ivory in the United States. . . . The new rules help fulfill President Obama's 2013 executive order on combating wildlife trafficking in the United States, while lending resources to help stem the problem in other countries."[29] The regulations permit the sale in the United States of genuine antiques only—including musical instruments, art, and jewelry—that have been imported legally and contain less than two hundred grams of ivory.

The Sheldricks are working with conservationists from mainland China and Hong Kong. They host visitors from both at the orphanage, and note that it comes as a surprise to many of their Chinese guests that elephants are *killed* for ivory. "We must educate," says Carr-Hartley. "We cannot treat China as our enemy—but we are in crisis." Sheldrick holds out hope that China can change.

Awareness in both the United States and China does seem to be increasing. By December 2015 the going price of illegal raw ivory in China was half of what it had been during a horrific price spike the year before. According to a 2015 report compiled by ivory researchers Esmond Martin and Lucy Vigne for Save the Elephants: "The news gives cautious hope that the unsustainable killing of Africa's elephants—driven by demand for their tusks—may eventually be reduced across their range." Furthermore, investigators found that, compared with last year, ivory carvers and vendors in China saw very little future in their business and no longer wanted their children to take up the profession.

However, according to the same report: "In Africa there is no indication that the ivory poaching crisis has slackened, and time is running out for many elephant populations. The Chinese government's strong statements have been a major driver in the drop in price, but this would likely be reversed if the ban is not implemented promptly and effectively."[30] On December 30, 2016, China went further, announcing it was "banning all commerce in ivory by the end of 2017."[31]

In July 2016 Martin and Vigne reported: "Vietnam is now one of the world's biggest illegal ivory markets. The number of items seen for sale [rose] by over six times from 2008 to 2015." And they note that "the overwhelming majority of raw tusks sold wholesale in Vietnam are smuggled in from Africa."[32]

I think of Lasayen, a one-month-old orphan elephant rescued by the Sheldrick Trust during my visit in September 2014. The keepers who flew out to fetch him administered an IV drip during the flight back. Once in the nursery, Edwin Lusichi drew blood, gave the animal antibiotics, put him on another IV drip, and tried bottle-feeding him. Lasayen was plainly terrified: I heard his cries, and they were wrenching. And yet watching this interaction, this care-giving, was as affirming as it was transfixing.

Today, according to the online journal entries of the Sheldrick Trust keepers, Lasayen is thriving, having survived the vulnerable teething stage. He and his pal Ndotto frolic constantly as they learn from older elephants how to be elephants.

Nick fostered an orphan elephant named Kilaguni in the name of his own mother—who for the rest of her life referred to Kilaguni as "my" elephant. Born in 2008, Kilaguni is now an adolescent, living at Ithumba and spending more and more time in the wild. In their blog entries, the keepers refer to him now as an "ex-orphan."

The future of the African elephant is precarious at best. In early September 2016, the findings of the Great Elephant Census (GEC)—which counts Africa's savanna elephants in eighteen countries in order to determine how many remain and where they are living—showed that the African population is dropping by 8 percent a year, primarily due to the ravages of poaching.[33] Some weeks after the publication of the census (and incorporating its findings), a status report was issued by the International Union for Conservation of Nature and Natural Resources (IUCN) African Elephant Specialist Group.

This report added data from the forests, using on-the-ground dung counts, and tallied remote savanna elephant populations (which had not been accounted for in the GEC's aerial counts).

The IUCN findings were presented at the CITES meeting of 182 nations held in Johannesburg in September to October 2016. The conclusion was heartbreaking: "Africa's overall elephant population has seen the worst declines in 25 years, mainly due to poaching over the past ten years . . . while habitat loss poses an increasingly serious long-term threat to the species."[34]

But that did not prevent two contentious decisions with deadly implications from being made at the meeting. I communicated about these decisions with Lee White, executive secretary of Gabon's Agence Nationale des Parcs Nationaux and Gabon's delegate to CITES. More than thirty parties in the African Elephant Coalition and Elephant Protection Initiative—both committed to a healthy and sustainable wild elephant population in Africa—supported a resolution that would, according to White, "close *all* domestic markets" for the sale of ivory. The proposed ban fell short of the necessary two-thirds majority vote. Instead, White says, what prevailed was a tragic compromise, only "urging all parties to close domestic markets that *contribute to the illegal trade* of ivory."

Along with the troubling issues of trade was a proposal to up-list elephants to "profoundly endangered" status—which CITES refers to as "Appendix 1"—a status that would stipulate that African elephants have more official protection from poachers.[35] On this subject, White offered an "intervention"—an impassioned plea for listing elephants at this most endangered status. He sent me a copy of this "intervention," excerpted here:

> I am in uniform today, to pay tribute to the 1,000 African wildlife rangers who have lost their lives over the last decade, mostly in the fight to save rhinos and elephants.
>
> Collectively as an international community we have failed to manage the ivory trade, resulting in catastrophic declines in many range states. In some African nations terrorists have benefited from this trade, and in certain tragic cases entire nations have been destabilized by poaching. . . . A vote against up-listing ALL elephants to Appendix 1 . . . will be seen as a green light by the poachers, traffickers, organized criminal networks and terrorists who make money off illegal trade in ivory. A vote for up-listing all elephants to Appendix 1 will make them see red. It will be a clear sign to the world that ivory cannot be traded. That the international community will come down just as hard on ivory, as we do on drugs, arms and human trafficking. It will be seen as a declaration of war on the forces that destabilize our African nations and who fund terrorism off natural resources.

This proposal to list the elephants as "profoundly endangered" (or Appendix 1) also failed.

One heartening decision did emerge from the CITES meeting: the procedure allowing a one-off sale of ivory stockpiles would not be renewed—that is, according to White, "at least until the next [conference] in Sri Lanka in three years."

On April 30, 2016, Kenyan officials burned the country's stockpile of confiscated and recovered tusks, representing six to seven thousand dead elephants: 105 metric tons of ivory, worth $105 million. Kenya's President Uhuru Kenyatta lit the pyre, stating: "No one, and I repeat, no one, has any business in trading in ivory, for this trade means death—the death of our elephants and the death of our natural heritage."[36]

FOLLOWING SPREAD: Schoolchildren visit orphan elephant Mzima, DSWT's Voi Rehabilitation Center, Kenya, 2010

THE PRESIDENT AND

Redwood National Park, California, 2008

PRAIRIE CREEK

"*F*orest is Mike's thing," says Nick, "and forest exploitation was no worse anywhere than with the clear-cutting of the redwoods. Mike missed out on the 'Redwood Summer' and the timber wars of the 1990s." Nick is referring to the summer of 1990, when environmental activists escalated their fight against logging. Their goal: protect the old-growth ancient redwood forests. The activists began through peaceful protest and civil disobedience (much as the Earth First anti-logging tree-sitters had done before them in Oregon, beginning in the mid-1980s). But the issues soon grew more contentious, the positions more polarized. In June 1990, following successful legal action by environmental groups, the northern spotted owl—which depends upon the old-growth forests for its habitat—was listed as a "threatened" subspecies under the federal Endangered Species Act, further inflaming the situation. The "timber wars" ensued.

"Mike missed out on Julia Butterfly," Nick continues. For 738 days, beginning in December 1997, Julia Butterfly Hill "occupied" a thousand-plus-year-old coastal redwood tree near the town of Stafford in Humboldt County, California. She lived on a platform built into the tree's limbs, about 180 feet off the ground, with the aim of preventing the Pacific Lumber Company from cutting the ancient tree down, while also protecting the surrounding grove from the company's ferocious clearcutting.

Despite the doggedness and commitment of the activists preceding him in the region, a decade later, Mike Fay saw for himself just how much of the old-growth forest tragically had *not* been saved. Whatever he already understood of the rape of this landscape, he was enraged by the destruction before him. It was staggering. On a visit to Northern California to do their "dog and pony show" about the Megatransect—at Humboldt State University in Arcata—Fay's mission became clear. "Mike was ready for combat conservation. He'd done it in Gabon, in the Central African Republic . . . but this was home, and he was angry."

The implications for the forests' wildlife were catastrophic. It was crucial, Fay determined, to examine the current state of the redwood forests. And so he proposed to *National Geographic* a "redwoods transect": he and naturalist Lindsey Holm would trek from Big Sur to just over the Oregon border.

National Geographic's editor-in-chief Chris Johns quickly agreed to the story. Nick came on board— but made it clear from the start that he did not wish to photograph Fay on another transect ("I'd just be repeating myself"). "And like Mike, I missed the timber wars and Julia Butterfly too. I would have *loved* to photograph the tree sitters, that energy, but this was long over. By the time we got there, the destruction, as horrible as it was, had become normalized. I spent months trying to see if I could photograph it in a powerful way. I got nothing."

Still, Fay believed that Nick should show the devastation already suffered by the forests—whether or not it was visually interesting—and shed light on what people were doing to counter that destruction; he felt that this would be aggressive, honest, and have a powerful effect. While Nick recognized that "the redwoods speak to incredible journalistic issues," and concurred with the advocacy spin, he had no desire to take a conventional documentary approach and photograph "tree stumps and people measuring trees and board feet, and restoration—reshaping the land to the natural contours, and fixing all of the other damage to the Earth after logging. . . . It's visually boring, it's not sexy, and it

Roosevelt elk, Prairie Creek Redwoods State Park, California, 2008 won't stick. I tried! I ultimately spent days photographing restoration in Redwood National Park. My photos were a disaster." Nick and Fay's positions regarding the visual approach to the redwoods story soon became irreconcilably polarized.

Nick is admittedly always thinking about his photographic objectives, how to be innovative, impressive. He is also certain that a spectacular "hallelujah!" depiction is a more seductive approach to capturing the imagination, to changing hearts and minds. To speak out for the future of the redwoods, these wild, splendid trees had to be glorified—the challenge was, how? Fay was virulently against this approach, which he saw as prettifying a calamitous situation, and he has lividly referred to it as a "hijacking" of his redwoods project. This dispute stabbed at some core differences between these two often ego-driven men. As Nathan Williamson (who assisted Nick on this story) put it in late 2016, on a phone call from Gabon: "Nick, the populist—he *needs* beauty and affirmation. He wants his song played on the radio and everybody to know it, to love it. Mike—he doesn't care. His is the protest record, and it must be made, at all costs."

Fay was, as ever, single-minded: he knew exactly what his goals were and how he wanted to achieve them. He and Lindsey Holm took notes and images of their arduous redwoods transect over the course of nearly a year, meticulously collecting data along the way. They looked at the condition of everything,

and gathered even anecdotal information—speaking with everyone who crossed their path—from biologists, foresters, tree-huggers and other environmentalists to people from the timber industry.

Fay and Holm started their eleven-month walk on September 2, 2007, and in late March 2008 Nick and Williamson made a three-week scouting trip, meeting up with them along their route. They were joined by Chris Johns. As Nick describes it, much of this logged terrain is "torturous": "some of the most brutally torn-up land on the planet. It can take hours to get around a fallen tree." Fay and Holm found themselves sometimes in landscapes of postapocalyptic bleakness.

During this visit, Nick also met Stephen C. Sillett, redwoods botanist, tall-tree-canopy pioneer, old-growth forest guru, idiosyncratic, lavishly and genuinely enthusiastic. Nick has described him fondly as "an energizer bunny: there is no 'off' button." He says that Sillett had "the perfect build for swinging around in the canopy—strong and compact." Sillett was with his frequent collaborator, biologist Jim Campbell-Spickler, who specializes in, among other things, canopy access and salamanders. Nick immediately recognized that Sillett's and Campbell-Spickler's relationship to these trees was like Fossey's to her mountain gorillas, Goodall's to the Gombe chimpanzees, and so on. Still, it took a while for that realization to evolve into a photographic concept, for him to see that it was again going to be about the individual.

Soon after his meetings with Sillett and Campbell-Spickler, Nick asked Reba to join him in California for the project. It would be a welcome change for the couple. Nick says that after decades of taking on projects that kept them apart for months at a stretch, "we just did not want to be separated anymore."

He was in his fifties, and had been working nonstop for years. Each project was in its way intense, elaborate, and—in both content and process—immensely demanding. The pace had left him with minimal time and space to pause, take some breaths, and rebalance. The physical requirements of some of the projects were also taking their toll, as were the stresses of sustaining—in every sense—LOOK3.

Having Reba with him made a difference for Nick. Her presence afforded him some much-needed equilibrium. As Williamson puts it: "There is no way Nick would be where he is now without Reba." He adds that not only has she provided him with a sense of solidity and moral support, but "she's also got a hell of an eye." Starting with the redwoods story, Reba would join Nick on all his projects, from start to finish.

Nick and Reba's sons were growing up: Ian had graduated from the University of Virginia and was working in Virginia while also shooting for *National Geographic*—stories on lowland gorillas[1] and the Goualougo chimps.[2] Eli was attending Humboldt State University (HSU). Nothing prevented Reba and Nick from rethinking certain givens in their lives, and that inevitably presented a range of challenges. When Ian and Eli were young, Reba had long accepted that she and their boys had two rhythms to follow: "We had the life with Nick, and the life without Nick." The transitions between the two lives weren't always easy. When home, Nick was a very large presence; as he himself concedes, he can sometimes take up all the air in the room. Reba, by contrast, is quiet and shy—while strong and steadfastly supportive—always providing essential family stability. From the beginning of their romance, Nick looked to Reba as his "Shelter from the Storm" (this time invoking Bob Dylan).

Reba's perspective on Nick is, of course, deeply personal. I asked her what her life had been like with a partner who travels constantly and is obsessive with his work, occasionally volatile, and (by his own admission) self-involved and fragile. With characteristic candor, she replied:

> With the kids, I did worry that . . . Nick wasn't there enough for them. Sometimes he would come off an assignment—and everybody's just waiting, all excited, for him to get home—but when he gets home, he's completely exhausted and falls asleep. . . . There was always that disappointment when he'd come home and was completely spent.

> I'm not sure he ever felt comfortable in the parent role. . . . He asserted or reclaimed his authority when he was home, and sometimes would blow up . . . or would be irrational instead of calm. . . . We would talk about it after, but when he was in the moment of anger you couldn't say anything. And when he knew he was behaving badly, he would just start crying. I think much of it was from stress.

When Nick and Reba decided to be together throughout the redwoods shooting, it took some getting used to. For eight months in 2008 and 2009 they lived in a repurposed chicken coop in the former logging town of Orick, California ("population six hundred and dropping," says Nick). Down the hill, Williamson lived in what he describes as "a mildew-infested trailer home."

Even with Reba's presence, however, work stresses prevailed: the demands of LOOK3 never seemed to abate, and, Reba says: "Nick was overwhelmed by how to make the story original." It was by no means the first story *National Geographic* had done on the redwoods, and he was desperate to dream up an original approach.

I traveled to Humboldt County in the autumn of 2012 to meet Sillett and Campbell-Spickler. We drove to the coastal Prairie Creek Redwoods State Park so I might understand the physical terrain, the environment that Nick and his team had taken on. Sillett and Campbell-Spickler were, to my great fortune, also determined to give me a sense of some of the world's tallest, oldest, wild trees—each one's distinctiveness, their clusters and groves, and the mini-ecosystems in their crowns of ferns, berry bushes, soil mats, and fungi—forests that host a surprising and large array of plant and animal, bird and amphibian life.

As we walked, Sillett offered a dramatic lead-up: "Here comes one of the great trees in the world, perhaps the most prehistoric of all trees. Right through there, the giant looming beast! Well over two thousand years old, probably." And when he spotted a tree he'd never seen before, the gracious enthusiasm of our morning jaunt gave way to pure zeal. He became an appealingly exuberant boy: "You guys, I'm seeing a tree that's freaking me out . . . okay, Jim, we're going to *have* to go up that one. Look at the trunk thickness—from this distance to see it that thick, that is *gigantic*! It's a *massive* crown . . . we are going to have to go there *right now*. Okay, we have a tree, Jim, which we have to do. Damn dude, look at its greatness. Ooh, baby!" This tree, he said, is one of those "that you keep in the back of your mind if you ever need a study tree, or you just have a hankering for awesome!"

Suddenly, Sillett grinned and issued an excited challenge: "Are you ready to bushwhack?" He raced ahead—shouting over his shoulder before disappearing into the bush of Prairie Creek: "Don't trust your feet!" And a second later, the chaser, from deep in the brush: "Use your hands!"

Campbell-Spickler gracefully demonstrated how to move through and around fallen trees: in dense redwood forests, you extend your arms first, *before* stepping, in order to grab limbs and other tree parts for stability. There is no trail. Your arms are working with your legs, everything on high alert in case something should give. The risk, according to my guides, is that you'll fall down a hole, "like Alice in Wonderland."

Wonderland it was, absolutely. The forest floor was surprisingly supple, responsive, softened by the layering of fallen trees and other natural debris, amassed over decades and decades. Everything I expected to register as solid was in fact textured, cushiony. Curiouser and curiouser. Along with being deceptive, the terrain is also unpredictable: rugged and tangled, or smooth and welcoming—shifting the sense of one's own mass so that walking can feel like gliding on clouds enveloped in silence.

I thought of Nick and his team as they began to understand this landscape, where things are not exactly what they appear to be. This was perhaps another "Lost World" for Nick. Not the redwood forests at large—they are anything but lost and unsullied: much of this land has been violently stripped by loggers. But these trees and the wondrous canopy remain protected and intact in this ancient stretch of continuous old-growth forest. It felt as if we were light years from the California coastline, which is only a few miles away. It seemed another "last place on Earth."

Sillett and his team were the first to map many of the trees in these forests. Like other scientists affirming the individuality of their subjects, Sillett named these olympian trees, first borrowing the names of Greek gods and goddesses and then drawing from Tolkien's universe. But as some of these trees have become celebrities, Sillett and Campbell-Spickler now publicly refer to them by an ever-changing number system, in the hope that this form of coding will safeguard them from what Sillett calls "the paparazzi." (Respecting that wish, I won't refer to our headliner redwood by name here.)

Sillett, Campbell-Spickler, and many of their colleagues yearn to protect these magnificent trees from negative impacts caused by untrained climbers who, often unwittingly, harm the trees. They feel a responsibility for the welfare of these wild beings that have so inspired and should outlive them. Their own scientific minds and superlative climbing skills are compounded by a questlike fixation and an abiding sense of wonder.

"Do trees have souls?" I asked as we walked among them. Campbell-Spickler's answer started out in relatively scientific terms, and then moved to the existential: "I view them in the same way I view any other organism that starts from a sperm and an egg. They have their own individuality. They are a being. They have a purpose. . . . They don't have the advantage of movement, so instead they endure. And because of that ability to endure, they are awe-inspiring to us."

Sillett went straight for the cosmic:

> When we're climbing the trees—because there's a peril associated with climbing—we're highly focused on the task. It's then that I can really get in tune with the trees and feel a

spiritual connection. Because I'm *participating* in this place. . . . The trees are on a different time frame: their movements are over such long stretches. . . . In a hundred years, what evidence will there be, from the tree's perspective, of my presence here? None.

During his years of working in jungles and woods and forests—in India, South America, all over Africa—Nick had never made what he considers to be an excellent photograph of a tree. What makes it so challenging? Nick says: "I'm not a still-life photographer, so trees are a killer for me." He adores exquisite landscape photography that is "more than illustrative, more than just pretty"—he mentions the work of Richard Misrach and Edward Weston. But, he says: "I can't do it. I can't see that way." How, then, would Nick see? If he was not going to photograph Mike Fay's transect or the ravaged forests, what *was* he going to do?

Finally, Nick thought he had found his footing in the forest. He began by making several vertiginous, scene-setting images of Sillett; his wife and fellow climber, botanist, and canopy-researcher Marie Antoine; Campbell-Spickler; and canopy-ecologist Giacomo Renzullo. In these photographs, the climbers seem to defy gravity, they are balletic tree-creatures: nimble, relaxed, and confident.

By the end of September 2008, Nick had been working with Sillett and Campbell-Spickler on these photographs for about three months, focusing mostly on a 330-foot-tall redwood in Humboldt Redwoods State Park. Campbell-Spickler regularly assisted Nick, both with the rigging and by transporting and setting up his gear. This allowed Nick to be completely focused on making the photographs— rather than worrying about the equipment, or worse, hurting himself in some way, stepping over an edge because he was after a particular perspective. Sillett and the team of researchers had perfected a technique they call "spider-climbing" that allows climbers to move about safely and with minimal impact—vertically, but also horizontally, and far out onto limbs—all without damaging the tree.

Nick's work in caves many years earlier, while a very different experience, helped to prepare him for some of the demands of the redwoods. Here again, he was moving about a precarious space, and working out a photographic process for revealing something otherwise unseeable, unknowable— harnessed to a rope most of the time and taking enormous care not to leave a trace of his presence. He made use of some of the painting-with-light techniques he had invented for the cave stories: the climbers carried flashlights that they pointed at parts of the trees, shifting their beams while he made long exposures—creating "brushstrokes" of light that helped him achieve depth and texture.

It all appeared to be working, sort of. But sometime in late November 2008, Nick broke down:

> I was painting myself into a corner. I literally had everybody in the trees. I'm in the canopy and can see everything, and we're working with all kinds of lighting, and . . . it just doesn't work. It all falls apart. I mean, I'd made some nice frames that give a sense of scale and beauty . . . but I hadn't yet pushed it far enough.

Sillett says that, although Nick made hundreds of images and seemed to know what he wanted, "he couldn't quite get it." Nick was demoralized, and shaky with increasing anxiety.

Nick has always recognized how lucky he is to be able to realize his projects more or less as he wishes, with tremendous time and resources at his disposal, and with such a dedicated editor in

Kathy Moran. But even with all this support, and Reba by his side, he felt like he was failing on all fronts. It sent him spinning into a black hole of despair, which was exacerbated by the strains of LOOK3. Smoking quantities of potent home-grown local marijuana only seemed to compound his depression.

At one point during this project, Williamson discovered Nick practically in tears, in a panic of self-doubt. "With Nick," he says, "even with all the beauty—and there is always beauty in these projects—there is *always* a darkness, some moment in the process where things break down, when he really freaks out. But it was the worst in the redwoods."

Moran has seen this side of Nick. He works, she says, from "a very personal place."

> You have to be prepared for his emotions. And when he goes dark . . . you have to be his safety net. You have to create that safe environment for him where he can expose his fragility. I don't do this work with anyone else. And to be honest, I'm not sure I *could* do it for somebody else. But I feel I have to give it to Nick.

Nick is quick to acknowledge that, beginning in 1993, Moran has been "my rock and my lifeline." It is rare for a photographer to work essentially with only one editor at *National Geographic*, but Nick understands that he "needed the consistency and clarity that came from Kathy. Her strength is mothering, protecting like a momma bear. I got her as an 'infant editor,' and we built strength and experience together." Most important, though, Nick has benefited from Moran's faith in his vision: "There is no trust like the trust that comes from showing raw unseen film or digital files to the person who must then represent the work and what the photographer is trying to say. The editor is the touchstone, and Kathy excels at all this."

But on the Redwoods project, Nick was sending Moran images in which he had little confidence. He was uncertain that they evinced the larger concept he wished to convey—what *was* that larger concept? His e-mails from the period are tormented in tone. Nick had yet to figure out his approach, how he would interpret, how he could bring his vision to the redwoods. His distress was palpable.

Nick is a photojournalist. He is also a portraitist. His subjects have almost always been, like him, charismatic animals (including Jane Goodall, including Mike Fay), in the midst of their own dramas, inhabiting extraordinary environments. And he has been able to observe many of his subjects day after day after day, ultimately creating experiential, revelatory narratives.

Now, he was in a national park with movie-star trees and trying to reconcile himself to the fact that there is no possible way to look at or render an individual tree in its entirety all at once. Nick wanted to manifest in his photographs something akin to the visceral intimacy that Sillett and his team have with these beings. He wanted somehow to translate their muscle and sensory memories, to fuse the sensuous with the intricate details of the trees, as conveyed in the scientists' computer-generated models that account for the multidimensional, anatomical sets of data they've collected.

Nick had to bring his own mode of long-term, nuanced, and focused observation to the redwoods, just as he had when he'd hunkered down in a hide for weeks at a time or set up a camera trap for months in order to make a portrait that gets under the surface of his subject. He needed to discover how to show these iconic trees as protagonists. If Fay understood the forest through the trees, Nick had to understand the trees through the forest.

He believed that reportage—even about the beauty of the coastal forest—could not really evoke any particular tree's essence. It was more like illustrating the *theme* of redwoods. It would not result in groundbreaking photographs. Nick isn't a theme guy. His photographs don't make reductive generalizations, they distinguish the specific and sui generis, whether an ecosystem, a family, or an individual.

It was time, he realized, to turn his focus to a single tree.

Sillett and Campbell-Spickler listened to Nick explain what he wanted to do. His idea was to create an intimate, detailed *portrait* of a tree, from base to top—despite the fact that it was not humanly possible to see a tree in its entirety in the forest in this way.

After much brainstorming, they understood how to help him achieve his goals. First, they had to decide on the tree—a very special tree. Nick had his eye on the tallest tree in the forest. Sillett, who is something of a helicopter parent to the trees, was worried about a few things. For one thing, he knew that the tree in question could not be accessed in such a way as to reveal itself as Nick envisioned. And there were other concerns:

> Nick wanted *the tallest* tree, and I wouldn't give it to him. National Geographic had just featured it on their TV program, so there had just already been so much trampling around this sacred tree! It's not my tree, but I felt like I was its caretaker. I had to consider the huge footprint consequences.

At first, Nick found Sillett's resistance repressive—and he took it personally. But Sillett had another tree in mind—one he called the "über tree"—a stupendous three-hundred-foot-tall beauty. Nick soon realized it was perfect for the portrait that was beginning to take shape in his mind's eye: it was positioned ideally to allow him the perspective he needed to ultimately render a tree in its entirety.

But there was one vast and agonizing drawback for Nick. The photographer James Balog had already photographed this über tree, and had selected it for precisely the same reason. It gnaws at Nick to this day that he "followed" in the footsteps of another photographer, although ultimately their respective translations of it diverge totally.

Balog is Nick's contemporary and has a similarly militant conservation mission; a well-known recent project is his "Extreme Ice Survey," focusing on climate change.[3] He is a powerful photographer whose work, like Nick's, is regularly featured in *National Geographic*. "Nick and I are definitely animated and captivated and moved and activated by the same things: a love of nature, wanting to see it stay alive," Balog told me. "We're kindred spirits in this brotherhood of trying to use photography to do something other than decorate."

In 1998 Balog set out to do a project on trees; in 2004 selections from the work were published in his book *Tree: A New Vision of the American Forest*.[4] Like Nick, he traveled to Prairie Creek Redwoods State Park. And like Nick, he worked with Sillett and Campbell-Spickler. It is not surprising, really, that both photographers would be led and drawn to the same tree: sublimely magnificent, it offered the best possibilities for rigging and for making the full-frontal portrait both men envisioned. The photographers needed to be able to access the optimal side of the tree and its crown, and then see it at every level—without the interference of another tree's limbs.

Balog's book features images of ninety-two remarkable trees spanning the North American forests— this heroic specimen is among them. His photographs are often composites that are constructed through layering or abutting multiple images. When Nick's story was published in *National Geographic*, in late 2009—with his portrait of this tree as a centerfold—Balog was vexed. He told me:

> What stung is that I had proposed a redwoods story to *National Geographic* years earlier. They had an eight-foot-tall print of my tree in the photo department offices for months. It was a killer, drop-dead, straight-down-the-center-of-home-plate idea—and they should have taken it. And they didn't.
>
> Then, a few years later, they do something practically identical to what I had proposed. I just didn't understand that.

Nick never saw Balog's print at the National Geographic offices, but acknowledges: "Balog was the pioneer. He was the one that made the groundbreaking picture first. I did something different, but to do so, I had to follow in his footsteps. And it killed me! We have a history of focusing on similar things, while taking very different paths. But the dance had never gotten this close before."

To make matters worse, the *National Geographic* story indicated, with regard to Nick's image, that this was the first time a tree had ever been photographed in this way. "That was just outrageous," Balog says. Nick concurs, adding: "I didn't invent how to move through the trees. Jim [Balog] didn't invent it. [Sillett and Campbell-Spickler] invented the technology for doing that. Jim and I used it." Describing the difference between Balog's approach and his own more specifically, Nick says: "Jim held the cameras in his hands, and was climbing a rope that was hanging off another rope—very hard and scary. And then he layered the images together wonderfully, making a composite. By the time I did it, [Campbell-Spickler] had come up with an approach that allowed for the precision I wanted."

Although the two men's images of the tree have certain inevitable resemblances, their photographic intentions—and thus their ultimate renderings—are remarkably distinct. Balog was not attempting to replicate nature, but rather to show the tree in a way that echoes human visual perception: we see Balog's tree as the sum of its parts. Our eye creates the whole from his multilayered mosaic. Nick, by contrast, was trying to transcend the way the human eye sees by depicting the tree *hyperliterally*: we see only the tree's detailed wholeness in all its complexity.

It was Campbell-Spickler who offered Nick the technical solution to achieving this explicitness. He suggested that they adapt an elaborate film-camera dolly—which had recently been used for a National Geographic television special on the trees—to accommodate Nick's still cameras. "That was the big breakthrough. It was similar to the technique Balog had used," Nick observes, "but because we took the human hand out of the equation, we were able to get absolute exactness." Later he worked with Ken Geiger, *National Geographic* magazine's deputy director of photography and a tech wizard, to "stitch" the individual images together on the computer and "rebuild" the tree, "to make visible," says Nick, "something you can't actually see." Nick has told me that "this would not have been possible technologically when Balog made his tree."

With Campbell-Spickler's help, Nick had figured out the *space* of the image. Now he had to consider *time*: how to transform a process and end result contingent on duration, into a still representation of a particular moment in the tree's life, in real time. (This recalled his work at the Grand Canyon, where he had made use of lightning, snow—anything that might indicate that this was a specific moment in the story of a landscape.) To achieve a truthful portrait, he felt it must be achieved in one continuous shoot.

Over the course of more than two weeks in March 2009, Nick and his team assembled by the tree at Prairie Creek each dawn. Three cameras would be mounted on the film dolly, which would start at the top of the tree and be lowered with absolute precision. As the dolly descended, the cameras—which were not positioned at the same level—would take photographs simultaneously, shooting again at increments of about six feet. The image of the tree would be amassed—first horizontally, the respective images stitched together by Geiger to create a panorama; and then vertically, when the panoramas were stacked, aligned perfectly, and also stitched together top and bottom.

Nick noticed that the bottom of the tree never got much light, so he placed Williamson in the adjacent tree holding a giant spotlight, powerful enough to match the daylight, but still with a warm glow to it. As the dolly was lowered, at a certain point Williamson would start moving the light down in sync with cameras, subtly alternating its direction each time. Illuminating the lower trunk in this way created a balance with the natural light in the higher parts of the tree and lent the base more texture. For every shoot, "I begged Jim [Campbell-Spickler—in red] and Giacomo [Renzullo—in yellow] to wear highly visible colors," recalls Nick. Sillett chose to wear green, and Marie Antoine was dressed in red and white. To give an idea of scale, Sillett, Antoine, and Renzullo were positioned at various points in the tree, while Campbell-Spickler was constantly moving about—so, surreally, he appears several times in the final image. Geiger, on the computer, accounted for all the necessary details for the composite to work, Humboldt State engineer Marty Reed worked the dolly, and Williamson took care of the cameras and worked the lights. Nick oversaw and directed the whole.

Day after day, they struggled with lighting conditions. If the morning fog and overcast burned off and the sky cleared, the light was hot, creating too much contrast. If there was a thick layer of clouds (usually the case), everything became flat. Gossamer clouds that diffused the harshness—yet still were radiant with the morning light—offered the perfect circumstance, if it lasted. Renzullo would climb to the treetop and radio news of the changing morning light to Nick and Geiger, who were at the base of the tree, watching everything on the computer monitor—wired to the three cameras—as the cameras photographed, and descended, step by step. This daily repetition drove Sillett crazy, Nick says. Although they were "treating this tree like a museum specimen," they inevitably trampled some of the surrounding ferns. "Steve doesn't want shoes to mess up that bark at all, and he is driving me nuts—even though he's right to be this way. Every second he's pointing out to me something bad I've done. . . . It's Mike's '100 Things Nick Did Wrong' all over again. When we left, we restored absolutely everything."

It was not until the eleventh attempt to shoot the tree that everything finally came together. In one move, lasting thirty minutes, eighty-four contiguous images were made. Nick and Geiger were on the computer monitor, adjusting and controlling the exposures, because even with Williamson lighting the lower part of the trunk there was still ten times more brightness at the crown. But then it happened: As the camera dolly reached a point near the middle of the tree, Nick suddenly heard Sillett say: "I feel it. It's *glowing*." Nick's heart was racing. The team was euphoric.

Geiger, responsible for stitching the images together, later explained the process:

> I took the multiple images in the sequence in which Nick photographed them, and fit them together. I overlapped them and then "feathered" the edges—all on the computer—to create one total, continuous tree. . . . At the time there was not a software program that could handle the intricacies and the fine detail of the branches going out in multiple directions. . . . So first we did a low-res rough just to see if the overlaps were good enough. The tree trunk was my guide as it is all on one focal plane.

"It took," he says, "a painstakingly long time."

The result is stunning. As Nick had done so often with the camera traps, he had had to envision the possibilities, the whole of this eighteen-hundred-plus-year-old being—without ever actually having seen it. His remarkably detailed image is revelatory.

"Redwoods: The Super Trees" was *National Geographic*'s cover story in October 2009.[5] For the first time in its history, the magazine allowed an image to break through its signature yellow border. The tree seems almost to be bursting the seams of the rectangle.

Nick at Prairie Creek Redwoods State Park, 2008. Photograph by Stephen C. Sillett

There was no afterglow for Mike Fay, who to this day feels betrayed by that *National Geographic* story. In addition to his own essay and Nick's photographs, the publication includes an essay by Joel K. Bourne Jr., and Michael Christopher Brown's images of Fay's redwoods transect. But from Fay's perspective, the piece as a whole is not what he had understood it would be. Indeed, he thinks it may even undermine his intentions— believing that Nick's work on the old-growth redwoods only speaks to the 3 percent. The concept, he told me with a glare, was *not* about the photographic challenge of these beautiful big trees.

Talking over pizza and beer in Libreville, Gabon, Fay spelled out for me what he had thought the *National Geographic* story was going to be:

It was about how you can cut down 97 percent of the most fabulous forest on Earth, the most dense and voluminous and tall forest on Earth, and you can let the timber barons steal all of that wealth from this place. . . . [The Redwood Forest is] one of the best examples on Earth of . . . what humans are capable of doing: destroying every single watershed, every single creek—all the fish are gone, the soil's pretty much all got wasted, all the trees got wasted.

Fay wanted to bring focus to that truth, and also to look at how subsequently—understanding what we had destroyed—"people are rebuilding this forest, bringing it back to life, and cleaning the creeks up. . . ." He believes that there are sustainable ways to cut, that it can be done without decimating the forests. Logging can take place in selective, strategic rotations where every ten to fifteen years a percentage of the weakest trees are removed. This strengthens the forest's genetics and the trees grow faster, while not compromising the harvest.[6] This approach supports those who depend on the forests, both economically (the timber industry) and ecologically.

For the *National Geographic* story, Fay wanted photographs that showed the devastation of the redwoods, and then bore witness to an ecosystem being restored. He wanted to offer a model in the United States that could be replicated elsewhere where forests are under siege. And what better place to do this than in one of the most celebrated forests? For Fay, gorgeous photographs of gorgeous trees are, more or less, strategically useless. For Nick, if people don't *care* about the trees, no matter how brilliant the conservation, how forceful the advocacy—nothing will change.

Steve Sillett had a dream.

There's a tree, he told Nick soon after the success of the redwoods story—an exceptional, prodigious, ancient specimen in California's Sequoia National Park—that is one of the largest trees on Earth. It is known as the President; it is 3,200 years old and still growing. It had never before been climbed or measured; indeed, no data had yet been collected beyond the tree's age. Since he'd first seen the tree in 1987, Sillett had been longing to climb it.

Nick was on it. He approached Chris Johns in late 2009 about a second portrait—this time, of the President. It was believed by many to be the oldest known living sequoia. "I started thinking of it as a companion to our [Prairie Creek] redwood," says Nick. "I saw them as a pair. The sequoia is the other great, giant tree of California—actually, of the entire world." His idea was to photograph the President in the snow, which he hoped would intensify its spiritual aura, and the overall "cathedral effect" of these grand trees. Johns agreed to the project.

Once all permissions for rigging, climbing, and photographing were gathered from the National Park Service (a feat in itself that began in March 2010—almost a year ahead of their shoot), Nick's next—and far more delicate—negotiation was with nature. He knew he wanted snow, but not just *any* snow: a thick, fresh fall of large snowflakes that would pile up on the tree's branches and stay there long enough to make the photograph.

In February 2011 it was frigid outside. Sillett and his team were especially vulnerable in these arctic conditions, even beyond the inherent risks of the climb. Moreover, unlike the trees at Prairie Creek, the President was unknown territory. (Sillett would not be able to measure and collect his data until the summer of 2011; he couldn't effectively work in the winter conditions Nick wanted for his portrait.) But Campbell-Spickler, Geiger, and the rest of the team had further developed the technology for shooting and rendering a tree in its entirety in the time since Nick's redwood portrait, and they continued to finesse it for the situation at hand, testing it over several days on-site. They felt as ready as they could be to create the image Nick envisioned on the anticipated day of a major snowfall.

Still, nothing could have prepared them for the blinding, all-enveloping whiteout blizzard that hit on February 26, the day of the shoot. It did not stop them from pressing forward—after so much preparation, it's hard to imagine what would.

Their first attempt failed. The communication system between the cameras and the computer kept breaking down. Nick and Geiger were working on the monitor in a kind of snow-cave tent the team had improvised. The climbers, shivering, were at risk of hypothermia, and visibility was diminishing quickly.

Despite the worsening weather conditions, they agreed to try one more time that day.

This time, everything was functioning. The team was positioned in the tree. It was show time. Nick had waited for snow, and here it was, as if on cue, falling like Niagara. They knew they had only a small window of time before the already perilous conditions would make proceeding

OPPOSITE: Nathan Williamson (left) and engineer Marty Reed preparing the camera dolly, Sequoia National Park, California, 2011; ABOVE: *National Geographic,* December 2012: "Sequoias: Scaling a Forest Giant"

impossible. As the snow engulfed them, they did it, slowly, and with tremendous care: one shoot of forty-five continuous minutes in the life of the President tree. That was it. Geiger checked to be sure that the file was good, and then Nick called everyone to come down out of the tree. The resulting portrait of the "snow tree" is a sublime partner for the earlier redwood portrait. It was published as *National Geographic*'s December 2012 cover story, "Sequoias: Scaling a Forest Giant."[7] Again, the image breaks through the confines of the yellow rectangle. The issue of the magazine was distributed with a many-panel foldout poster of Nick's hard-won image of the President.

Sillett later recalled:

> Moving through the frozen crown of this colossal tree required great care so as not to dislodge any snow, because documentation of the tree in full winter glory was Nichols's primary objective. One of my chief tasks was to deploy an access rope on the farthest edge of the crown near the tip of the tree's largest limb, over 60 feet away from the main trunk. The journey to this position, the view from there looking back on the mighty tree and its neighbors, and then rappelling 200 feet down from the limb into deep snow on the ground I will never forget.[8]

David Quammen contributed the essay for "Forest Giant." (Thanks to Nick, he had the "mind-blowing" opportunity to climb the President tree once the shoot was over.) I asked Quammen whether it was very different to have a tree, rather than an animal, as the subject of their story. He responded:

> No. It was very much like dealing with animals. . . . We both felt that this is a magnificent living creature—just the way a huge grandmother matriarch elephant is a magnificent creature. One of them happens to be able to move around, and another one is able to stand in one place for over two thousand years. But they're both extraordinary living creatures.

Quammen says, however, that Nick's role in the two tree stories was something new: "He was more a *director*." Certainly, Nick's years orchestrating camera traps and complex lighting had begun to prepare him for this role of setting up, but not actually holding the cameras, but these portraits pushed his ability to previsualize even further. Along these lines, the redwoods project was also the first time Nick proposed sharing the visual narration of a story with someone else—someone he might guide and mentor if need be. He understood that the narrative about the redwoods required a certain scope of coverage, and also knew that he didn't wish to take on every part of it. David Griffin assigned the young photographer Michael Christopher Brown to document the transect aspect.

Several people began to muse about Nick's next life as a wildlife filmmaker. (I'm reminded of the time I asked Nick which, if any, wildlife films had influenced him. His answer: *"The Big Lebowski* and *Gimme Shelter."*)[9]

While working among the redwoods, Nick made a marvelous image of a northern spotted owl, lustrous, flying toward his camera. More than fifteen years earlier, this captivating species had featured in the running conflict between ecologists and loggers in these ancient forests. The only viable habitat for the northern spotted owl is among the old-growth conifer forests of the Pacific Northwest. Environmentalists postulated that continued clear-cutting and destruction of these woods inevitably guaranteed the extinction of the popular bird. Their success in having the northern spotted owl listed as "threatened" ensured the protection of its habitat. Sadly, advocates—despite some successes with specific trees, groves, and stretches—had not previously been able to entirely save what little remained of these old-growth forests for the forests' sake. Instead, the swell of voices to save this bewitching little owl helped to block further destruction of the redwoods themselves, challenging the timber industry to do better environmentally in the process.[10]

Lowell Diller was a biologist for California's Green Diamond Resource Company, a timber enterprise that aspired to operate sustainably. Diller—whose expertise embraces the redwoods ecology, and who was an adjunct professor in the department of wildlife at HSU—was a consultant for Nick as he photographed the northern spotted owl. In 2016 Diller helped me understand the conservation balancing act in the redwood forests, especially with regard to this owl. Once an owl is listed under the Endangered Species Act, he told me, the timber companies can no longer harvest the trees that are its habitat.

> If you are a timber company, your whole sustainable economy is based on growing and harvesting trees. So you have this very interesting and intriguing conservation dilemma. Conservation of a species doesn't work unless it's ecologically sustainable *as well as* socially and economically sustainable. . . . How do we do timber harvesting in such a way that the company still stays in business, people still have jobs, we still get the wood products that we need from trees, and at the same time we're also protecting the natural resources, the habitat?

When Nick met him, Diller was monitoring and studying the northern spotted owl, which necessitated banding them. To catch them, he put a live mouse at the end of a stick as bait, and then, as a lure, mimicked the call of the owls. As the owl darts down to snatch the mouse, Diller does what he refers to as "the 'hand grab'—our preferred capture technique because it causes the least stress to the owl, but it can only be done with owls that are habituated to taking mice." Then Diller bands it—

Northern spotted owl, Humboldt County, California, 2008

trying to avoid getting bitten during the two- to three-minute process. When Nick learned of this trick, he decided to put a live mouse on a tray, on top of his camera. He told me that, since Diller felt it was ethical to use mice in this way for his study—in the interest of the forest's greater good—he felt he could replicate the process, adding: "Diller was careful not to bait the owls so frequently with the mice that the owls became dependent on them, or on his study, as a food source."

Nick used camera-trap technology, knowing that the human hand would not be able to release the shutter quickly enough to catch an image of a swooping bird coming in for the kill. Once Diller spots the owl on its perch, he can discern the arc of the owl's dip as it flies toward the mouse. He advised Nick where to locate the invisible beam. As soon as the flying owl broke through the beam, the camera was signaled to shoot. The remarkable lighting was achieved with strobes, brought in to stop motion, and to counter the darkness of the forest.

Habitat loss from logging has now ended, at least in California, says Diller, "where forestry practices are more protective of owls." (He's quick to add that the northern spotted owl is still vulnerable to logging on private lands outside California, and wildfire is also a potential danger throughout the remainder of the owl's range on private and public lands in the dryer inland areas of California, Oregon, and Washington.) But human incursion is not the only threat to this species. The northern spotted owl has natural enemies, too. Slightly larger, and much more aggressive, the barred owl is an invasive species, attempting to take over the northern spotted owl's territory, constantly trying to force it out of its habitat. It remains the next big menace to the survival of the northern spotted owl. Nick decided to try to photograph the barred owl as well. But there was no way to use the mouse-beam technique, as the barred owl was not habituated.

Their strategy instead was for Nick to camouflage himself. As Diller describes it:

> He would put an imitation barred owl on his head. Then we would play owl recordings and the resident barred owl–being very territorial and guarding its habitat—would act very aggressively toward any intruder. We were trying to mimic an intruder in their territory, so the barred owl would come down and attack it. Nick would be holding the camera as the barred owl would come in to attack the decoy on his head.

> This was the plan. We didn't know for sure if it was going to work. But I guaranteed Nick that the barred owls would attack his decoy.

As anticipated, the barred owls went for the imitation owl. Because of his unwieldy protective headgear, however, Nick couldn't see where they were coming from. (And, never having been studied, the birds' flight patterns were unpredictable.) Looking at a photograph of himself as owl bait, Nick now giggles at the goofiness of the plan: "It *so* did not work. Not only did I not make any photographs, I never even saw the owl!"

Nick attempting to photograph barred owl (seated behind him is Lowell Diller), Humboldt County, 2008. Photograph by Nathan Williamson. FOLLOWING SPREAD: Top: The President, Sequoia National Park, 2011; bottom: Coastal redwood, Prairie Creek Redwoods State Park, 2009. Both photographed by Nichols, composited by Ken Geiger

The northern spotted owl population continues to decline across the forests of the Northwest (the redwoods comprise only about 7 percent of this bird's total range). The primary culprit is indeed the barred owl.[11] According to a May 2015 *Newsweek* piece by Sarah Deweerdt, a controversial proposal from the U.S. Fish and Wildlife Service suggests killing about 3,600 barred owls in California, Oregon, and Washington. The article quotes Bob Sallinger, conservation director of the Portland Audubon Society: "The idea of killing thousands and thousands of these beautiful birds is unacceptable to many, many people. At the same time, having a species like the spotted owl go extinct is also unacceptable."[12] In August 2016, the northern spotted owl was listed as "threatened" under the California Endangered Species Act. Diller says he wouldn't be surprised if it is eventually up-listed to "endangered" status under the federal Endangered Species Act. To many—who are reconciled to the need for human intervention in that we are responsible for its habitat destruction in the first place—it seems only fitting that this accidental activist should have the highest protection and be allowed to live peacefully in the forests it helped save. During the past fifteen or so years there has been no significant loss of redwood-forest habitat, which would suggest that restoration and sustainability attempts—at least in the redwoods—are in fact working.

In the car with Sillett and Campbell-Spickler on our way back to Arcata after our day at Prairie Creek, we're just yakking.

The subject turns to Mike Fay, who is something of an intriguing hero to these two. "One day," speculates Campbell-Spickler, "Fay will just disappear. He'll be like one of those dogs who goes off into the woods to die, and you'll just never see him again."

Sillett considers this possibility, and then sums up his own opinion of the Fay/Nichols dynamic:

> I revere Fay. He's quirky, but he's astonishingly persevering. He's got the most endurance in the wilderness of anybody I know. He's like the John Muir of the twenty-first century.
>
> And Fay and Nick are kind of a perfect pair. Although Nick doesn't like fighting . . . he really hates it, hates yelling, but he'll get there. He'll get in your face. . . . He got so worked up when I got really pissed at him. But—I had to get used to the idea that he was going to be working there for *fifteen fucking days*. Literally. Standing by this amazing tree with a group of people, trampling, for fifteen days! The guy is so relentless. He was going to get that shot. After the eighth day, I'm like: "Okay, dude, you must have a decent one by now?" Little did I know it was going to be another *week* or something. God, it was just on and on and on. But that's the man. And I had to respect that. He wasn't going away, after all that effort, until it was perfect. Nick and Fay are relentless perfectionists. They don't give up. Ever.

HARVEST

Vumbi pride, warthog kill led by collared female,
Serengeti National Park, Tanzania, 2011

'm not going to go out and do 'greatest hits,'" Nick told me as we sat, tent-side, in March 2012, and had our first conversation for this biography. "I'm not going *random* on lions . . . everything I see makes me want to get more intimate." Getting more intimate always requires time.

In August 2011, Nick, Reba, and Nathan Williamson had returned to Tanzania for about ten weeks. It was the first of three trips they would make—adding up to eight months in the Serengeti, over about a year and a half—to photograph its charismatic big cat, the lion. Reba was now an official and integral member of the team, tasked with driving and with "spotting" the lions, who are so adept at blending into the landscape's palette, camouflaging themselves in plain sight. Williamson, now in his tenth year assisting Nick, was doing extensive video and sound work when not dealing with the tech and other challenges. Joining them twice for periods of about three weeks each was David Quammen, who would write two essays: one focused on the lion itself, the other on the tensions of living with them.

After the 2009 publication of his redwoods story, Nick had traveled to Kenya to photograph at the David Sheldrick Wildlife Trust elephant orphanage. Subsequently, in May 2010, he left Kenya for Tanzania to scout the lions story—considering possible camp locations, and meeting with Tanzanian officials regarding permits and other business. Rob Carr-Hartley, husband of DSWT's Angela Sheldrick, is a safari operator who knows Tanzania well. He advised Nick on some of the pragmatic challenges that lay ahead, such as how best to get around for photographing, while also suggesting where he might begin the journey—in order to have an overall sense of place.

Nick and the team were in the Serengeti under the auspices of the Tanzania National Parks Authority. Unofficially, they were also collaborating with the Serengeti Lion Project, initiated by biologist George Schaller in the mid-1960s. The study by now had some thirty-five prides in its scope. Over the course of several years, the project's longtime director, Craig Packer, had periodically met with Nick and Kathy Moran at National Geographic's offices in Washington, educating and advising them in preparation for Nick's time in the Serengeti, while also determining how to facilitate Nick's photographic needs and ideas as they continued to evolve.

On the advice of Carr-Hartley, the team acclimated themselves by first setting up camp in August 2011 in the northern Serengeti, in the area known as Lamai Triangle, or Lamai Wedge—bordered on the north by Kenya and on the south by the Mara River. The river ensures an abundance of wildlife. Over the course of about six weeks at Lamai, they regularly saw lions, but were unable to identify specific individuals with any consistency. As these lions were not in the Serengeti Lion Project's study group, none had been radio-collared for easy tracking and identification.

More than ever, Nick was convinced that in order to create an original project on one of the most iconic predators, in one of the world's most iconic parks, he would have to "lay siege" (as he puts it) on select prides inhabiting uniquely varied landscapes within the study area. This meant an intensive and long-term engagement: first habituating the animals to his presence, and then shadowing them day after day, getting to know their family and territorial histories, as well as particular prides' distinguishing behaviors. Nick had had it confirmed, over and over again, in almost every one of his stories, that it is all about the individual animal and the specifics of its family life and habitat.

The extensive time *National Geographic* afforded him once again allowed Nick to achieve a remarkable level of closeness with his subjects—a protracted courtship of sorts: what Edward Weston refers to in his *Daybooks* as "the flame of recognition":

> The flame started first by amazement over subject matter . . . the intuitive understanding and recognition relating obvious reality to the esoteric, must then be confined to a *form* within which it can burn with a focused intensity.[1]

Nick hoped that that uncanny recognition would now take place for him in the Serengeti.

George Schaller conducted his first, seminal baseline study of lions between 1966 and 1969. He looked at lions' behavior through their social interactions (the lion is the only cooperative, nonsolitary big cat), as well as in terms of territory and predation, while also focusing on prey populations. In his comprehensive 1972 volume *The Serengeti Lion*, Schaller writes:

> The Serengeti is a boundless region with horizons so wide that one can see clouds between the legs of an ostrich. It is a Pleistocene vision throbbing with the life of over half a million wildebeest and zebra, a stern yet lovely wilderness where man can renew his ancient ties with the predators that were once his competitors and the prey that gave him sustenance. . . . The predators are in many ways the park's most valuable resource for they are the ones which add excitement and authenticity to the natural scene, they are the symbol of this wilderness.[2]

Schaller, whose words are always authoritative and yet infused with wonder, goes on to speak about the Serengeti's ecological community at large, which depends on predators and the abundance of healthy prey. Predators, he maintains, are "the best wildlife managers." Essentially, Schaller considers the entire Serengeti ecosystem through the filter of the lion. His work was followed by Brian Bertram's 1969–73 study on lions' reproductive success, and then by Jeannette Hanby and David Bygott's 1974–78 investigations into the coalitions formed by male lions.

Craig Packer, the Serengeti Lion Project's director from 1978 to 2015, has a droll brusqueness about him that quickly gives way to a very real generosity. I followed up my 2012 visit to Tanzania with a battery of questions for him (over the next few years); invariably, he proved gracious with his time and knowledge. Before settling in the Serengeti, he worked with Goodall at Gombe. Goodall's chimpanzee study is the longest continuous field study of a mammal, and the Serengeti lion study is the second longest. In 2015 Packer published an assessment of the lions' current circumstances: *Lions in the Balance: Man-Eaters, Manes, and Men with Guns.*[3] The book deals not only with the prides themselves, but also with the reality of living with predators; the implications of corrupt and bureaucratic government officials; and trophy killing—among many other heated issues—while advocating concrete and measurable ways to potentially mitigate threats to the species' survival.

In the savannas and woodlands that comprise the habitats of the thirty-five prides of the Serengeti Lion Project, it is possible to observe individual lions and their prides on a consistent basis. Each pride has one radio-collared female. Every day during their time there, Nick, Reba, and Williamson would track a specific pride of lions and stay with them for hours and hours, each session inching closer, as permitted (or not) by the animals. These repeated visits in the Land Rover soon habituated the lions to their presence, which consequently allowed access to everything from the minutiae of the animals' daily lives (grooming, sleeping, playing) to the great dramas of survival (hunting for food, finding water, procreation, protecting cubs, securing territory), always informed by the Lion Project's comprehensive data on the background of each animal in its study group.

The scientific data proved invaluable for Nick. As he had with the chimpanzees, the Samburu elephants, the tigers Sita and Charger, and some of the mountain-gorilla groups, Nick had a detailed family tree at his disposal—in the case of the Serengeti lions, more than four decades' worth of genealogical information. This informs, for example, Nick's understanding of territorial shifts, dominance, and which males have sired cubs in which prides. Male lions will associate themselves with females in several prides (rather than engaging monogamously with one lioness or pride), and generally protect cubs they have sired. In an environment with infinite lessons on predation, longitudinal information about births and survival rates of cubs, numbers of lions in prides, and the prides' movements within the landscape is indispensable.

For Nick, appreciating these lions and lionesses as individuals with distinct histories makes this work inescapably personal, and fuels the frisson that breathes such raw authenticity into his portraits.

After their initial six weeks at Lamai Wedge, Nick, Reba, and Williamson packed into the Land Rover and made their way south, arriving two days later in the rich habitat of Seronera, where Schaller had concentrated his original three-year study. (The heart of the Serengeti and lion country, Seronera has since been overwhelmed by safari lodges and tourist vehicles.) From there, they continued south, following Daniel Rosengren, one of Packer's field assistants, who drove ahead of them through the short grass of the dusty savannas toward the arid Barafu Valley. Rosengren was going to introduce them to some of the lion study's prides that day, beginning with Semetu (whose resident males were known as "The Killers"), and then onward to Simba East, and then Vumbi (presided over by resident males C-Boy and Hildur). Packer explains the system of nomenclature: "Males [like C-Boy and Hildur] who enter the study area from elsewhere are given names . . . my Swedish assistants gave them Swedish names, the New Zealander named some after New Zealand rugby players." The lions born *within* the study area, however, "all have initials/numbers according to pride of birth."

As the team progressed, the landscape shifted, the brush giving way to sparse desert terrain, saturated greens turning to olive or sage. It was near the end of the dry season, when the plains ache for rain and survival is a daily struggle for the lions who live in this "marginal" habitat. Packer had briefed Nick, recommending that he experience and photograph the impact of the seasonal cycles, what the plains lions must do to endure. For these plains prides—whose habitat lacks a reliable water source during the dry season—it is literally feast or famine.

Proximity to water dictates much of lion behavior: their own physical need for water, and the fact that water attracts prey. The rains drive the timing of the yearly migration of more than a million wildebeest, along with hundreds of thousands of gazelles and zebras, throughout the ecosystems of Kenya's Masai Mara National Reserve and Tanzania's Serengeti. Before the rains and the migration, many of the plains prides are just barely surviving. As Packer put it: "The cubs will be mangy and half-dead, and the females will hardly be able to walk."

Each habitat places different demands on its residents. Packer had suggested that Nick also photograph one of the woodlands prides, the Barafu, whose habitat even in the driest periods has constant sources of water, guaranteeing a larger prey population. Packer told Nick that cubs were expected to be born to the Barafu pride within the next three to five months. The newborns' lives and needs, everyone agreed, would make for compelling storytelling when Nick, Reba, and Williamson returned as they planned to, in late January 2012. On this first trip in late 2011, however, Nick's attentions were elsewhere. The plains prides' precarious circumstances—the "famine" part of the cycle—demanded his focus.

On the afternoon they left Seronera, Nick, Reba, and Williamson followed Rosengren's vehicle as he tracked each pride's collared female within their respective territories.

Toward the end of the day, they spotted a group of lionesses that Rosengren identified as the Vumbi pride—*vumbi* is Swahili for "dust." The pride's habitat, in the sweeping, straw-toned grasses of the Barafu Valley, is randomly punctuated by rocky, gray kopjes (used strategically by the lions for surveillance and ambush), and acacia trees (for shade). The parched, loose surface soil tumbled about, at times coalescing in powdery apparitions shaped by the late afternoon breeze.

The lionesses had positioned themselves on a rise, each looking outward, encircling their cubs. "They were all so *thin*," remembers Nick. "We thought they were going to die." All was more silhouette than detail, illuminated by the sun, orange-yellow, descending through the endless horizon. Habituated to Rosengren and his vehicle, the lions remained aloof to their presence. Nick immediately began photographing.

Rosengren had a long drive ahead of him and was eager to get home before dark. Before departing, he offered either to lead them east to what would be their campsite for the next six weeks—a pristine spot on the rim of the Barafu gorge—or to leave them here with the Vumbi pride. Nick decided, with Reba and Williamson in enthusiastic agreement, that they could find their way to the campsite with GPS, and they should stay with Vumbi until sunset—if the pride continued to tolerate their presence.

Reba was peering through binoculars and noticed one of the females starting to pace, while looking especially intently into the distance. Another lioness did the same. "They've seen something!" Reba said. Something was happening, or was about to happen. They could all sense it.

One of the lionesses—the collared female—began trotting away from the group, and another followed behind her. "They went pretty far," remembers Nick, "could have been up to half a mile." The team rolled gingerly behind them in the Land Rover, Reba keeping her eyes on the animals through the binoculars. She watched as the lionesses fixed on two warthogs darting into one of the hundreds of holes marking the terrain. The lionesses pounced, digging furiously. "They were on them *immediately*." They inched the car a little closer so Nick could have better access.

Nick says:

> The wind is howling. By now, we know what's going on, and I'm excited—I can't *believe* that it can be possible to get the "cooperative kill" I wanted to photograph, and it's our first day! Serendipitous kills like this are what keep the plains prides alive during the dry season. I wanted to show how the pride works together.

> But we don't know how much they'll accept us. . . . We don't know if we can be close or must stay far away. They haven't eaten and there's dinner—and we *definitely* don't want to interfere with that. So we just set up a respectful distance from where they're all taking turns digging.

> The collared female was so intent. When the first warthog came out, she didn't blink. Everybody else dove into that food and was going crazy. She just stayed on top of the hole— knowing that there was another warthog down there. The lions were starving, and this was a life-saving meal of protein, and there was more, and the cubs needed to be fed. And she was right, and she got him.

> That was our first moment with the lions. When we got to camp that night, I was over the top!

One photograph Nick made that first day exudes exhilarating tension, like watching the frenzied athletic teamwork in a do-or-die effort to score the winning point. The lionesses' skeletal musculature reveals the toll of starvation, and the extreme physicality of this single-minded moment. The cubs— six months old at the time—fervently follow the lionesses' movements as the dust sprays. All this is set against the purple-hued, yellow-gray grasses in the now dusky light, a flicker of gold still glimmers as the sky slowly turns indigo.

This image was discussed at length some seventeen months later, in March 2013, as Packer, Quammen, Williamson, and Nick were reviewing the work at National Geographic's offices. The four of them were in Washington, DC, editing, captioning, and gathering picture-specific information for the lions story, which would run in the magazine's August issue.

It's generally agreed that a pride of lions hunts cooperatively—it's an effective strategy. Nick's rather extrapolative reading is that the collared Vumbi lioness who actually killed the warthog chose not to monopolize it: "After all, there were thirteen hungry lions." In other words, he believes that she was provisioning the pride. Packer's take was very different—reminding Nick that "it's very important to have Craig's filter on my 'Nick science.'"

Packer sees another dynamic among the lions in the image:

> All cats have a "killing bite." And she's going to focus on that animal through that killing bite to make sure it's dead. But in the meantime, everybody else gets to just go down and chomp on it. So they're all parasitizing *her*. It's not so much "I'm providing for everyone"; it's more

"Damn it—I've got to *kill* this thing!" And then it all gets eaten before she has a chance to eat anything herself!

It's a part of the conflict and the compromises that go on; the animal that catches [the prey] often doesn't benefit directly. . . . [But] she's not going to run off on her own. She can't say: "Well, I'm fed up with provisioning these slackers." If she tries to go off on her own, takes her cubs off with her, then she's going to be so much more vulnerable to the invasion by [other lions]. So she's stuck. She has to stay with these others. And there are other contexts besides hunting where she has to have the safety in numbers . . . so she has to endure all this.

Photojournalists who focus on human beings may have an insight into what motivates their subjects beyond primal instinct, a sense of how their subjects perceive themselves. Nick has no such information at his disposal. In fact, he knows very little about the self-awareness of his subjects.

Still, while empathy may be by definition unachievable, Nick's desire to understand and convey the interior lives of his subjects—even if at times reading and interpreting what he perceives as feelings, motivations, and thought processes in human terms—suggests in part why many of his images burn with such preternatural intensity and eloquence. His is a kind of unrequited love for an elusive, unknowable being. Nick recognizes that he will always remain "other" to his subjects—and his work is an ongoing improvisation between this and his lust to really know what will always remain outside his grasp.

In terms of both process and content, each of Nick's projects has evolved out of his previous ones. He tends not to make the same mistake twice. He incessantly challenges himself to do better—he is his own fiercest competitor—while never abandoning the moral core of his relationship to the wild. When deep into a project, he is haunted—sometimes at the expense of his health—by what he is *not* getting, *not* achieving. He is not interested in repeating himself, so each new project invites, insists on originality in every sense. At the same time, Nick is all-consumed by his pursuit of the protagonist, the concept, the plotline that will, as he is in the habit of saying, "tie the room together."

"Nick is always looking for Lebowski's rug," says David Quammen with a laugh, referring to the immortal conceit from the Coen brothers' film *The Big Lebowski*. "We both are. There has to be a Lebowski's rug." The allusion, he explains, is to "The Dude's groping, funny sense of coherence." For Nick, it also expresses the quest for the element or character that helps drive the narrative, making transitions fluid and the disparate connect. More than twenty years after his first story on the Lechuguilla Cave for *National Geographic*, and despite a couple of setbacks, Nick's project on the Serengeti lions can be seen as the Lebowski's rug within the context of his life's work.

Different metaphor: Nick considers the Serengeti project a "kind of the perfect storm, in terms of the team." Nathan Williamson, he feels, was "at the apex of his career with me. . . . We worked closely together on the video and photography—I wanted him to video precisely what I was photographing, to see the *exact* same thing from the same perspective through the video camera

Death is always near, and teamwork is essential on the Serengeti—
even for a magnificent, dark-maned male known as C-Boy.

THE SHORT
HAPPY LIFE OF
A SERENGETI **Lion**

Lions kill lions. C-Boy, defending his interests, confronts that peril on a daily (and nightly) basis.

ABOVE: *National Geographic*, August 2013: "The Short Happy Life of a Serengeti Lion"; OPPOSITE: Nick and Reba with Hildur, Serengeti National Park, 2012

that I was seeing through my camera, so that we could later marry the two together." Reba was invaluable on many levels, but was exceptionally skilled at identifying the individual lions within a given pride—all the while keeping track of the lion study's "who's who" of genealogical and other data. Finally, Quammen would, as always, provide the larger context. "I had David, and his voice is so important," Nick says. Quammen's essays, rich with experiential detail, as ever provide an ideal counterpoint to Nick's photographs.

Most important to the project, naturally, was its brilliant ensemble cast. Packer had told Nick about the handsome lion C-Boy, associated with the Vumbi, Simba East, and Kibumbu plains prides. Still, nothing had prepared Nick for the dark-maned rock-star, the quintessential king of beasts, whose portrait opens the August 2013 *National Geographic* story "The Short Happy Life of a Serengeti Lion."[4]

There, C-Boy is set against a dramatic sky of dark clouds and streaks of setting sun, at that moment of dusk when lions come to life—a propitious time for photographing. "I was always looking for this image," says Nick. He lies in sphinx pose on the savanna, head held high, gazing monarchically straight into Nick's lens. And Nick, photographing at C-Boy's level, meets that gaze: the strength of the image comes in part from this parity and clear visual engagement. And closeness.

Nick was lying down in the Land Rover when making the photograph: "I'm not more than four to five feet from C-Boy. Maybe closer. In the car we were silent. No movement. No fumbling with stuff."

Nick thinks that C-Boy was awaiting the arrival of another lion, Hildur—more flaxen-coated and seemingly mellower. The two males are what is known in lion-study parlance as "coalition partners"; Packer refers to their relationship more colloquially as a "bromance": "They've formed a team. They can take on the world." Together, they help defend the Vumbi pride and their territory as the Vumbi lionesses, with their *grande dame* radio-collared, care for their cubs. In Nick's series of images we see eight cubs, all of them born in April 2011 to several different mothers, due to synchronized estrus. The lionesses are in every sense extraordinary: the enormous energy, vigilance, and cooperation that go into raising and protecting their cubs "takes my breath away," says Nick. The Vumbi females would often form an elegant circle around the frolicking cubs—each lioness facing outward, alert and on the lookout for prey and other lions—striking in its geometric precision.

Nick remained resolute in his decision *not* to illustrate a checklist of "lion behavior" with cherry-picked indiscriminate images of lions throughout the Serengeti—whether or not they were in the study group, no matter the pride. The more time he spent with the Vumbi and later the Barafu prides, the more he saw the wisdom of that decision. Perhaps he gave up some representational

comprehensiveness with this choice. But he achieved an unprecedentedly intimate, individuating portrait of two prides and their resident males, as opposed to a generalized composite of a species. And as Nick himself says: "I didn't fall in love with lions in general—I mean, they're fuckin' cool—but I fell in deep, emotional love with some girls named Vumbi."

Rob Carr-Hartley had customized the team's Land Rover with a windshield that could be dropped down on the hood, enabling Nick to photograph from the driver's position if necessary; a raised roof strong enough to stand on; and Kevlar tires to guard against flats in the treacherous terrain. He told me about some of the vehicle's other special features:

> I made it so Nick could even lie on the floor and shoot at eye level [as he did with C-Boy]. And I placed a refrigerator in the back. He could stay out all night if he wanted—there is room for two people to lie down. There are shelves with basic foodstuffs; something for water. . . . The car is completely self-contained, and with the capacity to charge batteries and all that stuff onboard as well. In a simple way—without a lot of fancy stuff and gadgetry—it takes care of all the basic needs he'd have in the bush, and he can shoot out of any height and angle.

Williamson figured out how to mount, on the car's bumper, a low-tech mechanism with which the cameras—attached—could be tilted up and down and pan. The idea came to them after Nick missed

a charged flirtation and mating sequence because the camera was just too far away. This brought the cameras closer to the action, and they could be controlled from Williamson's and Nick's computers in the car. The only problem with these external devices was that the lions seemed to regard them as toys—"so eventually came close, to play with them."

The retrofitted Land Rover was designed to be a true extension of Nick's eye, allowing him to see in any direction or from any height without putting him in a compromising position. It was also sufficiently comfortable that he, Reba, and Williamson managed to spend eight to twelve hours in it almost every day they were in the Serengeti.

By 2011 advanced photographic technology permitted Nick to shoot during the dark of night, without visible flash, using infrared technology—and thus without disrupting the animals' activities. Biologist Luke Hunter, the president and chief conservation officer of Panthera, which is devoted to big-cat conservation, began his own work on the species back in 1992—mainly with efforts to reintroduce lions into areas where they'd been wiped out. He finds these unprecedented images riveting: "The lion work is really distinctive for showing lions at night, which no one ever really does, or they're just terrible flash photos that disturb the lions. Night is when most lion behavior happens. So Nick really pushed that envelope to get to things that you haven't normally seen about the cats."

Especially on the open plains, the Vumbi lions hunt best on moonless nights, under the cover of darkness. Their night vision is superb. At one point, Nick, Reba, and Williamson—working and living on lion time—spent six long, consecutive nights following the lions. After picking up the faintest beep from the collared female's tracking device, they followed the crescendo-ing signal in the Land Rover. Their own man-made "night vision"—a synthesis of viewing, lighting, and photographing tools and techniques—allowed them to operate in complete darkness. Infrared-filtered spotlights and strobes were attached to the car and pointed forward, and another infrared light mounted inside the car could be directed as they wished. (Nick quickly realized that this light didn't disturb the lions.) They wore heavy night-vision goggles for driving and used thermal monoculars to "see" the heat given off by mammals.

Nick and Williamson used digital cameras modified for infrared photography—their cameras' digital sensor filters were adapted to capture only the infrared spectrum. Because it's the sensor that sees the infrared, Nick could not look through the viewfinder—instead he had to look through the digital screen at the back of the camera. The process of the feed being translated to the screens created a slight delay, so he was never able to react to what was happening in the precise moment. In fact, says Nick, "I could not see what was actually happening, only what the infrared camera was seeing—even though it could be just feet away from us . . . very strange."

Ever anxious about influencing the behavior of the lions or their prey, the team kept some distance in the Land Rover. And all their tools allowed them to see without being visually obtrusive. But as Williamson notes: as well-fitted as the car was for facilitating photography when parked, and for traversing the jagged terrain, it was *not* silent. Rather, it was a "lumbering, diesel-belching vehicle that's rattling and banging around on this impossible terrain like its got pots and pans in it."

C-Boy (robot-camera photograph), Serengeti National Park, 2012

The cacophony was part of the reason Nick missed at least a few potentially good photographs. Williamson recalls a particularly painful loss—after five nights spent following the Vumbi pride, hoping to see another cooperative kill:

> We saw the lions heading out, and we started driving after them. Reba was looking through the thermals—and suddenly she saw this *wall* of heat. There were tons of wildebeests. It was really exciting: we were going to get another "kill shot" with Vumbi that we were after.
>
> But then the five lionesses split up. . . . So boom! There goes the idea of being right there when the kill happens. You don't know which one is going to bring it down, and you can't follow all five at once. . . . And we also realized that we are just too loud in this car. We will affect the prey. The wildebeests are shy of everything, because *everything* kills them. And they will hear us and run away. It was pretty deflating.

Nick's dream for the future, should he ever return, is for a quiet electric car that is otherwise similarly outfitted and tough enough for the terrain.

Even with the insights every outing afforded, and even with the successful images Nick knows he achieved, a central part of the lions' story eluded him: "All I was missing was having the Serengeti's incredible annual mythic migration come into my Vumbi frame." Nick continues:

> I wanted to connect the dots and see the Vumbi females hunting the migration, and C-Boy on his belly because he can't eat anymore, and everybody just lying around satiated.
>
> I never saw that. I never saw them so full that they couldn't even think about eating another bite. . . . We were with them so much, we knew when they had eaten, when they were hungry because they had not eaten for three days. We saw the famine, but never the amazing feast.

Because he had agreed to speak at the World Press Photo awards in Amsterdam in April 2012, he missed the Serengeti migration that spring. It came later than anticipated, delayed by capricious rains. Agonizingly, just as Nick was leaving Tanzania, driving through the Serengeti toward the airstrip in Seronera, *there they were.* The landscape teemed with wildebeest, gazelles, zebras—as far as he could see. Disheartened, but knowing he had to honor his commitment to World Press, he didn't stop. His plan was to return in the fall and stay through the following spring, with the specific goal of photographing Vumbi's interaction with the migration, to be with the pride during its feast.

Lions have no natural predators except other lions who want their territory. Then there is man. Lions are murdered by humans for trophies, for bushmeat, as ritual, or in retaliation, including when Maasai tribesmen bring their cattle into conservation areas—known and protected lion habitat—to graze, or because the lions roam into villages bordering parklands and eat livestock. Of course, a lion does not know when land management or boundaries have changed, or that animals may enter their territory who are not on the menu, or that he or she is no longer in a protected area.

Packer elaborates on the complexities of conservation efforts, which must take into consideration local populations and poverty in order to succeed:

> If people in the developed world want to conserve lions, they need to keep in mind that local people in Tanzania and the rest of Africa do not view lions as big fluffy animals with big brown eyes. . . .
>
> Human population growth is over 3 percent per year in areas immediately adjoining the Serengeti park. Poverty is the root cause of the high population growth and the reason why people eat bushmeat and engage in subsistence agriculture that is eliminating savanna habitat.

Nick knows that these conservation issues are central to what he is doing, and of course vital to the survival of the lions themselves. Although they are not issues he wants to address through *his* photographs this time, he does want them to be part of the larger story that *National Geographic* and David Quammen narrate: "I don't feel like I can blink with the natural history," Nick says. "I can't step away from it, not even for a moment. I just don't have enough time to do them both right."

With this in mind, he worked with Kathy Moran to arrange for photojournalist Brent Stirton to cover the conservation and social issues that surround living with predators. Stirton's photographs, accompanied by Quammen's words, were published in August 2013 as "Living with Lions,"[5] which complemented Nick's and Quammen's "The Short Happy Life of a Serengeti Lion" in the same issue.

Stirton's story, like Nick's, is informed by Craig Packer's science. Packer has been somewhat controversial in advocating that select Tanzanian parks be fenced "linearly" on specific, vulnerable borders, but not *enclosed* by fencing. Many people object to what they perceive as zoolike boundaries. Packer believes that as long as the human population continues to grow, the "romantics" who hope to recover once pristine areas are being naïve. Fences, he argues, function both to keep predators (and other animals) safely in the protected areas, and humans and livestock out. As he writes in *Lions in the Balance*, fencing has been proven effective in South African parks:

> I've worked [in east Africa] for forty years, and I never wanted to see fences either, but the sad fact is that fences work. . . . Education and living with lions sound great in theory, but these

BOTH IMAGES: From *National Geographic*, August 2013: "Living with Lions." Photographs by Brent Stirton

strategies will take generations—and the data suggest we might lose half of our populations in the next twenty years. We can't wait that long. . . .

Tourists may not like to see fences, but remember that the South Africans already have fences . . . and tourism is thriving in Kruger and the rest of South Africa's parks. Fences work: they protect neighboring communities from lions and elephants; they clearly mark out the land that belongs to the animals.[6]

Lions are also prime targets in legal safari or trophy hunting. The animal is baited into a range where he or she can be easily shot, after which parts of the lion's body may end up as a wall hanging—another conquest to be checked off the hunter's list. Safari hunting is a highly priced pastime that (somewhat illogically) is credited by many with helping to support conservation and the protection of wildlife, both financially and in terms of regulation. The trophy-hunting industry does provide resources to antipoaching efforts, and at times has played a role in the reintroduction of species into privately held land. Thus a species' numbers are increased, even if a percentage is allowed to be hunted. Enlightened self-interest on the part of the hunting industry, perhaps, but nevertheless beneficial.

Poaching accounts for the loss of more animals than legal trophy hunting does; and given poaching's lawlessness and complete lack of regulation, it has more lethal implications for certain species— among them elephants, rhinoceroses, and tigers. Moreover, the land controlled by legal safari hunting can create a buffer zone between parklands and villages, diminishing the threats and tensions of human communities abutting predator habitats.

The larger defense of the legal trophy-hunting industry—when it is well regulated, which it often isn't—is that managing parks and other wild spaces, and practicing conservation there, requires enormous sums of money. The hunting industry pays for a large percentage, employing thousands of people who might otherwise not have an opportunity for work. It is sadly ironic that advocates and practitioners of trophy hunting may do more to protect animals and bolster conservation efforts than those who are opposed to facilitated murder for profit, fun, and prizes. Many attribute any increase in wildlife—often citing South Africa and the United States as examples—to conservation models built around hunting.

That said, even while recognizing its perverse efficacy, scores of conservationists despise the very idea of trophy hunting, and are disgusted by the corruption and dishonesty that shroud this industry. They are also skeptical, to say the least, about its positive effects on the economics of conservation. When I spoke with Packer in 2013, he put it this way:

Trophy hunting is based on flawed economics. In most cases it doesn't generate nearly enough money to pay for the proper management (e.g., antipoaching patrols, community-engagement projects) of the hunting blocks. Historically, many countries have encouraged unsustainably high harvests of lions. And there is a great deal of corruption in the hunting industry in several African countries. Reform is urgently needed . . . international sanctions may help leverage reform.

Lioness of the Barafu pride, Serengeti National Park, 2012

The subject of trophy hunting was brought sensationally to the attention of the general public in July 2015, when an American safari hunter, on a $50,000 hunting vacation, shot a cherished Zimbabwean lion known as Cecil, who was part of a long-term wildlife study.

Jane Goodall wrote a statement in response to the killing of Cecil:

> I simply cannot put myself into the mind of a person who pays thousands of dollars to go and kill beautiful animals simply to boast, to show off their skill or their courage. Especially as it often involves no skill or courage whatsoever, when the prey is shot with a high powered rifle from a safe distance. How can anyone with an ounce of compassion be proud of killing these magnificent creatures? Lions, leopards, sable antelopes, giraffes and all the other sport or trophy animals are beautiful—but only in life. In death they represent the sad victims of a sadistic desire to attract praise from their friends at the expense of innocent creatures. And when they claim they respect their victims, and experience emotions of happiness at the time of the killing, then surely this must be the joy of a diseased mind?
>
> There are many ethical issues, which we seldom face up to, whenever an animal is killed. For example, is it "worse" to shoot a wild boar for food than to slaughter an imprisoned factory-farmed hog? Does the life of a wild turkey matter more than the life of a free-range domestic turkey? Is the person who grants a license to the hunter, or the one who authorizes that person, or the one who drafts the laws that make it legal to do this, as guilty as the person who pulls the trigger (or fires the crossbow)? These and many other such questions are seldom asked. And when they are, they sometimes seem impossible to answer.
>
> But trophy hunting is hard to defend. And the outpouring of anger and hatred occasioned by the killing of Cecil shows how many people feel that the days of the great White Hunter should be brought to a close.[7]

The public debate and anger Cecil's killing incited resulted in relatively quick, concrete protective action. In the United States, the Obama administration decided in December 2015 to list lions in central and west Africa as "endangered" under the Endangered Species Act. Lions in south and east Africa were reclassified as "threatened" under the same act.

The U.S. Fish and Wildlife Service, which administers the Endangered Species Act, cites "habitat loss," "loss of prey," "retaliatory killing due to increased human-lion conflicts," "inadequate regulatory mechanisms," and "weak management of protected areas" as its reasons for both of these classifications. According to the Fish and Wildlife Service: "'Endangered' means a species is in danger of extinction throughout all or a significant portion of its range. 'Threatened' means a species is likely to become endangered within the foreseeable future."[8]

As Erica Goode reported in the *New York Times* in December 2015, these new classifications for lions in Africa had an impact on the import/export regulations for animal trophies:

Hildur, C-Boy's coalition partner, Serengeti National Park, 2012

Both designations, the [Fish and Wildlife Service] said, will result in stricter criteria for the import of live lions and lion parts, like heads, paws or skins. Trophies from countries where lions are endangered will be "generally prohibited," except in very limited circumstances, the agency said. Trophies could still be imported from nations where lions are listed as threatened—like Tanzania, Zimbabwe and South Africa, all popular countries for American hunters—as long as they met the standards set under the special rule and the animals were killed legally.[9]

Goode observed that France had banned the import of lion trophies, and Britain may do so in 2017. "More than 40 airlines have also said they will no longer transport hunting trophies."[10]

Nick's work has always explored the man-nature dialectic. The Serengeti lion—like so many creatures for whom he has advocated through his projects—is vulnerable to the wealthiest and the poorest among us. The lion is prey to those for whom killing is about "sport" and trophies, and those for whom killing is perceived as a means toward quick and necessary cash, or retaliation for livestock that has been attacked.

Lion killing is also sometimes a matter of self-defense. And it is understood by some as a rite of passage. The Maasai view lion hunting as a measure of bravery and personal achievement. The Maasai Association (a community-based Kenyan NGO working to preserve Maasai culture and support economic stability and relief efforts) distinguishes the "rite of passage" symbolism of the Maasai hunt from the "hobby"

of trophy hunting. For the Maasai, they say, strict rules apply; foremost among them is a ban on killing lionesses. "Maasai believe that females are the bearers of life in every species. As such, it is prohibited to hunt a female lion—unless the lioness has posed a threat to human or livestock."[11]

Unfortunately, such prohibitions are not always heeded. In the first two weeks of April 2014, Maasai rite-of-passage rituals resulted in the killings of four lions. One of the victims was the Vumbi collared female so beloved by Nick and his team, as well as by Daniel Rosengren, who found her body. She had been speared to death—some of her claws removed as trophies. Rosengren suspects that two other Vumbi females have also been slaughtered in this way.

Within weeks, Craig Packer and Swedish biologist Ingela Jansson—whose work addresses lion-human conflict—put forth a new strategy in their ongoing efforts to resolve tensions between the Maasai and the lions. They proposed a system that financially rewards Maasai—an ever-increasing population that for years has been encroaching on supposedly protected parkland—for refraining from killing. As reported by Quammen on National Geographic's website, Packer and Jansson met with conservator Freddy Manongi of the Ngorongoro Conservation Area (NCA), "and discussed the possibility of a 'performance payment system,' as used in Jansson's native Sweden to mitigate conflict between the Sami people, the reindeer they keep as livestock, and the wolverines and lynx that sometimes prey upon those reindeer." This approach requires the approval of the Maasai elders in the NCA, but as Packer points out: "It's very sensible. . . . You're rewarding for conservation, rather than paying compensation for lost livestock. . . . Such a system would bring direct financial benefit to local Maasai for each lion they tolerate within their grazing lands."[12] Presumably, this tactic would also help discourage the Maasai from bringing their livestock to graze in protected lands where lions roam. It was hoped that this might curb both retaliatory and ritual killings.

Similarly, since 2007, the Lion Guardians, a community-based initiative in Kenya and Tanzania, is self-mandated to recruit and pay "young, non-literate Maasai and other pastoralist warriors to learn the skills needed to effectively mitigate conflicts between people and wildlife, monitor lion populations, and help their own communities live with lions."[13]

Recent land-rights challenges in Tanzania have resulted in pastoralist communities (such as the Maasai) and hunter-gatherer communities (such as the Hadzabe) gaining legal title to their ancestral lands in the Tanzanian Rift Valley. Resolving human-wildlife conflicts is more critical than ever, as is protecting the environment through continued and sustainable conservation.

For lions to thrive, water and prey must be plentiful; the ecosystem must be healthy and flourishing. In Packer's concise aphorism: "Keep lions happy, and you are being a good steward of the land."

The Serengeti lion lost one of its most devoted advocates when, in 2015, Packer was banned from Tanzania. He had brought charges of corruption and unscrupulousness in the enforcement of wildlife regulations against all levels of the Tanzanian government, including the highest.[14]

Concerned about the future of the Serengeti Lion Project, in August 2015 I contacted the Frankfurt Zoological Society, which since the 1950s has been deeply involved in the conservation of the Serengeti. They recommended that I get in touch with Dr. Simon Mduma, director general of Tanzania Wildlife Research Institute, which oversees wildlife studies in the country. I made several attempts to reach Dr. Mduma by e-mail in 2015 and 2016 regarding the status of the Serengeti Lion Project since Craig Packer's departure. To date, I have received no response.

Currently, Packer continues to study lions in various reserves in South Africa. In June 2016 I asked him about the fate of the Serengeti Lion Project. His answer:

> The Tanzanian government continues to meddle with the lion project, and it effectively ended in July 2015. . . . Safari Club International [a hunting club] quickly took over the lion house in Seronera, and they are pretending to survey lions in the park, but they have not monitored the lions in the long-term study area. Safari Club, of course, is only interested in perpetuating the status quo on lion hunting in Tanzania rather than conducting any sort of scientific research.

This bodes terribly for the Serengeti lions. Perhaps the new classifications by the U.S. Fish and Wildlife Service, and the new restrictions on imports, will make a difference—but only if those regulations are enforced.

More encouraging was a note I received in September 2015 from Daniel Rosengren. Although no longer working with the Serengeti Lion Project, Rosengren had joined the Frankfurt Zoological

Nathan Williamson, Nick, and Reba in the customized Land Rover, with Vumbi lionesses in the foreground (robot-camera photograph), Serengeti National Park, 2012

Society as its staff photographer. Before eventually leaving the Serengeti for another assignment, he was able to update me about C-Boy and Hildur:

> These two males, eleven years old this year, are still alive and looking really great. C-Boy being the most impressive male in our study area, with a long dark mane with long thick dreads. Hildur has a more blond mane, but still very long and impressive. Males usually live between ten to twelve years. So to look this strong and healthy at eleven is very impressive. They still occupy the same area as when Nick and Team were there.

When "Nick and Team" were working on the project in 2011 and 2012, and especially when they focused on the Vumbi pride, C-Boy and Hildur were a part of their daily lives.

I met up with Nick, Reba, and Nathan Williamson in March 2012 and stayed in the Serengeti with them for about ten days. I was bewitched by C-Boy the day after I arrived, when he broke the horizon line at dawn, as we searched for the Vumbi pride. The savannas appear to stretch infinitely, and C-Boy was far in the distance—but through the binoculars, his black mane and regal presence were unmistakable.

This was my first experience with Nick in the field. Every day, we awoke just before sunrise. A couple of Tanzanian and Maasai men were helping out at the campsite—keeping it supplied and preparing meals, among other tasks—and one of them would bring coffee as well as a bucket of hot water for washing to each of our tents every morning, as starry blackness slowly gave way to a hazy, limpid light.

The days were orchestrated to maximize Nick's time with the lions. Soon we were on our way, tracking Vumbi's formidable collared female and peering through the thermals until it was light enough to switch to ordinary binoculars. In the early mornings, when the lions were just returning from a night of hunting—especially if they had been successful—they would settle by a particular acacia tree, sometimes reveling in rambunctious play. The cubs blanketed the ground, romping acrobatically, rolling over, often joined by the lionesses, who might stretch blithely across the branches, bathed in morning light. When the cubs chirped, the lionesses would respond with throaty, exaggerated purrs—not quite roaring. That signature reverberating, penetrating roar comes only from the males, often when they are calling for the pride, or affirming their territory. The lionesses answer the call, and all is amplified as the sounds resonate across the savannas. During the night, as they hunt, this call-and-response increases with disquieting fervor.

Nick, while rarely daunted, is never cavalier about working with an apex predator, in the same way that photojournalists working in areas of potential hostilities remain vigilant.

One of Nick's closest friends is the photojournalist James Nachtwey. For decades, Nachtwey has committed himself to photographing in zones of often brutal conflict and social strife, and his images bear witness to some of humanity's most desperate, hellish experiences—from Rwanda to Somalia, Sudan, Bosnia, Romania, Chechnya, Kosovo, Iraq, Haiti, and countless other sites. To my mind, Nick and Nachtwey share an intense relentlessness, both in their belief in photography's ability to inspire conscience and change, and in their desire to do right by their subjects—all grounded in an ethical ideal. It seems clear that both men have felt crushed at times by the human capacity for evil. I know that Nick has also experienced sublime wonder, and perhaps Nachtwey has as well.

Of their friendship, Nick says: "We have nothing in common in our backgrounds, and what we look at is totally different, but I met him and immediately felt a strong connection. We connected out of what—drive? Ambition? Lust to document? . . . Jim has such focus and drive, and his vision . . . he has been so true to his mission. I have extreme respect for the cost that comes with his commitment. He has seen too much, and I can see it in his eyes." Nick told me that, as time has gone on, what they share—as people and as photographers—has become clearer: "Thirty-five years and mortality have made us both emotional about . . . 'Wow. We just spent a lifetime without blinking.' It takes a toll. And at this stage, I care so much about all of us who have done that long haul on the path to documenting our time."

It is possible that those few who have "done that long haul" feel an instinctive affinity for others who have been compelled to choose similarly demanding paths. Nachtwey's sense of this connectedness is eloquently expressed in a text message he sent Nick in 2012, after an unsettling dream. Nick was in the Serengeti at the time, and the note is included here in its near entirety:

> Lying awake at 4 am thinking of you and your work. At the most basic level, at the very bottom of it all, what links your work and mine, strange as it seems, is something primal. Very few photographers go there. There is what we tell ourselves we are doing, then there is what we are really doing whether we realize it or not.
>
> You go beyond time to the earth before humans existed. Then you relate it to human activity. But your core work and what will endure forever is what is primal. . . .
>
> My own work deals with what is primal in humans when the rules of civilization and socialization are broken. Then there is the law of the jungle. Violence and territoriality, with its cruelty, fear, suffering and base survival. It is dark and frightening and I think I try to apply something spiritual to it, primarily compassion. Maybe the way you apply something higher to animals. But it's really there. Only very few people know it. You show it to us.
>
> I had a dream about an animal, a big cat in fact, but not a lion, more like a leopard or big jaguar. Spotted. Totally aware. Unflinching. I could absolutely feel the irreducible feeding instinct. It woke me up by making the hairs on my neck stand up. Please be very very careful. I know it's nothing you have not thought about very deeply. Just sharing the thought and my affection for you.

Words not to be taken lightly. Indeed, there were moments I observed in the Serengeti when, for instance, a lioness, snarling, agitated, positioned herself as if to lunge into the open Land Rover. Then Reba's dulcet warning: "Nick . . . Ni-ick . . . she seems angry." We backed off, giving her whatever space she might need.

Nick, Reba, and Williamson (and at various points David Quammen, Kathy Moran, David Griffin, and I) had been regular trespassers in Vumbi's habitat, so it was only fair that the lions might pass through ours, out of curiosity, or simply because of the location of the camp, within the pride's territory. About 1:30 one morning during my time in the Serengeti—where the cool air and inky sky induce the deepest sleeps—I was jolted awake in my tent, not by a roar, but by a clamoring, squeaky and guttural chorus of lion noises. They sounded close—chillingly close . . . but Nick had told me that sounds carry far over the savannas. I tried to go back to sleep, telling myself that my sense of the animals' nearness was deceptive—they *must* be far away. But these sounds, which I had been hearing every day during our time with the Vumbi pride, seemed very much to be coming from just outside my tent: a large, heavy-duty canvas tent, yes, but positioned, not incidentally, at a little distance from the rest of the camp, separated from the other tents by a cluster of brush.

Then came a tugging at the ropes stabilizing my tent on one side.

This wasn't aggression. I knew that. Nor were the lions trying to get into the tent; I don't even know whether they perceived the inside/outside dynamic. They were always playfully nabbing things—for instance, Williamson had made canvas covers for the infrared lights mounted on the Land Rover's bumper (Nick: "When they stole one it was a party for thirteen, playing and chasing each other over the cat toy!"). Now, similarly, they seemed unable to resist the novelty of my tent's dangly ropes. I would have been charmed had I not been inside the tent, thinking how precarious my existence would suddenly become if, in their feline curiosity, they inadvertently pulled it down, exposing me.

A strange calm took over. As quietly as I could, I opened my nearby copy of Quammen's book *Natural Acts*,[15] and on the inside front cover scribbled some last words. Just in case. I wanted to let the park authorities know that they should not kill the lions that had killed me—after all, I was the intruder in *their* home. I certainly didn't want anyone to sue anyone; it was my choice to be there. And I didn't want Nick to feel guilty; in my note, I told him I'd never been happier. This is true.

The tugging and snuffling went on. I have no real sense of how much or little time passed. I remained silent, my stillness broken only by each breath I took.

A sonorous, drawn-out, distant roar suddenly penetrated my hyper-conscious state. Abruptly, the activity by my tent stopped. Beckoned, my nighttime visitors went on their way.

The next morning, we saw that the water bucket outside my tent had disappeared, its remnants found scattered nearby. The tent ropes were newly frayed—one was unknotted. And that was that. Now, when I look at the inside cover of my Quammen book, I smile and am momentarily transported back to the Serengeti.

The camp was entirely solar-powered (as configured by Williamson), which meant no noisy generator, no fuel-supply concerns, and a minimal footprint. Each day, the team recharged cameras, computers, everything. Only the Land Rover required fossil fuel. The team made a point of driving different paths to avoid creating a dirt road, and so the impact on the landscape was negligible.

After the morning's photo-session, Nick, Reba, and Williamson would return to camp for several hours, avoiding the midday heat as the lions napped. Williamson would examine and, when necessary, repair gear. Nick would edit the morning's images and, if the weather permitted a signal, dispatch e-mails, often writing to Moran how "Zenned-out" he was on this story. He would do some stretches for thirty minutes or so, in the hope of decreasing his backaches and knee aches, then take a shower, followed by lunch.

While I was there, I would interview Nick during these daily breaks, before or after lunch. It was during one of these conversations that he confided to me something of what was happening to him with this story:

> It's like this frightening metaphysical religious dream that I'm in right now. I'm scared to say anything, because it might go away. I'm anticipating. I'm in the right spot. I've spent my lifetime concentrating on wild. I'm totally tuned into it here.

On my second afternoon with Nick and team, we drove out in search of the Barafu pride (*barafu* means "icy wind" in Swahili). At the time, this woodlands pride was made up of six lionesses and half a dozen six-month-old cubs. The resident males were Hervé and Sammy. Packer's team, making its regular data-gathering rounds, had just days ago spotted two of the long-anticipated newborns. Unlike the Vumbi females, the Barafu lionesses did not, this cycle, share a synchronized estrus—which meant that their cubs might be born weeks or months apart. The cubs' different ages and varying needs and behaviors made cooperation among the lionesses more challenging. Nick was ready to focus on the Barafu pride—although Vumbi would continue to claim part of each day.

We never drove quickly on this uneven terrain, and as we entered the Barafu pride's territory we inched along, hyperalert in the taller grasses, pausing frequently to look through binoculars. Spotting something that looked like it might be the pointy tips of two little ears—but unsure if our eyes were fooling us—we searched for a lioness as confirmation. A mother of newborns will never leave her cubs exposed in the grass; she remains very close by. Then we saw her. We edged the car closer, still keeping our distance. The Barafu lions were not yet habituated to Nick's presence nor to the Land Rover, and having newborns nearby only increased their vigilance. Another set of small ears popped up, and we spotted a second lioness. We stayed still for a long while, until—wary of putting any unnecessary pressure on the two new mothers—it was time to retreat.

Every afternoon that week, we returned. Gradually, the lionesses allowed the car to get closer, snarling when we overstepped our bounds. In this setting, Nick photographed the early lives of what turned out to be six new cubs: three six-week-olds and three eight-week-olds. They were the size of lap dogs, looked to be about twelve to fifteen pounds, with determined but still uncertain gaits. Squealing, they hop-trotted about. To protect them—when not reposing *en famille* in the camouflaging grasses—their mothers concealed the cubs among rocks that edged the patchwork of puddles in the otherwise dry

ABOVE AND OPPOSITE: Lioness and cubs of the Barafu pride, Serengeti National Park, 2012

riverbed, or else in the bordering scrub. As I now conjure this scene, favorite e. e. cummings phrases come to mind from his poem "in Just-," when the world is "mud-luscious" and "puddle-wonderful."[16] Photographing the cubs' interactions was easier along the more exposed riverbed than in the taller grasses of the woodlands, where they were barely discernible except as nursing appendages to their mothers. Even in their infancy, it was evident which cubs were bolder, more curious.

Nick, Reba, and Williamson were unable to follow the Barafu lions at night as they hunted, the way they had with the Vumbi pride. The woodlands terrain is even more daunting than the savanna, and can be treacherous in the dark. Once the Barafu cubs were born, it was also too hazardous to be driving at dusk. Detecting the cubs in the brightness of day was difficult enough, much less as the light began to dim. The Barafu pride became a kind of foil for Nick, conveying how different its woodlands habitat—with its relatively lush vegetation and fairly reliable water source—is from the harsh and dramatic plains of Vumbi's territory.

Nick was looking to compose wide-angle, complicated images of lions—photographs that are not defined by lens choice, but comparable to the way we see with our eyes, including peripheral vision. Throughout his career, he has been reluctant to use telephoto lenses, given the lack of depth of field, and the sense of detachment in images made with them. Still, the telephoto sometimes becomes a necessary tool, offering a closeness that cannot otherwise be achieved. The Barafu newborns were one such case. Nick:

I was trying to see if I could get any complexity inside the telephoto—there is a way, but you just have to keep remembering to really *look* and *see* through it. It's got to be *you* seeing, not the lens, in order to get an image with any tension or depth, and that's about looking at the context too.

He achieves this poetically in his forest-primeval image of a Barafu lioness gently lowering and tilting her head to grasp a crouching cub in her mouth, while another cub follows close behind, encircled by the lioness's tail, seemingly reminding him not to lag. Or maybe the cub is being playful. His tail is up, eyes open wide, and his front legs slightly turned out. The threesome is highlighted in a soft gold with orange tones emerging from the shadows and dark greens of the woodlands. There is depth, movement, and emotion. It is a leonine answer to W. Eugene Smith's magical and hopeful 1946 image of his children, *The Walk to Paradise Garden.* In both photographs, instinctive trust prevails; innocence embodies strength.

Along with the customized Land Rover, Nick had dreamed up a few other tools to enable him to work from a low angle, meeting the lions at eye level. One was a small computer-guided robotic tank, upon which he and Williamson could deploy both the video and still cameras, side by side. It took several tries to get it right. (Eventually, Ken Geiger—*National Geographic*'s deputy director of photography and tech expert—called in what he refers to as "the bomb squad": a team of

fabricators based in North Carolina, who worked out the final kinks in the robot camera that Nick and Williamson used.)

Nick, Reba, and Williamson would drive within ten or fifteen feet of the Vumbi lions, set the tank on the ground, and guide it toward the animals. Again, it was a matter of habituation. At first the lions seemed wary of it, then they ignored it, then they slowly approached it, and ultimately they wanted to play with it, which made the robot-contraption at times difficult to retrieve. Reba remembers occasions when, at the end of the day, "Vumbi would follow it back to the car when we were ready to leave. They'd all surround it, and we couldn't get it back!"

In general, though, the pride seemed respectful of the little tank that joined them every so often: "Nobody ever flipped it over," Nick says. "Nobody ever really *bit* it. And when they touched it, it was very light—even the cubs would only tap it. . . . They know how to control their power, their strength."

Traditional camera traps installed in the landscape, however, turned out to be far less effective: "The lions really know their territory, and so anything new was quickly discovered, checked out, and ultimately dismantled by the cubs and the rest of the pride. I stopped using any equipment they could take apart early on, because I thought it might be dangerous for them."

It is worth noting that Nick is never secretive about his use of these tools; in fact, he wants viewers to know about them. Please understand, he is saying: in reality *no one* can possibly come that close to a lion. Nick doesn't want photography—his or anybody else's—to be a culprit in making the wild appear in any way "tame."

He employed less-high-tech methods as well, and initially, they could be just as disconcerting for the animals. The first time he stood on top of the Land Rover to photograph—breaking the silhouette that the lions were used to—it caused a bit of a stir among the big cats. But slowly, both the Vumbi and Barafu prides grew accustomed to this behavior. He hoped eventually to realize a photograph of the full bevy of Vumbi girls and their cubs sprawled on one of the kopjes. He knew he couldn't make a photograph looking *up* at them, against the sky, as there would be no context. Once the lions became acclimated to his standing atop the car, he would be able to capture the desired angle.

Another traditional method for getting the lions' attention—animal calls—proved amazingly simple and successful. Using his cell phone's recorder, Nick captured the sound of a male lion roaring. "And when I wanted to photograph C-Boy and his head was down," Nick says, "I could play another lion roaring . . . and he's going to look up." Knowing the effectiveness of this tactic, early one evening Nick positioned himself to photograph C-Boy, who was in particularly fine postcoital form: his black mane magnificent, like polished granite, his glorious face serene, confident. As expected, upon hearing the sound of another lion's roar, C-Boy looked up with interest, and Nick began shooting. The photo-session went on for a few minutes, and it was magical: C-Boy begins to roar himself, and a lingering lioness—in estrus—vocalizes coquettishly, approaches, and begins nuzzling him.

Vumbi pride with robot-camera tank, Serengeti National Park, 2012

The recorded roars ended, and suddenly the next tune on Nick's playlist started up: Neil Young's "Harvest," with its sway-inducing strum and Young's lilting falsetto:

Dream up, dream up,
let me fill your cup
with the promise of a man.

It was not an entirely unfitting backup for C-Boy's dalliance. (In Williamson's footage of this moment, we hear Nick break into quiet laughter: "All right, Neil!") The carnality in Nick's voyeuristic portraits is infused with a sense of triumph.

Nick primarily worked with black-and-white infrared from latest dusk to early dawn, and used color for all else. The Serengeti daylight can be very harsh for photographing—he calls it "angry" light: "It's much more interpretive if you work in the edges of the day."

My last morning with Nick, Reba, and Williamson visiting the Vumbi lionesses and their cubs was like a dream. On the ride back to camp, Nick put it into words:

This morning, with the Vumbi . . . was quiet. The day didn't rush upon us like it does when the sun pops up and burns. They were soft. We were soft. We were still kind of drowsy. We found them very easily. There was no drama. They were finishing their night's activities. And their play was fabulous.

You just want to take for granted that there's a place on the planet where lions roam with no tourist cars running . . . and where five lionesses named Vumbi and all their kids can have an amazing play session with no interference, before they go to sleep for the day.

About a month after I left, Nick departed Tanzania for the World Press gathering, and then went back to Sugar Hollow. He returned with Reba and Williamson to the Serengeti in the fall of 2012, with a plan to stay through the end of the year and into the next, in order to witness the migration in the spring of 2013. Williamson went home over the holidays to see his family, and would return in the new year.

But by January 2013 the Land Rover, which had broken down in December, still had not been repaired. Then Nick came down with a bronchial infection—fever, sweating, chills—and none of the medicines he had brought relieved his symptoms. On January 14, he and Reba flew home. The project came to an abrupt end.

At the time, missing the migration—such a vital part of the Serengeti's ecology—crushed him. The project felt unfinished. After a while, however, he made peace with himself about "the pictures that got away." This outcome was the consequence of decisions he made not to generalize or illustrate, but to stay primarily with Vumbi—decisions that he in no way regrets. To this day, his experiences with C-Boy and the Vumbi girls and their world live in his heart and his mind's eye.

Back home in Virginia, Nick's immediate task was the picture edit for the *National Geographic* piece. Then came the work on other platforms—the iPad in particular, but also National Geographic's website. Nick's Serengeti photographs received an exuberant response at a special showing of the project at National Geographic's DC offices in March 2013, and Williamson's video work was likewise warmly received. This presentation—to the magazine's creative and marketing staff, as well as others from National Geographic Society who wanted to attend—was beautifully contextualized by Kathy Moran.

Over the course of a few days, I had the opportunity to sit in on additional show and tells: I eavesdropped as maps were discussed, and the tablet iteration of the story was conceived; I sat in on a working conversation among Quammen, Packer, and Nick. And I watched Moran and Nick collaborating as they obviously had done so many times before: sequences unfolded, openers were suggested, some images didn't quite make the cut, and others were selected without question. The situation felt pressured, even frustrating at times, but never fraught. Rather, this was a familiar, organic process. I left my immersion at National Geographic with complete confidence that the lions story would be brilliant, and that Nick would ultimately be profoundly satisfied by having given months of his life so intensively to this groundbreaking project.

Some time after, I received an e-mail from Nick with the subject line "Sugar." His terse message: "they're putting a goddam dessert on the cover!"

The Serengeti lion—photographed by the magazine's poster boy—wasn't going to be the cover story of *National Geographic*? That the iconic big cat wouldn't preside over the yellow rectangle

C-Boy and consort (shot in infrared nonvisible light), Serengeti National Park, 2011

seemed inconceivable. People are crazy for cats in that eye-candy sort of way. They love Nick. They love Quammen. These were major ecological issues, a spectacular landscape, never-before-achieved proximity to these predators, and it was all rooted in one of the most important long-term scientific studies ever. The love-fest had seemed real enough at those meetings in DC. And I suspect Nick had always assumed that the cover was a given.

Another e-mail from him soon followed: "Someone in a committee meeting said 'people love cupcakes.' *Cupcake gentrification* is a term!"

And so the cover story of the August 2013 issue of *National Geographic* does not speak to wildness, to the magnificence of C-Boy, to the seductive beauty and intelligence of the Vumbi lionesses, but rather to . . . "Sugar: Why We Can't Resist It," with a lurid close-up of a red-frosted cupcake topped with white sprinkles.[17] In an article on National Geographic's website, Bill Marr, the magazine's creative director at the time, explained the choice: "We wanted a summery, easy-to-read photo of something luscious that you would just want to dive into."[18]

Kathy Moran was almost as distraught as Nick. She told me: "The thing that haunted Nick, and will always haunt him, was the cover. . . . When we talk about the magazine's history, we can't call this the 'lions issue.' He's enough of a pro . . . if it had been a cover he could have respected, he would have dealt with it . . . but a *cupcake?*" (It should be mentioned that *National Geographic* editions in other

ABOVE: Hildur and consort (shot in infrared nonvisible light). PAGES 330-31: C-Boy and consort (robot-camera photograph). Both Serengeti National Park, 2012

countries—Germany, Hungary, Iran, Japan, Latvia, Lithuania, Russia, and Ukraine—did feature the lions on the cover.)

I spoke at length with Chris Johns, then editor-in-chief of the magazine, about the choice of the "Sugar" cover story. He was entirely candid about the underlying reasons:

> I'd had a bad year in newsstand sales in 2013—and I'm going to own it. . . . But the cupcake cover actually was one of my best-selling covers of the year. . . . I could not take a chance on a lions cover when I had so much data that would tell me "don't do that." . . .

> Actually, I don't like the cupcake cover at all. But there are times when . . . you've just got to make decisions, when you're pretty sure this is going to sell significantly better.

In our conversations, Johns has always made it clear how deeply he respects and admires Nick and his work, and how much he values their friendship. "It was really hard on Nick," he said to me, adding: "The thing is, nobody, *nobody* has the string of stories that are as popular with our readers as Nick. Nobody is even close." The tradeoff in this instance was interior real estate: Johns gave the entire lions coverage, including Brent Stirton's reportage, fifty pages of the magazine.

As of this writing, more than three years later, Nick has more or less let it go—although "the cupcake issue" still comes up when he speaks publicly, as a wry punchline.

Toward the end of his time in the Serengeti, Nick had begun referring to this project, which felt so right, so Zen, and so climactic, as his "last waltz"—at least in terms of his work as a magazine photographer. In one of our conversations at the Barafu camp, he put it this way:

> "Lions" is my lifetime project. All my photography up until now, all the technical stuff, all the animal stuff, my ethics, my mission—"Lions" is drawing on my whole life of working in the wild. The desire to tell a big story is drawing on that.
>
> It has all come together on this one.

Maybe Nick would decide to return to the Serengeti one day and fulfill his dream of a trilogy on the larger Serengeti ecosystem—everything was open, anything was possible. But for now, he was tired of being away from home so much, even though having Reba with him made a huge difference. His back and knees no longer permitted him the ragdoll flexibility of his youth. He had been going nonstop for more than thirty years. He talked about being a better husband, a better father to Eli and Ian, and spending time with his mother, whose health was declining fast.

For the first time, no irresistible next story was germinating in Nick's imagination. Nothing was urgently pulling at him—except a desire to slow down, do right by his family, and center himself once again, back in the woods of Sugar Hollow. He told me with a smile that he was ready to "ride off into to the sunset," in the blaze of the Serengeti lions.

YOU CAN'T ALWAYS

Bison, Hayden Valley,
Yellowstone National Park, 2015

GET WHAT YOU WANT

You need a break. I don't think that we should be talking about anything related to work for a full year."

Those were Kathy Moran's words to Nick when he let her know, in the fall of 2013—after the publication of his Serengeti lions project—that he felt ready to retire as a magazine photographer. A month after *National Geographic* published the story, his book on elephants, *Earth to Sky*, came out with a packed publicity tour and other fanfare. With those major projects behind him, this seemed a perfect moment for Nick to take a breath at least, as Moran was suggesting.

But to many, it seemed inconceivable that Nick could stop: he had been running full-tilt for as long as most people could remember.

Chris Johns was one who didn't take the idea seriously at all. Furthermore, he had a project in mind and he wanted Nick to be the one to do it. The subject was the Greater Yellowstone Ecosystem. The U.S. National Park Service—an institution that National Geographic was instrumental in establishing—would have its hundredth anniversary in 2016. Johns wanted to focus on Yellowstone, the world's first national park, established in 1872 under the administration of Ulysses S. Grant, as a single-topic issue of *National Geographic*. When Johns first pitched the idea to him, Nick was decidedly resistant. "If I do anything, I want to go back to the Serengeti," Nick told him. "But I'm tired, Chris. I need time after 'Lions.'"

When I met with Johns in early 2014 (by which point Nick had agreed to take on Yellowstone), it was clear that he was obsessed with the project: "I believe in parks so deeply," he told me. "I knew Nick was tired . . . I understood that. So I said: 'Have some rest when you're done with your *Earth to Sky* book tour. Then, let's just go have some fun. Let's go on a road trip. I have a Ford pickup truck in Montana . . . we'll jump in that, and we'll go visit the superintendent of Yellowstone.'"

Johns managed to entice Nick out West in late 2013, although before leaving, Nick said to me: "What the fuck am I doing? My mother is dying, I'm losing my temper with the people I love, I'm beat—and I'm going to go with Chris. What's wrong with me?"

Just as Chris had hoped, the Yellowstone project proved irresistible. As they met with park administrators and conservationists, he could see that Nick was hooked.

> We're talking about wolves, bears, bison, elk, geysers . . . this really, really cool stuff. Nick is intensely into the conversations. I've agreed with him that the issue should have a single author, David Quammen, who lives in Montana. Nick loves working with David.

> It's like a switch went off in him . . . I started to see the obsessiveness. . . . He was as hungry as he was the first day that I met him.

Nick and Reba spent months reading and watching films about the national parks. Ken Burns and Dayton Duncan's television series *The National Parks: America's Best Idea* was a great resource. They delved into Frank and John Craighead's twelve-year study, begun in 1959, on Yellowstone grizzly bears. They pored over the images that came out of the Ferdinand V. Hayden Geological Survey expedition of 1871—including paintings by Thomas Moran and survey photographs by William Henry Jackson—which led to Yellowstone being named America's first national park.

They imagined conversations that transpired under the stars between John Muir—founder of the Sierra Club, and one of the staunchest advocates for national parks—and Theodore Roosevelt during their now famous three-night camping trip in Yosemite National Park, in 1903. Subsequently, Roosevelt, an avid hunter, created five national parks, fifty-one federal bird sanctuaries, four national game refuges, and 150 national forests during his presidency. As Muir saw them, the parks were how "over-civilized people" could get "in touch with the nerves of Mother Earth . . . rejoicing in deep, long-drawn breaths of pure wildness."[1] Despite their friendship, however, the two men must have agreed to disagree on certain matters. Muir despised hunting, referring to it as the "murder business," and reportedly asked Roosevelt: "When, Mr. President, will you set aside this infantile need to shoot and kill living things?"[2] Nick and Reba grappled yet again with the knotty conundrum of hunting and conservation. The paradoxical relationship between the two pervades discussions about the future of the Greater Yellowstone Ecosystem—22 million acres, with the 2.2 million-plus acres of Yellowstone National Park at its heart.

Nick and his mother, Joyce, 2012. Photograph by David Alan Harvey/Magnum Photos

The deeper Nick and Reba engaged with the subject, the more compelling the prospect became of calling Yellowstone home for fifteen months—through all the park's seasonal changes. And Nick was touched by Johns's enthusiasm. "It's so important to him," he said to me, as they prepared to head west. "I want to do Yellowstone for Chris."

And so, in late February 2014, Nick made his way to Yellowstone, with Reba following a couple of weeks later. Nathan Williamson would again lend his expertise, although this time only on the initial technological stages and setup of the project, after which he would return to Gabon to work as a videographer with Mike Fay. (About Williamson's ongoing Fay project, Nick said in 2016, "Nathan is a storyteller, and he really found his voice in video. His recent work in Gabon with Mike blows me away. I'm so proud of him.") Williamson had driven out before Nick, towing the efficient and light Airstream Bambi trailer for use when and if they were allowed to camp deep in the park.

The Greater Yellowstone Ecosystem is a mosaic of public and private lands spanning parts of Idaho, Montana, and Wyoming. It comprises two national parks (Yellowstone and Grand Teton), portions of five national forests, three national wildlife refuges, state, tribal, and private lands—managed by federal, state, local, and tribal governments, as well as by individuals unaffiliated with any government group.[3] It amounts to a disputatious amalgam of stakeholders and constituencies representing the full political spectrum and every other imaginable spectrum. Debates range from the esoteric to pugnacious pigheadedness, and are generally focused on fauna; flora, as well as the park's hydrothermal features and the trippy "geyser gazers" they attract, generally manage to stay out of the crossfire. For every animal tracked, admired, loved, or even fetishized by the "grizzly groupies" and "wolf watchers," there is someone who wants to hunt them down just beyond the park's boundaries, for reasons that range from retaliation to the thrill of the kill. For every hungry or migrating bison and elk that ventures out of the protected land of Yellowstone National Park to the public and private lands of the greater ecosystem, there's someone who deems the animal's presence problematic in some degree. Same thing with every wolf and bear. Some groups want more animals, others fewer.

Among the contentious, ever-changing issues that challenge Yellowstone are land use and wildlife management—including the listing and delisting of grizzlies and wolves, elk migrations, and bison boundaries—as well as climate change, invasive species, and much more. This ecosystem has far too many cooks, each in a special-interest kitchen concocting what collectively constitutes an often indigestible, even toxic, meal.

There is an ever-increasing number of visitors and vehicles, with accompanying emissions and noise. More visitors to the park can mean more bad decisions, bad timing, or bad luck. A hiker strays from the trail without bear spray, and encounters a female bear and her cubs. A visitor decides to take a swim in treacherous waters, or bathe in boiling thermals. The roadside circus photo-op has become especially hazardous—despite the fact that the park's rules don't permit visitors to get closer than one hundred yards to bears and wolves, and no closer than twenty-five yards to elk, bison, and other animals. The park rangers end up devoting huge amounts of their time to enforcing these regulations, while also attempting to keep animals away from the roads. It's critical that the wildlife remain fearful of humans, that they *not* become habituated, as they are fair game for hunters as soon as they leave the park. Still, people have been known to try to sit their small children on a bison—

somehow forgetting that these are *wild animals*, not pets. Ubiquitous "I-was-here" checklist self-portraiture inevitably invites the occasional death-by-selfie—backing right into the animal or geyser being appropriated as a prop and backdrop. (The danger of selfie-shooting is a problem so common now that anti-selfie signage is being developed globally as a graphic wakeup call.)[4]

At the north entrance of Yellowstone, in Gardiner, Montana, is the Roosevelt Arch, a tall stone structure with the park's founding premise inscribed at its top: "For the Benefit and Enjoyment of the People." But what about the wildlife? Every definition of Yellowstone—concept, intent, form, and content—inherently serves as a provocation. Those with varied interests in the larger ecosystem are often polarized. At the same time, Yellowstone and its animals are sometimes cast as scapegoats by landowners, hunters, ranchers, and tribes, all of whom harbor deep convictions about states' rights, notions of citizenship, dominion—in every sense—and manifest destiny.

For Nick to undertake this project with any hope of moving into new territory—especially given the plethora of previous coverage by *National Geographic*—he needed, as always, the cooperation of the scientists working on the ground, the majority employed by the National Park Service. But the park administrators' and scientists' relations with the media have long been strained. Time and again, Nick was told, Yellowstone had been duped by producers, by "talent" promising to be respectful of the landscape and the animals, and by photographers promising the park the use of their photographs. Over time, very few have lived up to those promises. Every scientist, administrator, and individual working in the park must strive to balance the priorities of both vulnerable ecosystems and the fundamental notion of a park that exists "For the Benefit and Enjoyment of the People." Too often, the goal of myopic media is sheer entertainment, requesting to ride a bison or run with the wolves or pet a bear. Not only is there no benefit to the park, but their spectacles pose the risk of encouraging visitors to behave equally irresponsibly.

Given this history, trust would have to be established over time between *National Geographic* magazine and the administrators and scientists at Yellowstone. To this effect, Chris Johns—with Nick's full concurrence—committed to sharing all the photographs from the project with the park, after the story was published. For the park to have access to superb photographs, representing in-depth coverage, for its many needs—from communication to education to advocacy to fundraising—would be helpful and would provide an incentive for extending itself to *National Geographic*. A deal was finally made, and the May 2016 Yellowstone special issue was under way.

In February 2015 I spoke with Dan Wenk, superintendent of Yellowstone National Park, who explained candidly why—despite the initial skepticism of some of the park's staff and resident scientists—he agreed to work with *National Geographic*:

> They were looking at doing something that *National Geographic* had never done before. First, they were looking not just at Yellowstone but at the Greater Yellowstone Ecosystem. Since *all* issues in Yellowstone are ecosystem issues, that was something I endorsed and supported 100 percent. . . .
>
> And second, I started to understand what *National Geographic* could do. . . . Nick, David Quammen, everyone would really spend the time, the energy, and make the personal

investment to tell the story of Yellowstone and the ecosystem . . . and what kind of a commitment it's going to take from all of us—not just the National Park Service, but the American public—to say: "What do we have to do to preserve this incredible place?" . . . I saw it as advocacy for wildness.

When they met, Nick liked Wenk immediately, seeing him as a "great leader" wholeheartedly devoted to the park. Nick also acknowledged that Wenk had a nearly impossible job negotiating all the factions clamoring around issues related to Yellowstone. "He truly tries to make things better," says Nick—adding what from Nick is a very high compliment: "He certainly has the soul of an artist."

Nick hoped to create the kind of unfettered access that he had enjoyed on many previous projects. He was also eager to apply some of the tools and methods he and his team had come up with in the Serengeti. But from the start, with very few exceptions, his requests for special access and use of technologies—such as aerial drones—were met with an emphatic "no." A few visitors had already used drones illegally, and the machines had often ended up in the park's fragile thermals, posing the potential to forever pollute and ultimately destroy them. The park—under constant monitoring from its various constituencies—could not agree to any unique access or methodology for the *National Geographic* team that it would not grant any other media or random visitor. Every decision the park leadership made regarding the *National Geographic* story they made through the lens of precedence. The only exceptions would be when the potential benefits of Nick's request would include an increase of data on a given species or landscape.

As has been the case with nearly all print magazines—and especially illustrated publications—*National Geographic*'s budget started to shrink during the first decade of the twenty-first century. Undaunted, Nick began to fundraise independently for his stories. With the Serengeti lion project, for example, he knew that, in order to realize his vision, he would need twice the budget Chris Johns had told him *National Geographic* could allot. Darlene and Jeff Anderson—Nick's close friends and supporters of many conservation causes—unhesitatingly came through for him in the Serengeti, and then again in Yellowstone.

Although he thus had the financial means to undertake the park story as he wished to, he was thwarted by access limitations imposed by the park, which frustrated and challenged him. On the Megatransect project, as Quammen notes, "nobody was there micromanaging you; it's out of sight, out of mind"; whereas in Yellowstone, "the jewel in the crown of the National Park Service, you are never out of sight and you're never out of mind." Generally in Africa, the treatment of the habitat and wildlife hinges on the ethics of the photojournalist, the production team, the conservationist, the writer. In Yellowstone, by contrast, Nick and his team would be observed and scrutinized around the clock, often by self-appointed whistle-blowers.

Yes, the park itself has all kinds of rules, to which there are no exceptions—not for *National Geographic* or anyone else. But Nick also had to contend with fanatically dedicated park devotees who track specific species with the obsessiveness of stalkers. Yellowstone abounds with them, spotting with their spotting scopes, constantly communicating with each other, and posting about who has seen which wolf, which

Wildlife managers darting a bull elk in order to remove rope tangled in the animal's antlers, Mammoth Hot Springs, Yellowstone National Park, 2014

338

bear, and where. These individuals monitor any possible interference with their species of interest, and their vigilance made it impossible for Nick (as well as the rest of the team) to have the untethered, up-close-and-personal engagement with the park that would help give his work a distinctive edge.

Among the people keeping an official eye on Nick were scientists Doug Smith, Yellowstone's principal wolf biologist, and Kerry Gunther, the principal bear biologist. Eventually, recognizing that Nick's photographs might in fact advance their scientific knowledge and understanding in some way—and observing the respect with which he and his team regarded the park and its wildlife—both scientists did their best to facilitate his work. Dan Wenk also realized that Nick's expertise could benefit the park's research:

> Nick and his crew . . . helped us to achieve some of our research goals—like with the setting of camera traps. . . . They [were], if you will, in search of the story. But [for us] it helps us with our research needs, whether about bears or wolves or bison. . . . They've become in some ways part of our team. But this is all because of Nick, and all his experience working with scientists and with wildlife that he brings to the table. . . . He does a great job of enlisting us all into the possibility of what can happen.

From the start, says Nick, the national parks project was to be the work of a team of photographers. "My promise was team leadership, and a portfolio of images." He was now in his early sixties. More than one person has noted his resemblance at this point to the scruffy Steve Zissou (the character played by Bill

Murray in Wes Anderson's 2004 film *The Life Aquatic*). Nick's body was failing him in various ways. In addition to a bad back, his left knee, after five meniscus surgeries, was weak: "I can't get up," he confessed to me at one point. "I get down to take a picture, and I can't get up." He needed younger photographers whom he could mentor, and who could function as his assistants and physical "surrogates" during the process of photographing. And he also needed seasoned photographers to join forces in the reportage. After thirty years of abusing his body while chasing the perfect image, the dream story, in Yellowstone he would assume a different role—one that evolved out of his directorial role in photographing the two trees: here he would be the "field marshal" (per some at *National Geographic*). Perhaps most important, as Quammen puts it:

> Nick is the dreamer, supplying the larger concept, and the integration. He's the guy with the huge imagination. He also has an imaginative heart and is acutely sensitive to other people's needs. He's always thinking about the whole package—what the writer needs, what the photographers need.

Moran and Johns, together with Nick, sketched out the ideas to be explored and interpreted by each of the participating photographers. Some had years of experience, others were just beginning their professional lives; the rest fell somewhere in between. Stories were grounded in each photographer's respective expertise, interests, and sensibilities, always with a view to telling the story of the Greater Yellowstone Ecosystem organically—in a way that felt responsive to the Yellowstone Nick was experiencing while living and working in the park. Because so much work on Yellowstone already

OPPOSITE: Tourists at Artist Point; ABOVE: Rutting bison, Lamar Valley. Both Yellowstone National Park, 2014

existed, any given project ran the risk of redundancy, or that it might illustrate preconceptions. By interacting regularly with the scientists and understanding their concerns, Nick believed he could help the magazine's team of photographers avoid conceptual clichés.

Wildlife photographer Charlie Hamilton James, for example, was brought into the Yellowstone project to depict aquatic creatures and invasive species, but this evolved into what Nick terms "wildlife dioramas"—beautifully composed, with a dramatic sense of space. David Guttenfelder agreed to address the issues facing the Greater Yellowstone Ecosystem, but his focus turned, says Nick, to "daily life"—the idea of living with the wild. His photograph of wolf biologist Doug Smith—surging forward in a snowy mist, helicopter still hovering—after shooting a gray wolf with a tranquilizer dart before collaring it, has the tense urgency of a war photograph. Joe Riis, photographer and wildlife biologist, was part of the *National Geographic* team too; for the past decade, Riis has been photographing and studying migrations of pronghorn, mule deer, and elk. His very close-up photograph of an elk herd—three-week-old calves following their mother—climbing a 4,600-foot slope after having swum across a river, with mountains far in the distance, feels as epic as the herd's journey.

Nick brought in two photographers to assist him on his own projects, as well as some of the more pragmatic tasks. Drew Rush helped to manage overall logistics—especially in the wintertime. He also worked on camera-trap photography of Yellowstone's mountain lions. The issue features Rush's beautifully lit image of a cougar. Ronan Donovan, who had previously spent time photographing in East Africa, would focus on the wild wolves when not assisting Nick with the camera traps and more. His photograph of wolves feasting on the carcass of a bison that has drowned in the Yellowstone River, everything dusted by snow, fur melding tonally with the still-uncoated patches of landscape, is remarkably painterly.

Erika Larsen, who shoots large-format film, was tasked with capturing "the voices of Yellowstone"—making more formal portraits accompanied by short quotations from her subjects. Her profile portrait of Superintendent Wenk, uniformed and gazing at the landscape he passionately strives to protect, reveals a dedicated believer. Larsen also photographed locals, from ninety-nine-year-old John Craighead, who with his brother Frank pioneered the early grizzly study in the park, to rancher and wolf-release critic Bill Hoppe. Larsen was assisted by Louise Johns (Chris Johns's daughter), a young photographer who undertook a project on one family's way of dealing with livestock-wildlife tensions, and whose image of a little girl chasing a red ball on a Montana ranch closes the issue.

Larsen credits Nick with many ideas, but is particularly grateful to him for reminding her to follow her own instincts. "He has made me believe I have the unique vision that is necessary for this project," she told me. "He has even gone as far as to offer his own funds for me to continue to create portraits he believes would be valuable to the final story. I think that represents a great team leader—guiding but also valuing the unique visions of its members to create the final work."

Apart from being the principal liaison with the park and trying to support the photographers on the team when necessary, Nick had to figure out how his own contribution to the Yellowstone issue would play out. He had to acknowledge to himself that he is neither a generalist nor a theme-driven photographer: whatever themes emerge in his body of work, he has arrived at naturally—through the unique filters of his character studies and narratives. In Yellowstone, he would be more of a hunter-gatherer; narrative would be replaced by a more illustrative comprehensiveness, resulting in a more strictly documentary body of work.

Nick decided to focus his own Yellowstone work on two ideas: "For the Benefit and Enjoyment of the People" and "Wonderland"—a common moniker for this spectacular environment even before its establishment as a park.

On an early, flurrying winter morning, just before Christmas 2014, Nick and I perch ourselves on a bench in front of Old Faithful. A sleek white coyote passes close by—our only company. Pockets of steamy earth stubbornly reveal themselves through the otherwise blanketing snow. We've timed our conversation to witness at least one eruption of the famous geyser, described by John Muir as "white torrents of boiling water and steam, like inverted waterfalls. . . . rushing up out of the hot, black underworld."[5] Nick would have to invoke a kind of photographic synesthesia in order to render the water's searing heat, these fierce forces beneath the Earth's surface.

Nick's images of Yellowstone's signature thermal features are some of his most illusory and enigmatic. He teases our sense of what is real, what is solid, what is day, what is night, what is

Tardy Geyser, Yellowstone National Park, 2015

fire, what is ice. In one image, a shadowy figure lends scale to the wintry tones under a rising sun. A surge of water, airborne—now vaporous, whirls: spectral dancers. In other scenes of winter's landscape, elemental and primordial, this gush momentarily crystallizes in flight. The wind whips the clouds, transforming the sky from opaque stormy grays to backlit pearly tones when touched with fitful sunlight.

Old Faithful presides over our conversation for several hours—two eruptions—before Nick and I, overcome by the cold, can no longer speak while sitting still. We reinvigorate by snowshoeing to another, less-reliable geyser where Nick hopes to photograph later in the day, if light, sky, and eruption align. His assistant Drew Rush is a Wyoming native who knows this terrain well—he will meet Nick at the site with the equipment packed on a sled.

The Yellowstone landscape is wistful and serene in the winter. The cars and tourists of the summer months are all but gone—only random clusters of snowmobilers during the day, and one open lodge and the visitors it accommodates disturb the otherwise hushed and sparkling environment. The snow is abundant yet revealing: animal and bird tracks appear everywhere.

We're moving forward slowly when we spot three bison, their faces masked by chunks of crusty snow. They have been desperately burying their heads in the ample whiteness, trying to dig deep for grass. They are hungry. These nomadic, grazing plains animals are not at this elevation by choice.

Nick tells me:

> The bison don't want this, but they are often killed if they leave the park to find grass. Lots of ranchers don't want them grazing where they graze their cattle. They say it's because bison carry a disease—brucellosis—that will infect their cattle. So do elk, but ranchers are fine with elk because they want to hunt them.

Many months later, in 2015, Nick told me that approximately seven hundred fifty bison had been culled:[6]

> It could be more the next year. It is an agreement the park has been forced to live with, as the states, particularly Montana, define bison as diseased livestock, and not wild animals—like elk. But since [people] like to hunt elk, they figured out how to manage them differently. It seems pretty arbitrary. There are a lot of activist groups trying to protect bison with civil disobedience, and they put out calls for "buffalo warriors."

There has never been a documented transmission of brucellosis to cows from wild bison, reported Christopher Ketcham in a February 2016 op-ed in the *New York Times*. Ketcham concludes: "Federal bison policy . . . has been captured by the politically powerful livestock industry." He proposes that wild bison should be managed in such a way that allows them "to restore themselves—through their ancient instinct to migrate—on their native landscape. . . . The sad irony here is that in order to allow Montana ranchers to graze their cattle, the park service is helping to slaughter a native animal so iconic that it is emblazoned on the park service's own logo."[7]

As of August 2016 the Interagency Bison Management Plan—which oversees the bison both in the park and throughout the Greater Yellowstone Ecosystem—has been investigating various ways of improving the conditions for the resident wild bison population. Among their goals is to provide migrating access to expanded, protected habitat outside the park's boundaries, as well as to relocate some of this population.

Yellowstone's Superintendent Wenk contends constantly with the park's "transboundary" issues. These encompass not just animals crossing borders—which, of course, they don't recognize—but all the government and nongovernment groups that manage these boundaries, or have a say about them, and that fungible area where management transitions.

Dan Wenk says:

> How do we deal with grizzly bears and wolves and elk and bison as they leave the park? . . . How do you manage, recognizing that bison can't go wherever they want to go across the western United States, that wolves and grizzly bears have limits in terms of conflict with people and places? Certainly we know that all the bison who leave the park in the spring would not return into the park unless they were forced back, as we do to help protect them. And boundaries are constantly changing—not because they are moving, but habitat changes, because of land development on the edges, and also climate change, for example. All this affects the greater ecosystem.

Photographer/biologist Joe Riis works with wildlife ecologist Arthur Middleton, looking at elk migration corridors. According to Middleton, the Yellowstone elk are not in the park itself for a large part of the year. For Riis, photographing the migrations supports his fundamental idea that "the parks are not big enough to support the population . . . the future of the parks and [their] wildlife depends on the people living on and managing the lands bordering the park."

The space constraints lead to genetic concerns. Those invested in the welfare of the bison, elk, wolf, and bear want the populations to be genetically strong, so that when they're subjected to natural stressors, they can continue to adapt, evolve, and thrive. As in the Serengeti and other ecosystems, so much depends upon the balance between predator and prey. The gray wolf was killed off in Yellowstone in 1926. It didn't take long before the elk population, suddenly without this principal predator, exploded. Partly for this reason, the gray wolf was reintroduced in 1995. Their proliferation has been so successful that today most human hunters in the Greater Yellowstone Ecosystem consider the wolves to be rival hunters of elk—which creates another conflict.

Riis grew up subsistence hunting in South Dakota for white-tailed deer, pheasants, and geese. He has "no interest in trophy hunting for head or hide: I think that the ethics of fair chase hunting are of utmost importance in the conservation debate. Long-range shooting, predator baiting, and trophy hunting are, in my view, unethical." But he accepts subsistence hunting as "important and often rooted in the culture in many places."

Middleton acknowledges the peculiar symbiosis between hunters and conservation:

> Hunters, inarguably to me, have played a tremendous role over a long period of time in funding and being spokespeople for very important conservation efforts across the United States, and especially in the West. The criticism would be that that there's a subset of species that get the benefit of that advocacy funding, and there are others, including some of these carnivores—predators—that don't. They don't because they're not what hunters want to hunt as badly as they want to hunt elk or deer or whatever else these carnivores or predators are eating. The carnivores, like the wolves, are therefore hunted and killed because they are perceived by the hunter as a competitor.

David Quammen takes the long view, discussing two possible perspectives on this issue:

> The concerns of population biology and conservation and the concerns of animal welfare and feelings are both legitimate ways of looking at this. But . . . they're not the *same* way of looking at it. People who are concerned about animal welfare and feelings of individual animals tend to assume that population biology is always on their side, and it's not.

> There are times when killing an animal *is* the best thing for the population. This might be through culling and might be by allowing a hunt.

> You can certainly make that argument about elk. The fact that people can hunt and kill elk means that the elk is the most popular animal in the Greater Yellowstone Ecosystem. There are hunters in Cody who kill an elk every fall, love elk and want there to be lots of elk in the woods, and favor the preservation of habitat for elk.

Quammen also believes that wealthy landowners can help preserve the ecologically rich Greater Yellowstone Ecosystem by keeping their large ranches intact and allowing them to be elk habitat in the winter. If, instead, the owners of big swaths of land decide to subdivide it for development or other purposes, the ecosystem disintegrates.

With the program since its inception, Doug Smith is the project leader for the Wolf Restoration Project (which oversaw the reintroduction of the gray wolf—the park's only wolf species—into Yellowstone beginning 1995). He's been the chief biologist for the park's resident 108 wolves in eleven packs (the 2016 count) for over twenty years. As always, Nick conferred extensively with him as he did with Kerry Gunther, the bear biologist, while planning the *National Geographic* project.

Smith tells me his first impression of Nick was "free-form"; he says he had a hard time following some of their conversations initially (it's true that Nick is not the most linear talker). But over time, he grew to understand Nick's intensity, his enthusiasm for the park, and his sense of mission. Smith also appreciated Nick's repeated assertion that he wanted to get the park's message out.

Smith has sharp features, a healthy crop of light-gray hair, and a moustache that is making its way to his jawline. He looks you straight in the eye when speaking. His passion for wolves is matched by his fear for the future of wild, if left to the whims of humans. "Our history is selfish," he says. "We are *takers*."

> We are at around 7.5 billion now . . . the population is going to grow and grow. Are you going to deny this family living space? Are you going to deny this logger a job? Are you going to deny this farmer a living—all because of these animals? Of course the answer is going to be no. They'll all get what they want at the cost of the wolf, the grizzly, the elk, the bison. . . . The one thing wolves need more than anything else is space. And eventually we're going to say, we ain't got it.

Although they may share little else, every community where Nick has photographed, including those involved in the divisive struggles around the Greater Yellowstone Ecosystem, has one thing in common: its challenges are based in questions of land use, and the rights of wildlife to have a safe habitat, and to roam. It is simple: to survive, wildlife needs space, often lots of it. Of course, the prevailing, yet often contested, assumption here is that wildlife in fact *has* rights.

In 2016, the revered biologist Edward O. Wilson, at age eighty-six, published *Half-Earth*: *Our Planet's Fight for Life*,[8] in which he advocates for dramatically increasing the percentage of the Earth's land and sea designated as protected reserves for wildlife. Instead of the current protected allotments—15 percent of land and 3 percent of sea—Wilson believes it is imperative that we set aside no less than *half* of the Earth's surface for wildlife to survive as it needs. He cites the disappearance of natural habitat, primarily due to human population growth and exacerbated by climate change, as the principal culprit in the planet's loss of biodiversity. He maintains that this 50-percent proposal does not displace people or undermine property rights.

In a March 13, 2016, op-ed piece in the *New York Times*, Wilson summarized: "This step toward sustained coexistence with the rest of life is partly a practical challenge and partly a moral decision. It can be done, and to great and universal benefit, if we wish it so."[9]

Doug Smith speaks to the same idea: "I'm hoping Nick and his team can help let people know that wild matters, and not to take it for granted as we may not always have it. You can't have wild without most of the native constituents of that particular area—and they need land."

Smith goes on to explain that the recovery of predators—so necessary for a balanced ecosystem—can no longer depend primarily upon parks. They will have to live on human-dominated landscapes, so "anything we can do to get wolves and bears and cougars to be able to live better with people is critical."

Coexistence with predators is at the heart of Smith's support for the removal of wolves from the endangered list, while still regulating how many may be killed annually. Kerry Gunther thinks similarly when it comes to bears. The listing and delisting of animals, according to the U.S. Fish and Wildlife Service, refers to the federal list of endangered and threatened wildlife. Species that are added to the list benefit from the protections provided by the Endangered Species Act. In brief, listing an animal means that the federal government enacts various controls regarding habitat use and protection, taking into account a given species' movements, to enable its population to increase to a sustainable and healthy level.

Both Gunther and Smith understand that, to accomplish their long-term goals for wolves and for grizzlies, delisting the animals may have more appeal to the local human population that's being asked to coexist and share their land with the predators. Otherwise, explains Smith, local hunters may be resentful at being told what to do, as well as distrustful, and they may kill anyway—illegally. When asking for local buy-in on wildlife management, there has to be a give and take.[10] (This echoes situations with conservancies in Kenya and other African countries.)

Smith spells it out very clearly, suggesting a more site-specific form of regulation than the federally imposed restrictions:

> You can't evict the people who live on the landscape now. You can't say: "Get off your ranch, we need it for wildlife habitat." What's the next best thing? You make wildlife habitat *compatible* with their lives. I know it's tough to understand—but compatibility occasionally means killing the wolf or grizzly. And the rancher is already killing elk and deer to eat. So now they can kill wolves when they cause a problem, and even hunt them for sport. . . .
>
> A lot of people do not like wolves and want to control them, and having them do that in an *unregulated* way is worse than in a regulated way. . . . An *angry* person in the woods with a gun is much worse than a person in the woods with a gun going: "I think they're managing wolves, so I'm not going to shoot every wolf I see." . . . This—and I know it sounds weird—is progress.

Smith is candid about the many dilemmas inherent in Yellowstone wildlife management, including the occasional need to make lesser-of-two-evils compromises.

Having spent most of my life in an environment far removed from any tradition of hunting, I ask Smith something I've been curious about: If you are not a subsistence hunter, what exactly is the draw? He responds:

> I hunt elk and deer, and it's very primordial. I hate to say it, but I'm trying to be honest with you—there's a thrill to the hunt and then the kill. It pulls at something deep within you. There's a kind of connectivity to the land, something ancient. . . .
>
> Now, there are a lot of hunters—I'm not one of them—who feel entitled: "I want my elk and deer every year, and if I don't get it, I'm mad because that wolf took it from me." I've had a lot of people who don't like wolves literally say to me: "I want to be the number-one predator.

I don't want the wolf to be the number-one predator. I don't want any competition. I want to be the prime hunter out there."

Not having ever felt this atavistic urge personally, I am a bit circumspect. Trying to reconcile this thrill with the simultaneous fact that Smith, for one, has committed his life to *protecting* animals confounds me further. Still, I accept him at his word, although I may remain forever flummoxed.

Not surprisingly, many conservationists and others are virulently opposed to the delisting, especially of grizzlies, believing that it will only expedite their demise.

Smith: "Basically, the future of wildlife is whatever we allow them to have."

It was with the hope of "improving the wolf's image," as well as gaining new biological insights, that Smith ultimately granted Nick's request to set up camera traps in Yellowstone. The intelligence and stealth of wolves allow them to be extremely elusive. And, sensitive to any changes in their environment, including an unexpected human presence, they are constantly on the move.

The camera traps would be strategically and unobtrusively placed around anticipated denning sites, where she-wolves might give birth to their pups in the spring. This installation would happen many weeks before the wolves came anywhere near the potential dens, which generally occurs in April. The timing did not work the first year, and the plan was abandoned so as not to risk influencing the wolves' behavior, or interfering with their denning. The biologists tracking the wolves understood that they were already too close to their potential dens.

But in March 2015, Ronan Donovan, working with Kira Cassidy (a research biologist under Doug Smith's supervision), managed to place extremely quiet camera traps in trees near six previously used wolf-den sites—but not too close, and never inside. Smith was keen to see how the new pups would interact with the rest of the pack when they first left the den. Of the camera traps, Smith said: "It will improve our data. . . . We might see behaviors we've never seen before. It could also help to connect people to the wolves."

In late summer, once they were certain that the wolves and their pups had left the dens, and were in fact miles away, Cassidy and Donovan checked the cameras. "By unlucky circumstance," recalls Cassidy, "*none* of the den holes we focused on were used by the packs. Some packs denned at other traditional spots, and one pack denned only 150 feet out of camera frame." Donovan adds, "They apparently had a lot more options than the biologists had thought."

Happily, this new scientific knowledge in itself proved to be extremely important. Even though the camera traps didn't yield, says Cassidy, "it was still a valuable photographic and scientific endeavor."

Raising pups is perhaps the most important task a wolf pack faces, and it may be that some of the females were extra wary about the camera boxes and moved to another hole just a little further away, to ease their suspicions. Given how much wolves have been persecuted, and in some places eradicated by humans, it is little wonder they have evolved to be cautious about everything in their environment.

Despite their wariness, clearly the wolves were not disturbed. Indeed, they are thriving, according to Cassidy, "with every pack producing and raising pups to the end of the year—adding thirty-five new members to the Yellowstone wolf population in 2015."

It was a different story with the bears. For one thing, bears are much less perturbed than wolves by the presence of humans. As Kerry Gunther says: "Bears adapt to people and human odors pretty well. I told Nick that after the first couple of times they saw the cameras . . . I think my exact words were: 'Nick, you could *piss* on that camera and it's not going to bother a bear.'"

The camera traps rendered some of the team's strongest bear images, including the pinup-like portrait of the adult grizzly in a *grand pas de deux* with an apple tree. Photographed in the front yard of a home near the northern boundary of Yellowstone National Park, this image also speaks to the expansion of the grizzly bear's habitat. Gunther says that it reaches "out to the very edges of populated urban areas. Managing bears and people in the wild-urban interface is a significant challenge."

Early in his time at the park, Nick gave a presentation at a Yellowstone Park Foundation Board meeting. There, he showed a collection of recent images taken in the park and its greater ecosystem, as well as photographs and footage from earlier projects—including Erin Harvey's marvelous footage of the tiger Charger bathing in his watering hole. For Gunther, seeing that clip triggered a decade-old memory—of discovering a research bear's radio collar that had come off in a pool of water in the woods. He went to check out the site.

There were four trails leading to the pool, Gunther told Nick, all with tracks and other evidence of use by bears. "So I knew bears came there and used it—I assume to soak in cold water on a hot day."

Nick and Gunther sent Ronan Donovan and a young bear researcher, Nate Bowersock, to scout the site in early August 2014. Nick instructed Donovan to place both a video and a still camera on trees about fifty feet from the pool. Donovan would keep adjusting and adding cameras over the next few months—always venturing out with two other people, all armed with bear spray.

With the first bear to come to the pool, they were hopeful—but he knocked the camera around, and no images came of it. Donovan subsequently secured the setup, and the cameras recorded lots of bear activity and remained untouched. Nick soon realized, however, that the cameras were placed too far away. In mid-September, he, Reba, and Donovan repositioned them right next to the pool. Soon they had footage of the grizzly "splashing and chuffing and throwing water all over the camera," Nick says. And then "he came out of the pool and, with his claws, slammed down two of our three cameras to the ground. When I first saw [the damaged equipment], I'm thinking, uh-oh—game over. But one camera, he didn't get."

The very next day, all the stars aligned. A grizzly mother bear brought her two cubs to the pool for a dip, and as Nick puts it: "She dove right in." In the resulting image, the mother bear glides blissfully through the water, hardly breaking its surface, propelling herself toward the camera with eyes open wide. Meanwhile, one cub dips its claws, about to join her, while the other looks on. The Yellowstone grizzlies are known as "silvertips" because their fur has a sheen of silver-gray, clearly seen in this picture. As Nick says: "The cubs literally glow, they are so silvery."

ABOVE: Grizzly bear (camera-trap photograph), near the northern boundary of Yellowstone National Park, 2014;
OPPOSITE: "Bear bathtub" (camera-trap photograph), Yellowstone National Park, 2014

Gunther and Nick came to call this pool "the bear bathtub." The photographs and video that Nick and his team shot there brought some new information to light. Gunther learned, for example, that both black bears and grizzlies use the bear bathtub—although never at the same time. Furthermore, Gunther says:

> They were also scent marking in a way that was new, that we'd not seen before. We've documented a lot of scent marking with bears using their feet, but these bears were using the sides of their chins, kind of like a cat. They did it all around the edge of the pond. And when other bears come in, you can tell they're sniffing around to see who's been there, and how recently.

Gunther was deeply influenced by the pioneering conservation work that Frank and John Craighead had started with bears here in 1959. His hope is that some future wildlife scientist will see Nick's and Donovan's work and be equally inspired. Gunther also hopes that the poignancy of the footage and the photographs will enhance the grizzlies' appeal.

Nick wanted the special issue of *National Geographic* to be a *revelation* of both the park and the Greater Yellowstone Ecosystem. He wanted to show their unique beauty as well as the conflicts and challenges confronting all species—including humans. He envisioned a probing examination of the role of a national park in the twenty-first century.

When I spoke with Superintendent Wenk, as the *National Geographic* story was still being photographed, it was clear that he felt similarly:

> I hope the images will contrast the wildness of the area with the visitor use of the area. And that people will start to ask: "What's acceptable here?"

> Is it acceptable to have the grizzly bear caring for her three cubs, while six hundred visitors encroach as close as they can . . . with their long lenses? We've changed the fishery so dramatically with our own intervention in the introduction of non-native species. What happens when the bears no longer function as they functioned historically in the park—when they no longer use the streams, when they change their diets? . . .

> What happens when a wolf who has spent 99 percent of his time in Yellowstone National Park, but ventures out one day during hunting season, gets shot? . . . What kind of limits should be put on that kind of situation? What does it mean when people hunt bison for food, or when we're shipping them off to slaughter because of population-control issues?

I hope the images make people think about what's the highest priority for a place like Yellowstone and an ecosystem like Greater Yellowstone's.

I rejoined Nick and Reba a few days before their departure from Yellowstone, in May 2015. The park in springtime is resplendently fecund, exhilaratingly awake. We saw newborn black bear cubs placed gingerly in a tree by their mother, who then lay below them to cushion their landing should they fall, as the little ones tentatively descended. The cubs plopped down on her from varying heights, after which they frolicked and nursed. Newborn bison calves, still bound to their mothers, followed them on untried legs. Grizzlies and their cubs, camouflaged, slinked through the sagebrush. And elk with velvety young antlers explored. Everyone was eating.

At dawn on one of those final days, we spotted wolves, lithe and quick and moving sinuously through the landscape. On another morning, Nick, Reba, and I went on an early morning walk with Tammy Wert, the park's Film and Fee Program Manager (or as she puts it, the "Whatever-the-Superintendent-Tells-Me-to-Do Manager"), and her partner, Steve Sarles. We were greeted by the songs of meadowlarks, and an occasional sighting of a reposing bison in the distance. I kept expecting Saint Francis of Assisi to appear around the bend.

On May 9, 2015, Kerry Gunther and his then-wife, Stacey Sigler—who ran the park's Research Permit Office—hosted a going-away party for Nick and Reba. Although much of the party food was set out on tables inside their home, the guests spilled out to their yard, where a grill was going, and a bonfire lent warmth and glow.

The party was also an extravaganza of cupcakes, from bite-size to D-cup, and in as many flavors as one could possibly imagine. There was an ad hoc photo booth where the multigenerational guests could pose with their cupcakes—often in mid-bite. It produced images framed with the *National Geographic* yellow border—less than reverent homages to the now-infamous "cupcake cover."

As we later settled ourselves in folding chairs outside on this cold and starry spring night—with a row of giggly children in front of us, tucked in their sleeping bags for the show—Tammy Wert gave the opening remarks. Teasingly, she reminisced about Nick and Reba's time in Yellowstone, and then moved back in time from Yellowstone, beyond the cupcake cover, all the way to Indiana Jones and then to Nick Danger.

Nick had been toasted and was pretty well roasted by the time he and a couple of the other photographers on the team gave presentations of their images. Nick's slideshow was accompanied by the Rolling Stones' 1969 tune "You Can't Always Get What You Want." A perfect metaphor, applicable to the demands, struggles, and challenges faced by humans and wildlife as they brush up against each other in the Greater Yellowstone Ecosystem, and to the photographic hurdles as well. Everything about the evening was fun and warmhearted, and sweetly reminiscent both of Nick's backyard slideshows and of LOOK3's vibe.

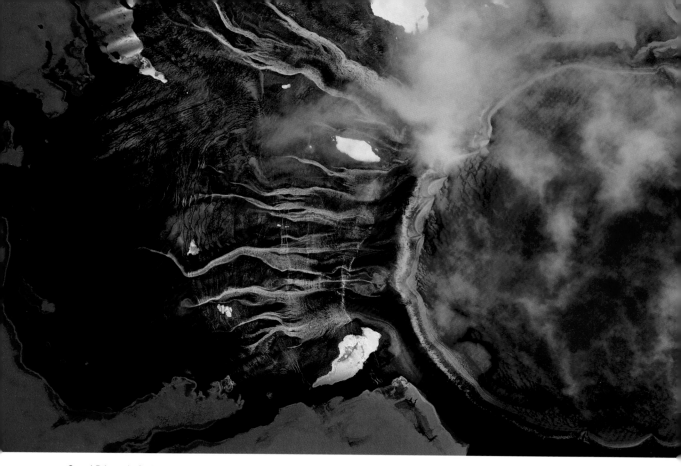

Grand Prismatic Spring, Yellowstone National Park, 2014

Reflecting later, Wert told me: "I've worked here long enough (almost thirty years) to be suspicious—or maybe cynical—about the things that come down from Washington." And then she admitted: "The *NGM* project fell into that category." She laughed, recalling some very loud

> advance conference calls with this guy—Nick—who always seemed to be telling us what he needed to do, use drones, camera traps, yadda, yadda. . . . We'd put him on mute, roll our eyes and say: 'Who *is* this guy?' The guy was the best person they could have selected to accomplish the project.
>
> As we got to know them—and he and Reba are pretty endearing—Nick impressed me with his dogged pursuit of doing it right, figuring out what the stories were, his options to document how he wanted to tell the story, how low he could actually go in a helicopter, apologizing to the right people when things didn't go right, and making us laugh a lot!

While he was working in Yellowstone, Nick learned that Kathy Moran, designer Bill Marr, photo-editor Sarah Leen, and Chris Johns had already begun considering some initial layouts for the magazine. It didn't sound as if their plans reflected the photo-essay approach he had envisioned for the issue, and Nick raised his concerns, assuming all would be addressed once he returned home to Virginia.

Along the way, he and Reba planned to pick up what Nick refers to as a "therapy dog"—a signifier, he says, that "now I'll *have to* retire." They fixed on a herding Australian cattle dog, otherwise known as a blue heeler. Nick wanted a female, and he settled on the name "Thermal." Reba gently indicated that this might not be an especially feminine name, suggesting instead Frida, after her heroine, Frida Kahlo.

Nick's response: "Stop! You're putting doubt in my goddam *feng shui*!"

They agreed to wait on the name until meeting her—they would pick the new dog up in Tennessee, on their drive back to Virginia.

Her name is Thermal, and she is lean, muscular, all puppy, and all teeth (while serving as Nick's "therapy dog," she's also known as the "land shark"). Her ears stand up when alert. Her coloring is a patchwork, from black at the tip of her snout to white to speckles of tan on her chest, around her jaw and her legs. A year later, in the spring 2016, they got a male Balinese kitten for Reba. He is a seal point cat with detailed markings. His vivid blue eyes gleam. The name? "He has no name yet," Reba told me at one point, "but depending on Thermal we might have to name him 'Run Forrest Run!'" They called him Cat. Then Catman. And finally Katman Dude (Nick explains: "First name Katman, family name Dude"). Reba wryly summed up the cat's presence some months later: "He ties the room together."

I left Yellowstone the day before Nick and Reba set off, their Airstream Bambi in tow. En route, they would visit with Tim Cahill in Livingston, and David Quammen in Bozeman. They would see a few Cardinals games in St. Louis, and pass through Muscle Shoals and Florence, Alabama, where Nick received the town's "Walk of Honor" recognition for his work. Before they knew it, they would be home in Sugar Hollow—in time to attend LOOK3 in mid-June.

Nick spent the summer going through his Yellowstone images, and those of the team. On October 5, 2015, he made a visual presentation of his work and the project at large at National Geographic's office—supported, as always, by Moran. By then, Chris Johns had been promoted to the chief content officer of the National Geographic Society. Replacing him as the magazine's editor-in-chief was Susan Goldberg, who asked Johns to serve as the guest editor of this single-topic special issue—as he had initiated the project and had nurtured it throughout its development.

The special issue of *National Geographic* did not, however, take shape as Nick had imagined it. There would be no sequence of interdependent photo-essays, celebrating each photographer's voice and sensibility. Of course editors, designers, photographers, and writers don't always concur on questions of form and content, and (as if in some meta-reflection of Yellowstone itself) there were a lot of cooks involved, with disparate ideas. Nevertheless, Nick was dismayed by what he regarded as the abandonment of these collectively unique visual perspectives. Furthermore, Johns and the other editors and designers chose to include many images—including some by Nick himself—that he perceived as uninspired or meaningless, especially when pulled out of context. And they had omitted what Nick felt were stronger photographs that spoke to the Yellowstone he had experienced.

Of one of his own Yellowstone images, which he saw hanging on the walls of National Geographic's offices at the time, he said:

Nick at Cascade Corner, Yellowstone National Park, 2014. Photograph by Ronan Donovan

They love it, and it's one of the most *boring* pictures I've ever seen! This is coming out of me, and it's my mistake. I'm not good at finesse, I'm not good at really fine aesthetics. I'm just a hammer guy. My pictures hit you over the head with a hammer. If they're not going to give me an essay, at least give me the hammer!

The visual approach seemed cliché to him. Nick felt that the editors and designers were imposing stereotypes of what the park was *supposed* to look like in their selection and sequencing of images. He expressed his apprehensions at magazine meetings several times, to no avail.

Finally, dispirited and disheartened, he wrote to Chris Johns, Kathy Moran, Bill Marr, and others. He had already stated his intention to retire from magazine photography at the end of this story, but *National Geographic* had offered to extend his contract through May 2016—the Yellowstone issue's publication date. In early December 2015, Nick sent an e-mail turning down that offer.

Its subject line was "Grace and Dignity." Despite the extensive time he had spent in Yellowstone, he said, his suggestions and perspective on the story had been ignored. He felt that the collaborative process that had always been essential to the success of his stories had been forsaken. He was now extricating himself entirely from the edit: "I simply feel it is detrimental to have any more contact while I am so emotional. I know it is a tough time for all."

Johns responded the following day with the reassurance that "the Yellowstone issue has always been about making a difference and I am confident it will."

"I truly hope," Nick replied, "that the publication has the effect that we dreamed of when we first went up the mountain."

In the end, he believes it does. But in the process deep and longtime collaborations and friendships were bruised.

The magazine opens with a visual overture foreshadowing the topics to be explored in later pages.[11] Subsequently, passages of images by each photographer evoke a sensibility and address a theme or idea. There is no compilation of photo essays, but the photographers are in no way diminished. David Quammen's text elegantly orchestrates all, creating bridges between ideas and territories, staying on trail, and then wandering into unexplored spaces. He reveals the park in all its complexities and challenges.

The "tough time" Nick had alluded to was very real. In September 2015 the magazine had issued an announcement that was, for many, nothing less than shattering. For $725 million, National Geographic Society had sold *National Geographic* magazine, along with its other media assets (including its book and map divisions), to a newly formed entity called National Geographic Partners, headed by 21st Century Fox. On September 9 a press release was issued, stating: "The new entity will be owned 73 percent by 21st Century Fox and 27 percent by The National Geographic Society."[12] James Murdoch (son of Rupert Murdoch) is the CEO of 21st Century Fox—which also owns the Fox Broadcasting Company, Fox News, and the 20th Century Fox movie studio.

The potential for this sale to undermine the magazine's journalistic integrity and its scientific credibility devastated many of the editors, photographers, and writers. Take climate change. *National Geographic* magazine had stalwartly reported from the frontlines of the global-warming crisis. The science is indisputable—and really, one just has to be paying attention to environmental happenings to know it is taking place—yet Rupert Murdoch has consistently and fervently proclaimed his skepticism about climate change, referring to it as "alarmist nonsense."[13] This, along with the often shortsightedly conservative and inflammatory propaganda from the Fox News Channel, understandably prompted many doubts about the new partnership.

Even if it may be supposed that editorial bias and other interference from the overseeing organization are minimal, many conservationists are already dismayed by the problematic content often generated by National Geographic's existing television partnership with Fox, which began in 1997, dismissing much of National Geographic's programming as ratings-driven "jaws and claws" sensationalism. Worse, this kind of entertainment television, when offered up as documentary "truth," can lead to damaging misunderstandings about species. Across a spectrum of disciplines—from scientists to activists to principled journalists and documentarians—many believe that the change of ownership compromises the future ethics and reliability of National Geographic Society's content. Others say we must wait and see.

After National Geographic's announcement, many staff members, photographers, and journalists feared for their jobs. And sure enough, in early November 2015, 180 people—that is, 9 percent of the staff—were laid off. As this unfolded, Gary Knell, appointed president and CEO of National Geographic Society in August 2013, attempted to assuage the concerns of his staff and colleagues, as well as the magazine's readers and the society's other constituents.

In the December 2015 issue of the magazine, he wrote in his "From the President" column:

> We'll still be the one National Geographic, committed to the highest standards of journalistic excellence and integrity but reorganized in a way that better empowers our efforts.

> We'll work to protect wildlife through initiatives to save elephants, big cats, and more. We'll document the at-risk species on Earth with the goal of helping to save them. We'll push for healthier oceans. . . . We'll nurture and support the world's best researchers, explorers, and educators. And we'll find new and powerful ways to share all our work through storytelling, journalism, and photography.[14]

For Nick, National Geographic's partnership with Fox became part of his retirement-from-being-a-magazine-photographer narrative. It wasn't the precipitating reason—he had spoken of retiring since at least 2013—but it solidified the timing of his decision. That said, Nick still believes in National Geographic, in Chris Johns and in Kathy Moran. There is so much history, so much love, and so much that has been accomplished. By late 2016, he was convinced that "National Geographic has not been compromised. It's actually getting better as far as TV content and programming." He adds:

> Photographers—working in any style—must cover the planet. It's not just the right thing to do—it is crucial. The animals, the trees . . . are losing a battle against humans they never asked to be in. Things must change now, or it will be too late. This is something all the voices of photography need to drive home.

FOLLOWING SPREAD: Moon-bow, Cascade Corner, Yellowstone National Park, 2014

CODA: THE WOODS

Thermal, Nick, Reba, and Katman Dude at their home in
Sugar Hollow, Virginia, 2016. Photograph by Ian Nichols

Without any warning, the light was suddenly eclipsed. It was a moment that would, from then on, define *before* and *after.*

By late January 2016, after the Yellowstone issue had been more or less finalized, Nick, Kathy Moran, and everyone else in his orbit had learned that Chris Johns was diagnosed with stage 4 lung cancer.

The illness of Nick's friend and colleague of more than twenty years superseded any lingering disagreement or sense of disappointment. What mattered mattered. Nick wanted only for Johns to be well and strong again—after which they might engage in new points of contention, of intense agreement, of collaboration . . . or they might just go for a walk.

And just as Nick was trying to come to terms with Johns's illness, another blow was struck. Reba—who had been having debilitating headaches and facial pain—was told that she had a small meningioma tumor in her brain. Very fortunately, not malignant. In the spring of 2016, she underwent a Gamma Knife radiosurgery treatment: focused radiation that maps and begins to shrink the tumor. Over time, the tumor's pressure on Reba's nerves—the source of her original symptoms—may be relieved.

As of this writing, Reba's tumor and Chris Johns's cancer seem to be under control. Reba's brain must be scanned every six months for assessment. As for Johns, he has undergone six months of chemotherapy and radiation, and thankfully his cancer appears to be in remission. But it has been a challenging stretch for each of them, as well as for those in their close circles.

When life gets harsh and out of his control, Nick's refuge is—as it has been since he was a child—the woods. He is now determined to spend all the time he can there with Reba. Accompanied by Thermal, bounding along, and on rare occasions Katman Dude, they take long walks, through the forests of Virginia's Pasture Fence Mountain, looking for animal tracks, identifying plants, savoring birdsongs. Together Nick and Reba muse about the transformation of these hilly woods surrounding their house in Sugar Hollow. It used to be a "black forest," rich in hemlocks. An infestation of woolly adelgid killed off most of the hemlocks years ago, but the new growth thrives: hardwood saplings, poplar, white oak, paw-paw, redbud. . . .

As they walk and talk, Nick and Reba configure their future, steadying themselves for life's ambushes, for more time at home, and for aging. Some additional retrofitting is to be done inside their already renovated farmhouse—removing a dicey staircase, for example, and installing one that is more user-friendly—anticipating possible issues with Nick's bad back and knees.

Their house, situated near the bottom of a hill and hugged by plantings and little garden ponds, was built in 1949 (although its foundations date to about 1820). It is constructed of concrete cinderblocks, made on the property using river sand. Bathed in sunshine, fed by plentiful spring water, the house has an open floor plan and many windows; the few doors lead either outside or to a porch. There's a short pathway to a screened-in pine A-frame structure, which they call "the sleeping house." In it is a bed suspended by ropes, where Nick and Reba sleep, except on the coldest winter nights. "Sleeping there is

Reba and Nick, 2015. Photograph by David Alan Harvey/Magnum Photos

very important to us," says Nick. "We stay close to the cycles of nature. Moonlight and bird and animal calls are not lost." It's also one of a couple of structures designated for Mike Fay whenever he might visit. Deeper in the woods, uphill, past Ian's lushly frenzied organic garden, stands "Fort Fay": a south-facing overlook constructed by Fay and Nathan Williamson, with an oak sleeping platform and sloping metal roof, optimally positioned to take in the view of Buck's Elbow Mountain in the distance.

Inside Nick and Reba's house, scattered throughout the space, are souvenirs from their travels and projects over the years. One favorite is a figure dubbed "Gus": a larger-than-life-size puppetlike initiation-costume from New Guinea, made of clay and straw, painted in earthy colors and covered with feathers. Gus hangs from the ceiling, as he has since their Berkeley loft days. Nick bought him after "Eater of Men," his early essay for *Geo* that took him down the Waghi River.

Nick's studio-office is in another renovated building at the end of the long, uphill driveway. Its white walls are dotted with family photos, some by Nick, others by friends and colleagues, as well as resonant "iconic images from 'the day,'" he says. Here is Charles Moore's devastating 1963 photograph of the Birmingham Alabama Fire Department fire-hosing demonstrators. And Philip Jones Griffiths's 1968 image of a seated American G.I. in Saigon, looking incongruously calm with his feet propped on the windowsill, as he exchanges fire with an unseen assailant outside. Here is Mary Ellen Mark's 1989 image of twin brothers from the Great Famous Circus in Calcutta—one holding a gorilla mask, the other wearing one, while cradling a sleeping puppy in his arms. (Nick tells me that Mark traded him this for a print of his 1991 photograph of Susie, the chimpanzee who was compelled to wear a tutu.) Nick met Jim Marshall when

Ian (left) and Eli Nichols, 2013

he first moved to San Francisco; here, Marshall's rock-and-roll photographs have a wall to themselves—images of the Allman Brothers, Bob Dylan, Keith Richards, and his signature Johnny Cash "Let's-do-a-shot-for-the-warden" flip-off photograph from San Quentin.

This building also houses Reba's painting studio, and Ian and Eli stay here when they're home. Nick and Reba are very happy that their sons live relatively close by. These days, Ian—who earned his BA in government from the University of Virginia—is working toward a PhD in conservation biology at Philadelphia's Drexel University. The lab he is working in is part of the greater Central African Biodiversity Alliance, and conducts research on Bioko Island, off the coast of west Africa, and in Cameroon. Ian's doctoral research is on chimpanzees in Cameroon, and his work relies on the use of camera traps. The lab's projects on Bioko, says Ian, are "about biodiversity, climate change, and education/outreach. I hope to continue my work in biodiversity both in Cameroon and Bioko." He tells me he plans to use photography for his work in Bioko as well.

As for Eli, he is currently managing an oyster farm on Chincoteague Island, off Virginia's Eastern Shore. This seventy-mile stretch of woodlands and wetlands, isolated from the rest of the state by the Chesapeake Bay, is about a five-hour drive from Sugar Hollow.

Here in his studio, Nick is working on his next big project. It is, in a sense, the most perfect entr'acte imaginable, as he transitions from being a magazine photographer to whatever may come next.

From June 27 to September 17, 2017, a traveling survey exhibition of his photographs premieres at the Philadelphia Museum of Art—*Wild: Michael Nichols*. Organized by the museum's curator of photographs, Peter Barberie, and myself, the show, says Barberie, "juxtaposes Nick's photographs with diverse, non-photographic works from the museum's collection, showing that the wild world has been a key subject for art across time and cultures. *Wild* invites visitors to contemplate humanity's role as nature's steward, tasked with safeguarding the wild places that perhaps once menaced us, but that we now risk forever destroying."

Separately, Nick has planned an exhibition with Jean-François Leroy's Visa pour l'Image photojournalism festival in Perpignan. That exhibition is scheduled to open just in time for Nick's sixty-fifth birthday, in September 2017.

As we discuss the Philadelphia show and settle on the final selection of images for this biography, we are again reviewing and codifying Nick's lifework. He and I discuss his Yellowstone photographs, which we agree are collectively not wholly successful. They do, however, complement the virtuosity of his lions epic, his elephants and great apes projects, his tigers and tall trees portraiture, and his revelations of the last unexplored places on Earth. Unlike those earlier projects, the Yellowstone narrative lacks a singular catalyzing central character. In Yellowstone, Nick isn't positioned to witness a family's daily life, a mother's challenges, the mind-blowing intricacy of a giant tree, an alpha male's ascension and leadership. He never falls in love. The Yellowstone images, in fact, contain minimal romance—and yet there is much wonder in them. If his work on the Serengeti lions is the apotheosis of Nick's unique sensibility, his comprehensive view of the Greater Yellowstone Ecosystem "ties the room together" if not photographically, then by setting forth and clarifying many of the conservation challenges he has encountered and taken on throughout his life and work. And this time, relatively speaking, it is in his own backyard.

If it could be condensed to a single message—although how reductive it would be to do so, given the complexities of the creatures and habitats he has covered, and all the hurdles overcome along the way!—Nick's statement is: *wild matters.*

In support of *wild*, a primary subject is land. We know that wild animals, globally, need protected habitat—lots of it, whether public or private—including migration corridors so they may roam as necessary, unthreatened.

The central question is: how? How to incentivize people living near protected wildlife habitat to attempt to coexist safely with wild animals, sometimes including predators—and to not hunt them for bushmeat or body parts, or in retaliation, or for ritual, or for the joy of killing? This may be about how and where livestock grazes; it may be about fencing; it may be about finding a way to offer people money for every animal *not* killed. Clearly, there needs to be a respectful give and take. Certainly it cannot be about displacement of local communities, nor of wildlife.

And, if a sustainable presence of wildlife is recognized as critical to a healthy planet, can we find a way to quantify the benefits to people? To effect those benefits pragmatically?

The Holy Grail in this fight for wild is ending the *demand* for animal parts once and for all—whether tusks from elephants; horns from rhinoceroses; skins, penises, and other organs from big cats; paws, skulls, and other parts from great apes; or living bodies for entertainment or often needless and brutal experimentation. Only by eliminating demand will the criminal slaughter of animals and the trafficking of their body parts cease. Until that point, what is the most effective way to focus on fixing this dire problem?

How may animals and people thrive interdependently, in relative safety? One imperative is to create alternative opportunities for humans living in desperate poverty who turn to poaching for quick cash, as a means of survival. Healthy ecosystems must function in tandem with healthy socioeconomic systems—meeting basic human needs, and ensuring that even the poorest people have agency.

As we consider the killing of animals for trophies—if trophy hunting is indeed as positive a force for conservation as some suggest—how do we mindfully, intelligently regulate it, while also contending with corruption and accountability in that industry? How can its proponents be persuaded to support honest, aggressive conservation? Is there a way to eliminate politics and greed from the listing and delisting of animals so that decisions are made with the primary goal of ensuring a given species' optimum numbers and health?

Will our worldview enable us to work toward a more balanced and respectful relationship with the Earth and the creatures with whom we share it? Or are we still so solipsistic as to believe that the Earth is ours alone—all other living things subordinate to humans? This kind of enslavement is death to wild. And it is equally toxic for humans, inextricably bound as we are to this ecosystem.

Ultimately, with existence on the planet should come rights—for big cats, great apes, rhinoceroses, elephants, bison, elk, wolves, bears, fish, birds, trees. . . . This is about much more than the wild world achieving standing in courts of law—although that, too, is critical, and many lawyers and conservationists continue to fight for this legal affirmation. Representatives of religious groups of myriad denominations have also affirmed the significance of all living creatures, and begun to embrace ecology into their teachings of faith and morality.[1] It is a state of mind, heart, and conscience. What can we do to help the Earth and all its inhabitants to flourish?

In his powerful 2016 exhortation *Half-Earth: Our Planet's Fight for Life*, Edward O. Wilson writes:

> Wildlands are our birthplace. Our civilizations were built from them. . . . The millions of species we have allowed to survive there, but continue to threaten, are our phylogenetic kin. Their long-term history is our long-term history. Despite all of our pretenses and fantasies, we always have been and will remain a biological species tied to this particular biological world. Millions of years of evolution are indelibly encoded in our genes. History without the wildlands is no history at all.[2]

Conservation is critical for *all* life. And we can still save threatened species and habitats. Conservation works, and there are many ways to consider, evoke, support, and speak out for its goals and its dependents, locally and globally.

On January 29, 2016, after receiving an update e-mail from Nick, Mike Fay wrote back to catch him up with his work in Gabon:

In the past three years we have never made more progress for conservation than for at least 10 years here in Gabon. We have accomplished what we thought would never be possible for parks. . . . we have brought lots of Gabonese with us on the path. . . . We did the impossible. Fish are coming back to the river mouths in droves. This year I am concentrating on elephants on a mission chasing every last poacher out of the last refuges. . . . Wonga Wongué is the masterpiece. We have taken a dying park with no chance and turned it into the most fantastic park in all of the forests of central Africa. . . .

"We will succeed," said Fay. "I am convinced."

Nick was elated after reading the e-mail, which goes on to describe Wonga Wongué Presidential Reserve's remarkably high population of chimpanzees and mandrills—all in "a landscape made in heaven." Fay's words and his enthusiasm affirmed so much. Nick has always shared Fay's passion and has, in his own way, committed to the same aspirations—even while following a different path toward their realization. Nick believes deeply in Fay's conservation work. He believes just as deeply in his own photography, and in the strength of the medium as a tool for interpretation, for storytelling, and for advocacy—however that action may take shape.

For Nick, the sense that he might actually be able to live his dream began almost four decades ago. In the fall of 1978—after receiving his first assignment with *Geo*—he wrote Reba a letter, filled with an aching hope for what he might accomplish. The letter ends with the words: "We're facing reality this time—no more pipe dreams—Hot damn."

From his childhood fantasies of faraway lands to his determination to become "the Mick Jagger of photography," an Artist with a capital A, to find his mission, his soul, his conscience, and finally his voice—so that he might *give* voice—Nick's dreams, coupled with his drive and talent, set him free. And they have allowed him to achieve so much.

Perhaps he and Reba will someday return to the Serengeti to continue working with the lions and realize his notion of a trilogy—a notion that still pulls at Nick in his daydreams. Maybe he will direct a film there: he whispers this idea to himself on those long walks in the woods, just to see what it sounds like . . . it's a nice sound.

Back in the Serengeti, he will look for thriving prides of lions. He pictures C-Boy's descendants, the next generations of the Vumbi lionesses. The savanna expands promiscuously before him. The lionesses, intensely aware but as aloof as ever, are dispersed in radiant repose on the smooth gray kopje, under a dramatic backlit sky. Watchful, waiting.

Hot damn.

FOLLOWING SPREAD: Vumbi pride, Serengeti National Park, 2012

MY BACK PAGES

EDITOR'S NOTES:
- In the interest of consistency, throughout this volume place names and transliterated terms (including names of indigenous African peoples) have been standardized following authoritative sources: the *New York Times*, *National Geographic* magazine, the writings of David Quammen. While the names of national parks overseas are often conveyed in the language of their country (e.g. Chad's Parc National Zakouma), here they appear consistently in English (e.g. Zakouma National Park), in accordance with the style of the online resource African-parks.org.
- The heading "My Back Pages" is taken from the 1964 Bob Dylan song of the same title.
- All quotes are from interviews and correspondence with the author, unless otherwise attributed.

FRONT ENDPAPERS
- Albert Camus, 1958 preface to "The Wrong Side and the Right Side" ("L'envers et l'endroit"; 1937), in *Lyrical and Critical Essays*, ed. by Philip Thody, trans. by Ellen Conroy Kennedy (New York: Vintage, 1970), p. 17.
- James Salter, *Light Years* (New York: Vintage International, 1995), pp. 23–24.
- Charles Bowden, "That Time in Paris," *PADDLEFISH 2014–2015*, no. 8 (2014): 17–29.

BACK ENDPAPERS
- Edward Abbey, *Postcards from Ed: Dispatches and Salvos from an American Iconoclast*, ed. David Petersen (Minneapolis: Milkweed, 2006), p. 257.
- Rachel Carson, "A Fable for Tomorrow," in *Silent Spring* (1962; Boston: Mariner Books, 2002), p. 3.
- Henry David Thoreau, "Walking" (1854), in *Walden and Other Writings*, ed. by Brooks Atkinson (New York: Modern Library, 1950), p. 597.

ENDNOTES
SOME GIRLS
The chapter title "Some Girls" is taken from the 1978 Rolling Stones album of the same name. Written by Mick Jagger and Keith Richards; produced by the Glimmer Twins; Rolling Stones Records.
1. "Illegal Wildlife Trade," U.S. Fish and Wildlife Service: International Affairs, accessed September 14, 2016, https://www.fws.gov/international/travel-and-trade/illegal-wildlife-trade.html.
2. Michael Nichols, *Gorilla: Struggle for Survival in the Virungas* (New York: Aperture, 1989).
3. Michael Nichols, *Earth to Sky: Among Africa's Elephants, A Species in Crisis* (New York: Aperture, 2013).
4. Barry Lopez, "Unbounded Wilderness," *Aperture* 120 (Summer 1990): 2–15.
5. Aldo Leopold, Part IV "The Upshot," in *A Sand County Almanac* (1949; New York: Ballantine, 1978), p. 239.
6. Ibid., p. 258.
7. Ibid., p. 239.
8. Ernst Haas, *The Creation* (New York: Viking Press, 1971).
9. Christopher D. Stone, *Should Trees Have Standing?: Toward Legal Rights for Natural Objects* (1972; Los Altos, CA: William Kaufmann, 1974).

MY HOMETOWN
The chapter title "My Hometown" is taken from Bruce Springsteen's song of the same name on his 1984 album *Born in the U.S.A.* Produced by Chuck Plotkin and Jon Landau; Columbia Records.
1. Jimmy Cliff, in *Muscle Shoals*, 2013, directed by Greg "Freddy" Camalier for Magnolia Home Entertainment, Los Angeles, 1 hour 51 mins., color.

2. See Charles Moore and Michael S. Durham, *Powerful Days: The Civil Rights Photography of Charles Moore* (Tuscaloosa: University of Alabama Press, 2007).
3. Mitchell J. Shields and Michael K. Nichols, "The Lure of the Abyss," *Geo* 1, no. 2 (June 1979): 74–93.

NICK DANGER
This chapter's epigraph is from Tim Cahill and Michael K. Nichols, "Nick Danger: Boy Photographer," *San Francisco Examiner Image–The Magazine of Northern California* (November 3, 1985): 18–23.
1. Shields and Nichols, "The Lure of the Abyss," *Geo*, pp. 74–93.
2. Ibid., pp. 81–86.
3. Ibid., p. 93.
4. Arthur Conan Doyle, *The Lost World* (1912; New York: Berkley, 1940), p. 34.
5. Tim Cahill and Michael K. Nichols, "Venezuela: Exploring a Lost World," *Geo* 2, no. 3 (March 1980): 58–99.
6. Cahill and Nichols, "Nick Danger," *Image*, p. 21.
7. Cahill and Nichols, "Venezuela," *Geo*, pp. 68–70.
8. Mitchell J. Shields and Michael K. Nichols, "Riding the Torrent," *Geo* 2, no. 8 (August 1980): 56–67.
9. David Roberts (and Michael Nichols), "Rafting the 'Eater of Men,'" *Geo* 6, no. 2 (February 1984): 58–71.
10. Among *National Geographic*'s many stories on the plight of the mountain gorilla was Dian Fossey's article "A Grim Struggle for Survival: The Imperiled Mountain Gorilla," *National Geographic* 159, no. 4 (April 1981): 501–5, 511–23.
11. Tim Cahill and Michael K. Nichols, "Gorilla Tactics," *Geo* 3, no. 12 (December 1981): 100–116.
12. Tim Cahill, "Love and Death in Gorilla Country," in *A Wolverine Is Eating My Leg* (New York: Vintage, 1989), pp. 17–18.
13. Patric Karuretwa, "Release of Rwanda's Mastermind of Death Promotes Genocide Denial," *Harvard Law Record*, December 4, 2009, http://hlrecord.org/2009/12/release-of-rwandas-mastermind-of-death-promotes-genocide-denial/. See also Diane Nienaber, "International Court Acquits Suspected Murderer of Dian Fossey," *Huffington Post* online, November 17, 2009, http://www.huffingtonpost.com/georgianne-nienaber/international-court-acqui_b_360379.html.
14. George B. Schaller, *The Mountain Gorilla: Ecology and Behavior* (Chicago: University of Chicago Press, 1963).
15. George B. Schaller, in Nichols, *Gorilla*, p. 20.
16. Ibid.

INDIANA JONES
1. Henri Cartier-Bresson's words describing Magnum are cited frequently. See e.g. the Magnum website: https://pro.magnumphotos.com/C.aspx?VP3=CMS3&VF=MAX_2&FRM=Frame:MAX_3.
2. "Missions impossibles," *Photo* 200 (May 1984): 158–71.
3. Tim Cahill and Michael Nichols, "Rope Tricks," *San Francisco Examiner Image–The Magazine of Northern California* (December 7, 1986): 31–36.
4. Tim Cahill and Michael K. Nichols, "Fear of Frying," *Rolling Stone* 457 (September 26, 1985): 35–40, 117–18, 124.
5. See Donna Ferrato, *Living with the Enemy* (New York: Aperture, 1991).
6. David Roberts and Michael Nichols, "A Labyrinth Called Lechuguilla," *Smithsonian* 19, no. 8 (November 1988): 52–65.
7. Benno Kroll and William Strode, "The Savage Pit," *Geo* 1, no. 11 (November 1979).
8. Michael Nichols and Anthony DeCurtis, "The Scorched Earth," *Rolling Stone* 546 (February 23, 1989): 40–49.

9. Tim Cahill and Michael Nichols, "Charting the Splendors of Lechuguilla Cave," *National Geographic* 179, no. 3 (March 1991): 34–59.

BRUTAL KINSHIP

1. Adam Janofsky, "Jane Goodall Brings Ape Activism to Campus," *Chicago Maroon*, May 11, 2010, http://chicagomaroon.com/2010/05/11/jane-goodall-brings-ape-activism-to-campus/.

2. Jane Goodall, foreword to *Understanding Chimpanzees*, ed. by Paul G. Heltne and Linda A. Marquardt (Cambridge, MA: Harvard University Press, in cooperation with Chicago Academy of Sciences, 1989), pp. xii–xiii.

3. *Brutal Kinship*, 1989, directed by Wolfgang Bayer for National Geographic Television, http://www.bfi.org.uk/films-tv-people/4ce2b793b4af8.

4. Jane Goodall and Michael K. Nichols, "Das Verhängnis, uns Menschen verwandt zu sein," *Geo* (German ed.) 13, no. 7 (July 1991): 66–88.

5. Michael Nichols and Jane Goodall, *Brutal Kinship* (New York: Aperture, 1989), p. 71.

6. Ibid.

7. Peter Miller and Michael Nichols, "Jane Goodall: Crusading for Chimps and Humans," *National Geographic* 188, no. 6 (December 1995): 102–28.

8. Michael McRae and Michael Nichols, "Orphan Gorillas: Fighting to Survive in the Wild," *National Geographic* 197, no. 2 (February 2000): 84–97.

9. Goodall and Nichols, "Das Verhängnis," *Geo* (German ed.), pp. 66–88.

10. Eugene Linden and Michael Nichols, "A Curious Kinship: Apes and Humans," *National Geographic* 181, no. 3 (March 1992): 2–45.

11. This issue of *National Geographic* would evolve into the book *The Great Apes: Between Two Worlds*, with Nick's photographs and texts by Jane Goodall, George Schaller, and Mary Smith (Washington, DC: National Geographic Society, 1993).

12. See James Gorman, "Chimpanzees in Liberia, Used in New York Blood Center Research, Face Uncertain Future," *New York Times*, May 28, 2015, http://www.nytimes.com/2015/05/29/science/chimpanzees-liberia-new-york-blood-center.html?emc=eta1&_r=0.

13. Francis S. Collins, "NIH Will No Longer Support Biomedical Research on Chimpanzees," National Institutes of Health, November 18, 2015, https://www.nih.gov/about-nih/who-we-are/nih-director/statements/nih-will-no-longer-support-biomedical-research-chimpanzees.

14. Peter D. Walsh, "Protecting Apes Could Backfire," *New York Times*, September 27, 2015.

15. John Berger, "Why Look at Animals?" (1977), in *About Looking* (New York: Pantheon, 1980), p. 19.

16. Ibid., pp. 21–22.

17. Cliff Tarpy and Michael Nichols, "New Zoos: Taking Down the Bars," *National Geographic* 184, no. 1 (July 1993): 2–37.

18. Bil Gilbert and Michael Nichols, "New Ideas in the Air at the National Zoo," *Smithsonian* 27, no. 3 (June 1996): 32–43.

19. Lynne Warren, Michael Nichols, and Fritz Hoffmann, "Panda, Inc.," *National Geographic* 210, no. 1 (July 2006): 42–59.

20. George B. Schaller, *The Year of the Gorilla* (1964; Chicago: University of Chicago Press, 2010), p. 259.

21. George B. Schaller and Michael Nichols, "Mountain Gorillas of Africa: Threatened by War," *National Geographic* 188, no. 4 (October 1995): 58–71.

22. Paul F. Salopek and Michael Nichols, "Gorillas and Humans: An Uneasy Truce," ibid., pp. 72–83.

23. Roméo Dallaire, *Shake Hands with the Devil: The Failure of Humanity in Rwanda* (Philadelphia: Da Capo, 2003).

24. See Gilles Peress, *The Silence* (New York: Scalo, 1995).

25. Philip Gourevitch, *We Wish to Inform You That Tomorrow We Will Be Killed with Our Families: Stories from Rwanda* (New York: Farrar, Straus and Giroux, 1998).

26. Sharon Begley and Brent Stirton, "A Globalized World's New Extinction Threats," *Newsweek*, no. 6 (August 6, 2007): 22–23.

27. Rachel Nuwer, "Grauer's Gorillas May Soon Be Extinct, Conservationists Say," *New York Times*, April 24, 2016.

28. Ibid.

29. Robert Draper and Brent Stirton, "The Battle for Virunga: Saving One of the World's Most Dangerous Parks," *National Geographic* 230, no. 1 (July 2016): 55–83.

30. Schaller, *Year of the Gorilla*, p. 259.

SITA AND CHARGER

1. Geoffrey C. Ward and Diane Raines Ward, *Tiger-Wallahs: Encounters with the Men Who Tried to Save the Greatest of the Great Cats* (New York: Harper Collins, 1993).

2. Michael Nichols and Geoffrey C. Ward, *The Year of the Tiger* (Washington, DC: National Geographic Society, 1998).

3. Geoffrey C. Ward and Michael Nichols, "Making Room for Wild Tigers," *National Geographic* 192, no. 6 (December 1997): 2–35.

4. Ibid., pp. 14–15.

5. Michael Nichols, "Sita: Life of a Wild Tigress," *National Geographic* 192, no. 6 (December 1997): 36–47.

6. Sharon Guynup, "Tigers in Traditional Chinese Medicine: A Universal Apothecary," *National Geographic* online, April 29, 2014, http://voices.nationalgeographic.com/2014/04/29/tigers-in-traditional-chinese-medicine-a-universal-apothecary/.

THE LAST PLACE ON EARTH

1. Michael Nichols and J. Michael Fay, *The Last Place on Earth*, with *Megatransect: Mike Fay's Journals* (Washington, DC: National Geographic Society, 2005). This boxed publication comprises two volumes: one featuring Nick's color photographs reproduced at large scale; the other with pages reprinted from Fay's journal entries during the fifteen-month Megatransect journey, from September 1999 to December 2000; the latter is illustrated with Nick's black-and-white photographs of Fay and the Megatransect team.

2. Fay, afterword to *Last Place on Earth*., n.p.

3. Melissa Harris, introduction to "The Forest Through the Trees: Dr. Mike Fay and the Mega-Transect in Africa," with photographs and extended captions by Michael Nichols, *Aperture* 167 (Summer 2002): 42–55.

4. Fay, in *Last Place on Earth*, n.p.

5. Eugene Linden, "Inside the World's Last Eden," *Time* 140, no. 2 (July 13, 1992): 62–69.

6. Douglas Chadwick and Michael Nichols, "Ndoki: Last Place on Earth," *National Geographic* 188, no. 1 (July 1995): 2–45.

7. Fay, afterword to *Last Place on Earth*, n.p.

8. Ibid.

9. Although William Graves was still the magazine's editor-in-chief at the time—Bill Allen would not officially step into that role until January 1995—Allen was the editor when the Ndoki story was published. Nick recalls: "Allen had been named and was already editor in everyone's mind. Even if Graves was still at the desk, Allen was making the decisions."

10. Fay is not the first or only conservationist to have played an instrumental role in creating protected areas in this region. Already protected by 1990 was the contiguous Dzanga-Ndoki National Park, and to a lesser degree the Dzanga-Sangha Special Reserve ("Special Reserve" designates an area where activities such as logging and/or hunting may be permitted), both in the Central African Republic. The conservationist Richard Carroll had initiated the protection of Dzanga Bai (in Dzanga-Ndoki National Park). Fay writes that he and his then-wife, biologist Andrea Turkalo, worked to "transform the Bai back into the mecca it had once been for the elephants of the forest." Turkalo's work is the longest-running study on forest elephants ever realized, and is still in process, despite ongoing threats from poaching.

11. "The Elephants of Africa: The Poaching Problem," *Nature*, PBS, November 16, 1997, http://www.pbs.org/wnet/nature/elephants-africa-poaching-problem/11367/.

12. Fay, afterword to *Last Place on Earth*, n.p.

13. Ibid.

14. *National Geographic*'s three stories on Mike Fay's Megatransect, all written by David Quammen with photographs by Nick, are as follows: "Megatransect," *National Geographic* 198 no. 4 (October 2000): 2–29; "The Green Abyss: Megatransect II," *National Geographic* 199, no. 3 (March 2001): 2–45; and "End of the Line: Megatransect III," *National Geographic* 200, no. 2 (August 2001): 74–103.

15. See Louis Sarno, *Bayaka: The Extraordinary Music of the Babenzélé Pygmies and Sounds of Their Forest Home* (Roslyn, NY: Ellipsis Arts, 1995); and *Song from the Forest: My Life among the Pygmies* (San Antonio, TX: Trinity University Press, 2015). See also the 2013 documentary film about Sarno, *Song from the Forest*, directed by Michael Obert, Tondowski Films & Friends, Germany, 1 hour 38 mins., color.

16. Fay, *Megatransect: Mike Fay's Journals*, in *Last Place on Earth*, pp. 7–8.

17. David Quammen, "Words," in *Last Place on Earth*, n.p.

18. J. Michael Fay, quoted in Quammen and Nichols, "Megatransect II," *National Geographic*, p. 5.

19. Ibid., p. 24.

20. Michael Nichols, "The Cast," *Megatransect: Mike Fay's Journals*, in *Last Place on Earth*, p. 141.

21. Quammen and Nichols, "Megatransect II," *National Geographic*, p. 24.

22. Ibid., p. 23.

23. David Quammen, *Spillover: Animal Infections and the Next Human Pandemic* (New York: Norton, 2012), p. 112.

24. Quammen and Nichols, "Megatransect III," *National Geographic*, p. 82.

25. Ibid.

26. Ibid., p. 97.

27. These developments are discussed in detail in David Quammen and Michael Nichols, "Saving Africa's Eden," *National Geographic* 204, no. 3 (September 2003): 50–77.

28. Ibid., p. 64.

29. Morgan and Sanz are principal investigators with the Goualougo Triangle Ape Project. When not in the park, Morgan is also a conservation research fellow at Chicago's Lincoln Park Zoo.

30. David Quammen and Michael Nichols, "Jane Goodall in the Wild," *National Geographic* 203, no. 4 (April 2003): 90–103.

31. J. Michael Fay and Michael Nichols, "Land of the Surfing Hippos," *National Geographic* 206, no. 2 (August 2004): 100–127.

PEACE, LOVE, AND PHOTOGRAPHY

1. Virginia Morell and Michael Nichols, "Kings of the Hill?" *National Geographic* 202, no. 5 (November 2002): 100–121.

2. Virginia Morell and Michael Nichols, "Our Grandest Canyon," *National Geographic* 209, no. 1 (January 2006): 36–55.

3. Walter De Maria, "The Lightning Field," *Artforum* 18, no. 8 (April 1980): 55–59, and cover image by John Cliett.

4. Photographer Will Kerner had produced all kinds of events in Charlottesville; Jessica Nagle is a cofounder of SNL Financial; Jon Golden is a photographer based in Charlottesville. In 2011, visuals editor and curator Scott Thode came onboard. In 2015, Deborah Willis—chair of the Department of Photography and Imaging, Tisch School of the Arts, New York University—joined, as did artist Phil Toledano, and Gina Martin of National Geographic Creative. David Griffin—now head of DGriffin Studio after leaving *National Geographic* and serving as visuals editor of the *Washington Post*—and Andrew Owen, now community events director, Instagram, joined the newly formed governing board in 2015, as did Brian Storm, founder of MediaStorm.

5. Other staff includes: Will May, exhibition producer; Chloe Delaney and Kaya Lee Berne, production assistants who also worked with Nick in his studio. In 2015, Mary Virginia Swanson was named executive director of the festival, succeeding Victoria Hindley, who held the position from the end of 2013 through the 2015 festival. As of fall 2016, Will Kerner is LOOK3's acting executive director.

6. Other artists who have been spotlighted since the festival's inception include: Sam Abell, Lynsey Addario, Nubar Alexanian, Christopher Anderson, Ernesto Bazan, Olivia Bee, Stephanie Berger, Julie Blackmon, Nick Brandt, Sheila Pree Bright, Mary F. Calvert, Cause Collective, Gregory Crewdson, Binh Danh, David Doubilet, Doug DuBois, Donna Ferrato, Larry Fink, LaToya Ruby Frazier, Ashley Gilbertson, Bruce Gilden, Nan Goldin, Stanley Greene, Lori Grinker, Monica Haller and the Veterans Book Project, David Alan Harvey, Walter Iooss, Graciela Iturbide, Jeff Jacobson, Lynn Johnson, Brenda Ann Kenneally, Josef Koudelka, Antonin Kratochvil, Tim Laman, Frans Lanting, Gerd Ludwig, Tom Mangelsen, Mary Ellen Mark and Martin Bell, Steve McCurry, Susan Meiselas, Richard Misrach and Kate Orff, Christopher Morris, Zanele Muholi, Vincent J. Musi, James Nachtwey, Piotr Naskrecki, Flip Nicklin, Martin Parr, Paolo Pellegrin, Gilles Peress, Sylvia Plachy, Joe Riis, Martha Rosler, Radcliffe "Ruddy" Roye, Joel Sartore, Callie Shell, Alec Soth, Maggie Steber, George Steinmetz, Hank Willis Thomas, Massimo Vitali, Alex Webb, Carrie Mae Weems, Steve Winter, and Joel-Peter Witkin. Interviewers have included: Donald Antrim, Leah Bendavid-Val, Chris Boot, Garnette Cadogan, Alex Chadwick, Geoff Dyer, Steve Fine, Vicki Goldberg, MaryAnne Golon, John Gossage, Darius Himes, Jean-François Leroy, Sally Mann, Kathy Ryan, David Quammen, David Levi Strauss, Scott Thode, Anne Wilkes Tucker, and Deborah Willis.

FAMILY TIES

1. See for example Alan Mairson, "Befriending Thugs Who Love the Planet," *Society Matters*, July 13, 2009, http://societymatters.org/2009/07/13/befriending-thugs-who-love-the-planet/.

2. Ruth Maclean, "Violence Erupts after Gabon Election as Incumbent Ali Bongo Named Victor," *Guardian*, August 31, 2016, https://www.theguardian.com/world/2016/aug/31/gabon-election-results-disputed-incumbent-ali-bongo-victor-jean-ping.

3. Dionne Searcey, "Gabon's Leader Gives Elephants Free Rein: Rural Voters Don't Forget," *New York Times*, August 26, 2016, http://www.nytimes.com/2016/08/27/world/africa/ali-bongo-gabon-election.html?_r=1.

4. On Fay's research, see David Quammen and George Steinmetz, "Tracing the Human Footprint," *National Geographic* 208, no. 3 (September 2005): 2–35.

5. Mike Fay, interview with Alex Chadwick, "African Flyover Reveals Impact of 'Human Footprint,'" *Radio Expeditions*, National Public Radio, aired August 17, 2005, http://www.npr.org/templates/transcript/transcript.php?storyId=4803547.

6. Charles Siebert and Michael Nichols, "Orphans No More," *National Geographic* 220, no. 3 (September 2011): 52.

7. Ibid., p. 54. For further information on elephant intelligence, see Ferris Jabr, "The Science Is In: Elephants Are Even Smarter Than We Realized," *Scientific American* online, February 26, 2014, http://www.scientificamerican.com/article/the-science-is-in-elephants-are-even-smarter-than-we-realized-video/.

8. J. Michael Fay and Michael Nichols, "Ivory Wars: Last Stand in Zakouma," *National Geographic* 211, no. 3 (March 2007): 34–65.

9. Luis Arranz, in Nichols, *Earth to Sky*, p. 74.

10. Fay and Nichols, "Ivory Wars," *National Geographic*, p. 54.

11. Ibid., p. 44.

12. Nichols, *Earth to Sky*, p. 50.

13. Bryan Christy and Brent Stirton, "Tracking Ivory," *National Geographic* 228, no. 3 (September 2015): 30–59.

14. Ibid., p. 37.

15. Ibid., p. 58.

16. Willy Lowry, "Ring of Elephant Poachers Broken Up by Tanzanian Authorities," *New York Times*, February 8, 2016, http://www.nytimes.com/2016/02/09/world/africa/ring-of-elephant-poachers-broken-up-by-tanzanian-authorities.html?_r=0.

17. David Quammen and Michael Nichols, "Family Ties: The Elephants of Samburu," *National Geographic* 214, no. 3 (September 2008): 34–69.

18. Nichols, *Earth to Sky,* p. 88.

19. Ibid., p. 89.

20. See Amy Yee, "Poaching Leaves Elephant Daughters in Charge: As Illegal Hunting Thins Out the Ranks of Matriarchs, Their Daughters Are Taking Over as Leaders of Their Social Groups," *New York Times,* July 4, 2016, http://www.nytimes.com/2016/07/05/science/female-elephants-follow-in-their-mothers-footsteps.html?emc=eta1&_r=0.

21. David Sheldrick was a forward-thinking national-park warden for more than twenty years who transformed the eastern area of Tsavo. He died in 1977, six months after being transferred to Nairobi to direct the planning unit for all of Kenya's wildlife areas.

22. Siebert and Nichols, "Orphans No More," *National Geographic,* p. 50.

23. Nichols, *Earth to Sky,* p. 138.

24. "Orphan's Project," DSWT website: http://www.sheldrickwildlifetrust.org/asp/orphans.asp. Accessed November 29, 2016.

25. The reference is to Joy Adamson's 1960 book *Born Free,* about the release of Elsa, an orphaned lion cub she and her husband George Adamson had raised, into Kenya's wild. The book was the basis of the popular 1966 film of the same title.

26. Charles Siebert, "An Elephant Crackup?" *New York Times Magazine,* October 8, 2006, http://www.nytimes.com/2006/10/08/magazine/08elephant.html.

27. See Ellen Nakashima and Steven Mufson, "U.S., China Vow Not to Engage in Economic Cyberespionage," *Washington Post,* September 25, 2015, https://www.washingtonpost.com/national/us-china-vow-not-to-engage-in-economic-cyberespionage/2015/09/25/90e74b6a-63b9-11e5-8e9e-dce8a2a2a679_story.html.

28. Ibid.

29. Jada F. Smith, "U.S. Bans Commercial Trade of African Elephant Ivory," *New York Times,* June 2, 2016, http://www.nytimes.com/2016/06/03/world/africa/elephant-ivory-ban.html?_r=1.

30. According to research by Lucy Vigne and Esmond Martin for Save the Elephants. The full study will be published in 2017.

31. Edward Wong and Jeffrey Gettleman, "China Bans Its Ivory Trade, Moving Against Elephant Poaching," *New York Times,* December 30, 2016, http://www.nytimes.com/2016/12/30/world/asia/china-ivory-ban-elephants.html?emc=edit_na_20161230&nlid=50687521&ref=headline.

32. Esmond Martin and Lucy Vigne, "Vietnam's Illegal Ivory Trade Threatens Africa's Elephants," *Save the Elephants* website, July 19, 2016, http://savetheelephants.org/about-ste/press-media/?detail=vietnams-illegal-ivory-trade-threatens-africa-s-elephants.

33. See Niraj Chokshi and Jeffrey Gettleman, "African Elephant Population Dropped 30 Percent in 7 Years," *New York Times,* September 1, 2016, http://www.nytimes.com/2016/09/02/world/africa/african-elephant-population-dropped-30-percent-in-7years.html?emc=edit_tnt_20160902&nlid=50687521&tntemail0=y. For more information, see the Great Elephant Census final results: http://www.greatelephantcensus.com/final-report. Accessed November 29, 2016.

34. "Poaching Behind Worst African Elephant Losses in 25 Years," IUCN website, September 23, 2016, https://www.iucn.org/news/poaching-behind-worst-african-elephant-losses-25-years---iucn-report.

35. The objection to this listing seems to have been grounded in interpretations of the CITES mandate, and the necessary biological criteria for such a listing. There were also concerns because of procedural rules allowing for "reservations"—which paradoxically might result in allowing for ivory trade not currently possible. According to Resson Kantai Duff of STE, there was "the widely held understanding that if the listing did happen, pro-trade countries would have taken a 'reservation.' This would mean that these countries would willfully step outside of the convention and exercise their right to trade. This would have been disastrous for elephants, far more disastrous than how it stands now." Lee White sees the threat of such reservations as "blackmail." For further information on this vote, see the Convention on International Trade in Endangered Species of Wild Fauna and Flora, "Reservations" page: https://www.cites.org/eng/app/reserve_intro.php. Accessed November 29, 2016.

36. Uhuru Kenyatta, quoted in Jeffrey Gettleman, "Kenya Burns Elephant Ivory Worth $105 Million to Defy Poachers," *New York Times,* April 30, 2016, http://www.nytimes.com/2016/05/01/world/africa/kenya-burns-poach...u-kenyatta.html?emc=edit_tnt_20160506&nlid=50687521&tntemail0=y.

THE PRESIDENT AND PRAIRIE CREEK

1. Mark Jenkins and Ian Nichols, "In the Presence of Giants," *National Geographic* 213, no. 1 (January 2008): 88–105.

2. Joshua Foer and Ian Nichols, "The Truth about Chimps," *National Geographic* 217, no. 2 (February 2010): 130–45.

3. James Balog's "Extreme Ice Survey" has been featured in a number of publications, including *Extreme Ice Now: Vanishing Glaciers and Changing Climate: A Progress Report* (Washington, DC: National Geographic Books, 2009). Balog's project was also the subject of the 2012 documentary film *Chasing Ice,* directed by Jeff Orlowski, Submarine Deluxe, U.S.A., 1 hour 15 mins., color.

4. James Balog, *Tree: A New Vision of the American Forest* (New York: Sterling, 2004).

5. Joel K. Bourne Jr. and Michael Nichols, "Redwoods: The Super Trees," *National Geographic* 216, no. 4 (October 2009): 28–59.

6. J. Michael Fay and Michael Christopher Brown, "The Redwoods Point the Way," *National Geographic* 216, no. 4 (October 2009): 60–63.

7. David Quammen and Michael Nichols, "Sequoias: Scaling a Forest Giant," *National Geographic* 222, no. 6 (December 2012): 28–41.

8. "Explorers Bio: Stephen Sillett," *National Geographic* online, http://www.nationalgeographic.com/explorers/bios/stephen-sillett/. Accessed October 31, 2016.

9. *The Big Lebowski,* 1998, directed by Ethan and Joel Coen and starring Jeff Bridges. *Gimme Shelter,* 1970, directed by Albert and David Maysles and Charlotte Zwerin, documentary about the Rolling Stones.

10. See Jes Burns, "Spotted Owls Still Losing Ground in Northwest Forests," *EarthFix,* December 9, 2015, http://www.opb.org/news/article/spotted-owls-still-losing-ground-in-northwest-forests/.

11. Ibid.

12. Bob Sallinger, quoted in Sarah Deweerdt, "Killing Barred Owls to Keep Spotted Owls Breathing," *Newsweek,* May 17, 2015, http://www.newsweek.com/killing-barred-owls-keep-spotted-owls-breathing-332540.

HARVEST

The chapter title "Harvest" is taken from Neil Young's 1971 song and album of the same name. Produced by Neil Young and Elliot Mazer; Reprise Records (released 1972).

1. Edward Weston, *Edward Weston: The Flame of Recognition,* ed. Nancy Newhall (New York: Aperture, 1965), p. 8.

2. George B. Schaller, *The Serengeti Lion: A Study of Predator-Prey Relations* (1972; Chicago: University of Chicago Press, 1976), pp. 405–6.

3. Craig Packer, *Lions in the Balance: Man-Eaters, Manes, and Men with Guns* (Chicago: University of Chicago Press, 2015).

4. David Quammen and Michael Nichols, "The Short Happy Life of a Serengeti Lion," *National Geographic* 224, no. 2 (August 2013): 28–61.

5. David Quammen and Brent Stirton, "Living with Lions," ibid., pp. 62–77.

6. Packer, *Lions in the Balance,* pp. 215–16.

7. Jane Goodall, "Jane Discusses the Horrors of Trophy Hunting," *Good for All News, Jane Goodall Institute,* August 20, 2015, http://news.janegoodall.org/2015/08/20/jane-discusses-the-horrors-of-trophy-hunting/.

8. "Listing a Species as a Threatened or Endangered Species," Section 4, Endangered Species Act, U.S. Fish and Wildlife Service, https://www.fws.gov/endangered/esa-library/pdf/listing.pdf. Accessed October 26, 2016.

9. Erica Goode, "After Cecil Furor, U.S. Aims to Protect Lions through Endangered Species Act," *New York Times*, December 20, 2015, http://www.nytimes.com/2015/12/21/science/us-to-protect-african-lions-under-endangered-species-act.html?_r=0.

10. Ibid.

11. "Facing the Lion: By Maasai Warriors," Maasai Association, http://www.maasai-association.org/lion.html. Accessed October 20, 2016.

12. David Quammen, "Can Good Come from Maasai Lion Killings in the Serengeti?" *National Geographic* online, April 29, 2014, http://news.nationalgeographic.com/news/2014/04/140428-serengeti-ngorongoro-conservation-area-tanzania-lions-maasai-craig-packer-lion-guardians-world/.

13. See the Lion Guardians website: http://lionguardians.org/about-us/. Accessed November 12, 2016.

14. Craig Packer, interview by Simon Worrall, "This Lion Expert Was Banned from Tanzania for Exposing Corruption," *Book Talk*, *National Geographic*, September 16, 2015, http://news.nationalgeographic.com/2015/09/150916-book-talk-simon-worrall-craig-packer-lions-serengeti-tanzania-trophy-hunting-africa-conservation/.

15. David Quammen, *Natural Acts: A Sidelong View of Science and Nature* (New York: Norton, 2008).

16. e. e. cummings, "in Just-" (first published 1923), in cummings, *100 Selected Poems* (New York: Grove Press, 1959), p. 5.

17. Rich Cohen and Robert Clark, "Sugar: Why We Can't Resist It," *National Geographic* 224, no. 2 (August 2013): 78–97.

18. Bill Marr, in Amanda Fiegl and Robert Clark, "Behind the Cover: August 2013," *National Geographic* online, August 2, 2013, http://news.nationalgeographic.com/news/behind-the-cover-august-2013.

YOU CAN'T ALWAYS GET WHAT YOU WANT

The chapter title "You Can't Always Get What You Want" is taken from the Rolling Stones song of the same name on their 1969 album *Let It Bleed*, written by Mick Jagger and Keith Richards. Produced by Jimmy Miller; Decca Records (UK) and London Records (USA).

1. John Muir, "The Wild Parks and Forest Reservations of the West" (1987), in *Essential Muir: A Selection of John Muir's Best Writings*, ed. by Fred D. White (Berkeley, CA: Heyday, 2006), p. 119.

2. John Muir, quoted in Patricia Randolph, "What We Can Do to Make a Difference," Madravenspeak, *Wisconsin Wildlife Ethic-Vote Our Wildlife*, April 19, 2009, https://wiwildlifeethic.org/2012/04/19/what-we-can-do-to-make-a-difference-17/.

3. With very few exceptions, the national parks, forests, and wildlife refuges do not have fences. Those that do—such as the National Elk Refuge between Jackson, Wyoming, and Grand Teton, which has a fence for a few miles along the western side where highway 89 runs north of Jackson—do so to keep animals from crossing the highway in that area, but they don't enclose the refuge. The private lands within the ecosystem boundaries (which aren't exact) are often fenced for cattle or sheep; but the fencing doesn't keep the wildlife out; it keeps the domestic animals from wandering away. Houses in the private land areas often have fences as well.

4. For examples of this no-selfie signage, see the Ministry of Internal Affairs of the Russian Federation, https://mvd.ru/upload/site1/folder_page/006/158/477/Selfie2015.pdf. Accessed December 5, 2016.

5. John Muir, "The Yellowstone National Park" (1898), in Muir, *Wilderness Essays* (Layton, UT: Gibbs Smith, 2015), p. 183.

6. See the 2015 *Annual Report of the Interagency Bison Management Plan*, p. 10, http://www.ibmp.info/Library/AnnualReports/2015_IBMP_Annual Report_final.pdf. Two hundred twenty-three bison were harvested in the public and tribal hunt (outside the park boundary); approximately 519 were captured at the Stephens Creek facility in the northern management area—inside the park—and shipped to processing facilities in Montana where they were killed, or died in confinement.

7. Christopher Ketcham, "The Bison Roundup the Government Wants to Hide," *New York Times*, February 15, 2016, http://www.nytimes.com/2016/02/15/opinion/the-bison-roundup-the-government-wants-to-hide.html?_r=0.

8. Edward O. Wilson, *Half-Earth: Our Planet's Fight for Life* (New York: Liveright, 2016).

9. Edward O. Wilson, "The Global Solution to Extinction," *New York Times*, March 13, 2016.

10. Currently wolves are managed by the appropriate state, tribal, or federal agencies. Management authority depends on status and location of subpopulations. No hunting is allowed in the park. Outside the park, regulated hunting is allowed in Montana and Idaho and managed by those states. In Wyoming wolf hunting was suspended in September 2014 due to a federal court ruling.

11. See David Quammen, Michael Nichols, David Guttenfelder, Charlie Hamilton James, Erika Larsen, and Joe Riis, "Yellowstone: America's Wild Idea," *National Geographic* 229, no. 5, special issue (May 2016).

12. "National Geographic Society and 21st Century Fox Agree to Expand Partnership," Press Room, *National Geographic*, September 9, 2015, http://press.nationalgeographic.com/2015/09/09/national-geographic-society-21st-century-fox-agree-to-expand-partnership/.

13. On August 26, 2015, Rupert Murdoch tweeted: "A climate change skeptic not a denier. Sept UN meets in NY with endless alarmist nonsense from u know whom! Pessimists always seen as sages." See David Wright, "Rupert Murdoch Links Regulations, Climate Change 'Nonsense' to Global Financial Turmoil," *CNN Politics*, August 27, 2015, http://www.cnn.com/2015/08/27/politics/rupert-murdoch-links-regulations-climate-change-nonsense-to-global-financial-turmoil/.

14. Gary E. Knell, "Our Unchanging Commitment," *National Geographic* 228, no. 6 (December 2015): 6.

CODA: THE WOODS

1. See "The Assisi Declarations: Messages on Humanity and Nature, from Buddhism, Christianity, Hinduism, Islam & Judaism," issued September 29, 1986: http://www.arcworld.org/downloads/the%20assisi%20declarations.pdf. See also Cormac Cullinan, *Wild Law: A Manifesto for Earth Justice* (Totnes, UK: Green Books, 2003); Steven M. Wise, *Drawing the Line: Science and the Case for Animal Rights* (Cambridge, MA: Perseus, 2002); Jo Edwards and Martin Palmer, eds., *Holy Ground: The Guide to Faith and Ecology* (Northamptonshire, UK: Pilkington, 1997); *Voices from Religions on Sustainable Development*, introduction by Gerd Müller (Bonn, Germany: German Federal Ministry for Economic Cooperation and Development, 2016); and John Grim and Mary Evelyn Tucker, *Ecology and Religion* (Washington, DC: Island Press, 2014).

2. Wilson, *Half-Earth*, p. 211.

SELECTED BIBLIOGRAPHY

MICHAEL NICHOLS MONOGRAPHS (in chronological order)

Gorilla: Struggle for Survival in the Virungas. Edited by Nan Richardson. Essay by George B. Schaller. New York: Aperture, 1989.

The Great Apes: Between Two Worlds. Texts by Jane Goodall, George B. Schaller, and Mary Smith. Washington, DC: National Geographic Society, 1993.

Keepers of the Kingdom: The New American Zoo. Essays by Jon Charles Coe, William Conway, David Hancocks, Jack Hanna, Edward J. Maruska, and Michael H. Robinson. New York: Thomasson-Grant & Lickle, 1996.

Nichols and Geoffrey C. Ward. *The Year of the Tiger.* Washington, DC: National Geographic Society, 1998.

Nichols and Jane Goodall. *Brutal Kinship.* New York: Aperture, 1999.

Nichols and J. Michael Fay. *The Last Place on Earth* with *Megatransect: Mike Fay's Journals.* Foreword by David Quammen. 2 vols. Washington, DC: National Geographic Society, 2005.

Earth to Sky: Among Africa's Elephants, A Species in Crisis. New York: Aperture, 2013.

ARTICLES FEATURING NICHOLS'S PHOTOGRAPHS IN MAGAZINES AND JOURNALS (in chronological order)

Shields, Mitchell J., and Michael K. Nichols. "The Lure of the Abyss." *Geo* 1, no. 2 (June 1979): 74–93.

Cahill, Tim, and Michael K. Nichols. "Venezuela: Exploring a Lost World." *Geo* 2, no. 3 (March 1980): 58–99.

Shields, Mitchell J., and Michael K. Nichols. "Riding the Torrent." *Geo* 2, no. 8 (August 1980): 56–67.

Cahill, Tim, and Michael K. Nichols. "Gorilla Tactics." *Geo* 3, no. 12 (December 1981): 100–116.

Shields, Mitchell J., and Michael K. Nichols. "The Rope." *Geo* 5, no. 2 (February 1983): 24–35.

Cahill, Tim, and Michael K. Nichols. "Berggorillas: Die Milden Wilden." *Geo* (German ed.) 5, no. 5 (May 1983): 88–102.

Roberts, David (and Michael Nichols). "Rafting the 'Eater of Men.'" *Geo* 6, no. 2 (February 1984): 58–71.

"Missions impossibles." *Photo* 200 (May 1984): 158–71.

Cahill, Tim, and Michael Nichols. "Fear of Frying." *Rolling Stone,* no. 457 (September 26, 1985): 35–40, 117–18, 124.

———. "Nick Danger: Boy Photographer." *San Francisco Examiner Image–The Magazine of Northern California* (November 3, 1985): 18–23.

———. "Rope Tricks." *San Francisco Examiner Image–The Magazine of Northern California* (December 7, 1986): 31–36.

Roberts, David, and Michael Nichols. "A Labyrinth Called Lechuguilla." *Smithsonian* 19, no. 8 (November 1988): 52–65.

Nichols, Michael, and Anthony DeCurtis. "The Scorched Earth." *Rolling Stone* 546 (February 23, 1989): 40–49.

Goodall, Jane, and Michael K. Nichols. "Das Verhängnis, uns Menschen verwandt zu sein." *Geo* (German ed.) 13, no. 7 July 1991): 66–88.

Cahill, Tim, and Michael Nichols. "The Splendors of Lechuguilla Cave." *National Geographic* 179, no. 3 (March 1991): 34–59.

Linden, Eugene, and Michael Nichols. "A Curious Kinship: Apes and Humans." *National Geographic* 181, no. 3 (March 1992): 2–45.

Tarpy, Cliff, and Michael Nichols. "New Zoos: Taking Down the Bars." *National Geographic* 184, no. 1 (July 1993): 2–37.

Chadwick, Douglas, and Michael Nichols. "Ndoki: Last Place on Earth." *National Geographic* 188, no. 1 (July 1995): 2–45.

Salopek, Paul F., and Michael Nichols. "Gorillas and Humans: An Uneasy Truce." *National Geographic* 188, no. 4 (October 1995): 72–83.

Schaller, George B., and Michael Nichols. "Gentle Gorillas, Turbulent Times." *National Geographic* 188, no. 4 (October 1995): 58–71.

Miller, Peter, and Michael Nichols. "Jane Goodall: Crusading for Chimps and Humans." *National Geographic* 188, no. 6. (December 1995): 102–28.

Gilbert, Bil, and Michael Nichols. "New Ideas in the Air at the National Zoo." *Smithsonian* (June 1996): 32–43.

Ward, Geoffrey C., and Michael Nichols. "Making Room for Wild Tigers." *National Geographic* 192, no. 6 (December 1997): 2–35.

Nichols, Michael. "Sita: Life of a Wild Tigress." *National Geographic* 192, no. 6 (December 1997): 36–47.

McRae, Michael, and Michael Nichols. "Orphan Gorillas: Fighting to Survive in the Wild." *National Geographic* 197, no. 2 (February 2000): 84–97.

Quammen, David, and Michael Nichols. "Megatransect," *National Geographic* 198, no. 4 (October 2000): 2–29.

———. "The Green Abyss: Megatransect II." *National Geographic* 199, no. 3 (March 2001): 2–45.

———. "End of the Line: Megatransect III." *National Geographic* 200, no. 2 (August 2001): 74–103.

"The Forest through the Trees: Dr. Mike Fay and the Mega-Transect in Africa." Photographs and extended captions by Michael Nichols. Introduction by Melissa Harris. *Aperture* 167 (Summer 2002): 42–55.

Morell, Virginia, and Michael Nichols. "Kings of the Hill?" *National Geographic* 202, no. 5 (November 2002): 100–121.

Quammen, David, and Michael Nichols. "Jane Goodall in the Wild." *National Geographic* 203, no. 4 (April 2003): 90–103.

———. "Saving Africa's Eden." *National Geographic* 204, no. 3 (September 2003): 50–77.

Fay, J. Michael, and Michael Nichols. "Land of the Surfing Hippos." *National Geographic* 206, no. 2 (August 2004): 100–127.

Morell, Virginia, and Michael Nichols. "Our Grandest Canyon." *National Geographic* 209, no. 1 (January 2006): 36–55.

Warren, Lynne, Michael Nichols, and Fritz Hoffmann. "Panda, Inc." *National Geographic* 210, no. 1 (July 2006): 42–59.

Fay, J. Michael, and Michael Nichols. "Ivory Wars: Last Stand in Zakouma." *National Geographic* 211, no. 3 (March 2007): 34–65.

Quammen, David, and Michael Nichols. "Family Ties: The Elephants of Samburu." *National Geographic* 214, no. 3 (September 2008): 34–69.

Bourne Jr., Joel K., and Michael Nichols. "Redwoods: The Super Trees." *National Geographic* 216, no. 4 (October 2009): 28–59.

Siebert, Charles, and Michael Nichols. "Orphans No More." *National Geographic* 220, no. 3 (September 2011): 40–65.

Quammen, David, and Michael Nichols, "Sequoias: Scaling a Forest Giant." *National Geographic* 222, no. 6 (December 2012): 28–41.

———. "The Short Happy Life of a Serengeti Lion." *National Geographic* 224, no. 2 (August 2013): 28–61.

Quammen, David, with Michael Nichols, David Guttenfelder, Charlie Hamilton James, Erika Larsen, and Joe Riis. "Yellowstone: America's Wild Idea." *National Geographic* 229, no. 5, special issue (May 2016).

FOR FURTHER REFERENCE: BOOKS (in alphabetical order)

Abbey, Edward. *Desert Solitaire: A Season in the Wilderness.* New York: Simon and Schuster, 1968.

———. *Postcards from Ed: Dispatches and Salvos from an American Iconoclast.* Edited by David Petersen. Minneapolis: Milkweed, 2006.

Berger, John. "Why Look at Animals?" (1977). In *About Looking,* pp. 1–26. New York: Pantheon, 1980.

Cahill, Tim. *Hold the Enlightenment.* New York: Vintage, 2003.

———. *Jaguars Ripped My Flesh.* New York: Vintage, 1987.

———. *A Wolverine Is Eating My Leg.* New York: Vintage, 1989.

Dallaire, Roméo. *Shake Hands with the Devil: The Failure of Humanity in Rwanda.* Foreword by Samantha Power. Philadelphia: Da Capo, 2003.

Douglas-Hamilton, Iain, and Oria Douglas-Hamilton. *Among the Elephants.* Foreword by Niko Tinbergen. New York: Viking, 1975.

———. *Battle for the Elephants.* Edited by Brian Jackman. New York: Viking, 1992.

Fossey, Dian. *Gorillas in the Mist.* Boston: Houghton Mifflin, 1983.

Gourevitch, Philip. *We Wish to Inform You That Tomorrow We Will Be Killed with Our Families: Stories from Rwanda.* New York: Farrar, Straus and Giroux, 1998.

Heltne, Paul G., and Linda A. Marquardt, eds. *Understanding Chimpanzees.* Foreword by Jane Goodall. Cambridge, MA: Harvard University Press, in cooperation with the Chicago Academy of Sciences, 1989.

Leopold, Aldo. *A Sand County Almanac, with Essays on Conservation from Round River.* New York: Ballantine, 1978.

Linden, Eugene. *The Ragged Edge of the World: Encounters at the Frontier Where Modernity, Wildlands, and Indigenous Peoples Meet.* New York: Viking, 2011.

Matthiessen, Peter. *The Tree Where Man Was Born.* New York: Dutton, 1972.

Moore, Charles, and Michael S. Durham. *Powerful Days: The Civil Rights Photography of Charles Moore.* Tuscaloosa: University of Alabama Press, 2007.

Muir, John. "The Wild Parks and Forest Reservations of the West" (1897). In *Essential Muir: A Selection of John Muir's Best Writings.* Edited by Fred D. White, pp. 119–26. Berkeley, CA: Heyday, 2006.

———. "The Yellowstone National Park" (1898). In *Wilderness Essays,* pp. 178–219. Layton, UT: Gibbs Smith, 2015.

Packer, Craig. *Lions in the Balance: Man-Eaters, Manes, and Men with Guns.* Chicago: University of Chicago Press, 2015.

Preston, Richard. *The Wild Trees: A Story of Passion and Daring.* New York: Random House, 2007.

Quammen, David. *Monster of God: The Man-Eating Predator in the Jungles of History and the Mind.* New York: Norton, 2003.

———. *Natural Acts: A Sidelong View of Science and Nature.* Revised and expanded edition, with a new introduction. New York: Norton, 2008.

———. *Spillover: Animal Infections and the Next Human Pandemic.* New York: Norton, 2012.

———. *Wild Thoughts from Wild Places.* New York: Scribner, 2004.

Sarno, Louis. *Bayaka: The Extraordinary Music of the Babenzélé Pygmies and Sounds of Their Forest Home.* Roslyn, NY: Ellipsis Arts, 1995.

———. *Song from the Forest: My Life among the Pygmies.* Foreword by Alex Shoumatoff. Afterword by Michael Obert. San Antonio, TX: Trinity University Press, 2015.

Schaller, George B. *The Deer and the Tiger: A Study of Wildlife in India* (1964). Chicago: University of Chicago Press, 1974.

———. *The Mountain Gorilla: Ecology and Behavior.* Chicago: University of Chicago Press, 1963.

———. *A Naturalist and Other Beasts: Tales from a Life in the Field.* San Francisco: Sierra Club, 2010.

———. *The Serengeti Lion: A Study of Predator-Prey Relations* (1972). Chicago: University of Chicago Press, 1976.

———. *The Year of the Gorilla* (1964). Chicago: University of Chicago Press, 2010.

Sheldrick, Daphne. *Love, Life, and Elephants: An African Love Story.* New York: Farrar, Straus and Giroux, 2012.

Smith, Douglas W., and Gary Ferguson. *Decade of the Wolf: Returning the Wild to Yellowstone.* Revised and updated edition. Guilford, CT: Lyons, 2012.

Stone, Christopher D. *Should Trees Have Standing? Toward Legal Rights for Natural Objects* (1972). Los Altos, CA: William Kaufmann, 1974.

Thoreau, Henry David. *Walden and Other Writings* (1854). Edited by Brooks Atkinson. New York: Modern Library, 1950.

Ward, Geoffrey C., and Diane Raines Ward. *Tiger-Wallahs: Encounters with the Men Who Tried to Save the Greatest of the Great Cats.* New York: Harper Collins, 1993.

Wilson, Edward O. *Half-Earth: Our Planet's Fight for Life.* New York: Liveright, 2016.

FOR FURTHER REFERENCE: ESSAYS AND ARTICLES
(in alphabetical order)

Begley, Sharon, and Brent Stirton. "A Globalized World's New Extinction Threats." *Newsweek,* no. 6 (August 6, 2007): 22–23.

Christy, Bryan, and Brent Stirton. "Tracking Ivory." *National Geographic* 228, no. 3 (September 2015): 30–59.

Draper, Robert, and Brent Stirton. "The Battle for Virunga: Saving One of the World's Most Dangerous Parks." *National Geographic* 230, no. 1 (July 2016): 55–83.

Foer, Joshua, and Ian Nichols. "The Truth About Chimps." *National Geographic* 217, no. 2 (February 2010): 130–45.

Fossey, Dian. "A Grim Struggle for Survival: The Imperiled Mountain Gorilla." *National Geographic* 159, no. 4 (April 1981): 501–5, 511–23.

Guynup, Sharon. "Tigers in Traditional Chinese Medicine: A Universal Apothecary." *National Geographic* online, April 29, 2014. http://voices.nationalgeographic.com/2014/04/29/tigers-in-traditional-chinese-medicine-a-universal-apothecary/.

Jabr, Ferris. "The Science Is In: Elephants Are Even Smarter Than We Realized," *Scientific American* online, February 26, 2014. http://www.scientificamerican.com/article/the-science-is-in-elephants-are-even-smarter-than-we-realized-video/.

Jenkins, Mark, and Ian Nichols. "In the Presence of Giants." *National Geographic* 213, no. 1 (January 2008): 88–105.

Linden, Eugene. "Inside the World's Last Eden," *Time* 140, no. 2 (July 13, 1992): 62–69.

Lopez, Barry. "Unbounded Wilderness." *Aperture* 120 (Summer 1990): 2–15.

McRae, Michael. "How the Nomad Found Home." *Outside* (October 21, 2011). https://www.outsideonline.com/1887471/how-nomad-found-home.

Quammen, David, and George Steinmetz. "Tracing the Human Footprint." *National Geographic* 208, no. 3 (September 2005): 2–35.

Quammen, David, and Brent Stirton. "Living with Lions." *National Geographic* 224, no. 2 (August 2013): 62–77.

Walsh, Peter D. "Protecting Apes Could Backfire." *New York Times,* September 27, 2015.

Wilson, Edward O. "The Global Solution to Extinction." *New York Times,* March 13, 2016.

INDEX

Page numbers in *italics* indicate illustrations.

ACKNOWLEDGMENTS

There are so many people to whom I owe thanks for their help in writing this book—some who didn't even know they were helping. I am forever grateful to the late Michael E. Hoffman, without whom, in so many ways, this book would not have been possible. Other forces of nature were also tremendously inspiring and are much missed: Lizzie Berger, with her fervent ideas on the notion of biography (and pretty much everything); Chuck Bowden, brilliant writer-warrior for the Earth and all its creatures and ecosystems; and Merce Cunningham, who taught me to see the most elemental in dance, and the dance in the wild. I am thankful to and for you all.

I have been enormously lucky. Writing a biography of a well-liked and admired individual such as Nick is an open-sesame: people are happy to speak about their experiences with him—in the field, growing up, as a friend, colleague, boss, husband and father, son and brother.

This biography was always meant to embrace Nick's life as a filter through which to speak to the critical conservation issues his work addresses. I am indebted to the many scientists, conservationists, and researchers I spoke with for their guidance and perspectives, as well as to their support staffs. My thanks go to the following scientists and their teams:

Regarding great apes: Jane Goodall and co.: Mary Lewis and Susanna Name; Bill Wallauer; Douglas Cress; Jenny and Jimmy Desmond; Hugo van Lawick ("Grub"); and Craig Sholley.

Regarding big cats: Alan Rabinowitz, Luke Hunter, and John Goodrich at Panthera; and Craig Packer—thank you all for being so available.

Regarding elephants: Luis Arranz; Iain Douglas-Hamilton and the staff at Save the Elephants, especially David Daballen, Gemma Francis, Resson Kantai Duff, and Jerenimo Lepirei—thank you also for the remarkable days at STE's research camp in Samburu. Daniel Lentipo kindly accompanied me to the STE camp and shared his recollections about working with Nick—thank you. I am grateful also to Angela Sheldrick and her husband, Robert Carr-Hartley, along with Edwin Lusichi—thank you for the extraordinary time at the David Sheldrick Wildlife Trust orphanage in Nairobi.

Regarding Yellowstone: Dan Wenk, Doug Smith and Kira Cassidy, Kerry Gunther, Arthur Middleton, and Tammy Wert—thank you all for your guidance and points of view, and for the time in Yellowstone.

Regarding Ndoki and the Megatransect: Dave Morgan and Tomo Nishihara, I am indebted to you both for making yourselves so accessible to me and for your many consultations and insights. Koumba Kombila, thank you for helping me to understand the issues behind Gabon Bleu. Lee White, I am grateful for your clarifications about recent decisions governing the ivory trade. And Jane Sievert, thank you for the reflections on your time with Nick and Mike Fay on the coast of Gabon.

Regarding tall trees: Steve Sillett and Jim Campbell-Spickler, endless thanks for your ongoing input, and for a most memorable day in the Prairie Creek forest. Steve, thank you also for letting us reproduce your photograph in this volume.

Lowell Diller, thank you for the discussion of Nick and the northern spotted owl. I am grateful to John Kramer for your memories of Nick's early river runs. Thank you to Richard Ruggiero for your recollections of Mike Fay and the early days as Peace Corps volunteers in the Central African Republic, and at the Bomassa camp.

Finally, regarding elephants, lowland gorillas, naïve chimpanzees, redwoods, transects, park building, coastal waters—really all things conservation: thank you, Mike Fay. It was in Washington, DC, back in 2012 that you first spoke with me about your work with Nick. And then—in spite of yourself—you allowed me to visit in Gabon where, over the course of ten days, you set forth so much of what matters to you. I am enormously grateful for your time, your insights, your passion, and your work.

I am deeply thankful to the many writers with whom Nick has worked, and whom I have harassed incessantly over the past several years. I'm especially indebted to David Quammen for your time on two occasions in Bozeman, for answering my endless queries via e-mail and phone, and for sharing with me parts of your Megatransect journals. This book has so benefited from your generosity and eloquence.

To Tim Cahill, thanks for the time you spent with me in Livingston recounting your gonzo adventures with Nick and looking through photographs of your time together—as well as all the ongoing follow-up.

Mitch Shields, thank you for your time and graciousness, and for recalling the experience of Nick's first published story almost as if it were yesterday. Doug Chadwick, Eugene Linden, and Geoff Ward: thank you all for your evocative memories of traveling and working with Nick.

As much as I bothered the writers and the scientists during the course of this project, Nathan Williamson—Nick's assistant, videographer, and all-around-everything in the field for over ten years—had to put up with more. Nathan, I suspect you didn't really know what you signed up for when you agreed to speak with me in the Serengeti back in 2012. Thank you for being so kind, candid, and for sharing your insights and observations, as well as for allowing us to publish your photograph of Nick at work.

All who have worked with Nick in the field—assistants, videographers, pilots, hide and blind builders, technical geniuses, and many others—have been extraordinary. Some are photographers whom Nick has mentored, and who are now established in their own right; others have gone on to conduct their own important wildlife research. All have been gracious and open as they have discussed their time working with Nick. Thank you: Neeld Messler, who assisted on so many early stories; Bryan Harvey, who shared journals and footage with me; Erin Harvey, who offered notes and footage as well; Daniel Rosengren, for answering my many questions about the Serengeti lions; John Brown, for your memories of the Megatransect; Roy Toft, for your vivid descriptions of working with Nick in India, as well as for your photographs from the field; and Ronan Donovan, for reflecting on your work with Nick in Yellowstone, and also for letting us reproduce your photograph of Nick.

Vince Musi, I am so grateful for your insights about LOOK3 and Nick's M.O. Thank you also to Will Kerner, Jessica Nagle, Andrew Owen, and Jenna Pirog for discussing the evolution of LOOK3, as well as many other ideas.

At Nick's studio, Chloe Delaney and Kaya Lee Berne were extremely helpful in the preparation of materials for this biography—thanks to you both. Nick's editors, curators, and colleagues at the publications and venues that have featured his photographs have also been wonderful and forthcoming. Jean-François Leroy, I so appreciate your discussing your friendship with Nick and ongoing work with him at Visa pour l'Image in Perpignan.

Regarding Nick's work for *Geo*, I am thankful to Elisabeth Biondi, Christiane Breustedt, Ruth Eichhorn, Steve Ettlinger, and Alice Rose George. Thank you to Laurie Kratochvil for speaking about Nick's work for *Rolling Stone*.

At *National Geographic*—Nick's home for more than a quarter of a century—I have spoken to many past editors, including Bill Allen, Kent Kobersteen, and Mary Smith. I am grateful for your reflections on Nick's growth as a photographer and on the importance of his stories. Ken Geiger spent time explaining to me how Nick's images of tall trees were "stitched" together. Susan Goldberg generously gave permission for us to reproduce *National Geographic* spreads and covers; and Gary Knell—soon after his arrival at National Geographic Society—kindly spoke with me about its mission and his hopes for the future of the organization. Thank you all.

For invaluable collaboration through this project: I appreciate the insights of David Griffin on so many aspects of Nick and his work, and thank you also for letting us reproduce two of your photographs in this biography. Chris Johns, you have been tremendously patient with my questions, and I am so thankful for your time and perspective. My greatest thanks go to Kathy Moran, Nick's editor since the 1990s. Your willingness to reflect back on your work with Nick, your clarity, openness, and generosity with my questions—even in tough moments—are a gift I will always remember, and are so important to this book.

Many of Nick's photographer friends and colleagues graciously discussed with me their take on him and his work. Thank you to James Balog, Charlie Hamilton James, Erika Larsen, and Joe Riis for your recollections. George Steinmetz and Steve Winter—I so appreciate your wonderful characterizations of young Nick, the early Berkeley loft days, and Nick and Reba's open-call slide shows. Donna Ferrato and David Alan Harvey, thank you for the many conversations, and I am very grateful to you both for allowing us to use your photographs. Brent Stirton, I appreciate the context you so often provided, as well as the use of your magazine spreads. Jim Nachtwey, I am very grateful to you for letting us include the beautiful and intense text message you sent to Nick in the Serengeti. Thanks also to photographers Glenn Baeske, John Burcham, Ines Burger, Dennis Dimick, Paul Fusco and his daughter Marina Nims, Jon Golden, Martin Gisborne, Steve Gullick, Mike McCracken, Clay Nordan, Eve Styles, and Peter Wilkins for allowing us to reproduce your photographs. Michelle Peel kindly let us include a photograph by her father, Charles Moore, inscribed to Nick.

For the Muscle Shoals sound, thank you Don Cash, Frankie Frost, Jamie and Ken Kelley, Chuck Lawler, Jean Schulman, and Shannon Wells (also for letting us use your photograph) for so generously sharing your vivid memories of Nick—growing up and later at the University of North Alabama.

I am truly happy that Aperture is my publisher, and grateful to the entire staff, especially my wonderful colleagues Chris Boot, Lesley Martin, Denise Wolff, Amelia Lang, Taia Kwinter, Richard Gregg, and Kellie McLaughlin. Susan Ciccotti and Sally Knapp, thank you in particular for your sharp eyes on the texts. Sarah Dansberger, I so appreciate your meticulous work on the endnotes and bibliography, and checking all the quotes against their sources. Thank you to Tom Bollier for your careful copy work, and to Nicole Moulaison and Nelson Chan for your critical attention to all production details.

I have had the great fortune and pleasure of collaborating with Yolanda Cuomo since the early 1990s—as the designer of so many books I've edited, as well as on *Aperture* magazine for more than a decade when I was its editor. For your superb eye, visual eloquence, friendship, and generosity of spirit, I am beyond grateful. Yo's associate, Bonnie Briant, is equally generous, as well as patient and talented. Bonnie, I am so thankful for your fastidious work on this book. Thanks, also, to Bobbie Richardson.

To Diana Stoll—my wonderful, deeply intelligent collaborator since the late 1980s when we first worked together at *Artforum*, then for nearly three decades at Aperture—I am eternally grateful and appreciative. You are an extraordinary editor and friend: sensitive, exacting, candid, tough but kind, insightful. Thank you doesn't begin to express it.

Aperture has always served a community of shared interests, an extended family of sorts. The extraordinarily generous individuals who joined forces to help make this book happen are members of that family. Nick, Aperture, and I extend our profoundest thanks to Darlene and Jeff Anderson; Lynne and Harold Honickman; Kellie, John, Julia, and Nate Lehr; Rhett Turner; the JST Foundation; and the Turner Foundation for their support, as well as to Chicago Title; Garrett DeFrenza Stiepel Ryder LLP; Gina and Mark Cousineau; Daniel MacMillan, Farmers and Merchants Bank; Mike Slinger; and the M3K Foundation for additional funding. Finally, we are grateful to Canon for standing behind its longtime ambassador. Thank you all for your continued commitment to Nick and his work, and for playing this crucial role in *A Wild Life*.

Mary Ellen Mark knew I was writing about Nick, and before her death in 2015 she was constantly extolling his courage and the unprecedented intimacy he achieves in his images. Her words on the back cover of this book mean so much to both Nick and me. Likewise, we are deeply honored to have the comments there of George Schaller—who has dedicated his life to several of the species and issues addressed in this book, and is the hero of so many of the scientists and conservationists with whom I spoke for this project. And Robert Farris Thompson—who has spent so much of his life steeped in African art and culture—my heartfelt thanks to you as well. That you both offered to be readers of *A Wild Life* and believe in this book means everything.

Many of my friends and colleagues (okay, all of them) have had to listen to me as I've waylaid conversations over the past five years with talk of this project. Many have contributed ideas and insights. I thank you all—Linda Azarian, Eunice Bet-Mansour, Pieranna Cavalchini, Robin Cembalest, Mary Charlotte Domandi, Tom Eisen, Debbie Freedman, Ella Harris, Jessica Helfand, Karen Hust, Liz Jonas, Fred Kaufman, Ben Ledbetter, Dennis Mullally, Ted Panken, Marianne Petit, Fred Ritchin, Kathy Ryan, Wendy Setzer, Meg Shore, David Levi Strauss, Anne Tucker, Deb Willis, and many others—for putting up with me. The individual who might have been most inclined to say *"Basta!"*—Mark Singer—not only didn't, but indulged every monologue, and in fact read, with his fine writer's eye, a late draft, offering superb feedback, for which I am profoundly grateful. My other ongoing reader was my dad, Stan Harris. To him and my mom, Renee Harris—well, I owe everything.

I am thrilled to be working with Peter Barberie and the Philadelphia Museum of Art on the survey exhibition *Wild: Michael Nichols*.

Finally, Reba Peck, Ian and Eli Nichols, Pat Charette, and the late Joyce Nichols—I am deeply grateful to you for embracing me into your world, for your openness, your time, and your engagement in this project. Over the course of almost five years, I was in many ways an ongoing imposition upon your lives, and yet you did everything you could to help me and facilitate this biography. Reba, your graciousness has helped me so much, and continues to move me enormously. Wow! Thank you. . . .

Nick: hot damn! Thank you for your trust in sharing your wild life with me, your belief in this project, and the extraordinary amount of time you've given it since 2012—not to mention the great gift of allowing me to spend time in the field with you. I hope with all my heart to have done you and your work justice, and that this book may make some difference for the animals, ecosystems, and individuals it celebrates.

—M. H., December 2016

A Wild Life
A Visual Biography of Photographer Michael Nichols
by Melissa Harris
Photographs by Michael Nichols

Aperture gratefully acknowledges the generous
support for *A Wild Life* from

Darlene and Jeffrey Anderson
Lynne and Harold Honickman
Kellie, John, Julia, and Nate Lehr
Rhett L. Turner

JST Foundation
Turner Foundation

Additional support has been generously provided by
Chicago Title
Garrett DeFrenza Stiepel Ryder LLP
Gina and Mark Cousineau
Daniel MacMillan, Farmers and Merchants Bank
Mike Slinger
M3K Foundation

Canon

Front cover: The tiger Charger (camera-trap
photograph), Bandhavgarh National Park,
India, 1996
Back cover and title page: Michael "Nick" Nichols,
self-portrait, Republic of Congo, 1999

Editor: Diana C. Stoll
Designer: Yolanda Cuomo
Associate Designer: Bonnie Briant

Production Director: Nicole Moulaison
Production Manager: Nelson Chan
Executive Managing Editor: Amelia Lang
Senior Text Editor: Susan Ciccotti
Assistant Designer: Bobbie Richardson
Editorial Assistant: Sarah Dansberger
Associate Managing Editor: Taia Kwinter
Proofreader/Copyeditor: Sally Knapp
Copy Work: Tom Bollier
Work Scholars: Giada De Agostinis, Jasphy Zheng
Luis Arranz's Spanish was translated by Paula Kupfer

Additional staff of the Aperture book program
includes: Chris Boot, Executive Director; Sarah
McNear, Deputy Director; Lesley A. Martin, Creative
Director; Kellie McLaughlin, Director of Sales and
Marketing; Richard Gregg, Sales Director, Books

On the occasion of the publication of *A Wild Life*, the
exhibition *Wild: Michael Nichols*, organized by the
Philadelphia Museum of Art, will be presented at the
Museum from June 27 to September 17, 2017.

First edition, 2017
Printed by Artron in China
10 9 8 7 6 5 4 3 2 1

Library of Congress Cataloging-in-Publication Data
Names: Harris, Melissa, author.
Title: A wild life : a visual biography of photographer Michael Nichols /
Melissa Harris.
Description: New York : Aperture, 2017.
Identifiers: LCCN 2016055093 | ISBN 9781597112512
(alk. paper)
Subjects: LCSH: Nichols, Michael. | Photographers--
United States--Biography.
Wildlife photographers--United States--Biography.
Classification: LCC TR140.N4855 H37 2017 | DDC
770.92 [B] --dc23
LC record available at https://lccn.loc.gov/2016055093

To order Aperture books, contact:
+1 212.946.7154
orders@aperture.org

For information about Aperture trade distribution worldwide, visit: www.aperture.org/distribution

aperture

Aperture Foundation
547 West 27th Street, 4th Floor
New York, N.Y. 10001
www.aperture.org

Aperture, a not-for-profit foundation, connects the photo community and its audiences with the most inspiring work, the sharpest ideas, and with each other—in print, in person, and online.

Melissa, Yellowstone National Park, 2014

MELISSA HARRIS is editor-at-large of Aperture Foundation, where she has worked for more than twenty-five years, including as editor-in-chief of *Aperture* magazine from 2002 to 2012; under her leadership, the magazine received many honors, including ASME's National Magazine Award for General Excellence.

Harris has edited more than forty books for Aperture, among them Letizia Battaglia's *Passion, Justice, Freedom—Photographs of Sicily* (1999, for which Harris also wrote Battaglia's profile); Charles Bowden's *Juárez: The Laboratory of Our Future* (1998); Merce Cunningham's *Other Animals: Drawings and Journals* (2002); Bruce Davidson's *Central Park* (1995); Donna Ferrato's *Living with the Enemy* (1991); Luigi Ghirri's *It's beautiful here, isn't it . . .* (2008); Graciela Iturbide's *Images of the Spirit* (1996); Josef Koudelka's *Wall* (2013); Sally Mann's *Immediate Family* (1992); Mary Ellen Mark's *Tiny: Streetwise Revisited* (2015); Richard Misrach's *Petrochemical America* (2012); Sylvia Plachy's *Self-Portrait with Cows Going Home* (2004); Eugene Richards's *Cocaine True, Cocaine Blue* (1994); David Vaughan's *Merce Cunningham: 65 Years* (2012 app, updated from Vaughan's 1997 book *Merce Cunningham: Fifty Years*, published by Aperture; app coedited by Harris and Trevor Carlson, Cunningham Dance Foundation, with an afterword by Bonnie Brooks); and David Wojnarowicz's *Brush Fires in the Social Landscape* (1994; rev. ed. 2015). She was also the editor of Michael Nichols and Jane Goodall's *Brutal Kinship* (1999) and Nichols's *Earth to Sky: Among Africa's Elephants, A Species in Crisis* (2013).

As a curator, Harris has organized photography exhibitions for Aperture, the Philadelphia Museum of Art; the Lumiere Brothers Center for Photography, Moscow; the Triennale di Milano; the Peggy Guggenheim Collection, Venice; Villa Pignatelli, Naples; and Visa pour l'Image, Perpignan, among other venues, often contributing essays to the exhibitions' accompanying catalogs.

Harris teaches at New York University in the Tisch Photography and Imaging department, and occasionally at Yale University. She served on New York City's Community Board 5 for several years, and is a trustee of the John Cage Trust.

"A world without huge regions
of total wilderness would be a cage;
a world without lions and tigers
and vultures and snakes and elk and bison
would be—will be—a human zoo.
A high-tech slum."

—Edward Abbey

"No witchcraft, no enemy action had
silenced the rebirth of new life in this stricken world.
The people had done it themselves."

—Rachel Carson